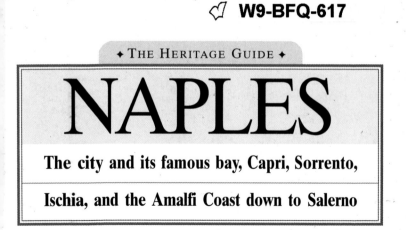

✦ THE HERITAGE GUIDE ✦

NAPLES

The city and its famous bay, Capri, Sorrento,

Ischia, and the Amalfi Coast down to Salerno

Touring Club of Italy

Touring Club of Italy

President and Chairman: *Giancarlo Lunati*

Chief Executive Officer: *Armando Peres*

Managing Directors: *Adriano Agnati* and *Radames Trotta*

Editorial Director: *Marco Ausenda*

Coordination: *Michele D'Innella*

Managing Editor: *Anna Ferrari-Bravo*

Senior Editor: *Cinzia Rando*

General Consultant: *Gianni Bagioli*

Jacket Layout: *Federica Neeff*

Map Design: *Cartographic Division - Touring Club of Italy*

Authors: *Leonardo Di Mauro* (The course of history; The artistic and cultural history; Naples and maritime Campania: instructions for touring; The places of the tour: chapters 1,2,3,4); *Gaetano Amodio* (The Sorrento peninsula and Capri. The Sorrento peninsula); *Concetta Picone* (chapters 9 and 10; Procida and Ischia); *Carlo Rescigno* (The Campi Flegrei, Procida, and Ischia, From Naples to Pozzuoli; From Pozzuoli to Cuma: Mount Vesuvius, Herculaneum, and Pompeii: The excavations of Herculaneum: The excavations of Pompeii: text of Paestum and Velia): *Armando Terminio* (chapter 8. The area around Mount Vesuvius. The Isle of Capri).
All practical information was compiled by the authors, except for details on hotels, restaurants, and parking.

Translation and adaptation: *Antony Shugaar*

Copy Editor: *Andrew Ellis*

Drawings: *Antonello* and *Chiara Vincenti*

Layout: *Studio Tragni*

Production: *Giovanni Schiona, Vittorio Sironi*

Picture credits: *S. Amantini/Laura Ronchi:* p.150; *M.Amendola/Franca Speranza:* 165: *G. Berengo Gardin/Action Press:* 55; *E.Caracciolo:* 21, 22, 25, 34, 44, 47, 48, 67, 87, 89, 103, 107, 108, 109, 140, 141, 144, 147, 149, 172, 193, 194; *Giuseppe Carfagna/Franca Speranza:* 23; *G. Cigolini/Image Bank:* 36; *P. Curto/Image Bank:* 175: *M. Fraschetti:* 40, 182, 188, 191: *A. Gallant:* 173; *R. Giordano:* 51, 53, 99; *Image Bank:* 26, 121, *Grazia Neri:* 27; *M. Pedone/Image Bank:* 93, 101, 104, 119, 158; *A. Pistolesi/Image Bank:* 111, 170: *Donata Pizzi/Image Bank:* 56,79; *L. Romano:* 33: *Laura Ronchi/Tony Stone:* 97, 133, 181; *G.A. Rossi/Image Bank:* 28, 38, 80,116, 130,137,151,153; *Scala/Firenze:* 12, 14, 16, 19, 20, 58, 63, 69, 77, 84, 91, 113, 123, 127, 135, 161, 169, 178, 186; *G. Veggi/White Star/Grazia Neri:* 64, 82.

Cover: *Aerial view of Naples, with Mount Vesuvius (D. Giaffreda/Marka)*

Picture p. 3: *The Duomo of Amalfi* (E. Caracciolo); pictures pp.4-5: *A Neapolitan theatre* (M. Caracciolo): *Galleria Umberto I, Naples* (Laura Ronchi): *View of Amalfi* (M. Caracciolo): *Tipical Neapolitan cakes* (M. Caracciolo).

Typesetting and colour separations: *Emmegi Multimedia - Milano*

Printed by: *G. Canale & C. - Borgaro Torinese (Torino)*

© 1999 Touring Editore s.r.l. - Milano
Code L2F
ISBN 88-365-1520-7
Printed in October 1998

Foreword

According to legend, Naples was founded on the tomb of a siren, who bequeathed her irresistible charm and mysterious appeal to the city. Legends aside, Naples has perhaps more to offer than any other city in Italy in terms of history, art, and sheer beauty.

The travelers of the eighteenth and nineteenth centuries who journeyed across Europe on the Grand Tour unhesitatingly acclaimed Naples as the most glorious and dazzling capital of the West.

Today's eternally sunny Naples rises majestically around a bay that offers one of the most memorable views of the entire Mediterranean: the islands of Procida and Ischia, the volcano of Vesuvius, and beyond it the promontory of Sorrento and the island of Capri. Cradled in this sweeping panorama lies the city of Naples, with its austere Aragonese castle guarding the port, its colorful Byzantine cupolas, imposing Renaissance palazzi, elaborate Baroque churches, Rococo facades, and network of lively sidestreets and steep avenues climbing to the hilltop vantage points of Castel Sant'Elmo and the sumptuous Bourbon palace of Capodimonte.

Amalfi: Duomo

The twenty-four itineraries detailed in this Heritage Guide take us first on a tour round this wonderful city – several times capital of the Mediterranean, where Greek was spoken until the age of Constantine, and whose past rulers include the Normans, Spanish, and French: these street-by-street tours are followed by excursions to the famous archaeological sites of Herculaneum and Pompeii, two Roman towns buried in the eruption of A.D. 79, and then down the coast of Amalfi and Salerno to the Greek temples of Paestum, solemn witnesses to a past glory we can only imagine. Other excursions take us to the islands of Ischia and Capri, and to that extraordinary "Versailles" of Italy, the Reggia at Caserta.

When Goethe reached Naples in February 1787 he declared that the sight of the bay, the islands and volcano, the castles and villas, exceeded all his expectations. "Anyone can be forgiven for losing his mind in Naples!"

Contents

Introductory Chapters

Excursions

Information for Travellers and Index of Places

Excursion Key Map
and Index of Maps and Plans

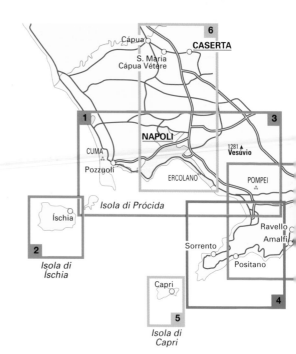

The numbers in bold indicate
the sequence of maps. The towns
marked include a street plan.

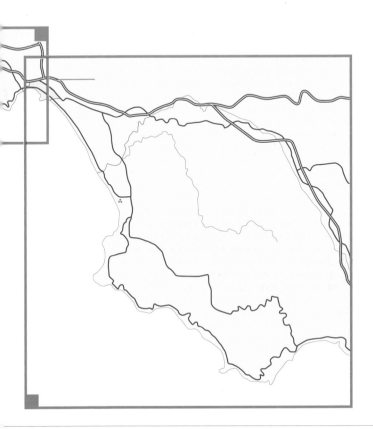

How to Use this Guidebook

■ We have attempted to use the original Italian names of all places, monuments, buildings, and other references where possible. This is for a number of reasons: the traveller is thus made more comfortable with the names as he or she is likely to encounter them in Italy, on signs and printed matter. Note also that maps in this book for the most part carry the Italian version of all names. Thus, we refer to Castel dell'Ovo and Via Toledo rather than to Ovo Castle and Toledo Street. On first mention, we have tried to indicate both the Italian and the English equivalent; we have renewed this dual citation when it is the first mention in a specific section of text. In Italian names, one of the most common abbreviations found is "S." for "saint" (and "SS." for "saints"). Note that "S." may actually be an abbreviation for four different forms of the word "saint" – "San", "Sant'", "Santo", and "Santa". Many other terms, while generally explained, should be familiar: "chiesa" is a church, "cappella" is a chapel, "via" is a street, "ponte" is a bridge, "museo" is a museum, "biblioteca" is a library, "torre" is a tower, "campanile" is a bell tower, "giardino" is a garden, "parco" is a park, "pinacoteca" is an art gallery, "teatro" is a theater, "piazza" is a square, "ospedale" is a hospital, "porta" is either a door or a city gate.

Maps and Plans. The itineraries and excursions described in this guide are accompanied by *route maps,* in which the suggested route is traced in yellow, with an arrow denoting the direction followed by the description in the text. All the main towns and cities have an accompanying *city map*; here the suggested itinerary is marked in blue. A key to the symbols used can be found on page 10. The principal monuments and museums together with the hotels, restaurants, and other public facilities are marked directly on the maps, and are followed by a reference to their location on the map or street plan (e. g., I, A3, meaning map I, square A3); hotels and restaurants are marked with letters in bold. The notation "off map" indicates that the monument or location

mentioned lies outside the areas shown on the maps. Floor plans of monuments are marked with letters or numbers for identification, and correspondingly linked to the descriptions in the text.

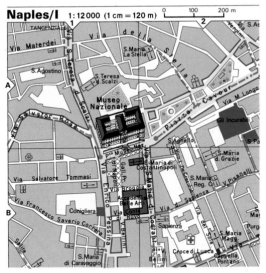

The Places to Visit. In all descriptions of monuments or landmarks differences in typography (names shown in **bold** or in *italics*) larger or smaller type size, and one or two asterisks (*) indicate the importance of each monument, museum, or other site. Written descriptions are illustrated with drawings and photos that help the reader to visualize works of art or architecture which he or she should not miss.

Information for travellers. A compendium of useful addresses, hotels and restaurants which suggests a selection of the finest hospitality facilities. Specific criteria are described on page 195. We provide information which is up-to-date as of the writing of this book. The reader should be aware that some subsequent changes may have occurred in hours or schedules.

Notice regarding telephone numbers. As of the 19th December 1998, each location's telephone code must also be dialled for local calls and are listed next to the symbol ☎ in the section Information for Travellers, page 195. For those calling from abroad, the local code (081 for Naples) must be dialled after international code for Italy, followed by the subscriber's number.

View of Agropoli

Conventional Signs Used in the Maps

City maps

Lines of communications

Throughfares

Main roads

Other roads

Pedestrian ramps

Pedestrian areas

Railroad lines and stations

Subway lines stations

Monuments and buildings

of exceptional interest

quite interesting

interesting

Other indications

Public offices

Churches

Hotels

Restaurants

Hospitals

Tourist information offices

Principal parking areas

Gardens and parks

Cemeteries

Excursion maps

Lines of communications

Excursion, with direction followed

Highway, with route number

Main roads

Other roads

Other indications

Places to see along the excursion

Other places

Urban area

Parks

Airports

Administrative borders

The course of history

For many centuries, the political, economic, cultural, and artistic history of the regions of southern Italy were identified with the history of Naples. In fact, as in few other cases in Europe (the Republic of Venice, the Grand Duchy of Moscow) the very name of the State – the Kingdom of Naples, or Regno di Napoli – is the same as the name of the capital.

A phenomenon that is of particular note from the 16th c. to the Unification of Italy, but which had its beginning with the decision of the Angevins to shift the capital of the capital of Sicily from Palermo to Naples, provoking the secession of the island from the great realm formed by the Normans in the 12th c., a kingdom whose northern boundaries were to remain virtually identical until 1860.

In ancient and medieval times, the territory that depended on the coasts of Campania (which we may divide into three large areas, the Phlegrean area, the Amalfi-Sorrento area, and the Cilento area) did not witness such a marked and lasting hegemony of one city over the others.

From Greece to Rome: a fusion of cultures

Characterizing this region was a lively dialectic between the coastal zones and those of the hilly and mountainous hinterland, which lasted over the centuries, pitting, with obvious exceptions, Greeks and Etruscans, Byzantines and Longobards one against the other.

The differentiation began during the Iron Age, when, alongside the cultures that buried their dead in ditches, found in ancient Cumae and in other areas, there was a survival of the practice of cremation in the interior (Vallo di Diano).

The earliest settlement of Greek colonists along the coast date back roughly to the middle of the 8th c. B.C., with the foundation of Pithecusa and the successive foundation of Cumae (the people of Cumae founded Parthenope in the 7th c. and Neapolis in the 5th c.) and then that of Posidonia (Paestum), by the Sibari around 600 B.C., and the Phocaean colony of Elea (Velia) in 540 B.C.

In the interior, in the meantime, the Etruscan colonization was triumphing over the local cultures (Ausonian) with major towns such as Capua, Nola, and present-day Pontecagnano near Salerno.

Conflicts between the coastal areas and the interior seem to have become less marked following the two Greek victories at Cumae (524 and 474 B.C.) over the Etruscans, followed by the invasion of the Samnites (and the Lucani) from the Apennines, who during the 5th c. spread their influence to the coastal cities as well. The reason for the Samnite conquest can be considered to have been the development of the "Campanina people," the Oscans,

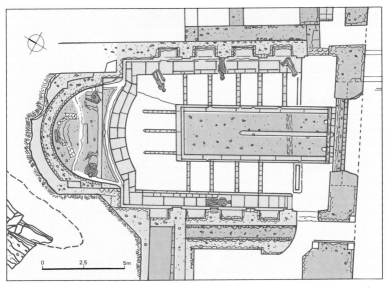

The nymphaeum at Baia, an important Roman complex

11

the product of the merging of the various cultures spread throughout the region. There still remained strong cultural differences between the peoples of the coast and the peoples of the interior, a contrast that allowed the burgeoning power of Rome to conquer Campania over the course of the three Samnite wars (343-290 B.C.).

The expansion and consolidation of Roman power in the region led to the settlement of many colonies in towns that already existed (Paestum) and the construction of important roads such as the Via Appia (ancient Appian Way), Via Popilia, Via Domiziana (ancient Via Domitiana), and the Via Traiana. Closely linked to Rome, the gulfs of Pozzuoli and Naples were dotted with sumptuous villas and possessed impressive commercial and military infrastructures.

In the 4th c. A.D. the region began to decline, with a progressive spread of marshes through much of the coastline and the subsequent abandonment of many towns (Paestum, Velia, Liternum).

St. Louis bestows the crown of the Kingdom of Naples on Robert of Anjou (Simone Martini, Museo di Capodimonte)

The Norman Kingdom

Campania was devastated between the fifth and sixth centuries by barbarian invasions, the Gothic war, and the Longobard conquest, which was halted only before the great coastal towns, solidly under the control of Byzantium. These cities (Gaeta, Naples, Sorrento, Amalfi, and Salerno) coincide with the dukedoms that, nominally under the rule of the Eastern Empire, were in fact autonomous, and opposed the Longobard dukedoms (later, principalities) in the interior (at first, only Benevento, then Capua, and finally Salerno, which was the only coastal city to be lost by Byzantium).

Enormous cultural and economic influence was wielded in these centuries by Benedictine monasticism, which was centered in the abbey, or Abbazia di Montecassino and, after 1020, with a further point of diffusion in the abbey, or Abbazia di Cava dei Tirreni. As the new millennium dawned in the year 1000, there arose a new factor in the political division of the region between Longobard princes and autonomous dukedoms, with the arrival of the first Norman knights and it was out of the conflict between Capua and Naples that there arose the formation (1030) of the first Norman county in Aversa. From here, the Norman knights went on, first to conquer Capua (1062), then other towns in Campania and Apulia, until they had achieved the unification of all of the Mezzogiorno d'Italia, or southern Italy, into a single kingdom (1130). The conquest was slow but ineluctable; in 1063 Gaeta fell, in 1077 Salerno followed and, last of all, Naples in 1137; to ward off conquest, Benevento had already placed itself under the protection of the Church in 1051 and, after the death of the last Longobard prince (1077), was ruled (until 1860) by delegates from the Pope.

The system of trade of the coastal dukedoms, based on the links with the Byzantine and Islamic east, and focusing on the city-state of Amalfi, entered a crisis that in time became irreversible. The feudal relationship became the tool used by the Normans to operate their political and administrative systems; the towns were a castle already existed were affected by new construction activity, while other castles were built. The castles, which served a twofold purpose, as the residence of the feudal lord and a military outpost, were spread throughout the kingdom of Sicily, becoming a permanent presence given the bond of continuity that was established between Norman castles and those of the Swabian, Angevin, Spanish, and Bourbon feudal lords.

Angevin and Aragonese Sovereigns

With the defeat of Manfred at Benevento in 1266 and the beheading of Conradin (1268) came the end of the Norman-Swabian dynasty and the beginning of the Angevin dynasty, which so profoundly marked the destinies of the kingdom and the city of Naples. The transfer of the capital from Palermo to Naples (which had already been chosen in 1224 by Frederick II as the site of the university) was one of the causes of the secession of Sicily and the war of the "Vespers," which between 1282 and 1302 devastated the Cilento and the Vallo di Diano. The transformation of Naples into a modern capital of a state changed its appearance and its destiny, and with that of the city, those of the areas that surrounded it. This led, during the years of the Angevin monarchy (1266-1442) to the slow marginalization of the interior areas; a process which, continuing in the second half of the 15th c. under the rule of the House of Aragón, was to accelerate ineluctably during the rule of the Spanish viceroys.

With Charles I of Anjou (died 1285) and his son Charles II (1285-1309) came the phase of the conquest of the kingdom and the consolidation of the Angevin dynasty, which elevated Naples to the rank of a great political and cultural capital. The final phase of the dynasty, with the Anjou-Durazzo, covered the reigns of Charles III (1381-86) and his children Ladislao (1386-1414) and Joan II (1414-35). Joan, in 1420, adopted Alfonso of Aragón, but in her last will and testament named Renato of Anjou as her heir; the war of succession that followed ended, in 1442, with the victory of the House of Aragón and the triumphant entrance the following year of Alfonso, known as Alfonso il Magnanimo, into Naples. The rule of the House of Aragón reached its greatest degree of expansion, assembling a cultural *koiné* that was to leave considerable trace in the regions of southern Italy. The role of Naples in the context of this Mediterranean empire was to prove central, and its cultural hegemony over the other cities of the south was to become even more powerful after the death of Alfonso (1458) and the succession to the rule over the Aragonese dominions in the Italian mainland by his son Ferrante I (1458-94). The last phase of the dynasty involved a series of rebellions by the barons and the succession of the reigns of Alfonso II (1494-95) and Ferrante II (Ferrandino, 1495-96), the descent of Charles VIII of France into Italy, the reign of Frederick (1496-1501), the brother of Alfonso II, and the final and definitive selection of Spain by the Neapolitans. Thus, with the entry of the first viceroy, Consalvo de Cordova, during the reign of Ferdinand the Catholic (died 1516), began the long succession of Spanish viceroys (1503-1707) that was to mark profoundly the destiny of southern Italy.

Two centuries of Spanish viceroys

In the first half of the 16th c., in the context of the immense empire of Charles V (1516-56), Naples was ruled by the viceroy Pedro de Toledo who reigned for quite an unusually long time (1532-53). During those years, the defensive works of the entire kingdom were strengthened and renewed, and in this context Naples was enlarged and surrounded with new walls. At the same time, with a view to better controlling the feudal lords, who incessantly plotted against the sovereign, their transfer to the capital was demanded; this was followed by the arrival of a number of craftsmen who worked hard to create the new appearance of the viceroy's capital. At this point the problem of overcrowding began (220,000 inhabitants in the middle of the 16th c.; 300,000 at the end of the same century), a problem that even at this early point appeared clearly as a fundamental problem of Naples; at the same time the rush of aristocrats and com-

The Guglia dell'Immacolata, or spire, in front of the Gesù Nuovo

moners into the capital contributed to the growing impoverishment of the outlying provinces, which were progressively being abandoned. This led to the identification between the city and the kingdom that was mentioned above; it now appears inevitable that – having lost its role as a capital with hegemonic control – Naples, after the century (1860-1950) in which it spent its considerable 'capital,' of culture and other intangible factors, accumulated over the centuries, is destined to downsize its various functions, returning to the surrounding provinces of the ancient kingdom that which geography and history have assigned them. In other, simpler words, the growth of Salerno, Benevento, Caserta, and Avellino, to remain only in the context of Campania, is taking place at the expense of the centralization that Naples had undertaken in previous centuries.

In the 16th and 17th c., the capital was populated as well with countless monastic complexes which, in part through a variety of fiscal easements, expanded, reducing the amount of space in which the increasingly numerous plebeians, could live. Despite the prohibitions issued by the viceroys, construction expanded outside the city walls, on a line with the main gates, resulting in the growth of the "borghi". At the same time, as the sole deterrent against growing social tensions, there arose numerous charitable initiatives, from the Pio Monte della Misericordia to the hospitals and conservatories which offered haven to a vast array of categories of the needy (orphans, "lost" or "straying" girls…). The 17th c. was a succession of dramatic events: the eruption of Vesuvius in 1631, the first eruption in centuries; the revolt against the Spanish in 1647, which spread the name of Masaniello throughout Europe; the plague of 1656 and the earthquake. The Spanish viceroyalty ended in 1707 with the occupation of the city by imperial troops; the 18th c. thus began with nearly three decades of Austrian viceroyalty. Still, the future of the city and the southern kingdom ("Mezzogiorno") were determined by the various European powers, and with the end of the war of Polish succession, the old kingdom of Naples was restored as an autonomous entity and was assigned to a prince who was half Spanish and half Italian, Charles of Bourbon, the son of Philip V and Elisabetta Farnese, destined to become the king of Spain, who served his apprenticeship, as it were (1734-59), in Naples.

The Bourbons of Naples

The city once again opened up to European influence; the queen, Maria Amalia, was a Saxon; the diplomats courted the young royal couple; travelers on the Grand Tour visited and described Naples and its famous surroundings: the mythical Campi Flegrei, or Phlegrean Fields, Mt. Vesuvius, in perennial eruption, what was then possible to see of the newly un-

earthed cities of Herculaneum and Pompeii. Charles modernized the appearance of the kingdom, with among other things the construction of a great royal palace at Caserta, as well as providing the city with the opera house, or Teatro di San Carlo; the palace, or Reggia di Capodimonte; and the immense poorhouse, or Albergo dei Poveri.

Having become the king of Spain (Charles III), he bequeathed Naples to his son Ferdinand IV who, succeeding to the throne at the age of eight, enjoyed an exceedingly long reign (1759-1825), during which he shifted from the utopian reforms of the colony of San Leucio to the ferocious repression of the Revolution of 1799 and the second restoration. In the wake of the French

Portrait of Charles of Bourbon, by Francesco Laini (Museo e Gallerie Nazionali di Capodimonte)

Revolution, Naples experienced during a few months in 1799 the Repubblica Partenopea ("Parthenopean Republic"), which ended in a fierce repression after the complete betrayal of the pacts according to which the revolutionaries had surrendered. Against the liberals and the better educated section of the aristocracy, moreover, the commoners had already displayed an unprecedented violence, to the point that many scholars believe that this moment marked the end of any determination for reform among the Neapolitan bourgeoisie in the 19th and 20th c., a bourgeoisie that was busy encouraging the worst aspects of the Neapolitan stereotype, depicting those aspects in literature, theater, and music.

The restoration of Ferdinand lasted only a short while, because by the beginning of 1806 he was forced once again to flee to Palermo by the French conquest of the mainland portion of his realm. Napoleon made his brother Joseph Bonaparte the king of Naples (1806-1808) and when Joseph took the throne of Spain, in Madrid, he replaced him with his brother-in-law Joaquin Murat (1808-15). During the decade of French occupation, there were created – either through the merger of existing institutions, or entirely anew – the botanical gardens, or Orto Botanico, an astronomical observatory, or Osservatorio Astronomico, a conservatory, or Conservatorio, and a city bank, or Banco di Napoli; the sense of renewal was made evident in the capital with the construction of roads to Capodimonte and Posillipo. Ferdinand, who had become, after the Congress of Vienna, Ferdinand I as the king of the Two Sicilies, was succeeded by his son Francis I (1825-30) and then by his nephew Ferdinand II (1830-59), whose reign was characterized by the repression of the liberal currents, which aspired to a constitution and by a series of technological and industrial innovations that put the kingdom of the Two Sicilies in the vanguard of all Italy (particularly famous was the first railroad, inaugurated in 1839: Naples-Portici). The constitution was conceded by Ferdinand II's successor, Francis II (1859-60) in June of 1860, when Garibaldi was entering the kingdom from Marsala.

From the Unification of Italy to the present day

Having lost its status as a capital, Naples experienced in the second half of the 19th c. a lively cultural life, but also a series of calamities, the most serious of which was the outbreak of cholera of 1884. The decision was made to solve the problems of hygiene and overcrowding with the great project of urban renewal known as the Risanamento; many of the buildings in the quarter that lay between the old center and the sea were demolished, and a new urban grid was created, with the great thoroughfare of the Corso Umberto. The ravaging continued under Fascism; the bombing of 1943 did terrible damage to the historic and artistic heritage of the city.

Over the course of the 20th c. – and in particular in the 1950s and the 1960s – Naples developed enormously over areas that for centuries had been renowned for their pleasant rusticity, the fertility of the land, the splendor of the landscape, and of which now nothing remains but a memory. A chaotic development, widely imitated in the smaller towns, which only exacerbated the perennial problems of the city. An attempt at renewal, at the end of the 1970s, was interrupted by the earthquake of 1980 and by the successive projects for reconstruction, in the course of which the mixture of enormous public funding and political corruption and organized crime produced not only rampant and uncontrolled development, poor and incomplete restorations, damage to the environment, and thefts of artworks, but also something close to an anthropological mutation. The problems of the city and the surrounding region, therefore, remain immense, and their solution, as the Marquis de Sade put it in the last line of his *Voyage d'Italie*, "is not a task that can be completed in a day, nor in a reign.".

The artistic and cultural history

The earliest and the richest evidence of human settlements along the coasts of Campania come especially from the islands in the Gulf of Naples, while priceless finds from the Iron Age have been unearthed at Pontecagnano. Between the ninth and the eighth centuries B.C., there appeared at Cumae and Capua the first products linked to Greek civilization. From that time on, the size of the settlements, the quality of the artistic products, the unbroken links among places, the historic events that took place in them, and the myths that were set there mark an historic, artistic, and cultural corpus that comprises: Pithecusa (Ischia), Cumae, Neapolis, Paestum, Velia, Capua, Pozzuoli, Baiae, Bacoli, Miseno, Sorrento, Stabiae. A territory that seems to be an inexhaustible "mine": in the 18th c. yielded up Pompeii and Herculaneum, in 1968 offered up, from the necropolis of Paestum the slabs from the Tomba del Tuffatore, or tomb of the diver.

The decline of the classical age and the high Middle Ages

The principal and the oldest evidence of early Christianity are the catacombs, and the baptistery of Naples, or the Battistero di Napoli; the complex of Cimitile; the sacellum, or Sacello di S. Matrona a San Prisco. All of these buildings show influences from the neighboring African coasts, mixing and combining with the influences from nearby Rome.

The arrival of the Longobard conquerors shattered the political and cultural unity that, with its ties to Byzantium, so characterized southern Italy. As we all know, the coastal areas remained Byzantine, while the interior was dominated by the Longobards. Benevento became the political capital of Longobard Italy, the center of a principality that was gradually to decline, with the secession of the principality of Salerno in 849 (and the reader should consider that the activity of the great Medical School of Salerno dates back to the 9th c., and continued until 1812) and with the Byzantine reconquest of territories in southern Italy. At roughly the same time as the arrival of the first Norman cavaliers came the foundation of the abbey, or Abbazia della SS. Trinità di Cava. Many of the large churches built in this period followed the model set by the Basilica di Montecassino; the prototype of the church built by Desiderius, ancient and yet at the same time innovative in terms of the meanings that it came to acquire, was soon imitated in the principal new foundations of southern Italy. The model of Montecassino was also imitated in the most important surviving monument of 11th-c. Campanian architecture, the cathedral of Salerno, begun by orders of Robert Guiscard and of the archbishop Alphanus in 1080. In the decorative array of the new foundations, there was a mix of Byzantine and Islamic style, as well as other styles that were closer to the Western Romanesque, in a syncretism that was to constitute the distinguishing feature of the artistic production of the 12th c.

Fresco of the Rites of Purification, in the Villa dei Misteri, Pompeii

The Angevin Gothic style

In the 13th c., with the shift of the center of political gravity northward from the Kingdom of Sicily, the European scope of the policies of Frederick II, and the vast changes that were underway in the commercial structure of southern Italy, due to the simultaneous economic growth of Pisa, Genoa, and Florence, there was a sharp shift in the affairs of the south. The reversal of role and status that had already occurred once in the Swabian era between the island and the mainland sections of the kingdom was further accentuated by the conquest by the House of Anjou, marking a fundamental transition in artistic terms as well, especially for Naples which became the capital in place of Palermo. In the wake of the conquerors came master craftsmen who updated, with a special predilection for the architectural style of southern France, the architectural vocabulary that had been sharply oriented in the Swabian era toward the Gothic. Throughout the kingdom, there was a reinforcement of all defensive works and full tribute paid to the restructuring of ancient religious foundations – in this way, Charles I arranged (with clear reference to his original feudal landholding and his own familiar memories) for the foundation of new buildings to bear witness to his own glory and that of his dynasty. The new capital was enriched with civil construction (Castel Nuovo) and religious foundations (besides S. Lorenzo, there was the cathedral, or Cattedrale, S. Domenico); in the university, founded by Frederick II in 1224, St. Thomas Aquinas taught; Naples witnessed a general reorganization of the entire coastal area, with a concentration of "fondachi," or entrepôts, and banks, with the creation of the Arsenal and the reconstruction of the Piazza Mercato. Overlooking this square was the church of S. Eligio, the earliest of the Angevin foundations; it clearly showed, as did the apse of the successive S. Lorenzo, marked features of the French Gothic. The adoption of styles from across the Alps took place as early as the reign of Charles II, and culminated in the foundations during the reign of Robert, in which there was the contribution as well of architects trained in Siena. At the same time, the city became increasingly open to the new ideas of Tuscan and Umbrian painting and sculpture, documented by the activity of Montano d'Arezzo and Pietro Cavallini. During the reign of Robert, Naples became a major artistic and cultural center, which still preserved strong ties with central Italy: Simone Martini painted (1317) a great altar piece for the canonization of Saint Louis, brother of the king; among others who worked here were Lello da Orvieto, Giotto with his workshop in 1329-32, Petrarch, and Boccaccio. Various masters who had learned their craft in the circle of Pietro Cavallini were responsible for the frescoes done in various phases in S. Maria Donnaregina over a long period (1319-1332), resulting in the creation of the greatest surviving series of paintings of the Neapolitan Gothic style. From the workshop of Giotto came the interesting Maestro della Cappella Barrile; among the Neapolitan followers of Giotto, the most illustrious was Roberto d'Oderisio; even during the reign of Joan I, the Florentine artist Nicolò di Tommaso was working in Naples. In the field of sculpture, as well, which saw in the earliest years of the Angevin conquest the work, in Ravello, of Niccolò di Bartolomeo da Foggia (1272), new ideas came from Tuscany, with the long stay in Naples (1325-37) of Tino di Camaino, who did the first royal Angevin tombs (of Catherine of Austria, ca. 1323; of Mary of Hungary, ca. 1325); the Tuscan influence was reinforced by the activity of Giovanni and Pacio Bertini, who created the great monument to Robert at S. Chiara. A masterpiece of French Gothic goldsmithery is the reliquary-bust of St. Gennaro (1304-1306).

The decades of Angevin-Durazzo rule, corresponding to the spread of late-Gothic currents, produced the funerary monuments and the frescoes of the church of S. Giovanni a Carbonara. During the same period, the figure of Antonio Baboccio da Piperno almost monopolized the production of sculpture, which was finally opening up to the new developments of the Tuscan Renaissance with the tomb, or Sepolcro Brancaccio in the church of S. Angelo a Nilo, the work of Donatello and Michelozzo, and with the activity of Andrea da Firenze. The most important works of painting are the late-Gothic frescoes of the chapel, or Cappella Caracciolo del Sole in the church of S. Giovanni a Carbonara, the work of the Lombard artist Leonardo da Besozzo and Perrinetto da Benevento.

The language of the Quattrocento and the Cinquecento

With the triumphant entry of Alfonso, known as Alfonso il Magnanimo, into Naples in 1443, there came about a sort of cultural *koiné* that was to leave considerable traces. In the context of this Mediterranean commonwealth, the role of Naples was central. The court of Aragón attracted such famous Humanists as Panormita (Antonio Beccadelli) and Giovanni Gioviano Pontano, as well as poets and men of letters, such as Sannazaro. The chief monument of this culture was, in Naples, the Castel Nuovo (in which Guillermo Sagrera worked, creating the splendid Sala dei Baroni) with its majestic triumphal arch.

The architecture of the 15th c. was marked by the late-medieval tradition, reinforced by the arrival of the modern style of the Tuscan Renaissance.

In the 15th c., it became common practice to cover the floors of the most prestigious rooms with glazed majolica tiles called "azulejos" or "rajolas," hence the term "riggiole," used in Naples to describe tiles.

In parallel with the painting of late-Gothic influence, and of various schools, there can be found – to the point of being dominant, in some cases – a style in which the more modern Flemish influences are revised with the styles of Burgundy and Provence and the early Italian Renaissance.

The links with Florence and with the culture of the Renaissance found instances in the "Tuscan" chapels of Monteoliveto, with the sculptures of Antonio Rossellino and Benedetto da Majano, in the chapel, or Cappella Pontano, in the Palazzo Como (Cuomo), in the presence, in the 1490s, of Francesco di Giorgio Martini, Fra' Giocondo, Giuliano da Maiano and in the *Tavola Strozzi* (now in Capodimonte), a panel bearing the most important depiction of the city in the 15th c. There were also numerous artists from the Po Valley, such as the sculptors Guido Mazzoni, Emilian, and Jacopo della Pila and Tommaso Malvito, Lombards both, who founded two of the most important Neapolitan workshops.

Among the architects of the early 16th c., we should mention Romolo Balsimelli, who designed the church of S. Caterina a Formiello to a plan – with a single nave, chapels, and a non-jutting transept – that was to be particularly successful in Naples, and Giovanni Donadio known as the Mormando. Of course, of considerable importance was the presence of such great "outsider" artists as Raphael and Titian in the church of S. Domenico, preceded by the altarpieces by Pinturicchio at Monteoliveto and by Perugino in the cathedral.

The 16th c. was marked by the activities of the Spanish viceroys, increasingly intent on the importance of the role of the capital and the modernization of the defenses of the kingdom. Naples was enlarged and renovated by the viceroy Pedro de Toledo, a number of streets were straightened and realigned, new enclosure walls reinforced the castles, in the place of the Angevin Belforte, the Castel S. Elmo was built, the Castel Capuano became the headquarters of the Tribunali. The viceroy who gave Naples its present-day appearance is buried in the church of S. Giacomo degli Spagnoli in an mausoleum by Giovanni da Nola, one of the most important sculptors of 16th-c. Naples, in collaboration with Girolamo Santacroce (the pupil of the Spanish sculptors Bartolomé Ordoñez and Diego de Siloe, who played a fundamental role in Naples).

In painting, as well, many of the most interesting figures were "outsiders," such as the Veronese Cristoforo Scacco, Antonio Solario, Pedro Fernandez, Polidoro da Caravaggio, Leonardo da Pistoia, Marco Pino, Giorgio Vasari, and the Spanish Roviale.

Mannerism and public buildings

Southern Mannerism at the end of the 16th c. and the early years of the 17th c. developed into various schools: the first was strongly influenced by the northern schools of art, because of the presence in Naples of Dirk Hendricks (known in Naples as Teodoro d'Errico, who did the ceilings of S. Gregorio Armeno and of Donnaromita) or Wenzel Cobergher, and is nicely exemplified by the work of Francesco Curia; the second is perfectly exemplified by the work of Gerolamo Imparato and clearly linked to the style of Barocci; the third was more tied up with the styles of a Counter-Reformation naturalism, almost the sort of "timeless painting" found in the work of Fabrizio Santafede. Present in many churches of Naples and neighboring town, they can now be seen in the large ceiling of S. Maria la Nova. A tireless decorator of walls and ceilings, active, in the wake of the Cavalier d'Arpino in the charterhouse, or Certosa di S. Martino, was Belisario Corenzio, who was still at work in 1640, thirty years after the death of Caravaggio.

The remarkable activity of decoration of the churches of Naples in the 16th c. was linked to the great transformation of the ancient monasteries undertaken following the Council of Trent. In Naples, moreover, the debate over religious subjects was particularly lively, and the danger that the Reformation might spread to the kingdom was a real one; in parallel, there was a growing number of new religious orders (Jesuits, Theatines, Oratorians) with buildings that were prestigious in terms of size and artistic importance (Gesù Nuovo, S. Paolo, and the SS. Apostoli by Francesco Grimaldi; the Girolamini by Giovan Antonio Dosio, etc.) and, in the case of the Theatines, the actual presence of the founder, St. Cajeton. Equally important for the city were the numerous foundations of hospitals, confraternities, conservatories, and in general of charitable institutions: in Naples, the Monte di Pietà, in which a number of the most important artists of the late 16th c. worked (the architect, Giovan Battista Cavagna, the Tuscan sculptors Michelangelo Naccherino and Pietro Bernini, the painter Ippolito Borghese, as well as Corenzio and Santafede, mentioned above) and the Pio Monte della Misericordia, founded in 1601 (architect, Francesco Antonio Picchiatti, sculptures by Andrea Falcone, paintings by Caravaggio, early followers of Caravaggio such as Battistello, and Mannerists such as Santafede and Azzolino).

No less interesting was the literary landscape between the end of the 16th c. and the first quarter of the 17th c.: in Sorrento, Torquato Tasso was born; in Naples, Giovan Battista Marino was composing the *Adone*, Giambattista Basile, the *Pentamerone*, Giulio Cesare Cortese various little poems and plays that rivaled those by Giambattista della Porta, the illustrious naturalist; in the field of music, Carlo Gesualdo, Principe di Venosa, was hard at work composing.

From Caravaggio to the cosmopolitan and enlightened 18th century

The 17th c. in Naples began with the construction of the new viceroy's palace, or Palazzo Vicereale, the work of Domenico Fontana, and with the arrival of the "outsider" Caravaggio, who, with his art, rejuvenated the art world of Naples, and laid the foundations for the remarkable flourishing of Neapolitan painting of the 17th and 18th centuries. He is the founder of that tradition of painters who, with different styles and in different periods, spread throughout Europe the reputation of the "Neapolitan school": Battistello Caracciolo, Bernardo Cavallino, Paolo Finoglia, Andrea Vaccaro, Francesco Guarino, Massimo Stanzione, Francesco Fracanzano, Aniello Falcone, Pacecco de Rosa, Salvator Rosa, and Domenico Gargiulo, all the way down to Mattia Preti and Luca Giordano. Alongside these artists are the other "outsiders," active for years in Naples, such as Jusepe de Ribera, Simon Vouet, Artemisia Gentileschi, Domenichino, and Giovanni Lanfranco.

Cosimo Fanzago – architect and sculptor, a Lombard, as was Caravaggio – was responsible above all for the renewal of architectural decoration; present in various roles in a countless array of construction projects, he developed formal models that were astonishingly successful for the rest of the 17th c. and even part of the following century. Another exceedingly active architect and worker of marble, or "marmoraro," was Dionisio Lazzari, the head of a flourishing workshop that did some of the most remarkable complexes of marble inlays of the century.

The Seven Works of Mercy, by Caravaggio (Pio Monte della Misericordia)

A fundamental figure in the transition from the 17th to the 18th c. is that of Francesco Solimena, a painter – influenced by Preti and Giordano, the two masters who emerged in the second half of the century, following the outbreak of the plague in 1656 – but also a fundamental figure in the formation of the generation of architects who were to dominate the first few decades of the 18th c.: Ferdinando Sanfelice, Giovanni Battista Nauclerio, Domenico Antonio Vaccaro (son of the sculptor Lorenzo, and himself an illustrious sculptor, as well, and painter). Solimena provided models for the great masterpieces of silver crafts-

19

manship; suffice it to consider the altar frontal or "paliotto," of the chapel, or Cappella del Tesoro, done by Giovan Domenico Vinaccia, one of the greatest artists in a sector in which Naples went unrivaled. And Solimena also influenced not only the painters he taught himself, such as Francesco De Mura, but also the most important sculptors after Vaccaro, such as Giuseppe Sanmartino, Matteo Bottiglieri, and Francesco Celebrano.

In the 18th c. the name of the city of Naples was known throughout Europe in the fields of philosophy, art, music, natural studies, and archaeology. Beginning in 1699, Giovan Battista Vico taught in the university, or Università; among his students were Ferdinando Galiani, Antonio Broggia, Pietro Giannone, and Antonio Genovese, who, in 1754, obtained the first professorship in a new subject, Economics.

The travelers of the Grand Tour, who came to visit the capital of a reign that had once again become independent returned to their homeland, often carrying with them *vedute* of the city and its surrounding areas. The Dutch artist Gaspar van Wittel, as early as the years between 1699 and 1702, had depicted Naples in drawings and paintings with a clear and precise hand, establishing the visual canons by which the city would be portrayed until the watercolors of Giovan Battista Lusieri and perhaps up to our present day, because in some cases it seems that the ideal and stereotypical image of the city – as if it were an immutable "postcard" – prevails over the reality of the situation.

Porcelain figures manufactured at Capodimonte (Museo Nazionale della Ceramica Duca di Martina)

In 1733, the year before the arrival of the young new king, Charles of Bourbon, Giovanni Battista Pergolesi composed *La Serva Padrona*, which later enjoyed a triumph in Paris, contributing to the creation of an indissoluble link between the name of Naples and the very idea of music, especially the music of the "commedia in musica," or Opera Buffa, which was to characterize the century, right up to the *Matrimonio Segreto*, by Cimarosa (1792).

Throughout the course of the 18th c. Naples was represented with sunny, musical, classical, luminous imagery; obvious the reality of the capital and the kingdom was not entirely that straightforward and that positive. And yet the 18th c. is popularly considered to have been one of the happiest centuries in the city's long proud history, a period that produced, aside from the artist and musicians already mentioned, such important figures as the minister Bernardo Tanucci and Gaetano Filangieri. In the artistic panorama, aside from the names that have already been mentioned, we should cite the names of the painters G. del Po, P. de Matteis, G. Diano, G. Bonito, and G. Traversi, and the architects N. Tagliacozzi Canale and M. Gioffredo.

The city was increasingly in contact with the rest of Europe, in part due to the presence of such major figures as Winckelmann, Mengs, Goethe, Saint-Non, d'Hancarville, Sir William Hamilton, Hackert, and Kauffmann.

Under Charles of Bourbon, there appeared in Naples the names of four architects who were completely extraneous to the local tradition: Medrano, Canevari, Fuga, and Vanvitelli, constantly preferred by the king for the new constructions he was undertaking, almost in opposition to Vaccaro and Sanfelice, heirs of that local tradition, and inevitably sought out by private and religious clients. These were the years of the construction of the royal palaces of Capodimonte, Portici, and Caserta, the immense Albergo dei Poveri, the Teatro di San Carlo, but also, given the remarkable emphasis laid in this century on the decorative arts, the establishment of a series of manufactories built at the behest of the king: the workshop of semiprecious stones, or Laboratorio delle Pietre Dure, and the tapestry manufactory, or Fabbrica degli Arazzi in 1737, porcelain at the Fabbrica della Porcellana di Capodimonte in 1743, silk at the Manifattura della Seta at San Leucio. These were also the years in which

Naples took on that Baroque appearance that so marked it until the earthquake of 1980, formed from the organic fusion in each building and in the environment at large of a decorative array that was the work of stucco artists and stone cutters working with piperno stone ("pipernieri"), with much of the crafts production adhering to the same esthetic canons. These were the years of the creation of the famous crèches, or "presepi," in which the celebration of Christmas served as a pretext for the self-depiction of a festive people. Lastly, these were the years of the long-devastated villas of Mt. Vesuvius, the excavations of Herculaneum and Pompeii, the foundation of the Accademia Ercolanese, and the development of a new science of archaeology.

From 19th century to the loss of harmony

The cultural vitality of Naples was encouraged by the scientific institutions founded during the decade of French occupation, ranging from the Botanical Gardens, or Orto Botanico, to the Observatory, or Osservatorio Astronomico. The 19th c., which began in Naples with the Neoclassical transformation of the present-day Piazza del Plebiscito ended with the major project of urban renewal known as the Risanamento. It was then that the city took on the appearance that characterizes its historic quarters and which saw the construction of many of the most interesting buildings of 19th-c. Naples, from the Floridiana to the facade of the Teatro di San Carlo, the Accademia di Belle Arti. With the great urban renewal project, or Risanamento, there was undertaken at the end of the 19th c. a true gutting of the city, while the special law ("legge speciale") that accompanied this project, the first in a series concerning Naples, allowed vast speculation and wildcat development along the coastline from Mergellina to S. Lucia, and in the hills from Corso Vittorio Emanuele to the Vomero.

For the painting of the 19th c., the prime "glory" of Naples was constituted by the school of Posillipo, or Scuola di Posillipo, comprising such interesting landscape painters as Giacinto Gigante, Pitloo, Vianelli, Vervloet, Duclère, Carelli, Fergola; that school was followed, shortly after the Unification of Italy, by the so-called school of Resina, or "Scuola di Resina." Dominating the field of Neapolitan art between the last few decades of the 19th c. and the first decades of the 20th c. would be such painters as Filippo Palizzi, Domenico Morelli, Gioacchino Toma, Antonio Mancini, and Francesco Paolo Michetti, and such sculptors as Vincenzo Gemito and Francesco Ierace.

Figurine of the Neapolitan comic, Totò

After the Unification of Italy, Naples, no longer a capital city, enjoyed a lively and fertile cultural life that had its greatest representative in the philosopher and historian Benedetto Croce.

The popular modern image of the city, of its inhabitants and those of the vast territory that surrounds it – even those who do not reside in the city, like the "regnicoli" of the centuries past, present themselves elsewhere as "Neapolitans" – is based on the tradition of poetry in dialect, theater, and song, ranging from Salvatore Di Giacomo to Raffaele Viviani, from Eduardo De Filippo to Totò and to "O sole mio," a tradition that blends tragedy and irony. For many, however, the most accurate image of modern Naples is that provided by *Hands over the City* (*Le Mani sulla Città*), a film made by Francesco Rosi in 1963, which clearly and objectively illustrates the causes and effects of the urban devastation of the period following World War II and the definitive loss of a harmonious city.

Naples and maritime Campania: instructions for touring

In spite of the fact that Naples, its gulf, its islands, and the coasts of Campania have formed for at least three centuries a "place" that is one of the best known in international tourism, the modalities of visiting and staying are now quite different in the many different locations. In the past, Naples tended to concentrate all interest in the field of tourism as well, so that tourists would leave the city to visit the "surrounding areas"; nowadays, it would seem that the city of Naples has become a sort of "surrounding area" (and of little more than marginal interest), outranked by Capri, Ischia, Sorrento, Amalfi, and Positano, modern "capitals" of international tourism.

Naples over the last thirty years has experienced a decline in the tourist sector, worsened by the earthquake of 1980 and by the impossibility for a tourist interested in history and art to visit churches and palazzi that are closed for endless restoration projects. A city in which the general impression was that there was nothing left to see or to tour that was not fraught with daunting problems and complications, a city that was thus often skipped by tourists who would land at the airport or pull in by train, or even drive in to the city, and would immediately head for the hydrofoil dock and then sail off to the true destinations of his or her visit to Campania. The only relationship with the city seemed to be that of a visit to the Museo Nazionale Archeologico by tour buses that picked the tourist up at his or her hotel (in Sorrento or Amalfi) and then dropped them off at the main entrance of the museum, for a brief guided tour of what seemed to have become the "Museum**" in the surrounding area which you should not miss." Tourism has flourished in Naples only on the occasion of the major exhibitions that have been held here from 1979 to the present day, or on the occasion of an event like "Napoli Monumenti Porte Aperte," which, for just two days, made it possible to move through the streets of the historic center, the churches, the palazzi, and the museums, with the same enjoyable naturalness – and crowds – that tourists normally find in Florence and Salzburg, Toledo and Palermo.

Since the beginning of 1994 it is easier to visit many of the churches in the historical center – now partially a pedestrian zone – that are no longer used for worship; they are open from 10 am to 4 pm (closed Sundays and holidays) and guarded by city employees.

When to go

The pleasant climate and the lack of any particular major seasonal events mean that any time of the year is good for a trip to Naples. It is obvious that spring and fall are the best seasons to enjoy the beauty of the surrounding areas. July and August, the months in which

Street-side theatricals in the center of Naples

most Italians take their holidays, might be a good time to visit the city of Naples, but are decidedly the worst time to go to places like Capri and Pompeii and the Amalfi coast, crowded beyond belief.

Among the events that are truly "genuine" and not prompted purely by modern-day tourist trends, we should mention, besides the various feasts of patron saints (S. Costanzo on Capri on 14 May, S. Gennaro, with the event of the miracle of the liquefaction of the blood in the ampoules in May and on 19 September, the Madonna dell'Arco in the Vesuvian sanctuary, or Santuario della Madonna dell'Arco, and with numerous events throughout the region, including the festival of S. Anna, or St. Ann, on Ischia on 26 July; S. Pantaleone at Ravello on 27 July; the Assunta, or Our Lady of the Assumption, at Positano on 15 August; the Immacolata, or Our Lady of the Immaculate Conception, at Torre del Greco on

Historical regatta of the Maritime Republics, held at Amalfi

8 December; S. Michele, or St. Michael, at Ottaviano; Carnevale, or Carnival at Capua and at Palma Campania; the celebrations of Good Friday at Procida, Amalfi, Ottaviano, and Somma Vesuviana; the Festa dei Gigli, or feast of the lilies, at Nola on 28 June; the Festa dei Quattro Altari, or feast of the four altars, at Torre del Greco from 27 to 29 June; the Festa della Madonna del Carmine at Naples on 16 July with the feigned burning of the campanile of the church of the Carmine Maggiore; Easter Monday at Forio and Ottaviano.

How to get there

The network of roads in Campania is good and quite extensive. Therefore, driving to Naples is easy and fast; the real problem is what to do with your car once you reach the city. Cars are everywhere in Naples, like in no other city in Italy. There are the problems of traffic jams, finding parking, and break-ins and thefts. Something has begun to move in the early months of 1994 in terms of efforts to control traffic, but the use of a private car, especially for a tourist on a first visit or in a hurry, is strongly discouraged. Once you have reached Naples, the best thing is to leave your car in the hotel parking lot or garage. And this is true for the other cities as well, Caserta and Sorrento and Salerno, which are best visited on foot.

For those who choose to go by train, in Naples they will need to learn how to get from one to another of the four train stations (Napoli Centrale, Piazza Garibaldi, Mergellina, Campi Flegrei) which the Italian railroads, or Ferrovie dello Stato, use almost interchangeably for express and long distance trains ("treni rapidi," "treni di lunga percorrenza" – at least until February 1994). They are all linked by a interchange line, which serves as a sort of subway (the stops in the historic center are Mergellina, Piazza Amedeo, Montesanto, Piazza Cavour, Piazza Garibaldi; the last-named station is under the station of Napoli Centrale). The airport of Capodichino is not a destination of major importance; in part because of the proximity of Rome's Fiumicino airport; you can reach it by taking the 14 bus, black and red (nero & rosso) or by taxis, which should be carefully monitored by the passenger (for more on this subject, read the paragraph on transportation).

Arrival in Naples by sea is a common occurrence because of the shipping lines for the islands of the gulf, the many cruise ships, and above all, the links with Sardinia, the Aeolian Islands, or Isole Eolie, and Sicily (travel by ship – as opposed to travel by rail – is the most comfortable way of reaching and returning from Palermo). The Stazione Marittima is in the heart of the city, adjoining the Molo Beverello from which ferryboats and hydrofoils depart, with different schedules and intervals in the various seasons, for the islands of the gulf, with links to Salerno, Pozzuoli, and Casamicciola, and, Capri along, with Sorrento, Amalfi, and Positano. There is a useful connection by sea Naples-Sorrento and, in the right season, even Naples-Positano. Local newspapers usually provide a page with the schedules of city public transportation and the main trains.

Information

The dwindling in tourism in the city of Naples has led to a decline – if not the complete disappearance – of the services providing information for tourists that we offer here under the heading of The Other Places. If in Naples you do not wish to inquire directly at the main tourist office (Azienda Autonoma di Soggiorno, at Palazzo Reale, Piazza del Plebiscito), the only information kiosk that is actually in operation can be found in the Piazza del Gesù, the point of departure for the most common itinerary of touring the old center, along the thoroughfare of Spaccanapoli and the other *decumani*.

Transportation

Since we previously advised against using your car, the traveler/reader will now, no doubt, expect great praise of the efficiency of public transportation; well, it is not possible to offer that praise.

And yet Naples, in the first three decades of the 20th c., possessed a complex and functional system of public transportation that was virtually abandoned, and is now completely inadequate to the city's needs. Aside from the single line of the subway, or "metropolitana" mentioned in the paragraph about reaching the city, we should add, often with transfer stations, four funiculars or cableways (the Funicolare Centrale, the Funicolare di Montesanto, the Funicolare di Piazza Amedeo, all three of which run up to the Vomero with way-stations at Corso Vittorio Emanuele and beyond; the Funicolare di Mergellina for upper Posillipo), and the railroad, or Ferrovia Circumvesuviana (with a terminal station in Corso Garibaldi, linked directly with the main railroad station (Ferrovie dello Stato) in Piazza Garibaldi), the Ferrovia Circumflegrea and the Ferrovia Cumana (with a terminus in Piazza Montesanto and urban way-stations at Corso Vittorio Emanuele). Surface transportation, with the almost total suppression of the once-extensive trolley system (the sole exception is the trolley, or tram, of Line 1, which runs from one end of the city to the other, east to west, near the waterfront), is now based on buses, which are perennially swamped in the city's chaotic traffic. A modern subway line is under construction; the stretch that links the Piazza Vanvitelli to the hospital zone of the Colli Aminei is now in operation.

There are plenty of taxi stations; a tourist should just be careful only to ride with licensed drivers, and in some cases and for certain trips – to the airport, for instance – determine the fare in advance, and keep an eye on the meter.

Food and fine dining

Naples and Campania are universally renowned for a number of distinctive local products and dishes: pasta, mozzarella, and pizza. Alongside these staples, there is a vast array of "specialties," which sadly are rarely offered by trattorias and restaurants, which tend to level out to a standard cuisine, almost devoid of genuine links with tradition, and "original" at times only in the juxtaposition of flavors that are extraneous to the products of the region. For certain dishes, you will just have to angle for an invitation to enjoy some "home cooking" or else order in advance in a restaurant.

The best way of approaching the Neapolitan cuisine is the observe its bask ingredients directly on the stalls of the many markets (Pignasecca, S. Anna di Palazzo, Lavinaio, Borgo S. Antonio) dominated by great basins of seafood (especially on Sunday, a day in which fish and shellfish are preferred) and the products of the exceedingly fertile "Campania Felix" (tomatoes, artichokes, peppers, zucchini, eggplants, fennel, broccoli rabé, crab-apples, oranges, lemons, figs, melons, hazelnuts…). As always, the products determine the typical dishes, so that we have the clam sauce of "vermicelli alle vongole" or the clam broth of the "zuppe di vongole" and other "frutti di mare"; "parmigiana di melanzane," "peperoni imbottiti," "zucchini alla scapece," "friarielli" (a variety of broccoli sautéed in a pan)… Among the first dishes, or "primi," the king is still pasta, from the simplest "spaghetti al pomodoro" to the far more demanding "maccheroni al ragù" – a ragù, or meat sauce, which has a complete literature all its own – and lasagna (obligatory at Carnevale, or Carnival) and "pasta e zucca"; then there is the "sartù di riso" and the famous soup, or "minestra maritata"; the pasta is present as well in "frittatine di maccheroni," and in the "timballetti"; among the "rustici," or rustic dishes, note the "casatiello" which has a variant, in the "panino napoletano" and the "taralli sugna e pepe"; among the "secondi piatti," or entrees, there is the "braciola" (a stuffed "involtino" with raisins and pine nuts, cooked in a tomato sugo, or sauce), the octopus, or "polpi affogati," the rabbit, or "coniglio alla cacciatora" (typical of Ischia); among the side dishes (for Christmas) the salad, or "insalata di rinforzo"; among the dairy products, mozzarella ("di bufala"), "butirri" and "provole" cheeses.

Neapolitan pastries are renowned and are ever present because of the respect of tradition, which – here at least – is still respected by the Neapolitans; every festivity in fact, is distinguished by one or two special pastries, and this sort of "seasonal cycle" is preserved, especially by the most illustrious pastry shops, who thus manage to avoid routine production. At Christmas, it is customary to have "strùffoli," "roccocò," "susamielli," "mostaccioli," "raffiuoli," and little colorful pastries made of "pasta reale"; at Carnevale or Carnival, the "sanguinaccio" and the "migliaccio"; at Easter, the "pastiera" and the "casatiello dolce"; for St. Joseph's Day, the "zéppole di San Giuseppe," named after the saint, described by Goethe among others; and for the Day of the Dead, the "torroni morbidi." The renowned "sfogliatelle," both "sfogliatelle frolle" and "sfogliatelle riccie" (the latter also have a Santa Rosa variant) are eaten throughout the year, and do not have any ties to special holidays, much like the "babà" and the "torta caprese."

Pizza, perhaps Naples' most celebrated "invention"

Among the red wines, we should mention Gragnano, Aglianico, Taurasi, Ravello Rosso, Falanghella, Pere e' Palummo; among the white wines, Asprino, Falerno, Lacrima Christi, Epomeo, Greco di Tufo, Sanginello, and Biancolella.

Naples, and not only Naples, by night

In Naples and in the surrounding areas, in the islands of the gulf, people live by night, indeed at certain hours of the night even the automotive traffic in the streets of the center seems like the daytime traffic in other cities. Perhaps it is the Spanish heritage, perhaps it is the climate, perhaps it is the old cliché of the "dolce far niente," but one thing is certain, and that it is that at four in the morning (with the possible exception of during the winter) it is possible to find nightspots in which to linger, and even restaurants in which to dine. In all probability, Goethe was right when he noted: "If in Rome one can study with pleasure, in Naples one does not wish to do anything but live; we forget ourselves and the universe; as for myself, it is a rather odd sensation to have dealings only with men interested in pleasure and nothing else."

Although Naples is the only city overlooking the sea that has not reserved (with a very few exceptions) the most splendid stretch of its beach front real estate for luxury car dealerships, the modern heart of Neapolitan night life has traditionally been in the area lying between the sea and the thoroughfare comprising Via Chiaia, Via Filangieri, Vie dei Mille, and Via Vittoria Colonna. In particular, there is a considerable concentration of restaurants, bars, discotheques, sandwich bars, and so on, in the area around the Piazza Amedeo, the Via Martucci, and the Piazza S. Pasquale. The Riviera di Chiaia, an exceedingly busy thoroughfare at all hours, from the Piazza Vittoria (with the adjoining Piazza dei Martiri) as far as Mergellina is punctuated with bars and clubs; and, in particular, the area of Mergellina, especially during the summer, given its proximity to the waterfront of the tourist marina ("porto turistico") and the entrance of the roads that run along the hill of Posillipo (Via Posillipo, Via Petrarca) all the way to Marechiaro and the Parco di Posillipo.

The village at the foot of the Castel dell'Ovo is quite crowded, with cars as well as pedestrians, because of its central location and its proximity to the hotels of the Lungomare.

In the historic center, which since 1994 has once again been playing its proper role in a city so loaded with memories and art, great popularity is enjoyed by the various spots (bars, clubs, "circoli" offering good music) between the Piazza Dante, Piazza Bellini (greatest concentration), and the Via Paladino; in an area revolving, therefore, between the Accademia di Belle Arti, the Conservatorio, and the university campuses.

There is a fairly lively theater industry, especially in the small "alternative" theaters of the historic center (Galleria Toledo, Teatro Nuovo); for music, aside from the temple of international fame, such as the Teatro di S. Carlo, Naples offers the concerts of the Associazione Scarlatti, the Settimane di Musica d'Insieme, and the events in the RAI Auditorium. There are a good number of movie houses. There are many summer events throughout the region; we should at least mention the Wagner concerts, or Concerti Wagneriani di Villa Rufolo in Ravello, and the Incontri Internazionali del Cinema in Sorrento.

It is almost embarrassingly obvious to point out the salient aspects of night life in the Gulf: places like Capri and Positano seem, in name at least, to boast decades of social life, elegance, and fast living. In these towns, as well as in Sorrento, Amalfi, Ischia, Sant'Angelo, and Forìo, night life has a number of historically sanctioned sites (the Piazzetta di Capri, the Buca di Bacco in Positano, where the entire stretch of waterfront near the beach is a lively center of night life, the right bank of the port at Ischia); in some cases, there is a very close relationship between the places in which night life flourishes and the places for beach life, but the passing tourist should always remember that in the best known resort towns, the true night life takes place in the most exclusive villas and aboard sailboats and yachts.

In all of the other seaside towns in the summer, there are plenty of discotheques – as is the case everywhere – including some spontaneous ones; also in the summer there are plenty of events (concerts, shows, festivals…) staged everywhere that tourists come in large numbers.

The Campania countryside

Despite the size of the territory and the remarkable beauty of a number of renowned sites, Campania is not one of the Italian regions with a particularly high number of protected areas. A number of large parks (Mt. Vesuvius – devastated in 1993 by vast forest fires – and the Cilento) seem to exist only on paper, by law, and in the intentions wherewith they are lovingly visited by tourists who are particularly interested in environmental and naturalistic matters.

For information on nature preserves (Oasi Protette): Lega Ambiente Campania, Comitato Regionale, Vico Cinque Santi 27, Naples, tel. 455459, 210683; WWF, Villa Pignatelli, Riviera di Chiaia 200, Naples, tel. 660140.

The itineraries of this guide run through the nature preserves listed here, all operated by the former Azienda di Stato per le Foreste Demaniali, with offices in Salerno (tel. 089/224458). The nature preserve, or Riserva Naturale Statale degli Astroni, situated in the Phlegrean Fields, or Campi Flegrei, beyond Pozzuoli, constitutes, with its ancient extinct volcano and two small lakes, a remarkable example of volcanic activity; it extends over 250 hectares, from elevations of 10 to 230 meters above sea level. It houses the Centro Recupero Fauna Selvatica. To tour the preserve, telephone 081/5883720.

The Riserva Naturale Valle delle Ferriere, in the territory of Scala (SA), occupies 465 hectares of a steep valley studded with streams and architectural relics from the old iron works of Amalfi. The Parco Naturale del Vesuvio, the large volcano that looms over the Gulf of Naples, can be easily reached from Herculaneum or Torre del Greco, and it extends over volcanic rocks, some ancient, some recent (1944), for more than a thousand hectares, in a fertile and impressive setting. Upon request, the Servizio Foreste (Forestry Department, tel. 081/5521181) issues a permit to tour the preserve, or Oasi dell'Isola di Vivara, the sole and luxuriant remains of an ancient crater. The island can be reached from Procida.

Tourists venturing along the edge of Vesuvius

The places of the tour

It is difficult, as we prepare to tour Naples (elev. 10 m, pop. 1,062,208), its renowned surroundings and the coasts of Campania, not to be influenced by the thousand ways in which these places have been described by previous travelers and the role that they play in what we might well describe as the "collective tourist imagination." We may apply to Naples, the great Mediterranean metropolis, what Predrag Matvejevich wrote of the sea that laps at its shores: "The image of the Mediterranean has been deformed by fanatical tribunes or by fatuous analysts, by scholars without convictions or by preachers without faith, by official chroniclers and poets for great occasions. [...] The debate over the Mediterranean has suffered from its own prolixity." The first invitation, to those who approach this city and its surrounding areas, to this "Land of Sirens," is to preserve your ability to see, to observe, to tour, and to love Naples as a "normal" city; this is the only way in which you will be able – in time – to perceive and appreciate its particular qualities.

Goethe, one of the "discoverers" of Naples on the Grand Tour

It is necessary then – and it will be useful for tourists, but even for the inhabitants themselves – to free ourselves of many of the commonplaces concerning volcanoes and the Baroque, unbridled passions and crèches, "feasts, flour, and gallows," or "feste farina e forca" and the wild life of Capri, the Bourbons and the Piedigrottas of every sort, "the last days of Pompeii" and pizza, Camorra and porcelain, emotional scenes and popular songs, and plenty of other clichés. All important factors, to be taken into consideration, alongside of which, however, we should also recall that the Middle Ages and the 16th c. have left indelible marks here, that Spanish viceroys have also governed elsewhere, that the travelers of the Grand Tour had words of admiration for other cities as well, that the 18th c. left its mark on other parts of Europe as well, and that Campanian cuisine is part of the cuisine of the Mediterranean (from Valencia to Marseilles, from Tunis to Rhodes)…

Considering these aspects, the "forestiero," or outsider, can finally look the Neapolitan siren right in the eyes, with the conscious risk of remaining "fatally wounded," or he or she can think of Naples as an abnormal city, alluring as a siren, because the city – according to a myth – was founded on the tomb of a siren. Goethe wrote the following lines on 27 February 1787, just two days after his arrival in Naples: "Today, I enjoyed myself, devoting all my time to these incomparable beauties. One may try to describe or paint these things – but they are beyond any description. The beach, the gulf, the inlets, the sea, Mt. Vesuvius, the city, the suburbs, the castles, the villas! This evening we went to the Grotto of Posillipo, at the moment when the sun is setting and its rays pass through to the other side. I then forgave everyone who loses their head over this city, and I tenderly remembered my father, who had preserved an unforgettable impression of the objects that I was seeing today for the first time. And just as they say that anyone who has seen a ghost can no longer be happy, just so we might say that anyone who can return, in their mind, to Naples will never be entirely unhappy." In the text of the tour itineraries, the *italics* and **bold** characters indicate monuments and places of particular note; an asterisk* is set alongside features that are important in their category or in any case of special interest.

The information concerning population of townships are taken from the census of 20 October 1991. We do not give the population of villages ("frazioni").

1 Naples: the center of the city and Via Toledo

The center of Naples is formed by three adjoining squares (Piazza del Municipio, Piazza Trieste e Trento, and Piazza del Plebiscito); here are the headquarters of the city's political and administrative power, and here the main city arteries all converge. Created in various eras, they are all the result of the decision made by Charles I to establish in this area the residence of the Angevin court, the Castel Nuovo (literally the "new castle"), the initial nucleus of the "Reggia di Napoli" (or Royal Palace of Naples), the monumental structure that joins the three squares. From Piazza Trieste e Trento begins Via Toledo, the chief thoroughfare of the 16th-c. expansion ordered (1536) by the viceroy whose name it bears (for many Neapolitans, the street is simply called "Toledo").

The Via Toledo is still one of the chief streets of the city, bustling with crowds and traffic at all hours of the day; it has always captured the imagination of foreign travelers for its liveliness and for its size (it is more than 2 kilometers in length, and quite broad; for centuries it had no equal in all Europe). It presents a fairly uniform character in terms of the architecture of its palazzi, and it has no particular monumental features, showing with the almost total lack of religious structures that it is a street founded in "modern" times, extraneous to the ancient and medieval core of the city, where most of the religious foundations are concentrated.

Along the western side, toward the hill, or Collina di S. Martino, is the dense grid of streets of the working-class Quartieri Spagnoli, traditionally seen even by the local middle-class as one of the areas that – for better or worse – most clearly manifests the old and trite stereotypes of "napoletanità," or Neapolitan-ness (the most extroverted cordiality, the art of "getting by," the festoons of laundry lines, life in the street, hoodlums, purse-snatchings…).

1.1 The center

The itinerary (see plan on p. 30) runs through the three squares in the political and administrative center of Naples, around the Palazzo S. Giacomo, Castel Nuovo, and the Palazzo Reale. Because of the proximity of the Stazione Marittima and the Molo Beverello (where the ferryboats and hydrofoils for the islands dock and depart), the central funicular, and the main terminus of public transportation, this is an ideal starting point for any other itinerary through Naples, and since it not only con-

Aerial view of the Castel Nuovo, showing the Arco di Trionfo di Alfonso

tains monument that are representative of the various phases of the city's history, but also overlooks the renowned panoramic vistas of the Gulf of Naples, Mount Vesuvius, and the hill, or Collina di San Martino, its an excellent introduction to an overall visit of Naples.

Piazza del Municipio (I, E2). This square, with a regular layout, adorned by tree-lined flower beds, looks south toward the sea and a panoramic view of Mount Vesuvius. Due to its proximity to the Stazione Marittima, once used for docking ocean liners, this square appeared – until only a few decades ago – as a city "gate"; it still preserves its character as a "tourist" center, since here and in the surrounding area are located the offices of many airlines, shipping companies, and travel agencies.

It is overlooked by the *Palazzo di S. Giacomo*, now the headquarters of the city government ("Municipio"), but originally built (1819-25) by S. Gasse to house the offices of the Bourbon Ministries, incorporating in its right wing the church of S. Giacomo degli Spagnoli; on either side of the portal are two epigraphs with the names of the «Martiri del '99»; on the staircase is an ancient female head, popularly known as "Marianna 'a capa 'e Napule," or "Marianna, the head of Naples," formerly located in a street near the market, or Mercato, and later placed here because it was considered to be one of the symbols of the city. At the center of the square is an *Equestrian monument to Victor Emmanuel II*; on the eastern side stands the *Teatro Mercadante*, formerly the Teatro del Fondo, built by F. Securo in 1778 (the facade dates from 1892) and inaugurated in 1779 with *L'Infedeltà Fedele* by Cimarosa.

The square seems to extend out into the sea with the *Molo Angioino*, which separates the basin, or Bacino Angioino from the Bacino del Piliero, which forms part of the large commercial shipping port, founded by Charles II in 1302, and repeatedly enlarged and rebuilt up until the major renovations of the 20th c., which involved the construction in 1936 of the *Stazione Marittima dei Passeggeri* (ferry and boat station), to plans by C. Bazzani.

S. Giacomo degli Spagnoli (I, E-2). This church was built in 1540 at the behest of the Viceroy Toledo by F. Manlio, adjoining the hospital established for the Spanish troops. The interior abounds in 16th-c. artworks (in the atrium, note two tombs by M. Naccherino) and relics of the Spanish occupation of Naples; behind the main altar note the *Tomb of the Viceroy Pedro de Toledo and his consort Maria** (1539, but assembled in 1570), a majestic creation of Giovanni da Nola and assistants.

Castel Nuovo** (I, E-F2). The construction of this castle, the most important civil structure in the Angevin and Aragonese city, at the behest of Charles I, and undertaken in 1279, was made indispensable by the inadequacy of the other two older royal residences, the Castello dell'Ovo and the Castello di Capuana; the former being excessively isolated along the water, the latter being too distant from the coast. The architect was Pierre de Chaule and the new residence, completed in 1284, was called the "Chastiau neuf," to distinguish it from the other, older castles. Nothing survives of the original Angevin structure, with the exception of the Cappella Palatina (Palatine chapel); fires, wars, and sieges had damaged it badly, and so Alfonso il Magnanimo (Alfonso the Magnanimous) decreed (1443) the immediate reconstruction of the castle/palace, a reconstruction that followed some semblance of organic fidelity only following the arrival (1449-50) of the architect from Majorca, Guillermo Sagrera. A remarkable decoration of the bases, based on scales and channels, with all sorts of inclinations and angles, characterizes the five new towers, better suited to a more modern system of defense: the main tower, or "torre maestra," overlooks the sea, and is known as the Torre del Beverello (p. 32, G) – over it for centuries fluttered the banner of the monarch; the Torre di S. Giorgio (F) and – protecting the entrance – the Torre di Mezzo (B) and the Torre di Guardia (A), and lastly, the Torre dell'Oro (L), the only tower that shows its tufa stone structure, without the piperno facing that can be found on the other towers.

Between the Torre di Mezzo and the Torre di Guardia stands the **Arco di Trionfo di Alfonso***, or Arch of Triumph of Alfonso (C), the most notable ornament of the palace and a fundamental monument in the history of 15th-c. art in southern Italy, in the moment of transition from the Gothic style to the Renaissance. The structure is made up of two stacked arches; these are round arches, each flanked by twin columns; it was built (1453-68) to commemorate the triumphal entrance into Naples of Alfonso the Magnanimous (26 February 1443), modeled after its ancient counterparts, and depicted in the principal frieze, with *Triumph* over the lower arch (to the right, note the

Naples/I

1:12000 (1 cm = 120 m)

Naples/I   1:12 000 (1 cm = 120 m)

beginning of the procession, with musicians on horseback, at the center is the king on a carriage covered with a baldachin, on the left, dignitaries and ambassadors). The entire figurative repertory used by ancient Roman art in structures of this sort is present in this complex decorative machine, culminating with the four *Virtues* in the attic, two *river deities* in the pediment, and a statue of St. Michael, protector of the southern regions as far back as the Longobard era.

At the base of the sub-arch, note two bas-reliefs that are traditionally interpreted as the *Departure for War* and the *Triumphant Return of King Alfonso*; in a niche in the gate (D, originally closed by bronze doors dating from 1462-68, by Guglielmo Monaco) is an unfinished bas-relief depicting the *Coronation of Ferrante I.*

The arch, in which Renaissance elements from the Venetian-Lombard area are blended with late-Gothic proportions and a matrix of Burgundian culture, was the work of a group of artists of varying provenance, known to us from original sources (scholars, however, disagree as to the attributions of the diverse parts). Among those artists are the Milanese Pietro di Martino, who worked in every phase of the project, the Dalmatian Francesco Laurana, the Roman Pietro Taccone, Isaia da Pisa, the Lombard Domenico Gagini, Andrea dell'Aquila, Antonio di Chelino, and the Catalan Pere Johan.

Immediately following the arch is the vestibule (E), its ribbed vault with tierceron ribs, and keystones bearing the heraldic devices of King Alfonso. In the courtyard, which was renovated in the 18th c., an exterior staircase, typical of the Catalan architecture of the 15th c., leads to the largest and best known room in the castle, the **Sala dei Baroni*** (I), nowadays housing the Consiglio Comunale, or town council; it is named the hall of the barons because, in 1486, it was the site of the arrest of the feudal lords who had conspired the year before against Ferrante I. The hall, the Neapolitan masterpiece of Sagrera, is an almost perfect cube (26 m on each side, and 28 m high), and features bare walls surmounted by a vault with heavy ribbing which forms an enormous star-shaped pattern, penetrated at the very top by an oculus. Sadly, the carved decorations were destroyed in the fire that in 1919 devastated the hall (there still survive a number of *hanging capitals* and – badly damaged – the bas-reliefs of the *portal*).

Overlooking the courtyard is the facade of

31

the **Cappella Palatina*** (Palatine chapel; H) adorned by Renaissance portal with sculptures by Andrea dell'Aquila and a rose window by Matteo Forcymania. Founded in 1307, this chapel is the only structure surviving of the Angevin castle; it was frescoed by Giotto and his workshop (1329-30) with a cycle of frescoes that had already been destroyed in the 15th c., of which precious traces have emerged (*friezes* and *small heads* attributed to Maso di Banco) in the embrasures of the windows, following the restoration work that eliminated the 18th-c. decorations of the chapel; the chapel, when the castle was devoted exclusively to military use, was dedicated to St. Barbara, patron saint of munitions. From a small door on the left side you can reach the spectacular 15th-c. *spiral staircase*** that leads to the Sala dei Baroni. The interior, which has been restored to the forms of Angevin Gothic, features the frescoes and sculptures of the Museo Civico, founded in 1990 with the installation in the chapel and on two floors of paintings, sculptures, and *objets d'art* owned by the township, in part taken from the chief monumental complexes of the city.

Among the sculptures dating from the 14th and 15th c. there are – once belonging to the same chapel – a tabernacle with a *Virgin Mary with Christ Child and Donors*** by D. Gagini, a *tabernacle* by J. della Pila, and a *Virgin Mary with Christ Child*** by F. Laurana (formerly on the portal). Also by the latter, a *Virgin Mary with Christ Child*** from the church of S. Agostino alla Zecca. A number of the frescoes, largely detached from the Castello di Casaluce, are by Niccolò di Tommaso. In the halls, paintings from the 15th to 18th c. (including the altarpiece by M. Cardisco, formerly on the altar of the Cappella Palatina) as well as an extensive and important collection of work by 19th-c. Neapolitan artists.

In the 16th c. the castle was surrounded by an enclosure wall with bastions that incorporated earlier structure and determined, with the excavation of broad ditches, a sweeping transformation of the surrounding areas. The 16th-c. fortifications were demolished between 1871 and 1939, and were replaced with avenues and flower beds (among them stands the old Aragonese entrance to the castle). In the same period, the imprecise term of "Maschio Angioino" (Angevin keep) began to circulate, and that term is still used to describe the castle, since it was generally stated that not all of Castel Nuovo had been demolished, but only the structures that surrounded the oldest part of the castle (which was extensively restored during the same years); all the same, that structure was little if at all Angevin in origin, and it had in any case never served the functions that are normally attributed in military architecture to the "maschio" or "mastio" – "keep" or "donjon."

The gardens, or *Giardini del Palazzo Reale* are closed along Via S. Carlo by a fence whose main entrance is flanked by two groups of Horse Tamers, by Clodt von Jürgensburg, a replica of other groups executed for St. Petersburg and Berlin, a gift from Czar Nicholas I in commemoration of his state visit in 1845 (epigraphs in the bases).

Teatro di S. Carlo* (I, F1). This world-renowned opera house was built in just a few months during the first years of the reign of Charles of Bourbon; it was inaugurated (4 November 1737) on his saint's name day, and was named after the patron saint, with a performance of the *Achille in Sciro* by D. Sarro, libretto by Metastasio. It was built by A. Carasale to plans by Medrano; the facade was added in 1810-12 by Niccolini, who also rebuilt the interior following a terrible fire in 1816; in the hall, with six orders of boxes, the painting on the ceiling, depicting *Mount Parnassus*, is by G. Cammarano. Among its directors were Rossini and Donizetti; world premieres held here include *Mosè in Egitto* (1818) and *La Donna del Lago* (1819) by Rossini, and *Lucia di Lammermoor* (1835) by Donizetti.

Palazzo Reale* (I, F1-2) or royal palace. The earliest nucleus of the "modern" of the Reggia di Napoli was begun (1600-02) by D. Fontana (who left his signature at the base of a column of the facade) adjoining the older Palazzo Vicereale (viceroy's palace, from then on known as the "old palace," or Palazzo Vecchio) which filled the surface of the little opening toward Via Toledo, overlooked by the sides of the theater and the

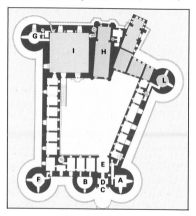

Plan of the Castel Nuovo

Interior of the Teatro di S. Carlo opera house

"new" Palazzo Reale. The palace, which was designed in a grandiose style and in modern forms for a visit of the king (which had been announced, but never took place), was restored and enlarged in the 18th and the 19th c. The facade, with three orders, largely preserves its original form; the most notable changes were made in the portico, whose arcades, for considerations of static engineering, were alternately walled up (1753) by L. Vanvitelli and adorned with niches which were later made to house – in 1888, at the command of King Humbert I – statues of the most representative monarchs of the various dynasties that ruled over Naples – the work of eight different sculptors. From the left, note *Roger of Altavilla* (Hauteville), *Frederick II of Swabia*, *Charles I of Anjou*, *Alfonso I of Aragón*, *Charles V* (of Gemito), *Charles of Bourbon*, *Joaquin Murat*, and *Victor Emmanuel II*.

At the center of the facade note the heraldic crests of the king of Spain and the viceroy, who founded it; there is a further heraldic exaltation of the Spanish monarchy in the metopes of the frieze, which bears the components of the sovereign's crest and depictions of his various realms (note the Visconti serpent of the Duchy of Milan).

From the courtyard you can reach the **Museo dell'Appartamento Storico di Palazzo Reale***; on the left you may note the monumental stairway, or Scalone d'Onore, built by F. A. Picchiatti (1651) and decorated by G. Genovese in 1837

with marble entirely taken from quarries of the kingdom; it leads into the deambulatory that in turn leads to the little *court theater*, installed by F. Fuga in the Gran Sala delle Feste. Although it was damaged during the ww II (vaulted ceiling rebuilt) it still preserves its 18th-c. decorations, culminating in twelve papier-maché and gesso statues by A. Viva. Following this is room 2, with an *Allegory of the Virtues of Charles of Bourbon and Maria Amalia*, by De Mura (1738) in the ceiling; the doors, like all the other doors in the historic apartments, were painted in the 18th c. A number of rooms still feature, in their vaulted ceilings, the decorations done at the behest of the various Spanish viceroys: in room 4 frescoes by Corenzio (*Military Triumphs of the House of Aragón*), in room 8, or Antica Galleria, *Triumphs of the House of Austria*, by Corenzio and assistants, in room 11 *The Deeds of the First Viceroy, Consalvo di Cordova* by Caracciolo.

The room 6, or Sala del Trono, or throne room, still preserves the location and the shape of the baldachin dating from the reign of Charles of Bourbon. The ceremonial halls are closely adjoined by the apartments of the sovereigns, where the original furnishings have since been replaced. In the vaulted ceilings of the two rooms between rooms 26 and 34 are frescoes by D. A. Vaccaro. Among the paintings, which date to the period running from the 16th c. to the 19th c., one should note in particular works by A. Vaccaro, Giordano (*Canvases*

33

from the church of *S. Maria del Pianto**, 1664), M. Preti (*The Prodigal Son*), Guercino, Schedoni (*various paintings** including the *Charity of St. Elizabeth*); Flemish portraits (room 12); cartoons for the tapestries of Bonito; still lifes and view paintings of the 18th and 19th c. Of particular interest and value, porcelains, watches and clocks, se-

The Scalone d'Onore in the Palazzo Reale

mi-precious stone inlays, Neapolitan tapestries (*Stories of Psyche* by P. Duranti), a large 17th-c. French carpet in the Salone d'Ercole (room of Hercules), the furniture brought by the family of Murat to Naples, signed by A. Weisweiler (room 13) and the remarkable rotating lectern made for Maria Carolina (room 23) and executed by G. Ulrich (1792). A wooden door dating from the 16th c. and painted in false bronze – almost certainly one of the rare remains of the furnishings of the Palazzo Vecchio – leads to the royal chapel, or Cappella Reale that was built by F. A. Picchiatti in the middle of the 17th c. The interior remains as it was in the 19th c. (on the ceiling, note the *Assumption of the Virgin Mary*, by D. Morelli). Of particular note due to its excellent artistic quality and the great value and craftsmanship of the semiprecious stones set in gilt copper frames is the *high altar**, by D. Lazzari, executed (1674, doors date from 1691) for the church of S. Teresa agli Studi, moved here in 1806. In the display windows, note the liturgical furnishings, ob-

jects in silver, and reliquaries that once belonged to the chapel.

In the Appartamento delle Feste, or party suite, built by G. Genovese (1837-48) and decorated by painters and ornamentalists of the Accademia Napoletana, the **Biblioteca Nazionale "Vittorio Emanuele III"** has been installed and is now housed. It takes its origin from the Fondo Farnesiano (Farnese collection), inherited by Charles of Bourbon; subsequently many other historic libraries were added to it. The Biblioteca Nazionale, the leading library in southern Italy, now preserves 1,785 papyri from Herculaneum.

Piazza del Plebiscito, and S. Francesco di Paola* (I, F1). The square (the ancient, irregular Largo di Palazzo, used especially for popular ceremonies and festivals) was "regularized" beginning in the end of the 18th c. with the construction of the Palazzo del Principe di Salerno, the symmetrical palazzo, to the north, now housing the prefecture, and above all with the construction of the Doric hemicycle ordered built by Murat (1810, architect, L. Laperuta) at the center of which is a basilica, a monumental votive offering of Ferdinand I for the reconquest of his kingdom after a decade of French occupation. Begun in 1817 by P. Bianchi, it was completed in 1846 in the latest forms of the neoclassical style; with the hemicycle and the nearby facade of the theater, or Teatro di S. Carlo, it constitutes one of the most important Neapolitan examples of this style. The church harks back to the shape of the Pantheon; inside it, there are statues and paintings from the same period, except for the main altar, a recycling of the 17th-c. altar that once stood in the church of the SS. Apostoli, and canvases (in the sacristy, note the *Circumcision* by A. Campi, 1586) which in part come from churches that once stood in the Largo di Palazzo.

Isolated in the square, set on simple pedestals, are *equestrian statues** of Charles of Bourbon and Ferdinand I (the former is by Canova, as is the horse in the latter, in which the figure of the king is by Antonio Calì).

S. Ferdinando (I, F1). This church, which appears to have been incorporated into the structures of the adjoining Galleria, was founded in 1622 with the title of S. Francesco Saverio, for the Jesuits, and following their expulsion, was given to the Knights of Constantine, who renamed the church in honor of the king. Inside one may note *frescoes** by Paolo De Matteis, sculptures by Lorenzo Vaccaro, and the tomb of the Duchess of Floridia, the morganatic bride of Ferdinand I, by T. Angelini; every Good Friday, the Stabat Mater composed by Pergolesi – for the Arciconfraternita to whom the church has belonged since 1837 – is performed here. Until 1919 the square had the same name, but has since been known as the Piazza Trieste e Trento; this is also a fundamental crossroads, marking the beginning of Via Toledo.

Galleria Umberto I (I, E-F1). This is one of the most representative buildings of late-19th-c. Naples, built (1887-90) to plans by E. Rocco, with decorations by E. Di Mauro, who made use of a design by A. Curri and a glazed iron roof by P. Boubée. On the main facade toward the theater are statues by the Carrarese sculptor Carlo Nicòli.

1.2 Via Toledo, the Quartieri Spagnoli, and Piazza Dante

The itinerary (see plan on p. 30) follows the route of Via Toledo as far as Piazza Dante, with the Spanish quarters on the left. The itinerary also reveals a number of aspects of the social life of the city, from solemn centers of economic power, with the major banks, to the streets crowded with shop windows (including a number of shops corresponding to "historic businesses," including old pharmacies and pastry shops, with late-19th-c. and Liberty decorations) and thriving streets and alleys, busy with working-class life.

Via Toledo (I, C-D-E-F1). Along the initial stretch of this street, you will note on the left the Palazzo Berio by L. Vanvitelli and the little square ("piazzetta") that takes its name from the Teatro Augusteo (by P. L. Nervi), and which is overlooked by the lower station, or Stazione Inferiore of the central funicular to the Vomero.

At the first crossroads on the right, you will take a short detour in the street (Via di S. Brigida) which takes its name from the church of S. Brigida, which was begun in 1640 and built very slowly until roughly 1726, then extensively restored in 1856 and again following the bombardment done by an Austrian dirigible in March of 1918; this church contains a virtual art gallery of 17th-c. art, with paintings by Stanzione, G. Farelli, and G. Simonelli (sacristy) and many works by Luca Giordano, who was buried here in 1705: the *Glory of St. Bridget* in the dome, and the *Biblical Heroines* in the spandrels (1678), as well as a *St. Nicholas** (1655) and *St. Ann* on the altars of the first chapels and of the left transept, Scenes of the *Last Judgment* and the *Passion* in the sacristy (1704-05). The dome is quite remarkable, standing only 9 m tall so as not to hinder the artillery of the neighboring Castel Nuovo; it culminates in a little spiral lantern.

We continue along Via Toledo. Immediately to the right is the *Banca Commerciale Italiana*, formerly the Palazzo Zevallos e Carafa di Stigliano, with a portal by Fanzago. On the interior (the banking hall is taken from the original courtyard with an interesting solution in the eclectic style) are neoclassical rooms, and paintings by Caravaggio (*St. Ursula Impaled**, 1610), De Mura, and Coccorante. Next comes the modern *Banco di Napoli*; on the left (no. 317) is the *Palazzo Lieto* and on the right (no. 148) is the 16th-c. *Palazzo Capece Galeota* (formerly Palazzo di Tappia), rebuilt in 1832 by S. Gasse; across the way are buildings corresponding to the structures originally ordered by the Viceroy Toledo for the quartering of the Spanish troops, until the middle of the 17th c., giving the present-day name to the area (the Quartieri Spagnoli) and the orthogonal layout of the street grid.

Of greater note is the monumental complex of **Montecalvario** (whence the name of the quarter) comprising the Franciscan church founded in 1560 (entrance from the Piazza di Montecalvario; on the interior, among other 16th-c. paintings, you should note the important *Triptych**, dating from the 1570s, the work of the Maestro di Montecalvario, now considered to be the Venetian painter Giovanni de Mio) and the church of the *Concezione a Montecalvario** (entrance from Via Concezione a Montecalvario), a masterpiece by D. A. Vaccaro (1720-24), who also did the paintings and stuccoes that adorn the luminous interior.

At the corner with Via Concezione a Montecalvario is the church of *S. Maria delle Grazie a Toledo* (rebuilt in 1835; on the interior, neoclassical paintings and altar dating from 1759 with sculptures by G. Sanmartino); following it, also on the left, are the

35

Palazzo Cavalcanti (no. 348) by Gioffredo (1762) and the *Palazzo del Nunzio* (at no. 352, site of the Nunziatura Apostolica, or Apostolic See, ever since the 16th c.).

The road opens out into the *Piazza Carità* which marks the beginning of the market, or Mercato della Pignasecca (see below). On the left, at no. 6, note the *Palazzo Mastelloni*, by Tagliacozzi Canale, which, with the adjoining *Palazzo Trabucco* at no. 1 of Via S. Liborio, constitutes a fine and well-preserved example of 18th-c. civil architecture (stairways at the far end of the courtyards). An-

Street market in the Spanish quarters

other palazzo adorned by interesting 18th-c. stuccoes stands at no. 368 of Via Toledo; across the way is Via Caravita, built in 1749, in accordance with an overall plan by Gioffredo, who designed the buildings that overlook the street, which frames the facade of Monteoliveto.

S. Nicola alla Carità (I, D1). Built by O. Gisolfi (1647) with a facade designed by Solimena, this church's interior provides a vast panorama of Neapolitan painting between the 17th c. and the 18th c. In the vaulted ceiling, note the *frescoes* by Solimena (1701), who also did the canvases in the cross vault (*Virgin Mary and Saints Peter and Paul**). In the presbytery and at the entrance, canvases by De Matteis; in the chapels, artwork by De Mura, A. d'Aste, and G. Diano, and a wooden *Crucifix* by N. Fumo.

Palazzo Carafa di Maddaloni (I, C1). Overlooking Via Toledo is one side of the palazzo (the monumental entrance portal is on Via Maddaloni), one of the most important of the Baroque era because of the prestige of its owners, its artistic importance, and its

overall size. Founded at the end of the 16th c., it became property of the Carafa di Maddaloni family, which had it enlarged and redecorated by Fanzago; in the sumptuous apartment on the main floor is a vast hall, its vaulted ceiling painted by F. Fischetti.

Palazzo Doria d'Angri (I, C1). Directly across the way from the previous palazzo, and built by C. Vanvitelli to plans by his father, Luigi (1755), this is one of the most important palazzi of the 18th c., in part because of its remarkable urban setting, at the intersection of two major thoroughfares, emphasized by the architect with the elegant composition of the facade (damaged during WWII). On the interior, on the second floor, are various rooms which preserve, to a greater or lesser degree, the 18th-c. decorations (gallery frescoed by F. Fischetti, with carvings, stuccoes, and mirrors; *boudoir* with remarkable carvings; ceilings painted by artists from the circle of the Vanvitelli); from the balcony of this palazzo Garibaldi – who lived here during the days of his dictatorship – proclaimed on 7 September 1860 the annexation of the southern regions to the Kingdom of Italy.

Spirito Santo* (I, C1). Founded in the 16th c. and rebuilt by Gioffredo – it is his masterpiece – this church was completed in 1774. In the large and luminous interiors are major artworks dating from the 16th c., taken from the previously existing church (sculptures by Naccherino, paintings by Santafede), and others executed in the 18th c. (paintings by De Mura, F. Fischetti, F. Celebrano). Atop it rises one of the most elegant domes in the city, which can best be admired from the little square at the end of the Vico de' Bianchi, site of the *Arciconfraternita dei Bianchi allo Spirito Santo*, one of the best-preserved structures of its kind.

Overlooking the little square is the elegant facade in piperno stone of *S. Maria Materdomini* (1573), once adorned with a *Virgin Mary with Christ Child** by F. Laurana (now on the interior, near the *Tomb of Fabrizio Pignatelli** by M. Naccherino); the church is connected to the hospital, founded by Pignatelli in the 16th c. to house pilgrims, and later enlarged; in the courtyard is the church of the **SS. Trinità dei Pellegrini**, built by L. Vanvitelli, and completed by his son Carlo. It has a handsome *interior** with an octagonal plan, with a rectangular presbytery, succeeded by a smaller octagon for the Confratelli; canvases from the 17th c. (*St. Januarius Praying for Naples* by O. Palumbo and D. Barra, with a lovely view of the city) and 18th c.

The Via Porta Medina leads to the 17th-c. church of *S. Maria di Montesanto* (A. Scarlatti is buried here), which gives its name to the quarter. In the square with the stations of the Ferrovia Cumana (with an iron shed) and the funicular that runs alongside the most extensive remains of the enclosure walls from the viceroyal period, against the backdrop of Castel Sant'Elmo; here once stood the Porta Medina, demolished in 1873. The sense of a "city gate" that the place still preserves (not far off is a subway station) can be seen in the vast crowds that daily fill Via di Porta Medina and by the survival of the old and popular Via Pignasecca market.

Via Montesanto (on the right in the nearby Vico Spezzano is the Palazzo Muscettola, which has been fitted with the 16th-c. doors from the demolished old Palazzo Vicereale) and Via Tarsia lead back to Via Toledo. Via Tarsia and Salita Tarsia partly bound one of the largest, most complex and most sumptuous princely palaces of Naples, so elaborate that it has been left unfinished and so large that it gave rise to a small quarter: the *Palazzo Tarsia*, built by D. A. Vaccaro in the 1730s for the Spinelli family, and in the 19th c., extensively transformed with the insertion of a neoclassical exhibition pavilion, which in turn became the Teatro Bracco. It is possible to see of the original structure the much decayed but very large courtyard (now the Piazza Tarsia) bounded by a hemicycle over which extends the enormous terrace-belvedere, offering a sweeping panoramic view.

S. Michele a Port'Alba* (I, C1). One of the jewels of 18th-c. Naples, this church was built by D. A. Vaccaro, and has a beautiful interior. Built between 1729 and 1735, it is a reconstruction of an earlier church; after the death of Vaccaro (1745) other fine features were added, such as the handsome font (1768) in the sacristy, intact in every item of furnishing. Vaccaro, who was a painter as well as an architect, is also thought to have done the canvases on the altars (with the exception of the main altar, featuring an older St. Michael, attributed to Marulli).

Piazza Dante (I, C1). This square was once called Piazza del Mercatello after the market that was held there from 1588 on. It is bounded by the hemicycle of the *Foro Carolino** built by L. Vanvitelli to serve as a setting for an equestrian monument to Charles of Bourbon, that was never built; its attic is decorated by 26 statues depicting a great array of virtues of that sovereign. In the large center niche was opened the entrance (1861) to the Convitto Nazionale Vittorio Emanuele II, housed in the rooms of the old monastery, or Convento di S. Sebastiano, of which it is still possible to make out (the church collapsed in 1939) the two cloisters; the older of the two cloisters is a rare relic of Naples between the Romanesque and Gothic eras (note the capitals). To the left of the hemicycle, the gate, or Port'Alba was built in 1625 in an older tower-keep, set in the viceroyal walls, adorned by a statue of St. Gaetano that once stood on the Porta Reale, since demolished. At the center, note the monument to *Dante* (1872) with a statue by T. Angelini. Across the way is the 17th-c. church of *S. Domenico Soriano* (inside is the tomb, or Sepolcro Falcone, by Sanmartino), the *Palazzo Ruffo di Bagnara* (at no. 89) and the church of *S. Maria di Caravaggio*, with an elliptical plan, the work of G. B. Nauclerio, with a façade dating from the earliest decades of the 18th c.

Close by is the only surviving suburban Aragonese villa, the *Conigliera di Alfonso II*, whose structures can be easily singled out at the end of the courtyard of the palazzo, with entrance from Vico Luperano no. 7.

The curved facade abutting Piazza Dante, created by Luigi Vanvitelli

2 Naples: the old center of the city

One of the chief monuments of Naples is the layout itself of the urban grid in the oldest center, almost perfectly preserved: a unique case for a city that has been inhabited without interruption, especially if we consider that for many centuries, Naples – along with Paris and Constantinople – was one of the largest cities in Europe. This center is based on three axes running east-west (*plateiai*, to use the ancient Greek term, or in Latin, *decumani*) intersecting at right angles with axes that run north–south (respectively *stenopoi* or *cardines*); they thus form blocks ("insule") that are rectangular in shape (160-180 x 20 m). In some cases, these blocks have been consolidated into "insule" that include two, or more, of the original blocks especially due to the presence of large religious complexes which – during the years of the Spanish viceroy, which coincided with the Counter Reformation as well – had the right to expand at will, at the expense of civil constructions. The plateau upon which ancient Neapolis once stood can be clearly made out, and a long "promenade" along its perimeter, besides along the visitor to see a number of ruins of the en-

Aerial view of the center of Naples, showing the straight groove cut by the "Spaccanapoli"

closure wall from the 5th or 4th c. B.C., allows one to reconstruct, mentally and "sensorially," the shape of those walls: you can still perceive (in spite of the extensive modern transformations) the drops toward the broad valleys that surrounded the plateau and you can follow streets whose routes follow that of the ancient walls. This walk can be repeated in quest of successive expansions dating back to Roman times, the Angevin and Aragonese periods and the time of the viceroy.

The city's hilly topography determined the future expansions of the enclosure walls, which were always minimal to the north, due to the ideal natural defensive position of Caponapoli and the waters that poured down in torrents from the nearby hills, and to the east, due to the presence of marshes. Naples grew during the Roman era and the high Middle Ages toward the sea, beginning a westward expansion that was continued under the Angevin kings. After becoming the capital of the kingdom under Charles I of Anjou, Naples continued to be enriched with the buildings that mark a true capital; it was to the immense efforts made by the Angevin rulers that we owe the creation of the new palace, the plan of the quarters toward the sea, the final appearance of the Piazza Mercato, and above all the construction of the cathedral and of nearly all the large churches. To the point that, as late as 1632, as one remarkable French traveler, J. J. Bouchard, noted, it was still common to hear the Neapolitans say (with clear anti-Spanish intent): "In short, we should say that Naples is French, for it was they who made her what she is."

While most of the religious architecture of the city dates back to the Gothic era, most of the private civil architecture was founded in the 16th c. Indeed, almost all of the palazzi are constructed around a core – which can be made out clearly beneath the many and varied encrustations – which involves a courtyard, to one side immediately within the main entryway, an open stairway, and, facing the entrance, a low loggia, often adjoining the garden. Another noteworthy feature of the Neapolitan palazzo is found in the importance taken on by the portal in the context of the facade: because of the shortage of space (the streets were the same ones that had been laid out by the ancient Greeks) the entrance was endowed with all of the significance of a "status symbol," and was therefore continually renovated. The daunting and almost simultaneous construction of so many palazzi in the 16th c. can be explained by the policies of the viceroys in favor of the transfer into the capital of the barons who still lived in the provinces. There then ensued the mass immigration of masons, artisans, and an entire populace who left the increasingly impoverished feudal holdings for a capital where the taxes were less burdensome (in the interests of public order) and it was always possible to eke out a living, until the population had risen to 300,000 by 1595. The pleasant city of orchards and vegetable patches and gardens changed before the astonished eyes of the old inhabitants into an unrecognizable and crowded metropolis, leading to the human and structural overcrowding that seems such an intrinsic part of our very idea of Naples, clearly visible in the streets of the oldest nucleus of the city.

2.1 Spaccanapoli: the lower decumanus

The itinerary (see plan on p. 30) runs through much of the historic center, linking two of the principal churches (Monteoliveto and the Annunziata) along a route that is largely constituted by the thoroughfare of the lower *decumans* of the ancient city and its westward extension, commonly called "Spaccanapoli" – literally, "Naples-splitter" – because from the vantage points of the Certosa and Castel S. Elmo it seems to divide (at least until the turn of the twentieth c.) the city into two nearly equal parts.

This thoroughfare is an unbroken succession of squares, churches, spires, and palazzi, some of the most important in Naples (the church of Gesù Nuovo with its spire, S. Chiara and its cloisters, the Piazza S. Domenico and the Cappella Sansevero, the statue of the Nile and Via S. Gregorio Armeno) which have most served to codify and stereotype the tourist's idea of Naples as a "city of art"; monuments which are certainly wonderful, but which are not all the city has to offer.

Along with the variations in architecture and artworks, you may note sharp changes in the social settings, which shift gradually from Monteoliveto, location of the large barracks of the Carabinieri, or paramilitary police, to Forcella, in the narrow lanes of which it seems that one can almost detect a different atmosphere from the rest of the city, crossing the Piazza del Gesù, and the Piazza S. Domenico, close to the various university campuses and the center of student life.

There are also a variety of commercial activities: at S. Biagio dei Librai books are no longer sold (as the name might suggest), and instead old jewelry is traded, perhaps because of the proximity of the ancient Monte di Pietà, or church-run pawn shop, while in Via S. Gregorio Armeno there is a

long succession of crafts shops selling crèches and artificial flowers.

Monteoliveto* (I, D1). This church is also known by the name of S. Anna dei Lombardi because, with the suppression of the monastery, it was assigned, at the turn of the 19th c., to the Confraternita dei Lombardi. Founded in 1411, it was a favorite of the Aragonese court. The monastery stood in an area outside of the city proper, pleasant and abounding in gardens and vast empty spaces, allowing numerous expansions over the centuries, traces of which remain – even after extensive demolitions – in a cloister, with two orders of pillars (with entrances from Via Monteoliveto and Via Battisti).

The facade is characterized by the facing, in piperno stone, of two Renaissance chapels, which flank a Catalan arch; in the atrium, note the tomb of the architect D. Fontana. The interior is a full-fledged museum of Neapolitan sculpture from the 15th and 16th c. A particular importance are the three Renaissance chapels, with marked Tuscan forms, due to the close links of the Aragonese court with the Medici court, the presence of Tuscan artists, and the purchase of artworks from Florence: in the first chapel (*Cappella Piccolomini**), note the exact replica of the chapel, or Cappella del Cardinale di Portogallo from the Florentine church of S. Miniato al Monte, as well as the *Tomb of Mary of Aragón*, by A. Rossellino and B. da Maiano, and, also by Rossellino, the *Nativity and Saints* on the altar; in the second chapel (*Cappella Tolosa**) which is particularly reminiscent of Brunelleschi's style from the Sagrestia Vecchia, note the Della Robbia tondos and the frescoes; in the third chapel (*Cappella Terranova**) note the *Annuncia-*

tion with Saints* also by Maiano. Among the most noteworthy artworks, we would point out, as well, in the counterfacade the altar, or Altare Del Pezzo* (to the left) by G. Santacroce, the altar, or Altare Ligorio (to the right) by Giovanni da Nola, and the late 17th-c. organ, flanked by frescoes by Battistello Caracciolo. To the right of the presbytery stands a large chapel with a renowned group in terracotta of the Lament Over Christ** by the Modenese artist Guido Mazzoni (1492); on the walls, note the frescoes with Bible Stories by a Spanish painter, Roviale. From here, you will enter the Old Sacristy*, formerly a refectory, a splendid room with vaulted ceilings frescoed (1544) by Giorgio Vasari and assistants, and on the walls, wooden inlays* by Fra' Giovanni da Verona, once in the Cappella Tolosa. In the presbytery, with its 16th-c. apse, note the marble-inlaid altar by the Ghetti brothers, executed to designs by Vinaccia and a wooden choir dating from the 16th c.

Palazzo Gravina (I, D1-2). This palazzo stands in Via Monteoliveto, facing Largo Gravina, which terminates in the fountain built by D. A. Cafaro, with a statue of Charles II of Spain as a boy. This is an example of Tuscan and Roman styles unknown in Naples, and was built in the first half of the 16th c. by Gabriele d'Angelo for the family of the Orsini di Gravina, with a portal rebuilt by Gioffredo. The building is currently used by the department of architecture; destroyed more than once, it preserves of the old decorations only tondos with heraldic crests and portraits of the Orsini family by V. Ghiberti (in the courtyard).

Guglia dell'Immacolata * (I, C2). This spire is one of the most important products of 18th-c. Neapolitan sculpture, and was the work of the sculptors F. Pagano and M. Bottigliero and the architects G. Genoino and G. Di Fiore; it was built at the behest of the Jesuits, who wanted to celebrate one of the most important points in their preaching and, at the same time, the Company of Jesus itself (the sculptures in fact depict Jesuit saints and Life of the Virgin Mary). It appears, like the other "guglie" or spires, as a "petrification" of one of the countless "festival machines" that on a wide variety of oc-

The 18th-century Guglia dell'Immacolata

casions were assembled, modifying periodically the appearance of the Baroque city.

Gesù Nuovo * (I, C2). This large Jesuit church was built (1584-97) with the incorporation of the structures of the large Palazzo Sanseverino di Salerno, built in 1470 by Novello di San Lucano, who left his "signature" in the epigraph that interrupts on the left the compact diamond-point rustication of the facade (uncommon in Naples but quite frequent in the provinces of the kingdom); the Baroque portal incorporates the Renaissance portal of the palazzo. The church, with central plan, and with a "scodella" dome (replacing the original dome, which collapsed) has an interior that has been sumptuously sheathed with marble facing, stuccoes, and frescoes. Among them, we would point out, in the counterfacade, the Expulsion of Heliodorus from the Temple* by F. Solimena (1725), the vaulted ceilings of the nave (Corenzio and De Matteis), the pendentives with the Evangelists* by Lanfranco, the Life of the Virgin Mary, by Stanzione in the vault of the tribune, Life of St. Ignatius and St. Francis Saverio by Corenzio and De Matteis in the vaults of the transept. Almost all of the most important marble workers, sculptors, and painters active in Naples between the end of the 16th c. and the middle of the 19th c. have left their marks in the church: in the chapel, or Cappellone di S. Francesco Saverio (right transept) canvases by Giordano, and sculptures by Fanzago; in the facing chapel, or Cappellone di S. Ignazio, architecture and sculptures (David and Jeremiah) by Fanzago; in the presbytery, note the main altar (1851-57) with a statue of Our Lady of the Immaculate Conception, to whom the church is dedicated (Immacolata). In the chapels, note paintings Stanzione, Azzolino (Virgin and Saints, 1st on the left), S. Conca, G. Imparato (Nativity, 2nd on the left); sculptures by G. B. Gallone and D. Di Nardo (wooden reliquaries, chapel at the end of the left side aisle, where there is also a handsome altar by G. Bastelli), F. Mollica, T. Montani, M. Naccherino, P. Bernini, and G. D'Auria. In the sacristy, devastated by a fire (1962), note the frescoes by Aniello Falcone, the altar and basin by D. Lazzari, and cabinets that were probably designed by Fanzago.

S. Chiara** (I, C2). This church was built at the orders of Robert of Anjou and Queen Sancha in 1310 by Gagliardo Primario; it was linked to convent of Clarissan nuns, and was to be used as a "pantheon" of the monarchs of Naples, and is one of the best-known churches in the city. Its immense nave was transformed (1742-69) into one of the most astonishing interiors of 18th-c. Italy, but it was completely destroyed by fire following a bombardment in 1943; all that survived was destroyed by the restoration (completed in 1953) that "gave it back" its Gothic form.

You enter the monastic complex through a portal made of piperno stone; the facade of the church, with a pronaos with three apertures, is adorned only by an enormous rose window. The interior is unified, simple, and immediately comprehensible in its spatial articulation, as is appropriate for a Franciscan church, and it comprises a single nave covered with a truss roof (now the trusses are made of reinforced concrete), with ten chapels on each side, surmounted by a continuous tribune, and ending in a flat wall that serves as a filter linking up with the nuns' choir. With a few exceptions, the artworks that were moved here date from the 14th and 15th c. In particular, note the royal tombs, or *Tombe Reali**: on the far wall, there looms the giant remains of the *Sepolcro di Roberto d'Angiò** (tomb of Robert of Anjou), the largest single funerary monument of medieval Italy, the work of the Florentine brothers Giovanni and Pacio Bertini (1343-45); to the left is the tomb of Maria of Durazzo, by followers of the Bertini; to the right are the tombs of *Charles of Calabria* (ca. 1330-33) and *Mary of Valois* (ca. 1333-38), both by Tino di Camaino. Tino di Camaino also created what remains (7th chapel on the right) of the tomb of their daughter Mary. On either side of the entrance are the tombs of Clemenza and Agnese of Durazzo (on the right, by an unknown sculptor influenced by Tino, from the early 15th c.) and the *tomb of Onofrio and Antonio Penna* (on the left) by A. Baboccio (1407-14). In the 8th chapel on the right, fragment of the tomb of *Ludovico of Durazzo* by P. Bertini (1344).

Among the other works of art, we would point out, in the 10th chapel on the right, tombs of the Bourbons, the *tomb of Philip of Bourbon*, to plans by Fuga with putti by Sanmartino, and the *tomb of Maria Cristina di Savoia* (Marie Christine of Savoy), the wife of Ferdinand II; on the altar, panel by the Florentine G. Macchietti, in the floor and on the walls, epigraphs concerning the buried sovereigns and their relatives; the *Gothic main altar* is surmounted by a wooden *Crucifix*, dating back to the foundation of the church, the tomb, or *Sepolcro Longobardo* (10th chapel on the left) by G. T. Malvito; in the 9th chapel a sarcophagus with a depiction of the myth of *Protesilaus and Laodamia* (4th-3rd c. B.C.); in the 7th chapel the tombs of Balzo (14th c.) and S. Francesco by M. Naccherino.

To the right of the presbytery area, you enter the sacristy (in an adjoining room, large *embroidered cloth* dating from the 17th c.) and to two rooms which then lead to the nuns' choir, or Coro delle Monache and to the convent: the former (A) is faced with majolicas similar to those of the cloisters, while the latter preserves its 16th-c. frescoes. From here, through a 14th-c. *marble portal*, you can reach the **Coro delle Clarisse***, the work of Leonardo di Vito, designed as a separate church and standing as one of the most important Gothic monuments in Naples; with its two solitary pillars it is almost reminiscent of a chapter hall ("sala capitolare"). Following the extensive damage suffered during the war, it was stripped of the sumptuous decorations accumulated over the centuries, and it is now adorned only by the *funerary slab* meant for the provisional burial of King Robert and by fragments of a *Lament Over the Dead Christ*, the sole surviving sections of the cycle that

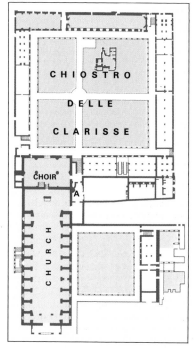

Plan of the Convent of S. Chiara

was frescoed in this church (1328-30) by Giotto and his assistants.

The **Chiostro delle Clarisse****, or cloisters of the Clarissans, was a result of the 18th-c. projects for the renewal of the Angevin complex; D. A. Vaccaro preserved the Gothic deambulatory, creating in its center a refined, "secular" rustic garden, decorated with majolica figured tiling* by Giuseppe and Donato Massa, devoid of any reference to holy matters, in which the dominant colors – yellow, green, and light blue – are the

The Chiostro delle Clarisse at S. Chiara

same as the sky and the grapevines and the lemons that grow between the pillars that support the pergolas.

In the setting of the immense monastery, still undergoing restoration, it is possible to see the cloisters, or *Chiostro dei Francescani*, in its intact medieval form, the hall, or *Sala Maria Cristina* with detached 14th-c. frescoes, and the rooms that now contain the museum, or *Museo dell'Opera di S. Chiara*, where you can see the remains of a bath house dating from the first or second c. A.D., as well as an array of artifacts that tell the history of the complex.

Once you emerge from the enclosure of the convent citadel, you may note the campanile that, over the first 14th-c. floor, features two stories dating back to the late 16th c.

Via Benedetto Croce (I, C2). This street begins at the church of S. Chiara (a view back at Castel S. Elmo). At no. 12 is the *Palazzo Filomarino della Rocca*, of 14th-c. origin (remains along the walls of the staircase), but rebuilt in the 16th c. by Di Palma (monumental courtyard), restored in 1650 and again in the 18th c. (portal by Sanfelice); Benedetto Croce lived and died here (1952); the apartment on the main floor houses

the Istituto Italiano di Studi Storici which he founded.

At no. 19 is the *Palazzo Venezia*, the headquarters of the ambassadors of the Serenissima from 1412 until the fall of the Venetian Republic (plaques in the courtyard).

Piazza di S. Domenico* and the Guglia di S. Domenico (I, C2). This square was built by Alfonso I, who also ordered the construction of the large stairway in piperno stone (rebuilt in the 19th c.) alongside the apse of the Dominican church. The eastern side, irregular in the context of the older urban layout, corresponds to the circuit of the ancient Greek walls. At the center is the *Guglia* (spire), begun in 1658 as a votive offering for deliverance from the plague, by F. A. Picchiatti and completed by D. A. Vaccaro in 1737.

This square is bounded by noteworthy instances of civil construction. Facing the apses of the church is the *Palazzo Sangro di Casacalenda*, begun by Gioffredo in 1766 and carried forward by L. Vanvitelli; one bay of the structure was demolished in 1922 to make way for the expansion of the adjoining Via Mezzocannone; on the main floor note a number of rooms frescoed by F. Fischetti; on the western side of the square stands the 15th-c. *Palazzo Petrucci*, which preserves from that period the marble portal and the loggias in the courtyard; it was the headquarters between 1698 and 1806 of the Banco del Salvatore (literally, "Bank of the Savior," see bust of the *Savior* in the entryway). Across the way is the *Palazzo Corigliano*, now housing departments of the Istituto Universitario Orientale; built in the 16th c. and traditionally attributed to Mormando, it was enlarged and rebuilt in the 18th c., and again in the 19th c., by G. Genovese; it still preserves its 16th-c. forms in the base and sumptuous rooms with decorations (1734-41) that culminated in the *Cabinet del Duca**, one of the loveliest and best-preserved Rococo interiors in all Naples.

S. Domenico Maggiore* (I, C2). The square is dominated by the apsidal section (into which opens the usual entrance) of the large church built at the behest of Charles II and built (1283-1324) by incorporating the existing church of S. Michele Arcangelo a Morfisa, toward the portal of which (which mixes Gothic and Renaissance styles) climbs the staircase, on the left. The vast monastic complex, Casa Maggiore dell'Ordine dei Predicatori nel Regno di

Napoli, was the headquarters of theological studies for the university of Naples, and its guests have included St. Thomas Aquinas and Giordano Bruno. The facade, as in other churches founded during the Angevin period, overlooks a courtyard (with entrance from the Vico S. Domenico) and reveals the complex stratification that characterizes the church.

The interior has something of the sweep and span of a cathedral (nave and two side aisles, with side chapels) and presents the appearance given it during the "restoration" undertaken by F. Travaglini (1850-53), who replaced the 16th-c. and Baroque decorations with neo-Gothic decorations (with the exception of the flooring, the ceiling of the nave, and the balustrades of the chapels), including among the modern stuccoes, 14th-c. sculptures.

The tour of the church, one of the richest in artworks in all Naples (a truly imposing series of tombs from the 14th to 19th c), begins to the right of the counterfacade, in which you will find the Renaissance chapel, or Cappella Carafa di Santaseverina by R. Balsimelli, with the remarkable 19th-c. tomb, or Sepolcro Saluzzo. In the 2nd chapel on the right (see plan below, 1, Brancaccio) *frescoes** by Pietro Cavallini (1308-09) with *Life of St. Andrew, Mary Magdalene, and St. John the Evangelist*. In the 4th chapel (2) paintings by Marco Pino (*Baptism of Christ*), Teodoro d'Errico (*Resurrection*), and P. De Rosa; in the 5th chapel (3) *Madonna dell'Umiltà** by Roberto d'Odorisio.

Next comes the chapel, or *Cappellone del Crocefisso** (A), with various Carafa family tombs, with sculptures dating from the 15th to the 18th c., by various artists, including J. della Pila and the Malvito. To the right,

Resurrection, by V. Cobergher. On the far wall, between the *Deposition** by Colantonio and the *Calvary** by Pedro Férnandez (both of which are currently in storage, for considerations of security) is a reproduction of the *Crucifixion* (mid-13th c., in storage), venerated because supposedly its Christ is alleged to have spoken to St. Thomas. To the left of the altar, note the chapel, or *Cappella Carafa di Ruvo** (4), one of the most refined artworks of the Renaissance in Naples, by R. Balsimelli (1511) with wooden crèche statues by P. Belverte (1507), the *Tomb of Ettore Carafa* by G. T. Malvito and frescoes in the dome by P. Férnandez, and a chapel for which Raphael painted his *Madonna del Pesce*, now in the Prado. Once you return to the nave, you can enter the *sacristy** (B), which is famous for the elegant homogeneity of the Baroque setting (wooden furnishings designed by Nauclerio, *Triumph of Faith*, by Solimena, 1706, in the vaulted ceiling, frescoes by G. del Po, 1711, in the chapel, or Cappella Milano, 5, which terminates the sacristy; altar of the Ghetti) and because it contains, all around the walkway (this is unique in all of Europe) the tombs of 10 Aragonese and Spanish sovereigns and 35 dignitaries, including the Marchese di Pescara, Ferrante d'Avalos, victor in the battle of Pavia (1525); in the floor, note the modern funerary slab of the first Catholic bishop of New York, who died in Naples immediately after his consecration, while waiting to leave for America. From the transept, you will enter the old church of S. Michele a Morfisa which houses, among many others, the tomb, or *Sepolcro Vicentini* (8) by Bottigliero and the tomb of the composer Nicola Zingarelli (7). In the left transept, note the *Tomba Pandone** (6; 1514, by G. T. Malvito with lunette by Giovanni da Nola), and, higher up, the front of the tomb of John of Anjou (Sepolcro di Giovanni d'Angiò) by Tino di Camaino. In the presbytery, dominated by a large 18th-c. organ, note the *monumental altar** with marble inlay in lively polychromy by Fanzago, a Paschal candelabrum dating from 1585, in which are recycled the statues of the Virtues, by the workshop of Tino di Camaino, for the tomb, since dismembered, of Philip of Anjou (Filippo d'Angiò, 9). In the left transept (1st chapel, 10, copy by A. Vaccaro of the *Flagellation* painted by Caravaggio for this church, now in Capodimonte) tomb of R. Del Doce by G. T. Malvito and Giovanni da Nola, and higher up, a funerary *slab from the tomb of Philip of Anjou*, by Tino di Camaino (11). Return down along the left side aisle and you will find, at the be-

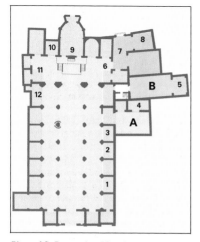

Plan of S. Domenico Maggiore

ginning, the altar of the *Madonna della Neve** by Giovanni da Nola (12; 1536) and the cenotaph of the poet G. B. Marino.

Cappella Sansevero* (I, C2). Overlooking the nearby Via De Sanctis is an aristocratic chapel (S. Maria della Pietà or Pietatella) that until 1889 was linked to the Palazzo Sangro with an aerial passageway. This is one of the most interesting 18th-c. complexes in Naples, and is strongly marked by the personality of the Principe Raimondo di Sangro, who, between 1749 and 1771, oversaw the reconstruction of the chapel, which was founded in 1590. On the interior, with frescoed vaulted ceilings (F.M. Russo), are the Sangro family tombs, largely executed in accordance with the iconographic indications of the client, by A. Corradini (sculptures to the left of the entrance; *Veiled Modesty**), F. Queirolo (medallions set between the windows; *Liberality, Sincerity, Disillusionment**), F. Celebrano (main altar with a *Deposition*, monument to *Cecco di Sangro* at the entrance), P. Persico (*Pleasure of the Marital Yoke*), F. M. Russo (*cenotaph of Raimondo di Sangro*). The stretch of pavement with a labyrinth lying before the cenotaph was designed by Raimondo himself. Among the other artworks, we should mention the renowned *Veiled Christ**, formerly in the crypt, a masterpiece by Sanmartino (1753), two ovals on copper by C. Amalfi, and four tombs that existed prior to the 18th-c. renovation, including a *monument to Paolo di Sangro** (1st chapel on the left) by B. Landini (marble work) and G. Mencaglia (sculptures). In the crypt, note two 18th-c. *anatomic machines*, which contributed to the reputation as inventor and "sorcerer" of Raimondo, a remarkable figure of a scientist and man of letters, as well as a Masonic Grand Master.

S. Angelo a Nilo (I, C2). At the entrance to Via Mezzocannone is this small church, founded in 1385 as an aristocratic chapel of the family of the Brancaccio. Its exterior and interior appearance dates from the 18th-c. renovation done by A. Guglielmelli (*portals* from the 14th and 15th c. with wooden doors dating from the turn of the 16th c.). Among the

Statue of Veiled Modesty in the Cappella Sansevero

numerous funerary monuments you should note (to the right of the presbytery) the *tomb of Rinaldo Brancaccio***, the founding cardinal, completed in Pisa in 1426-28 by Donatello, Michelozzo, and Pagno di Lapo Portigiani, and sent to Naples by sea; an outstanding work from the transitional phase between a lingering Gothic style and a Renaissance style of a startling modernity (the openwork of the bas-relief of the *Assumption**, the only part that can be attributed with certainty to Donatello). Adjoining is the *tomb of Pietro Brancaccio* by J. della Pila; on the altar, note the *St. Michael* by Marco Pino (1573), across from which is the monumental Baroque tomb of Francesco and Stefano Brancaccio by B. and P. Ghetti. In the chapel, or Cappella di S. Candida, a canvas by C. Sellitto.

Piazzetta Nilo (I, C2). This little square takes its name from the statue of the River Nile, dating from the Hellenistic period, and found on this site; it was later set on a pedestal in the adjoining Largo Corpo di Napoli. The square was the site of the Seggio di Nido, the remains of which may perhaps be in the loggia that was incorporated into the church of *S. Maria dei Pignatelli*, an aristocratic chapel ("cappella gentilizia") which, under its 18th-c. appearance, preserves Gothic features; on the interior, note the fine chapel with marble facing that dates from the 16th century. At the beginning of Via Nilo at no. 26 is the *Palazzo del Panormita* later known as Palazzo Capece Galeota (heraldic crest in the vault of the entryway), one of the most important and best preserved examples of architecture dating from the 16th c. in Naples.

Palazzi Carafa (I, C3). At the beginning of Via S. Biagio dei Librai, at no. 8 stands the *Palazzo Carafa di Montorio* – characterized by a monumental cornice and built in the 16th c. by joining two existing buildings (it still shows signs of the damage caused by fire in 1944) – and, across the way, at no. 121, one of the most important civil buildings of the Neapolitan Renaissance, the *Palazzo Carafa di Maddaloni**, built in 1467 for Diomede Carafa, a Humanist who was in contact with

Lorenzo the Magnificent. The taste for collections of antiquities that distinguished the owner of this palazzo can be seen in the surviving busts, set, with a statue of Hercules, as decorations of the *portal*, and in other works of marble in the courtyard. The palazzo, faced with a flat rustication (now darkened by the elements, but originally marked by a Gothic-style polychromatic decoration, with ashlars alternating in a yellow and a dark tufa-stone, covered with pinkish plaster), clearly shows the mixture of Italian and Catalan architectural elements that so marked the latter half of the 15th c. in Naples (basket arch in the entryway, foliate capitals, portal showing clear influence of Leon Battista Alberti). Particularly noteworthy are the wooden doors of the portal, carved in a late-Gothic style, with the heraldic emblem of the Carafa family.

S. Nicola a Nilo (I, C3). This little church, built to a central plan, has a vibrant Baroque facade; running up to that facade are two "pinzer" staircases, which are always crowded with vendors selling objects of all sorts, a little "flea market" that, along with the flower-covered pergola that adorns a votive aedicule at the side of Palazzo Carafa, the monumental buildings, and the ancient commemorations (*stele* with a Greek epigraph at the beginning of the Vico S. Nicola a Nilo), all help to make this stretch of the lower *decumanus* one of the most picturesque places in Naples.

S. Maria Donnaromita (I, C2-3). A short way after the Baroque facade of the church of the *SS. Andrea e Marco a Nilo* is, on the right, the Renaissance facade of the church that was linked to the medieval monastery of Donnaromita, rebuilt by Di Palma in 1535. The interior, stripped of its Baroque decorations, presents the distinctive features of the Neapolitan Renaissance; the prime ornament of the church is the splendid carved *ceiling** with paintings by Teodoro d'Errico. On the counterfacade and alongside the windows are canvases by De Mura; in the dome, note a fresco by Giordano. There is a rare relic of Naples of the ducal era in the tomb, or *Sepolcro del Duca Teodoro* (A.D. 719-29).

S. Maria di Montevergine (Monteverginella; I, C3). This church too is linked to a monastery founded during the Middle Ages (1314), completely rebuilt in the age of the Counter Reformation (1588), as can be seen by the distinctive forms of the church's facade, punctuated by simple pilaster strips made of piperno stone. On the interior,

note the frescoes and canvases by D. A. Vaccaro (who also designed much of the marble work), F. Di Maria, 17th-c. choir and organ. In the 5th chapel on the left, note the *Madonna della Vittoria*, a remarkable panel dating from the 16th c., in the background of which is depicted the Battle of Lepanto, surmounted by the tiara and keys of St. Peter, transformed into cannons which fire at the Turkish fleet. In the large convent, note the handsome cloisters.

Cortile del Salvatore and the Gesù Vecchio (I, C3). A little further along, on the right, is the elegant entry portal (fastigium by Fanzago), leading into the monumental *Cortile del Salvatore*, part of the Collegio Gesuitico, or Jesuit college, incorporated into the complex of buildings of the main campus of the university, or Università.

The courtyard stands alongside the church, which was begun in 1564; on the sumptuous interior, on the altars of the transept, on the right, note the *Isaiah** and *Jeremiah** by Fanzago and the canvas by C. Fracanzano; on the left, Joshua and Gideon by Matteo Bottigliero, and the canvas by F. Solimena, in the chapels, artworks by Battistello Caracciolo (2nd on the left), Ghetti and Vinaccia (3rd on the right), G. Cenatiempo (1st and 4th on the left).

SS. Marcellino e Festo (I, C3). On a line with the portal of the Cortile del Salvatore is a lane, or "vico" that, with a handsome view of the distant campanile of S. Agostino alla Zecca, leads to the silent Largo S. Marcellino. The church of the SS. Marcellino e Festo, adjoining the nearby monastic complex (now housing university institutes) created (1566) from the merger of the monasteries of S. Marcellino and S. Festo, dates back to the 8th c. On the interior of the 17th-c. structures, done however in the Renaissance style, there extends an array of 18th-c. decorations that stands out for the refined polychrome assortment of marbles (designed by L. Vanvitelli) and the elegance of the wooden carvings in the jalousies, which are linked to the 17th-c. carvings in the ceiling (the paintings have since been removed and put in storage). Of considerable importance is the *ancona** of the main altar, adorned with statues and marble inlay by D. Lazzari (1666).

On the interior of the vast *cloisters** – which shows in the use of pillars, in the absence of one side (in order to allow the building to open out in a panoramic view of the sea), and in the gentle slope of the jutting balconies, the distinctive features of much of the monastic typology of Naples in the Counter Reformation – you will find a handsome garden beyond which, from a terrace, you can see at a lower elevation the *Oratorio della Scala Santa*, an oratory built by L. Vanvitelli.

SS. Severino e Sossio* (I, C3). One of the oldest, largest, and richest monasteries in Naples, founded by the Benedictines in the high Middle Ages and rebuilt from 1490 on. In 1835, in this vast monastery, the Grande Archivio del Regno, now the Archivio di Stato (state archives, see below) was installed. The 16th-c. church begun by Di Palma has an 18th-c. facade by G. del Gaizo (in the church courtyard, note the transennas made of piperno stone by G. B. Nauclerio in 1737). Dominating the vast and handsome interior, abounding in artworks, are the vaulted ceilings frescoed with *Life of St. Benedict**, a masterpiece (1740) by Francesco De Mura, who also painted the canvases beside the large windows (*Saints and Pontiffs*) and in the counterfacade (*Supper in the House of the Pharisee*). In the 16th-c. flooring (the only example of its type surviving in Naples) you may note a succession of funerary slabs. In the chapels (many of which were frescoed by Belisario Corenzio, who did the frescoes in the vaulted ceiling of the nave, which collapsed following the earthquake of 1713, and by G. A. Criscuolo) are works* by Marco Pino (to the right in the 1st, 3rd, and 6th chapels, the *Nativity of the Virgin Mary*, *Our Lady of the Assumption*, the *Epiphany*, and frescoes in the vaulted ceiling; to the left in the 1st chapel, *Nativity*). And there are others by G. A. Tenerello (marble ancona and tomb in the 2nd chapel on the right), G. A. Criscuolo (*Annunciation* in the 5th chapel on the right), Giovan Bernardo Lama (*Deposition* in the 3rd chapel on the left), Andrea da Salerno (*polyptych* in the 2nd chapel on the left, taken from the lower church). On the right, following the chapels you will see the vestibule of the sacristy with, on the left, the Medici chapel, or Cappella Medici (*Virgin Mary and Saints*, by F. Santafede, 1593, sculptures by G. D'Auria and frescoes by A. Nucci). To the right, facing it, is the *Tomb by Andrea Bonifacio**, a masterpiece (1518-19) by B. Ordóñez with an epigraph dictated (as was the case for the handsome tomb, or *Tomba Cicara*, by the Tuscan sculptor Andrea Ferrucci, facing it) by Sannazaro. The Tomba Bonifacio, done for a child that died at the age of six, has a highly original layout, with putti supporting the body of the dead child, while others hold up the cover of the sarcophagus, which resembles that in the

lovely *Lament Over Christ*, on the base. From here, you can descend to the older lower church, or Chiesa Inferiore (on the exterior side, note the remains of Gothic arches) with a Renaissance appearance. From the right transept (floor in marble inlay, 1697, *Deposition* from the *Cross* by G. Imparato, *Nailing on the Cross*, by C. Smet) you will pass into the chapel, or *Cappella Sanseverino** with the *tombs of Ascanio, Jacopo, and Sigismondo Sanseverino*, three brothers who were poisoned by their uncle in order to gain possession of their feudal holdings, a highly original work by Giovanni da Nola and assistants (1539-45); on the floor, behind the altar, is the handsome tomb, or *Tomba della Madre Ippolita de' Monti*. The sumptuous presbytery is enclosed by a balustrade of inlaid marble designed by Fanzago, who also completed the *altar** (1643, extensively renovated in 1783), in the vaulted ceiling (the central panel has been redone) note the frescoes by Corenzio (who died in his eighties, falling from the scaffolding, and is buried in the church, beneath the Greek epigraph near the 2nd pillar on the right in the nave); a splendid *carved choir** (1560-73) by B. Tortelli; a monumental wood-and-papier-maché organ (1774). To the left of the presbytery is the chapel, or Cappella Gesualdo with the *tomb of Carlo Troya*; in the left transept, note the *tomb of Vincenzo Carafa* by M. Naccherino and a *Calvary* by Marco Pino (1577). In the 7th chapel on the left you may see the Crucifix donated, before the battle of Lepanto, by Pope Pius V to Don John of Austria.

Monte di Pietà* (I, C3). This austere, compact palazzo was built by Cavagna (1597-1605). A solemn but airy atrium, lined with pillars, frames at the end of the courtyard the chapel, or Cappella della Pietà, one of the most noteworthy and well preserved complexes of art in Naples in the transition between the 16th and 17th c. In the facade, note sculptures by P. Bernini and M. Naccherino (1601); on the interior, note the frescoes by B. Corenzio, amidst gilt stuccoes and paintings by I. Borghese, G. Imparato, and F. Santafede; in the ante-sacristy, the Monumento Acquaviva by Fanzago; the sacristy (with furnishings, floor, and ceiling painted by G. Bonito) and the hall, or Sala delle Cantoniere are perfectly preserved 18th-c. rooms.

Via S. Biagio dei Librai (I, B-C3). At no. 31 in this street is the house in which G. B. Vico was born and where Vico's father had his bookstore, one of the many bookstores that lined this street, which takes its name from the church of the confraternity of the booksellers. *Via S. Gregorio Armeno*, characterized by the hanging campanile of the church of S. Gregorio Armeno, is traditionally the heart of the Neapolitan crafts tradition and is one of the best known streets of the historic center, for its market of statues and articles for crèches, which takes place in November and December.

S. Gregorio Armeno* (I, B3). This vast monastery is one of the oldest and one of the richest in artworks in the area; it was founded in the 8th c. by nuns who were fleeing the iconoclastic movement of Byzantium, and was completely rebuilt, after the Counter Reformation, by G. V. della Monica, who assisted Cavagna in the reconstruction of the church (completed in 1580) with its single nave, chapels, and dome over the square presbytery, and a simple facade in which there is a porticoed atrium with pillars supporting the choir (handsome carved

View down Via S. Gregorio Armeno

door dating from the 16th c.). The interior of the church, sumptuously homogeneous in its green and gold colors, despite the fact that it was decorated between the 16th and 18th c., is dominated by a stupendous carved-wood *ceiling**, painted from 1580 on by Teodoro d'Errico and his workshop, covering the length of the church, including the nuns' choir, hidden by a lovely 18th-c. jalousies. Over the entrance are frescoes by Luca Giordano (1679) depicting *The Arrival in Naples of the Nuns with the Relics of the Saint** (probable self-portrait in the figure of the man showing the nuns the way to the refuge). The *main altar** with splendid inlays in semiprecious stones was done to a design (ca. 1650) by Dionisio Lazzari; note the lovely speaking grate. Completely the decorative array are 18th-c. artworks executed under the supervision of Tagliacozzi Canale: the carved jalousies, the spectacular wooden and papier-maché choir lofts, the balustrades with iron bars on all the chapels. Among the paintings, works by S. Buono (*Our Lady of the Immaculate Conception*, near the en-

trance), Giovan Bernardo Lama (*Ascension*, on the main altar and in the 3rd chapel on the left), P. De Rosa (*Annunciation*, 1st chapel on the right), F. Fracanzano (*Life of St. Gregory the Armenian and Tiridates** on the sides in the 3rd chapel on the right, 1635).

In the last chapel on the right are housed the remains and other relics of Saint Patricia (taken from the convent dedicated to her, since suppressed), greatly venerated by the Neapolitans, to the point that this church is popularly known by her name.

If you skirt the high enclosure wall, absolutely without openings, continuing past the bell tower, you will reach the entrance to the convent, with a long easy stairway that climbs up to the vestibule: even here you can sense the remarkable wealth of the convent in the frescoes by G. del Po on the walls of the vestibule, the marble benches, the sumptuous "wheel" forms on either side of the entrance, the furnishing of the atrium. The *cloisters**, lovely and noteworthy for their remarkable state of preservation, set on pillars and open to provide a panoramic view of the gulf, has in its center, amidst the rows of citrus trees, a large *marble fountain** lined with life-size statues depicting the meeting at the well of Christ and the Samaritan woman, by M. Bottigliero (1733). The secular and theatrical flavor of the whole (so common in Neapolitan cloisters of the 18th c.) is enhanced by the spectacular Rococo background that masks the view of the cisterns and the Cappella dell'Idria (the sole, exquisite remains, redecorated, of the medieval convent). From the cloisters you can enter the nuns' choir, which is at the same elevation; from here you can pass into other intact rooms of the convent (corridor with little altars) enriched over time with artworks of every period, brought as "dowries" by the girls who were becoming nuns, members of the most illustrious families of Naples; this array of artwork now constitutes a perfectly preserved "devotional museum." Among these rooms, note the Salottino della Badessa, or parlor of the abbess, a Rococo jewel.

Archivio di Stato (I, C3), or state archives. One of the largest archives on earth (over 50,000 m of shelf space) and of fundamental importance to the history of southern Italy from the 10th c. to the present day, is located in the old monastery of the SS. Severino e Sossio (see above), in which there are four cloisters dating from the 16th and 17th c.; on two sides of the cloisters, or Chiostro del Platano, note the *Life of St. Benedict** frescoed by Antonio Solario, called the Zingaro, no later than the first decade of the 16th c.

Pulcinella among crèche figurines in a workshop window in the center of Naples

Palazzo Como and Museo Civico "Gaetano Filangieri" (I, C3). Built in the second half of the 15th c. for the Florentine merchant A. Como (known to everyone in Naples as Cuomo), near the Aragonese court, this is one of the most interesting palazzi of the century because of its adherence to the style of the Tuscan Renaissance. At the turn of the 17th c., a monastery was situated here, adjoining the church (on the side) of *S. Severo al Pendino*, which during the work on the expansion of Via Duomo (1879) was deprived of its facade and the first few chapels; the palazzo was demolished; its facades were rebuilt (1881) on the new street front, and in the rebuilt palazzo was housed the museum donated to the city by Gaetano Filangieri, inaugurated in 1888. The original collections were for the most part destroyed in 1943; the museum was reopened in 1948 with the surviving collections and new donations and loans, preserving its varied nature, typical of a private collection. Of special note is the late-19th-c. layout and arrangement of the halls of the museum, set around two large halls on the ground floor and on the second floor. Among the collections, we would point out the European and Oriental arms and armor, the fabrics, the coin collection, the porcelain, a number of sculptures, and – among the paintings – works by B. Luini and Ribera.

S. Giorgio Maggiore (I, B3). One of the oldest churches in Naples, it was found between the 4th and 5th c. by Bishop Severus, and was then rebuilt by Fanzago, completed and reduced in size during the work on the construction of Via Duomo. At the entrance is the *early-Christian apse** (the ancient church was oriented differently) featuring columns that follow a motif that was adopted in the Baroque renovation of the church. On the first altars, two enormous canvases by F. Peresi (1713), and in the left side aisle, a *triptych* frescoed by Solimena, with, at the center, a *Crucifix* by N. Fumo; in the nave, the so-called throne of St. Severus, or Cattedra di S. Severo; in the choir, large canvases by A. d'Elia (behind the one of the left, *St. George and the Dragon*, a fresco by Aniello Falcone).

Forcella (I, B4). The last stretch of the lower *decumans*, after Via Vicaria Vecchia, twists to the right, forming in fact the "forcella," or dogleg, that gives its name to the street, the heart of a distinctive old working-class quarter.

SS. Annunziata* (I, B4). The Santa Casa dell'Annunziata is one of the chief charitable institutions in the city, already in existence in 1318 and intended for the care of abandoned infants. The church was rebuilt (1760-82) by Luigi and Carlo Vanvitelli, the latter taking over following the death of his father. Badly damaged during World War II, it was restored, and is now closed for work to repair damage caused by the earthquake of 1980. The interior is large and well lit, with a single nave and three chapels on either side; note the high dome; this is one of the greatest masterpieces of L. Vanvitelli; set against the white marble and stuccoes (*Virtues*, by G. Sanmartino, A. Viva, and G. Picano) stand out the large altarpieces by De Mura (1761), F. Narice, and G. Starace. On the right are the rooms that survived the fire: the chapel, or *Cappella Carafa di Morcone*, with decorations of marble inlay by Iacopo Lazzari, the lovely sacristy decorated with frescoes by Corenzio (1605) and *carved cabinets** with *Stories of the New Testament* and *Prophets*, by G. d'Auria and S. Caccavello (1577-80), the *Treasure*, designed by G. A. Dosio. The lower structure, with a central plan, is by L. Vanvitelli. To the left of the facade is the 16th-c. campanile, with a monumental portal by T. Malvito (note the handsome wooden doors, carved by P. Belverte and Giovanni da Nola, 1508) leading into the courtyard of the hospital.

2.2 Via dei Tribunali

The itinerary (plan on p. 30), beginning at Piazza Dante, winds along the central *decumanus* of the ancient city, called Via dei Tribunali because it ends in front of Castel Capuano, since the 16th c. the "Palazzo di Giustizia," or hall of justice. This itinerary allows one to visit exquisite Gothic, Renaissance, and Baroque churches and a virtual art gallery, from the paintings by Mattia Preti in S. Pietro a Maiella to the splendid Caravaggio of the Pio Monte. A brief detour leads to the cathedral, a remarkable assembly of structures and artworks dating from the 4th to the 19th c.

Conservatorio di Musica (I, B-C2). This musical conservatory has been located since 1826 in the Celestine convent of S. Pietro a Maiella. The Conservatorio, one of the most important conservatories in Italy, had its origin during the decade of French occupation, when all the existing conservatories were joined in one institute, including those founded in the 16th and 17th c., which had had as pupils and teachers D. Cimarosa, N. A. Porpora, A. and D. Scarlatti, F. Durante, G. Paisiello, G. Spontini, G. B. Pergolesi, and N. Iommelli. Among the directors of the unified (1808) Regio Collegio di Musica we might mention N. Zingarelli, G. Donizetti, F. S. Mercadante, and F. Cilea. Aside from the memorabilia, old musical instruments, and works of art, the conservatory, as a relic of the city's glorious musical past, boasts one of the most notable musical libraries in Italy. In the courtyard, note the *monument to Beethoven* by F. Ierace.

S. Pietro a Maiella* (I, C2). Built at the end of the 13th c. and dedicated to Pietro Angeleri, the hermit who lived on the Maiella and became pope (Celestine V, 1294) and saint. The exterior is characterized by the tripartite, cusped campanile (in accordance with an exceedingly widespread typology in the region), beneath which stands the main entrance. The Gothic interior, with nave and two side aisles and side chapels, transept with apse and chapels with straight end walls, of clear Cistercian derivation, one should note in particular the *ceilings**, slightly modified by restorations that eliminated the Baroque decorations, with canvases with *Life of St. Celestine V* (nave) and *Life of St. Catherine of Alexandria* (transept), some of the greatest masterpieces (1656-61) by Mattia Preti. Among the other artworks, one should note the 14th-c. frescoes in two

chapels (*Life of St. Martin* by the Maestro della Cappella Leonessa, *Life of Mary Magdalene*); a floor with enameled tiles (*azulejos*) of a type that was common in Naples under Aragonese rule, but nowadays quite rare; an *inlaid wooden choir** dating from the 16th c.; Renaissance sculptures and tombs (G. da Nola); canvases by Stanzione, De Mura, and G. del Po, frescoes by De Matteis, and lastly the refined Baroque decoration in *marble inlay** of the presbytery (balustrade by Fanzago, main altar by the Ghetti).

S. Maria Maggiore (La Pietrasanta; I, B2). This church, rebuilt in the Baroque style, and constructed on one of the oldest early-Christian basilicas in Naples, looms up high and somehow incongruous because of the gutting of the city undertaken for the construction of the Policlinico. Founded in the 6th c. by Bishop Pomponius, it was originally preceded by a porticoed atrium which connected with the Romanesque *campanile* (in brick with recycled marble work; it is the oldest surviving bell tower in Naples) and the 15th-c. chapel, or Cappella Pontano. Rebuilt on a central plan by Fanzago (1653-67), it was badly damaged by wartime bombardments, and only recent restored. The church is generally known as the Pietrasanta because it housed the original stone of its consecration in a little altar set in the church courtyard.

Cappella Pontano* (I, B2). This is one of the prime monument of the Neapolitan Renaissance, and was built in 1492 as an aristocratic chapel ("cappella gentilizia") for the Humanist G. Pontano. As the architect of the chapel – with a rectangular plan, and set atop a podium, punctuated by pilaster strips, and thus complying perfectly with the Vitruvian canon for small temples – attributions have been ventured, for Fra' Giocondo and Francesco di Giorgio Martini. Standing out against the piperno stone is the marble of the portals and the epigraphs with Latin mottoes; on the interior, note a polychrome flooring made with some of the best-preserved 15th-c. majolicas.

Via dei Tribunali* (I, B2-3-4). In the central section of this street, there is a succession of buildings of particular importance. At no. 362 is the *Palazzo Spinelli di Laurino*, the product of the merging (1767) of two buildings dating from the 16th c., at the behest of the client T. Spinelli, who developed a number of original architectural solutions (circular courtyard adorned with stuccoes and statues in terracotta; monumental staircase with the exaltation of the illustrious women of the dynasty).

The street, in this section, runs along the site of the Greek *agora* and the Roman *forum*, widens into the Piazza San Gaetano, with a monument to St. Cajetan, built by the Theatines in 1737.

Purgatorio ad Arco* (I, B2). One of the prime Baroque monuments in Naples, built during the 17th c., when the cult of the dead was reaching its peak, and unfailingly dear to the hearts of those Neapolitans who have maintained – in spite of the prohibitions of the church elders – a remarkable veneration for the remains of the dead. It was built at the behest of a confraternity established in 1604 with the intention of gathering funds meant for the celebration of special masses for the souls of the departed; funerary motifs recur, therefore, in the facade, on the exterior (with skulls and crossed tibias in bronze, often adorned with fresh flowers) and on the interior. The architect of the first order of the facade was Fanzago, who is also said to have created the remarkable motif of *skulls and crossbones* behind the main altar. Of considerable interest, as well, are the *tomb of Giulio Mastrilli* (principal benefactor) by Andrea Falcone, the *Virgin Mary with the Souls of Purgatory*, by Stanzione (ca. 1630) on the main altar. Along a stairway to the left of the entrance, one can descend to an enormous hypogeum (actually, another church) in which there are more-or-less ancient burials, the object of popular veneration.

S. Paolo Maggiore* (I, B3). Set high atop a stairway, which happens to coincide with the elevation of the podium of the ancient temple upon which it was built, is one of the most important churches in Naples, adjoining a monastery that was established by St. Cajetan (S. Gaetano) himself, in 1538. It was founded between the 8th and 9th c., in the cella of the *temple of the Dioscuri*, the ruins of which date back to a restoration done in the 1st c. A.D., but which was first founded earlier still. The Theatines had it rebuilt between 1583 and 1603 to plans by the confraternity member F. Grimaldi, with a Latin-cross plan, with a nave and two side-aisles and side chapels; in the facade (slightly set back) was incorporated the pronaos of the temple, echoing in the capitals of the pilaster strips the design of the

motif (celebrated, and studied by Palladio, among others) of the ancient columns; the link between structures of different eras led, after the earthquake of 1688, to the collapse of the pronaos, of which only two columns, which stand, with base and capitals, almost 11 meters tall.

Cavagna and Di Conforto were also active in the work that went on for years on the original project; many of the most important artists working in Naples in the 17th and 18th c. took part in decorating this church. Badly damaged by bombing during the war, the church has been restored. Despite the extensive destruction (the apse and the vaulted ceiling of the transept have been completely rebuilt) the vast interior* still glitters with ornamentation. The vaulted ceiling of the nave, frescoed by Stanzione (1644) with *Lives of Saints Peter and Paul*, was exposed for many years to serious leakage, and now presents huge gaps. The side chapels are in many cases organically linked with the decorative array of the bay that stands before it; on the right in the 6th chapel, note paintings by Stanzione and P. De Rosa, where there once hung a painting by Luis de Morales depicting the *Madonna della Purità* (Our Lady of Purity, in storage for security considerations, replaced by a copy), a recurrent image in Theatine foundations, and, with ancient copies, in various Neapolitan churches; in the preceding bay, note four statues by Andrea Falcone (*Prudence and Temperance*) and N. Mazzone (*Justice and Strength*). Of particular importance are the two chapels beside the apse; on the left is the *Cappella Firrao** with a *Virgin Mary with Christ Child* by G. Mencaglia on the main altar, and on the sides the *tomb of Cesare Firrao* by G. Finelli (1640) the tomb of *Antonio Firrao* by G. Mencaglia (1643), in the vaulted ceiling frescoes by Aniello Falcone and splendid marble work from the workshop of the Lazzari; on the right is the Cappella di S. Andrea Avellino with stuccoes by A. Viva, substituting the original decorations in silver, and the altar by D. A. Vaccaro; in the presbytery, main altar designed by Fuga with sculptures by A. Viva and a lovely *ciborium* designed by A. Cangiano (1608). In the nave, note the *Guardian Angel** by D. A. Vaccaro. Note the splendid sacristy with *frescoes** by Solimena, a masterpiece of the years 1689-90. In the crypt, which is normally officiated, note the bas-reliefs with *Life of St. Cajetan* by D. A. Vaccaro.

S. Lorenzo Maggiore** (I, B3). One of the leading monumental complexes in terms of the exemplary architectural stratification and the density of historical traditions and memories (in this church Boccaccio met Fiammetta, for this church Simone Martini and Colantonio painted the altarpieces now in Capodimonte; in the monastery, Petrarch stayed, and it was here that the meetings of the Parlamento del Regno took place). The church, founded in the 6th c. and rebuilt after 1270-75 by Charles I, was stripped of its Baroque decorations during modern restoration. Incorporated into the facade built by Sanfelice (1742) is the large original *portal*, commissioned by Bartolomeo di Capua (1324), which preserves its original *wooden doors*; on the right is the monastery, with a 15th-c. portal (high up, alongside the symbols of the city, are the heraldic crests of the Sedili di Nido, Capuana, Montagna, Portanova, Porto, Forcella, and Popolo, which were placed here in the 19th c.) and campanile.

This church has a single nave, covered with a truss roof and with side chapels and a *polygonal apse** with a deambulatory and radial chapels; in the flooring, metal elements indicate the layout of the early-Christian church. On the interior (restored to its Gothic appearance, with the exception of the facade, which was completely rebuilt in the 18th c.), which is expansive, luminous, among the loveliest of medieval Naples, one can clearly see the difference between the forms of the older apsidal part and those of the nave; the former was influenced by the use of French craftsmen, the latter with the use of local craftsmen and the progressive abandonment of the models from across the Alps, following the death of Charles I and the reign of Charles II.

At the entrance, note the *Franciscan Allegory*, by F. Curia; in the first chapel on the right, (A) note the tomb, or *Sepolcro di Ludovico Aldomoresco* (1421) by A. Baboccio. The 3rd chapel, the *Cappella Cacace** (B), is one of the most exquisite 17th-c. settings in Naples (1653): marble inlays designed by Fanzago, sculptures by A. Bolgi, paintings by Stanzione. In the right transept is a *Nativity* (C), which, with the *Dormitio Virginis*, facing it (D) was meant to form part of the cycle of stories of the Virgin Mary, frescoed by Montano d'Arezzo (1305-11). If you walk along the deambulatory, you can see the tomb of Catherine of Austria, or *Sepolcro di Caterina d'Austria** (ca. 1323; F) by Tino di Camaino (he also did the *Virtues* holding up the case) and assistants; the frescoes with *Life of Mary Magdalene* (ca. 1295-1300) by an unknown artist in the 1st chapel of the deambulatory (E), the funer-

ary slabs, the frescoes with *Life of the Virgin Mary* (ca. 1333-34) in the 6th chapel (H), by the Barrile, hence the name of the Maestro della Cappella Barrile for the unidentified painter of the school of Giotto; the tomb, or *Tomba di Maria di Durazzo* in the 9th chapel (I). The main altar (G) is adorned with an ancona with statues of *St. Lawrence, St. Anthony, and St. Francis** and three bas-reliefs with *Lives of the Saints* (in the background, you can pick out Neapolitan monuments), the work of Giovanni da Nola (ca. 1530). In the left transept, note the other *Gothic tombs*, in the chapel, or Cappellone di S. Antonio (L), set amidst intarsias by Fanzago, note a 15th-c. panel by an unidentified painter, with *St. Anthony Surrounded by Angels*, and two canvases by M. Preti. Finally, there are numerous 16th-c. tombs.

Detail of interior of S. Lorenzo Maggiore

Before the left transept, a door leads into the cloisters (M; note on the immediate left the handsome tomb, or *Sepolcro Puderico*, 1466) where you will find the entrance to the chapter hall, or *Sala Capitolare*, whose Gothic structures (with recycled columns, like all the others in this church) were frescoed by L. Rodriguez, with the *Exaltation of the Franciscan Order* (1608); on the walls and in the display vitrines, there are remains of the mosaic floor of the early-Christian church, marble work, and ceramics. Rodriguez himself decorated the vaulted ceiling of the large (45 x 10 meters) *refectory* (which held the sessions of the parliament, or Parlamento, in the 17th c.), with an adjoining room with a vaulted ceiling, set on columns, an unusual example of structures from the Swabian age of Naples.

Beneath the church and the convent have

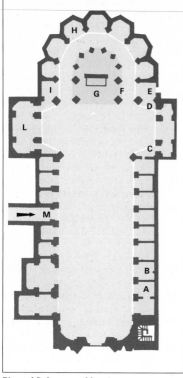

Plan of S. Lorenzo Maggiore

been uncovered important ruins of the Graeco-Roman and early-medieval city, including those of the *Macellum*, the city market, which dates back to the second half of the 1st c. B.C., and upon which was built the early-Christian basilica and, on a line with the chapter hall, an early-medieval construction. At the center of the cloisters you can still clearly make out the circular layout of the structures set in the middle of the rectangular portico upon which the shops looked out.

Along a stairway set between the chapter hall and the side of the building, formerly the outside of the refectory hall, you will climb down into the area of the **excavations*** where you can see a section of some 60 meters of the *stenopos*, aligned with the present-day Vico Giganti. Among the rooms that overlook this are, of particular note are those identified as the headquarters of the Erario (where the city treasure was stored) with an entrance decorated by pilaster strips supporting a brick tympanum.

Girolamini* (I, B3). The immense monastic complex of the Oratoriani, which occupies almost all of two "insule" of the ancient center, was developed between 1588 and

the first few decades of the 18th c. The church was built (1592-1619) by the Florentine G. A. Dosio in accordance with the Tuscan Classical style, with a nave and two side-aisles, divided by columns. The facade, built by D. Lazzari, was greatly modified by Ferdinando Fuga (1780); it is adorned by statues by Sanmartino.

The interior is homogeneous, even in the chapels, at behest of the of Oratorian order, with the recurring presence of artist of Tuscan, Roman, and Emilian formation, such as Dionisio and Jacopo Lazzari, P. Bernini, the Pomarancio, Guido Reni (*St. Francis*; in the sacristy, *St. John the Baptist and the Baptism of Christ*), Francesco Gessi (*St. Jerome*), and Pietro da Cortona (*St. Alexis Dying*). Alongside these artists, there are also works by such Neapolitan artists as Belisario Corenzio, Fabrizio Santafede, Azzolino (the *"Madonna della Vallicella"* on the main altar), Luca Giordano (*Expulsion of the Money-Lenders from the Temple*, 1608, in the counterfacade, *S. Maria Maddalena de' Pazzi*, or Mary Magdalene), Solimena, De Mura, and De Matteis. Among the sculptures there are lovely *torch-bearing angels* by Sanmartino at the sides of the presbytery. In the sacristy, 18th-c. decorations, flooring and cabinets done to designs by A. Guglielmelli, who also did the overall project of the lovely setting.

In the monastery (entrance at no. 142 of Via Duomo) there are two cloisters (the work of Dionisio di Bartolomeo and D. Lazzari), the library, or Biblioteca, and the art gallery, or Pinacoteca. The **Biblioteca*** is of particular importance because of the volumes it contains (including the libraries of Giuseppe Valletta and Carlo Troya) and for the beauty of the 18th-c. *Sala*, or reading room; designed by A. Guglielmelli, it was opened to the public in 1586. The **Pinacoteca** comprises works donated by benefactors and by the monks themselves, especially during the 17th and 18th c.

Cathedral** (I, B3). This cathedral, dedicated to Our Lady of the Assumption, stands on the site of the episcopal seat of St. Aspren the first bishop of Naples, where as early as the 4th c. there stood the twin cathedrals of S. Restituta and the Stefania, with their adjoining baptisteries and oratories. Many of these buildings were demolished or were incorporated during the construction of the Angevin cathedral, on which work probably began as early as the reign of Charles I, despite the fact that the sources attribute to Charles II the foundation of this large Gothic church, which was completed during the reign of King Robert. Damaged by earthquakes (1349, with the collapse of the facade and the campanile, 1456, 1688, 1732...), the church was repeatedly restored and renovated in its decorative array. The facade was rebuilt in a Neo-Gothic style to plans (1876) by E. Alvino; the *portals*, by A. Baboccio (1407), are old; in the central portal you can still see the 14th-c. pillar-bearing lions and the *Virgin Mary with Christ Child* by Tino di Camaino (in the lunette). The interior is built to a Latin-cross plan, with a nave and two side aisles, lined with chapels; the 16 pillars that support the round arches are flanked by 110 ancient granite columns; the first bay of the left aisle was stripped (1969) of its decoration, and offers an instance of a structural palimpsest, hidden by the marble and stucco that uniformly cover the interior. The height of the nave and the transept was diminished by the carved and gilt wooden ceilings (1621) which frame paintings by late-Mannerist painters. Giordano and his workshop did the *Saints* that stand between the large windows (with the exception of two by Solimena on the sides of the apsidal arch) as well as the tondi, lower down, of the *Patron Saints of Naples*. Set on each pillar is an aedicule with busts of the earliest bishops. In the counterfacade there is a monument to *Charles I, Charles Martel, and Clemenza of Hapsburg* by D. Fontana (1599). On the left is a handsome baptismal font (1618) and the episcopal throne (1376). In the 2nd chapel on the right, note the important tombs from the 14th and 15th c., partly dismembered or recomposed, with a *Strength* by Tino di Camaino; next comes the monumental "facade" of the treasury, or *Tesoro di S. Gennaro*. In the transept, on the right, note the tomb, or *Sepolcro Sersale* by Sanmartino, an altarpiece with Our Lady of the Assumption, painted by Perugino (1506) for the main altar on commission from the Cardinal Oliviero Carafa (portrait below). Adjoining is the chapel, or **Cappella Minutolo****, one of the best-preserved Gothic rooms in all Naples. Built in a second phase (as can be seen by the small size of the entrance and especially from the buttresses of the adjoining chapel, jutting to the left), this chapel is entirely frescoed: the older scenes (vaulted ceiling and walls) are attributed to Montano d'Arezzo; on the socle is painted (perhaps by Roberto d'Oderisio) a series of kneeling *Minutolo knights*; in the apse (1402) is the large *tomb of Enrico Minutolo*. On either side of the altar are the older *tombs of Orso and Filippo Minutolo*. This latter tomb, on the right, has Cosmatesque decorations similar to those found in the 13th-c. floor. This was the site where Boccaccio set his celebrated novella of the *Decameron* concerning the misadventures of Andreuccio of Perugia.

In the next chapel, the *Cappella Tocco*, with handsome ribbed vaults set on foliate capitals, note, in the socle, the *frescoes* attributed to P. Cavallini and, on the walls, *Life of St. Aspren* by A. Tesauro (1517-19); *Virgin*

The Biblioteca dei Girolamini, with its sumptuous 18th-c. decor

Mary with Christ Child and a handsome tomb of *Giangiacomo Tocco* by Diego de Siloe. Presbytery and apse, already rebuilt at the end of the 16th c., were rebuilt again to plans by P. Posi (1744-45) who created, along with P. Bracci, the altar upon which stands *Our Lady of the Assumption*, in marble and stucco, by Bracci with canvases by S. Pozzi (who also painted a number of the frescoes) and C. Giaquinto (on the left); the only features that are older are the choir, dating from the 17th c., and the Romanesque *Crucifix*.

Two stairways lead up to the **higher church****, one of the most noteworthy creations of the Renaissance in Naples, built at the behest (1497-1506) of Oliviero Carafa, to provide a worthy resting place for the relics of St. Januarius, formerly at Montevergine. The remarkable technical complexity of the depth of the chapel beneath the dizzying Gothic apse and the originality of the composition have recently persuaded scholars to attribute the design to Bramante. Tommaso Malvito, documented as the artist who did the founts, his son Giovan Tommaso, and their workshop certainly did the marble sculptural decorations of the chapel, divided into a nave and two side aisles by columns that support the flat ceiling; near the entryways, with handsome bronze doors adorned with the insignia of the Carafa family, is a statue of *Oliviero Carafa praying* before the altar, which contains, in a terracotta urn, the remains of the patron of the church.

In the left transept is the chapel, or Cappella del Sacramento (or Cappella del Galeota), with frescoes by Andrea de Leone) which echoes, in the Gothic structure of the ribbed umbrella vault the shape of the much larger vault that once covered the

apse, a genuine wonder of the builder's art, damaged by earthquakes and demolished for safety in the 16th c.

In the chapel, or Cappella degli Illustrissimi, symmetrical to the Cappella Minutolo, note the *Jesse Tree**, a fresco by Lello da Orvieto (ca. 1315), and, on the architrave of a little door on the right, *Stories of the Passion*, by an unknown painter, who reveals the culture of Avignon. Next is the *tomb of Innocent IV*, or Sepolcro di Innocenzo IV (Sinibaldo Fieschi, pope from 1243, tutor of Conradin of Swabia, died in Naples in 1254), and the *tomb of Andrew of Hungary*, or Sepolcro di Andrea d'Ungheria (born 1345); high up, note the *organ doors*, painted by Vasari (1546-48, many of the figures are portraits of the Farnese family). In the sacristy, decorated with portraits of the bishops, is the *Rest on the Flight into Egypt*, by Aniello Falcone (1641). From here, you can step out into the courtyard, to see the exterior of the transept, a stretch of paved Roman road, the handsome 18th-c. courtyard of the archive, or Archivio Diocesano, and, behind glass, a room with ancient columns, which some have identified as the atrium of the Stefania, the early-Christian basilica that was demolished (note a *marble calendar* of the 10th c., reworked in the 12th/13th c.).

Along the left aisle is the chapel, or Cappella Brancaccio by Dosio, with statues by P. Bernini and a *Baptism of Jesus* by F. Curia; in the 2nd chapel note the painting by Marco Pino and in the altar frontal, a 16th-c. *Deposition*; in the middle is the entrance to **S. Restituta***, a 4th-c. basilica, founded under Constantine, with a nave and four side aisles set on columns, transformed in the Angevin period with the creation of chapels in the outer side aisles and the demolition of the bays closest to the facade. The bases of the ancient columns, with handsome recycled capitals, are hidden by the floor which was raised in the 14th c. (it is possible to see the actual size of one column, at the end on the right). In the apse, note the Romanesque fresco with the *Deesis*, in part, repainted; the Baroque appearance of the interior dates back to the restoration by A. Guglielmelli following the earthquake of 1688. In the left side aisle is the chapel, or *Cappella di S. Maria del Principio*, adorned with a mosaic of the *Virgin Mary and the Saints Januarius and Restituta**, signed by Lello da Orvieto and dated 1322; on the side walls, note *two slabs** carved with Stories of Joseph (left) and Stories of Samson, St. Gennaro, and other saints, by a late-Romanesque Campanian sculptor. Among the

Interior of the Duomo, or cathedral

countless works of art preserved here, we should mention, near the entrance, an altar by D. A. Vaccaro and the cenotaph of A. S. Mazzocchi with a bust by G. Sanmartino. From the right side aisle, you enter the *baptistery** (S. Giovanni in Fonte), built between

Precious bust of St. Januarius in bishop's vestments

the end of the 4th c. and the beginning of the 5th c., with a square plan, and with splendid *mosaics** from the same period (*Monogrammatic Cross* and *Evangelical Stories* in the dome, *Saints* in the octagonal tambour, *Symbol of the Evangelists* in the pendentives, interspersed with fascias with flowers, fruit, and birds).

Facing S. Restituta, in the right side aisle is the monumental entrance, as if it were the facade of a church, to the chapel, or **Cappella del Tesoro di S. Gennaro***. It was (1608-37) to fulfill a vow taken by the entire city during the outbreak of the plague in 1527, without concern for expense, and with the contribution of the most important artists of the period, and with the Certosa, it is certainly the principal monument of the Baroque era in Naples. Two aedicules with *Saint Peter and Saint Paul*, by G. Finelli, stand alongside the large brass *gate*, by Fanzago and G. Monte (1628-65). The chapel, built to a Greek-cross plan with a dome, and built to the design of F. Grimaldi, glitters with marble, silver, and paintings. In the dome, note the *Paradise* by Lanfranco (1641-43); all the other frescoes in the vaulted ceilings, in the lunettes (*Life of St. Januarius*), and in the pendentives, are by Domenichino (1631-38), who also did the paintings on copper on the altars (a complex that is unrivaled in terms of size), enclosed in splendid frames, with *Scenes from the Life and Miracles of the Saint*, with the exception of the marvelous *Miracle of the Saint Emerging Unharmed from the Furnace*, by Ribera, on the right-hand altar. We should mention, in the apse, the small door of the balustrade, the bronze statues of the patrons, the main altar with a silver altar frontal, a masterpiece by Vinaccia, and, on the altar, large silver urns with flowers; note the statues, also in silver, of *St. Michael* and of *Tobias with the Angel*; on either side of the tribune, note the two large silver candelabra ("splendori"). Set on brackets, all around, are the silver busts of the countless patrons of Naples, done between 1605 and 1856. From the chapel on the right, you can pass into the sacristy and the chapel, or Cappella dell'Immacolata, which are equally lavish.

On the recurrence of the feast of St. Januarius and the supposed miracle of the liquefaction of the saint's blood, in May and September, the *reliquary bust** of the saint is displayed (a masterpiece of Gothic goldsmithery, done in Naples in 1304-05 by the French masters Etienne, Godefroyd, Guillaume de Verdelay, and Milet d'Auxerre), in part covered because it is draped in episcopal vestments, and the *reliquary of the blood*, a little 14th-c. temple containing the ampoules that are inserted in elements dating from a later period.

Guglia di S. Gennaro (I, B3). This spire, built in the Piazza Riario Sforza, is the oldest of all the Neapolitan spires. Built in 1636 as a votive offering for the salvation of the city during the eruption of Mt. Vesuvius in 1631, it was completed in its base (1645) to plans by Fanzago, and was inaugurated in 1660.

Pio Monte della Misericordia* (I, B3). This important and venerable old (1601) charitable institution, founded to perform works of corporal charity, and still in operation, is housed in the building erected by F. A. Picchiatti (1658-70). The solemn and austere facade opens out at the base with a portico – in accordance with a typology that is uncommon in Naples – in which you will find the entrances to the courtyard and the church (invisible from outside), designed to house the needy and to emphasize the character of the construction. It is adorned by a major sculptural complex by Andrea Falcone (1666-71); at its center is the *Madonna della Misericordia* and two *allegorical figures* on the sides, alluding the seven works of charity. The plan of the church also refers to these seven works of charity; it is octagonal, covered with a dome, and with six chapels, as well as the main chapter (note the elegant and whimsical holy *water founts*, by Andrea Falcone). On the main altar is one of the greatest masterpieces of Caravaggio, *The Works of Mercy***, which also provides an incomparable image of the daily life of the Neapolitan people in the early 17th c.: the painter portrays, beneath the image of the Virgin Mary with Christ Child amidst Angels, episodes taken from the Bible, ancient history, and everyday life, repre-

Altar of the church of the Pio Monte della Misericordia

senting the works of corporal charity. These charitable works are the subject, though individually, of the paintings on the altars of the various chapels, the work of Battistello (*Liberation of St. Peter from Prison**, 1615), G. B. Azzolino, F. Santafede, G. V. Forli, and L. Giordano.

The adjoining *Pinacoteca*, or art gallery, features paintings of the Neapolitan school of the 17th and 18th c., including works by Francesco De Mura, willed to the congregation, and by Luca Giordano, Andrea Vaccaro, and Agostino Beltrano.

Castel Capuano (I, A-B4). The view along Via dei Tribunali culminates in a tower, adorned by the insignia of Charles V, surmounting the entrance to the Castel Capuano, founded, according to tradition, by William I; on the site there already existed, in all probability, a fortified structure defending the gate which – though it shifted its location by a few dozen meters – has always been called the Porta Capuana.

This was a Norman palace; it was restored by the Angevin occupiers, and it maintained its role as a royal residence even with the Aragonese dynasty, losing all military connotations, now that it was enclosed within the new city walls. Donated by Charles V to the Principe di Sulmona, it was expropriated by the Viceroy Toledo, who assembled the Tribunali Cittadini (1540), or civic tribunals here, thus transforming it into the Vicaria, the Palazzo di Giustizia (hall of justice), a function that it still serves. The adaptation of the building was entrusted to F. Manlio; other work was done here over the centuries; the castle has thus lost its old appearance, but preserves various old rooms. In the 16th-c. **Cappella della Sommaria***, the most exquisite room in the complex, where the walls and ceilings, amidst elegant grotesques and gilt stuccoes, are frescoed with *Evangelical Scenes* and *Scenes of the Last Judgment*, by the Spanish painter Pietro Roviale (or Ruviale; ca. 1547); on the altar is a *Pietà*, also by the same painter.

S. Caterina a Formiello* (I, A4). To the left of the castle, one has a fine view of this Renaissance church, one of the most important, in part because of the monumental position in the urban landscape. The name comes from its proximity to the old "formali d'acqua." It was begun around 1510 by the Tuscan architect R. Balsimelli and was completed in 1593. On the interior, note the moldings in piperno stone (visible in a few areas) which were covered with a refined and uniform decoration culminating in the frescoes by L. Garzi (vaulted ceiling of the nave, counterfacade, and the pendentives of the dome, 1695-97) and by G. Borremans (vaulted ceilings of the transept and the choir, 1708-1709). In the chapels, there are artworks from the 16th and 18th c. (*Life of St. Catherine* by G. del Po in the 5th chapel on the left). The 2nd chapel on the left contains the relics of the Martiri Idruntini (martyrs of Otranto; the inhabitants of Otranto killed by the Turks during their occupation of the town in 1480), which were transferred to Naples at the behest of Alfonso II. The large chapels of the transept, dating from the 18th c., are all a glorification of the Dominican order: on the left is an altar by Sanfelice, sculptures by G. Colombo and M. Bottigliero, a canvas by G. del Po; on the right is a complex designed by P. Schisano with sculptures by P. Benaglia and marble decorations by F. A. Gandolfi. The presbytery serves almost as an enormous aristocratic chapel: at the base of the pillars of the dome (frescoed by De Matteis) are six *tombs of the Spinelli** family, done in the last few decades of the 16th c., the work of G. D. and G. D'Auria, S. Caccavello, and S. Longo; the main altar itself was built at the behest of the Spinelli family. Note the remarkable wooden choir by B. Tortelli and assistants (1566).

On the church courtyard, note the *votive*

aedicule of St. Gennaro, with a bust of the saint, by D. A. Vaccaro (1709).

Porta Capuana* (I, A4). At the foot of the handsome side of the church is a statue of *St. Cajetan* that once stood atop the aedicule that was erected as a votive offering in the wake of the plague of 1656, on the adjoining gate, or Porta Capuana, one of the main gates of the city and the chief ornament of the *Aragonese walls*, built in the last few decades of the 15th c., and one of the last examples on earth of a typology that would shortly thereafter be rendered obsolete by the use of artillery. Between the two towers, one named "Honor" and the other named "Virtue," is the lovely marble arch designed (1484) by Giuliano da Maiano.

2.3 From Via Carbonara to the Museo Nazionale: the upper decumanus

This is the most elevated area of the ancient Neapolis, set between Via Anticaglia, with ruins of the Roman theater, Via Costantinopoli, and the Piazza Miraglia; from the 19th c. on, it has been transformed from an acropolis, first pagan and later Christian, with a high concentration of monasteries, into a huge hospital zone, with a progressive – and ongoing – adaptation of numerous monasteries. Other monasteries have been transformed into the academy of fine arts, or Accademia di Belle Arti (in the 19th c.) and departments of the school of architecture Facoltà di Architettura (S. Antonio a Port'Alba, 1992). The itinerary (see plan on p. 30) ends at the Museo Nazionale, one of the most important museums of antiquities in the world.

S. Giovanni a Carbonara* (I, A3). Built between 1343 and 1418, this church became the "pantheon" of the last Angevin rulers. It stands at the far end of a broad street whose name indicates the site that was used in the Middle Ages as a dump for refuse, but also as the site of tournaments. The church has no facade, and the one that you can see actually belongs to the chapel, or Cappella di S. Monica, which connects at a lower elevation with the nave of the church; in turn, the structure with a central plan that concludes the church is not actually an apse, but is the chapel, or Cappella Caracciolo del Sole which – before Sanfelice had built the "pinzer" staircases and the architectural backdrops on either side of S. Monica – characterized the whole, with its buttress-

es surmounted by statues and its marble heraldic crests.

To the left of the chapel of S. Monica is a church courtyard, upon which the portal of the church opens; the interior of which is dominated by giant *monument to King Ladislao**, built by his sister Joan II, upon which are depicted *Ladislao and Joan enthroned*, and, higher up *Ladislao on horseback* and – something wholly uncommon in a church – with his sword unsheathed. The monument, which dates from 1428, is traditionally attributed only to Andrea da Firenze, but is actually the work of a number of Tuscan and northern artists. Passing under it, you will enter the chapel, or *Cappella Caracciolo del Sole** built in 1427 at the behest of Sergianni Caracciolo, a great seneschal and the lover of Joan II, killed in 1432 and buried here in a tomb carved (after 1441) by Andrea da Firenze and assistants. The chapel, with a central plan, is frescoed (ca. mid-15th c.) with *Lives of the Hermits* and *Life of the Virgin Mary*, on which Leonardo da Besozzo and Perrinetto da Benevento both worked, and with flooring in 15th-c. majolica tiles.

To the left of the presbytery is the chapel, or *Cappella Caracciolo di Vico***, which also has a central plan and is covered by a dome; this is one of the most notable products of the architecture of the 16th c. in southern Italy. Founded in 1499 and completed in 1516, this is a remarkable structure, with great equilibrium of its various members, revealing, at a very early date, the presence in Naples of the earliest forms of the Roman Renaissance. The attribution to G. T. Malvito, based on documentary sources, should be limited to the marble work; the design, on the other hand, should be laid to an architect who was well informed concerning the work then being done by Bramante and Sangallo. At first, the sole ornament was the marble altar, on which work was done by the Spanish sculptors Diego de Siloe and Bartolomé Ordóñez. On either side, shortly thereafter, were placed the *tombs of Nicolantonio and Galeazzo Caracciolo* (on the left), the work of A. Caccavello and G. D. D'Auria; set between the twin Doric columns are statues and busts depicting other members of the family, done in the 16th and 17th c. by G. D'Auria, E. Ferrata, and G. Finelli.

Along the nave you may note the altar, or *Altare della Madonna delle Grazie* by M. Naccherino and, facing the entrance, the monumental altar, or *Altare Miroballo** (practically a chapel in terms of the complexity of the decoration), the work of various Lombard sculptors (J. della Pila, T. and G. T. Malvito, and Pietro and Francesco da Milano). Facing the presbytery is the entrance to the chapel, or *Cappella di Somma* (1557-66). On the right are the chapels, or Cappella Recco and Cappella dell'Epifania, with the *tomb of Gaetano Argento*, by F. Pagano (1730). From the church courtyard, you enter the chapel, or Cappella Seripando, where there is a *Crucifix* by Vasari (1545); you will then return to the stairway (from the landing, there is a handsome view of the dome and the campanile of the SS. Apostoli), and you can enter the Gothic chapel of S. Monica through a portal that has been attributed to a pupil of Andrea da Firenze, who signed, on the interior, the *Monumento Sanseverino*. At the foot of the stairway, between the flights, is the entrance to the Baroque lower church, the Consolazione a Carbonara, in which you may note the large altar (formerly in the upper church) designed by Sanfelice with sculptures by Sanmartino.

SS. Apostoli* (I, A3). Founded in the 5th c., it was completely rebuilt (1609-49) by the Theatines to plans by F. Grimaldi. The dome was stripped of its majolica-tile sheathing. In the harmonious interior, the gilded stuccoes frame a major series of *frescoes**, among the masterpieces of Lanfranco (1638-46), along the entrance wall (*Piscina probatica*, with trompe-l'oeil architecture by V. Codazzi), alongside the large windows, in the vaulted ceilings of the nave, transept, and apse (*Martyrs and Glory of the Apostles*;

Prophets, Patriarchs, and Virtues) and on the pendentives of the dome (*Evangelists*). On the arches of the chapels, note the Saints by Solimena; in the dome, Paradise by G. B. Beinaschi. In the chapels, there is a full-fledged art gallery of the 17th and 18th c. In the left transept is the altar, or *Altare Filomarino** built at the behest of the Cardinal Ascanio who, closely tied to the court of Pope Urban VIII, wanted to make this altar a manifesto of his taste and style in Naples, entrusting the work to Roman artists and craftsmen; designed by Francesco Borromini (ca. 1640) with sculptures by F. Dusquenoy, G. Finelli, A. Bolgi, and G. Mencaglia, and with mosaics by G. B. Calandra (to models by Guido Reni).

Sepulcher in the old church of S. Maria Donnaregina

In the presbytery, note the lamp-bearing angels and the *bronze candelabra** with the symbols of the Evangelists by A. Bolgi and G. Bertolino (1653), 17th-c. ciborium and choir, canvases by Lanfranco. In the right transept, note the *Altare Pignatelli* designed by Sanfelice, which reproduces the altar across from it, by Borromini. On the walls of the transept, canvases by Giordano.

S. Maria Donnaregina* (I, A3). Set atop a staircase is the facade (which has been restored to its original polychrome version, in *faux marbres*) of the 17th-c. church of S. Maria Donnaregina, which belonged to a convent that was rebuilt after 1293, at the behest of Mary of Hungary, on an earlier, existing foundation. The monastery was enlarged and modernized in the 17th c. and the 14th-c. church was incorporated into the cloistered section, or "clausura'; the present-day appearance of the complex is the result of a restoration done (1928-34) by G. Chierici, who separated the structures of the "two" churches, creating a distinction that historically had never existed, since, in the 17th c., the "old" church was structurally integrated with the "new" church, comprising in part its choir. After the damage caused by the war and the years of neglect and thefts, which left considerable scars, the **Chiesa Nuova**, or "new" church, undergoing restoration (1997); it will become the site of the new Museo Diocesano. The interior, which has a single nave, presents a refined marble decoration and, in many chapels, you may note the recurrent depiction of floral still lifes (present in other convents of the 17th c., such as the Croce di Lucca). The vaulted ceiling of the nave was frescoed by Francesco de Benedictis (1654); the dome (the pendentives have been lost) is by Agostino Beltrano (1655); in the presbytery (devastated by thefts) note the main altar, designed by Francesco Solimena and canvases by Luca Giordano. In a room to the left, in which the little speaking chamber opens out, note the tombs dating from the 16th c. and the base upon which was set the tomb of the queen Mary, until the restoration work done by Chierici; in the nuns' choir, reduced in size during the work done to separate the two churches, note the handsome stuccoes and frescoes by Solimena. You will enter the **Chiesa Vecchia**, or "old" church, from the Vico Donnaregina; in it and in the rooms of the old monastery, partially demolished to make way for the construction of Via Duomo, is the school for restoration of monuments, or Scuola di Specializzazione in Restauro dei Monumenti dell'Università. The 14th-c. *church** – preceded by a porticoed courtyard (ca. 1766) with various traces of the previously existing structures – presents a remarkable layout, with a single nave, covered with a truss roof (hidden by a lacunar ceiling by P. Belverte dating from the early 16th c.) and terminating in a pentagonal apse with high windows. The nuns' choir, with a highly original solution, is located in an elevated position, supported by pillars which create the effect, immediately inside the entrance, of a church with three aisles of equal height, with decorated vault-ed ceilings (like those in the apse) featuring the Angevin lilies and the white-and-red bands of Hungary, the heraldic symbols of the queen who founded the church. To the left is the *monument of Mary of Hungary** (died 1323), a masterpiece by Tino di Camaino (with the assistance of Gagliardo Primario) and a prototype of the Angevin tabernacle tombs; on the front of the sarcophagus are portraits of the queen's many children including, at the center, St. Louis, set between King Charles Martel of Hungary and King Robert of Naples. Facing it is the chapel, or Cappella Loffredo with frescoes dating from 1315-20. You can then leave the church, taking a staircase on the left, and climb up to the antechoir (which also has 14th-c. frescoes) and to the nuns' choir, on the walls of which is the most extensive cycle of 14th-c. *frescoes** surviving in Naples. Executed over a period of at least ten/fifteen years, beginning in 1318-20, they depict, on the counterfacade, the *Last Judgment* (culminating in the Madonna of the Apocalypse, hidden in the lacunar ceiling), *Lives of St. Agnes and St. Catherine* on the right wall, *Scenes from the Passions* and *Life of St. Elizabeth of Hungary*, on the left wall, Prophets and Saints on the walls close to the apse. The frescoes, the work of various unknown painters who must have been close to Pietro Cavallini, have been altered in their coloring by a terrible fire on the roof (1390).

S. Giuseppe dei Ruffi (I, A3). The church, founded by a number of ladies of the Ruffo family, was begun in 1669 by D. Lazzari; the open facade, which contains the stairway, was designed by A. Guglielmelli and was completed (1721) by his son Marcello. On the interior, note the extensive *marble inlays** allowing the visitor to see various phases of this art that was so important in Naples during the Baroque age.

Via dell'Anticaglia (I, B2-3) Following two overhead passageways that connected the old Palazzo Caracciolo d'Avellino with its 17th-c. expansion, the old *decumanus* takes the name of Via dell'Anticaglia (Street of the Antiquities) for two high Roman walls (beginning of the second c. A.D.) in brickwork. These walls were built to support the facade of the Roman theater, or *Teatro Romano* (largely preserved and incorporated into the buildings on the left) which probably stood on the Greek theater; this theater has a maximum diameter of 102 meters and must have been able to hold some 8,000 spectators; it is famous because the emperor Nero, as Suetonius tells us, performed here as a Greek singer.

Ospedale degli Incurabili (I, A2). This old hospital, founded by Maria Longo, was inaugurated in 1522 and continually enlarged until the 18th c. The stairway on the right in the courtyard leads to the renowned pharmacy, or **Farmacia***, a splendid 18th-c. room, the only structure of its kind to be preserved virtually intact in Naples. Rebuilt (1747-51) by B. Vecchione, it is arranged in two halls in which, on the shelves of a sort of sideboard made of walnut and briar wood, are arranged the *vases* (there were originally 480 of them) made by Donato Massa and assistants, depicting Bible scenes and allegories; at the center of each wall are display cases with carvings (by Gennaro di Fiore) and Rococo ornaments (note the remarkable "sutured wound," an allegory of Cesarean birth); in the great hall, or Sala Grande, note the flooring in terracotta and majolica by Giuseppe and Gennaro Massa, and, in the ceiling, *Machaon Tends to the Wounds of Menelaus,* by P. Bardellino (1750). Another 18th-c. stairway, near the main entryway, leads to the chapel, or *Cappella di S. Maria Succurre Miseris,* the headquarters of the company, or Compagnia dei Bianchi della Giustizia, established to assist those sentenced to death, with a macabre wax sculpture, *La Scandalosa,* from the end of the 17th c.

S. Maria Regina Coeli* (I, B2). After you pass the octagonal hanging campanile, you will see the elegant late 16th-c. facade of this church, probably designed by G. F. Di Palma, but only completed in 1594. A stairway runs from the atrium, with vaulted ceilings painted by the Flemish artist L. Croys at the end of the 16th c. The stupendous interior, notable especially for its exception state of conservation – with a single nave, chapels, dome, and choir behind the presbytery – shows clear signs of the untiring work of embellishment that was undertaken between the 16th and 19th c. On the walls, faced in the late 18th c. with polychrome marble work, is the lovely reflection of the gilt wooden ceiling, in which there are three canvases of subjects pertaining to the *Virgin Mary** by Stanzione (1640-47), while between the large windows are *Saints* by D. Gargiulo and L. Giordano; the latter also did the canvases and frescoes in the 2nd chapel on the left and the canvases in the 4th chapel on the left; in the 2nd chapel on the right, note the St. Francis by P. Brill.

S. Maria delle Grazie a Caponapoli* (I, B2). Caponapoli is the highest point in the ancient city, where the acropolis was situated and where, in the high Middle Ages there stood many monasteries. At the end of the street extends a small square, or "largo," with the simple facade of S. Maria delle Grazie a Caponapoli, one of the most splendid Neapolitan churches dating from the 16th c., devastated (1980-92) by an unbroken series of instances of vandalism and thefts, and currently (1997) closed. Despite this, it still preserves intact many of its architectural decorations and a considerable number of artworks (many of which have been removed by the Soprintendenza, or commission of fine arts) which make it one of the chief monuments of Naples. Built (1516-35) by Di Palma, the church has a single nave with chapels and transept; the *fornices* of all the chapels are framed by twin columns supporting a continual entablature, in sandstone, completely carved with figures of victories, grotesques, heraldic crests, and ornaments of every sort, comprising one of the most important decorative complexes of the Renaissance. Among the sculptures that survive in the church are works by G. D'Auria, S. Caccavello, Giovan Tomaso Malvito (tomb, or *Sepolcro di Joannello de Cuncto and his wife Lucrezia**, 1517, chapel to the right of the presbytery), Giovanni da Nola (*Madonna delle Grazie**, also from 1517, on the altar of the sacristy, which was one of the loveliest and richest in the city; *Deposition** in the first chapel on the left), G. A. Tenerello (*Annunciation,* altar of the left transept), and G. Santacroce (*Incredulity of St. Thomas,* 6th chapel on the left); M. Bottigliero is believed to have done the tomb, or Sepolcro Colacino.

Adjoining is the little church of the *SS. Michele e Omobono,* belonging to the confraternity of the tailors (note the scissors carved into the portal), at the altar of which was set the polyptych of St. Michael (*Politico di S. Michele**), attributed to Francesco Pagano (ca. 1492).

S. Andrea delle Dame (I, B2). This monastery was founded in 1583 by four sisters of the Palescandolo family, and built by their brother Marco, a Theatine architect. From a frescoed atrium you enter the cloisters, set on pillars, with handsome rows of very tall palm trees, and on the right you enter the church, with a single nave, decorated with frescoes by Corenzio (surviving in the counterfacade, on the triumphal arch, and in the presbytery); the handsome decoration of the *presbytery** in marble inlay is by D. Lazzari (1676); majolica flooring by Ignazio Giustiniani (1729); canvas by G. Diano in the ceiling.

Via S. Maria di Costantinopoli (I, B2). This is one of the most monumental streets in Naples, both for its size (we are at this point well outside of the ancient layout) and because it is lined by many monasteries and palazzi from the period of the viceroys. It was built in the context of the expansion plan undertaken at the behest of the Viceroy Toledo and it originally led to a city gate. It begins from the Piazza Bellini, which is adorned at its center by a *monument to Bellini*; at the other end, a stretch of the ancient *Greek walls* (4th c. B.C.). Behind the monastery of *S. Antonio a Port'Alba*, there are long stretches of the Angevin and Aragonese walls. At no. 99 is the Palazzo Firrao, one of the main constructions of the 17th c., in part because of the unusual arrangement of the facade, an heraldic exaltation of the Spanish sovereigns and royal family. In the entrance of the palazzo at no. 101 is reassembled the upper section of the late-Gothic *portal of S. Maria di Mezzo Agosto*, which was demolished in the 19th c. Next comes the church of *S. Giovanni Battista delle Monache*, built in 1673-84 by F.A. Picchiatti who was in time replaced by G. B. Nauclerio, who built the monumental facade; it has been closed for many years. In 1864, with the construction of Via Conte di Ruvo, it was separated from the monastery

and behind it, in the new street, was built the *Teatro Bellini* (1876-77).

Accademia di Belle Arti (I, B1-2), or academy of fine arts. This is one of the most interesting structures of 19th-c. Neapolitan architecture, a masterpiece of the Neo-Renaissance school, characterized by a refined use of tufa-stone ashlars; it is the work of E. Alvino who renovated (1864) the monastery, or Convento di S. Giovanni, to use as the site of the Accademia, making original use of the old structures. The main facade overlooks the parallel Via Bellini, the center of the 19th-c. quarter that developed (1857) from the suppression of the old Fosse del Grano.

S. Maria di Costantinopoli (I, B1-2). At the end of this street is the church which gives it its name. Originally founded in the 16th c. as a token of the cult of the Madonna of Constantinople, who protected against epidemics, the church was rebuilt in the early years of the 17th c. by Fra' Nuvolo. The interior was renovated in the 18th c.; at the corners of the ceiling is the heraldic crest of the Piazza del Popolo (the "P" of "Populus" is in black on the gold-and-red shield), because the church was built at the expense of the public. The complex "decorative machine" of the presbytery (frescoes by Corenzio) was originally conceived by Fanzago (who also did the statues of *St. Roch and St. Sebastian*, who were also protectors against the plague) and was reno-

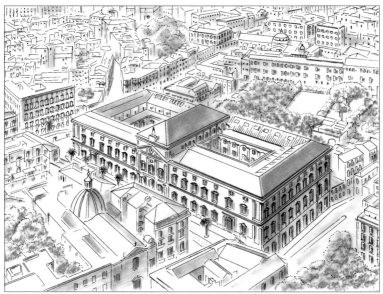

The late-16th-c. palazzo housing the Museo Archeologico Nazionale

vated in the 18th c. (main altar by D. A. Vaccaro).

The church is partly surrounded by the structures of the eclectic *Galleria Principe di Napoli*, roofed in iron and glass (1870-83).

Museo Archeologico Nazionale** (I, A1). The decision to turn the *Palazzo degli Studi* – built in 1585 as a stables and converted in the 17th c. into the main university building – into a museum, dates back to 1777 and was made by Ferdinand IV, who ordered the installation in the new museum of the Farnese collection and the finds from Herculaneum and Pompeii. The prima Farnese collection had been started in 1547 by Alexander Farnese (the future Pope Paul III); the most important artworks, however, were the product of the tireless collecting activities of his nephew, the Cardinal Alexander, who had planned to use them as furnishings for Palazzo Farnese in Rome. The excavations of Herculaneum and Pompeii provided the other core collection, which from 1750 to 1822 was displayed in the Palazzo Reale of Portici. Other historic collections were added over time (Borgia and Picchianti collections) along with finds that came to light in excavations undertaken in Campania and elsewhere in southern Italy. The entire array of materials has thus given rise to the most important museum of ancient art in the south, both in terms of the history of the collections and for the marvelous objects that make up those collections; the current installation is intended to highlight the history of private collecting and, on the other hand, to place the individual finds in their original settings.

The marble sculptures are, for the most part, Roman copies of classical and Hellenistic originals and, in many cases, the soul surviving document of masterpieces that otherwise would have been lost forever. One example is the group of the **Tyrannicides Harmodius and Aristogiton***, whose original, in bronze, bears the signatures of Kritios and Nesiotis (circa 477 B.C.). Of exceptional value is the statue of the *Doriphorus*** by Polycletus (second half of the 5th c. B.C.), found in Pompeii in 1797; of the *Farnese Hercules**, found in the 16th c. in the baths of Caracalla in Rome, Lisippus created the original in bronze in the second half of the 4th c. B.C., while the statue in question was signed by the "copyist" Glykon on its base. In the same public complex, archaeologists found the **Farnese Bull***, one of the largest sculptural groups to survive, the copy of an original from the Rhodian school, from the end of the 2nd c.

B.C. The collections also include the so-called *Psyche** of Capua (it was unearthed in the amphitheater of that city), the *statue of Antinous* (2nd c.), a bronze statuette of a *Dancing Faun* (Hellenistic age), a rich collection of Greek and Roman portraits (of particular interest are the head of Homer and the colossal statue of Antoninus Pius, a portrait of the *princeps* following his deification); the Astarita collection contains a fragment of high-relief (2nd c. B.C.) from the altar of Zeus at Pergamon.

The gem collection, another historic collection of the Museo, comprises some 2,000 pieces, which come both from finds in Campania and from the Farnese collection. The **Farnese Tazza****, a product of Alexandrian art of the 2nd c. B.C., is the most exquisite example, both in formal terms and in terms of the complexity of depiction. Also worthy of note however are a late-Eastern-style Achemenid *seal* (end of the seventh c. B.C.), a carnelian (Apollo Triumphing over Marsias) attributed to Dioskourides, a fragment of *cameo* (Centaurs) signed by Sostratos, and an *amethyst* with Artemis, done by Apollonios.

Through the epigraphs (over 2,000 of them, most in Latin, though there are also documents in Greek, Oscan, and Etruscan) many aspects of life in the ancient world have been reconstructed. These too are largely from the Farnese collection – though many are examples found in the 18th c. in Campania and in the rest of the kingdom of Naples – and are now arranged by cultural area. Among the exceptional documents are the bronze tables, or **Tavole di Eraclea*** (end of the 4th c./beginning of the 3rd c. B.C.), concerning the administration of the lands of sanctuaries; also noteworthy are the little *gold laminae* (4th c. B.C.) linked to the Orphic cult, epigraphs in the Oscan language (mid-4th c./3rd c. B.C.) discovered in the sanctuary near the Fondo Patturelli in Capua, a copy of the cippus, or *Cippo Abellano*, and an ovoid *funerary stele* from Bellante (6th c. B.C.) with inscription in the Sabellic language. Illustrating the progressive Romanization are judicial and agricultural laws, boundary stones, mile columns, and *calendars**, which indicate the days of the year, the feasts, the signs of the Zodiac, the length of the days and the nights.

The Egyptian collection developed out of the combination of the Borgia and Picchianti collections, which were formed between the 18th and 19th c. in accordance with the prevailing tastes of the period; this original nucleus was expanded with finds from Pompeii and other sites in Campania. The materials, often of unknown origin, range from 2700 B.C. (Old Kingdom) to the Roman-Ptolemaic era (3rd/1st c. B.C.). The oldest piece of statuary is the so-called *Dama di Napoli*, or lady of Naples, along with *ushabti* – in wood, stone and faience – *sarcophagi* for the preservation of papyri, epigraphs with the different types of writing used in a single period and over the centuries, artifacts in the Egyptian style, which document the development in the peninsula of Eastern cults from the end of the 1st c. B.C.

The mosaics date from the period between the 2nd c. B.C. and the 1st c. A.D., and for the most part they come from Pompeii, Herculaneum, and Stabiae. Most notable of all is the mosaic depicting the **Battle of Alexander the Great Against Darius****, remarkably large (3.42 x 5.92 m), found in the Casa del Fauno, at Pompeii.

A section is dedicated to the **Villa dei Papiri***, with the finds unearthed in 1750-65 in a residence in Herculaneum that is still underground. The sculptures have been repositioned in accordance with the original decorative array, a document of the Hellenization of the culture of Campania and the owner of this villa at the end of the 1st c. B.C. Note the interesting *machine* used to unroll the charred papyri found in the ancient residence.

Of the vast collection of pottery and vases, a selection is on display (black- and red-figure ceramics, of both Greek and Italic production; examples of local ceramic workshops from southern Italy), while the topographic section illustrates the prehistory and early history of the Gulf of Naples and of inland Campania, as well as the Colony of Cumae, from its foundation to the Roman era.

Paintings**, another notable part of the collections of the Museo, come from the Roman cities buried by the eruption of A.D. 79 and constitute a collection of remarkable value; dating from the 1st c. B.C. to the 1st c. A.D., and for the most part detached from their original sites between the 18th and 19th c., they are copies of Greek originals.

The Farnese Hercules (Museo Archeologico Nazionale)

The fragments on display come from the villa of Fannius Synistor at Boscoreale, from the Basilica of Herculaneum, the villa of Agrippa Postumus at Boscotrecase, and from the possessions of Julia Felix in Pompeii; they illustrate *mythological and literary themes, still lifes*, landscapes*, scenes of everyday life* and *portraits*, including the very famous one of Paquius Proculus and his wife** (end of the reign of Nero). Rarer are the examples of **painted architecture**, depicting – with trompe-l'oeil perspectives – false backdrops that open out onto green spaces, or niches or marble inserts of various colors, in which are inserted isolated figures or paintings. The paintings with a funerary subject were, on the other hand, found in tombs and can be dated back to the 4th/2nd c. B.C.

The idea of reconstructing the original setting was the inspiration for the arrangement of the hall of the temple of Isis, or **Tempio di Iside**, where you can see – although not in their precise original location – frescoes and other finds unearthed in Pompeii in 1764-66. This array includes both architectural ornaments and fragments of paintings, both the product of the reconstruction of this place of worship following the earthquake of A.D. 62.

Completing the collections is a *model** made of cork (scale 1:100), done in 1861-79, which reproduces a plan of Pompeii, a number of pieces of *silver work*, largely from Herculaneum and from Pompeii (no fewer than 115 items in one complete set* found in the house of Menander, in Pompeii), *objects made of ivory and bone*, having to do with games or with women's possessions, Egyptian or Egyptian-style glazed terracottas, glass objects, in part from the Farnese collection and in part from the towns surrounding Mt. Vesuvius (of particular note is the specimen from Pompeii known as the Vaso Blu), Greek and Italic arms and armor, found in the sanctuaries of Magna Graecia, or in Campanian and Samnite sites.

3 Naples: the expansion to the sea

This is one of the areas that has been most heavily transformed over the last hundred years by the projects for the renewal and reconstruction of the Corso Umberto (the Rettifilo, literally, the "straightaway"), bombardments, and reconstruction. It begins (see plan on p. 30) to the west with Via Medina, and it comes to an end in the east with the church of the Carmine, whose campanile, for centuries and right up until the construction of the tall buildings in the new office center, had long marked the extreme southeastern edge of the city. Along the arc of this area, you can have some idea of the considerable size that Naples had already attained by the 14th c. There have been profound changes – to an even greater degree than has been the case in the western section – in the relationship with the sea, now distant, separated by the commercial port from the everyday life of the city. A bit out of place – behind the backdrops of the Rettifilo and Via Marina – are the surviving fragments

Interior of the church of S. Maria del Carmine

of the old urban fabric (marked by the elongated shape of the blocks of the Angevin expansion, which only partly survived the general demolition), once the site of the various communities of foreign merchants, attracted to the numerous city gates that opened onto the sea, through which goods of all sorts were brought (the place names remain, such as Via Porta di Massa), or else the sites of the concentrated activities of an entire category, as is still the case even today (Piazza degli Orefici).

A vast square, disfigured by war and by the property speculation described in *Le Mani sulla Città* (*Hands over the City*) by Francesco Rosi (1963) this is Piazza Mercato; for centuries, this was the center of commercial life in the city, and it was built here at the orders of the Anjou; it has been the site of the most important events in the history of Naples, from the beheading of Conradin (Corradino) to the revolt led by Masaniello to the mass executions of 1799.

From Via Medina to the Carmine along Corso Umberto

Via Medina (I, D-E2). This street is named after the Spanish viceroy who ordered the renewal of what had been the Angevin Largo delle Corregge. On the right, at no. 24, note the 18th-c. *Palazzo Fondi* and the church of the Pietà dei Turchini; across the way are the churches of the Incoronata and of S. Giorgio dei Genovesi, now in the shadow of a tall building and other buildings dating back to the period of government under Mayor Lauro (1950s). Next come the *Palazzo d'Aquino di Caramanico* and the *Palazzo Giordano*, both by Fuga. Behind them ex-

tends the modern quarter built in the old Zona dei Guantai (area of the glove-makers), where only the church of the *SS. Pietro e Paolo dei Greci* survives (with iconostasis dating from the 18th c.). On the right is the *Palazzo Carafa di Nocera*, built in the 16th c. but transformed in the 19th c., and the church of S. Diego all'Ospedaletto. Behind that, there survives a rare fragment of the medieval city, based around Via S. Bartolomeo (where you will find the church of *S. Maria della Graziella*) and the Rua Catalana. This whole area was the site, during the Angevin rule, of Fondaci and Logge (the structures used by non-Neapolitan merchants, whence comes a vast series of place names linked to the Genoans, Catalans, Pisans, Greeks…).

S. Maria Incoronata* (I, E2). This church was built at the behest of at the behest of Joan I with the title of "Corona di Spine" or crown of thorns (depicted in the portal) after a relic that was donated to the church; it features a remarkable layout with two naves, covered by cross-vaults; this layout has generated a vast array of theories. The church is now stripped of all furnishings and every decorative element, with the exception of the Baroque altar and a series of frescoes*; those on the arches of the nave are particularly important (*Biblical Stories*) as are those in the 1st bay (*Triumph of Religion and the Seven Sacraments*) by Roberto d'Oderisio (in two phases 1340-43; 1352-54). In the nave there are frescoes, by a master from the Marches, in the early 15th c., detached from the chapel, or Cappella del Crocifisso (on the left), still with their preliminary drawings.

Pietà dei Turchini* (I, E2). This building originated with the establishment (1583) of a conservatory to house "lost" boys; it was decorated by many of the principal artists of the 17th and 18th c., including Battistello, Juan Do, F. Vitale, Giordano, D. Lazzari (altar in the right transept), G. Farelli, L. Vaccaro, and G. Diano (*canvases* in the left transept, 1781). The name of the church comes from the turquoise ("turchino") outfits worn by the children housed in the conservatory, where they were taught music and singing as well (among them was A. Scarlatti).

Palazzo delle Poste e Telegrafi (I, D1-2). This is certainly one of the most handsome and important buildings erected in Naples in the 20th c. It stands at the center of a modern quarter, or "rione," created with the "renewal" of the Quartiere S. Giuseppe. Built (1935) to plans by G. Vaccaro and G. Franzi, who won the competition of 1929 for the project, it takes its inspiration from European examples of the Modern Movement; of special interest is the curvilinear facade, the vestibule, the large stairway, and the two large halls on the ground floor.

S. Maria la Nova* (I, D2). This church is called "Nova" to distinguish it from another similarly named church demolished for the construction of the Castel Nuovo. It was built in 1297 near an old tower and was rebuilt at the end of the 16th c. with an austere and distinctive facade, with two orders of pilaster strips, reminiscent of solutions that were used in the city's civil architecture (Palazzo Giusso, for instance). On the left is the chapel, or Cappella di S. Giacomo della Marca (1504), which, in the sharp clarity of its volumes is reminiscent of the chapel, or Cappella Pontano. The interior is one of the most remarkable and exquisite in the city, and boasts a particularly splendid *ceiling* (1598-1603) adorned with 46 paintings by various artists; this is of special importance because it shows all of the schools of painting in Naples just prior to the arrival of Caravaggio. The nave is marked by the presence on the various pillars of *little altars* under the patronage of various families (in three of them, notice paintings by G. Imparato). In the chapels, there are artworks by B. Caracciolo, Teodoro d'Errico, G. Santacroce, Giovanni da Nola, and F. A. Altobello. We would mention in particular, as masterpieces of the art of marble inlay, the *altar frontal* in the 5th chapel on the right and the *pulpit* by F. Balsimelli (1617-20). In the presbytery, before the handsome altar designed by Fanzago, note the *funerary slab of Joan III of Aragón*; in the chapel on the left, note the vast Baroque silver decoration. In the enormous chapel of S. Giacomo della Marca (nearly another church), note the frescoes by Stanzione, and the *tombs of Odetto di Foix viscount of Lautrec* and that of *Pietro Navarro* (two condottieri sent by Francis I to reconquer the Kingdom of Naples in 1528), the work of A. Caccavello; in the side chapels, note artworks by G. D'Auria and Ercole Ferrata.

S. Maria Donnalbina* (I, D2). This church, which existed as early as the ninth c., was rebuilt in the early years of the 17th c. The interior constitutes an organic complex dating from the years spanning the end of the 17th c. and the beginning of the 18th c., considering the marble inlay on the main altar, the stuccoes, and the splendid carvings in the choir loft; the canvases by N. Malinconico (in the handsome carved ceiling over the nave), and by F. Solimena (in the transept). In the counterfacade, note the *tomb of G. Paisiello* (died in 1816). One curious aspect is the invention of the journalist and writer on Naples, Matilde Serao who, playing on the sounds of the names of three major monasteries, tells the tale of three girls in the same family, all in love with the same man, who urges them to become nuns, persuading them to found three convents that take the names of the unhappy girls: Donna Regina, Donna Romita, Donna Albina.

Palazzo Penna* (I, D2). It was built in 1406 by Antonio Penna, the secretary of King Ladislao, and it is the only to survive in good condition from the period of Durazzo. The facade, with a handsome portal and original wooden doors, is adorned with rustication that repeats the insignia of the owner (feathers, after his name; "penne") alternating with the insignia of the king. Adjoining it is the *Palazzo Casamassima* (with an entrance from Via Banchi Nuovi), which still faithfully maintains the layout of the 16th c. (open staircase, double loggia in front of the entrance); it was enlarged in the 18th c. (in the vaulted ceiling of one large hall, note a handsome fresco by G. del Po). The chapel, or *Cappella Pappacoda* (1415), has a spectacular late-Gothic *portal* by Antonio Baboccio, which has been restored to its original polychrome form, and a small bell tower, interesting for the coloring of the materials of which it is made and decorated (tufa, piperno stone, and marble) and for the use of both medieval and recycled marble work.

Piazza Bovio (Piazza della Borsa; I, D2). This square, set at one end of the huge 19th-c. boulevard ripped through the heart of the city ("Rettifilo"), is adorned at its center by a fountain, the *Fontana del Nettuno*, by M. Naccherino and P. Bernini (1601), moved here in 1898. Overlooking it is the *Palazzo della Borsa* (stock exchange, 1895) with a great hall in the Eclectic style. The building includes (with an entrance from the left side) the little church of *S. Aspreno al Porto*, founded in early times, and articulated on two levels. In the modern vestibule, there are columns taken from

Piazza Bovio and Corso Umberto I

the demolished cloisters of S. Pietro ad Aram; in the upper church are carved transennas from the 9th/10th c., some of the most important relics of Naples in the ducal period; The lower oratory is set in an interesting old room from a Roman bath; the altar has been dated back to the 8th c.

If you head straight down toward the sea from this square, you will find the church of **S. Maria di Portosalvo** (I, D3), which stands, completely out of place in its surrounding. The only surviving structure out of all those that once surrounded it is the 18th-c. church of the Immacolatella (Our Little Lady of the Immaculate Conception; surrounded by sculptures linked to the Virgin Mary) built at the behest of Charles of Bourbon to plans by D. A. Vaccaro and now confined beyond the enclosure of the harbor, or Porto. The church was built by sailors in the 16th c.; on the interior, note the painting by Battistello in the ceiling, statues by A. and G. Viva and a *balustrade** of marble inlay. Alongside it stands an obelisk erected to celebrate the return of the king in 1799, following the repression of the revolution, and the Repubblica Partenopea.

Corso Umberto I (Rettifilo; I, D3, C3-4, B4-5). This long broad avenue, built, beginning in 1889, in the context of the urban renewal project that came in the wake of the great epidemic of cholera in 1884, which had been especially brutal in the old quarters, or "quartieri bassi," the result of the medieval expansion, set between the hill, or Collina del Monterone and the sea. The palazzi that overlook it show a homogeneous Neo-Renaissance and Eclectic appearance, especially evident in the so-called "quattro palazzi," or "four palazzi," which mark off the boundaries, at the intersection with Via Duomo, of the Piazza Nicola Amore (named after the mayor during the renewal). Almost at the beginning of the street stands the *Palazzo dell'Università degli Studi* (1897-1908), adorned in its pediments by reliefs depicting important moments in the history of the Neapolitan university, or Studio Napoletano, which was founded in 1224 by Fredericl II: at the center (by F. Ierace) the *Reading of the Diploma of Foundation*, on either side (by A. D'Orsi) *G. B. Vico Teaching*, and *Giordano Bruno in Disputatation with the Dominicans*.

S. Pietro Martire (I, D3). Founded in 1294, this church was rebuilt around 1750 by Astarita. It was restored following very serious damage sustained during the war (a bay on the left shows the Renaissance decorations that have been covered up in the rest of the church by stuccoes). It features artworks by Mario di Laurito (1501), J. della Pila, B. Ordóñez, G. B. Azzolino, G. del Po, G. Diano, S. Conca, and F. Solimena.

S. Agostino alla Zecca* (I, C4). A stairway climbs the difference between the elevation of the "Rettifilo" and that of the street in which, near the Zecca, stands this church. Damaged by the earthquake of 1456, it was rebuilt in two phases by B. Picchiatti (1641-97) and by G. De Vita and G. Astarita (1756-70): the former did the facing of the campanile and large nave, while De Vita built the cross vault and Astarita was responsible for the singular solution of the dome that is transformed into an apsidal cupola. In the church (closed for restoration since 1980) there are major artworks, including: in the spectacular apse, *canvases** by G. Diano and a group with *St. Augustine Trampling Heresy, between Charity and Faith* (1761) by Sanmartino; in the chapel to the left of the presbytery is buried Nicolò Jommelli; in the adjoining Cappella Tufarelli note the relief by P. Bertini; there is a handsome pulpit by A. Caccavello; in the lovely sacristy, note the frescoes by G. Diano. The palazzo at no. 174 in the Corso Umberto incorporates a part of the monastery; after you climb a couple of stories, you can enter the column-lined *cloister* (roofed over, and now a university classroom) with decorations by the Picchiatti, and to the remarkable *chapter hall** in a pure Gothic style, with vaulted ceilings with pronounced ribbings, supported by two columns adorned with handsome recycled Swabian *capitals*.

S. Maria Egiziaca a Forcella (I, B4). This church was founded 1342, and was rebuilt in 1684 by D. Lazzari to an elliptical plan. It was – until a serious theft (1993) of paintings by Giordano, A. Vaccaro, and Solimena, which decorated it – of the most homogeneous and important pieces of Baroque art and architecture. What remains to be admired is the elegance of the architectural space and the refined wooden carvings and marble inlays.

S. Pietro ad Aram (I, B5). This church, built on the site in which an erroneous tradition had it that Saint Peter converted Saints Candida and Aspren, it was rebuilt in the second half of the 17th c. The monastery was de-

molished to make way for the construction of the Rettifilo and the church, which survived, was renovated in a 19th-c. style; as a side portal, a *portal* was recomposed that came from another demolished monument, the Conservatorio dell'Arte della Lana. In the vestibule, beneath an aedicule designed by M. Nauclerio (1711), stands the so-called altar, or *Altare di S. Pietro* (12th c.); on the wall, note the *Mass of St. Peter*, a fresco dating from the 16th c., with one of the oldest views of the city ever painted, in the background. Next to the church, note the walled-up door, which was opened to celebrate the Jubilees in 1526, 1551, 1576, the years fol-

Fish vendors' stalls near Porta Nolana

lowing the celebration of the true Holy Year in Rome; this privilege was abolished in 1600. In the vestibule of the sacristy, note the tomb, or *Sepolcro Ricca* by Gian Giacomo de Brixia (Brescia).

Porta Nolana (I, B5). Set between two towers names "Faith" and "Hope," this gate is adorned in its exterior front only by a marble arch and a relief depicting *Ferrante I on horseback* (an indirect confirmation of the relief on Porta Capuana in the Aragonese ring of walls); in the interior facade is the usual bust of St. Gaetano. Nearby is one of the most crowded and vital markets of the city. You may then continue along the Corso Garibaldi or else follow the old Via del Lavinaio.

S. Maria del Carmine* (I, C5). This is one of the most important churches in the city, in terms of historic and artistic interest, and it is one of the most beloved, because of the Neapolitan's love of the Madonna "Bruna," or Brown Madonna; this is the center of one of the best known Neapolitan festivals (16 July, Madonna del Carmine) during which fireworks are used to simulate a fire burning the campanile (the tallest bell tow-

S. Maria del Carmine

er in Naples, 75 m high, built in several phases and completed by Fra' Nuvolo in 1631). It existed as early as the twelfth c., and was rebuilt between 1283 and 1300. Nowadays, the only surviving trace of the Gothic church is in the cross vault over the presbytery, because even in the facade the building features the style of the 18th c.; in the interior, decorated by Tagliacozzi Canale, the modern ceiling is a reproduction of the original ceiling, which was entirely destroyed during the war. Beneath the triumphal arch is a hanging platform, with a tabernacle in which a greatly venerated Gothic *Crucifix* is stored; it is venerated because, according to tradition, during the siege of the Aragonese in 1439, it ducked its head, just avoiding a projectile (still preserved) that had penetrated into the church, and it lost only its crown of thorns. In the chapels, note the artworks by Preti (2nd chapel on the right), Bottigliero (5th chapel on the right), F. Solimena (6th on the left), and P. De Maio (1st on the left). In the nave, beneath the pulpit, which stands on the same place as the pulpit from which Masaniello in 1647 harangued the crowd just before being killed in the monastery, a handsome *statue of St. Michael*, dating from

the 16th c. In the arms of the transept, note the frescoes and canvases by Solimena; the presbytery has a sumptuous marble facing by the Mozzetti; behind the altar it is possible to observe from close up the greatly venerated image of the Madonna della "Bruna," a painting that dates from the 14th c., enclosed in a marble aedicule dating from the 16th c. In the handsome sacristy, note the frescoes by F. Falciatore (1741). To the left, in the nave, is the *monument to Conradin of Swabia*, buried in this church with his cousin, Frederick of Baden) by P. Schoepf, to a model by Thorwaldsen, donated in 1847 by Maximilian of Bavaria. On the interior of the cloisters, handsome pergolas with lemon trees.

Piazza del Mercato (I, C4-5). Established as the marketplace by the Angevins, this square is bounded to the north by a low exedra at the center of which stands the church of *S. Croce al Mercato*; both of those structures were the work of F. Securo (1786), and were built after a fire in 1781 destroyed all of the vendors' stalls and the chapels erected on the site of the execution of Conradin and the ditches in which the victims of the plague 1656 were buried. On either side are two *fountains*, devastated, dating from the 18th c. From the beheading of Conradin (1268) on, this was the site of executions, and it has always been the center stage of Neapolitan history beginning from the "revolt" of Masaniello.

S. Eligio Maggiore* (I, C4). The apses of this church close off the square on the west. This is the first church founded by the Angevins in Naples, and it adjoins a hospital and a bank. It was damaged by bombs during the war, and has been restored, with the elimination of every trace of the Baroque decorations. You enter the church from the side, through a *portal** in the purest French Gothic style, which stands next to the 15th-c. arch, or *Arco dell'Orologio*. The interior has a nave and two side aisles with a transept, and it is an architectural palimpsest. The restorations have uncovered all of the various "works in progress" along with the traces of the various transformations. In the 16th c., a fourth aisle was added by linking one of the Gothic rooms of the hospital to the left-hand side aisle, through large arches made of "piperno" stone.

Not far away is the church of *S. Giovanni a Mare*, which already existed in the 12th c.; this Gothic church has recycled columns, and has been closed for decades.

4 Naples: the expansion outside the old city walls

Despite the prohibitions of the viceroys, who wanted to prevent the construction of buildings outside the city walls, Naples soon expanded beyond the enclosure. In the 19th c., massive public works (renovation of Piazza Cavour and Via Foria; construction of the road to Capodimonte and the Corso Maria Teresa, later Corso Vittorio Emanuele; construction of the Corso Garibaldi and the Piazza Carlo III) transformed the appearance of these places.

The area to the north, between Mater Dei and Piazza Carlo III, because of its unusual topography, can still be considered by parts, which often take their names from their principal church.

To the west, on the hill, or Collina del Vomero, development came later, if we leave aside the buildings erected along the streets that run up here. The Vomero as it is today, a genuine city within the city (many of the inhabitants of this section refer to the historic center as "Naples"; for that matter, for the inhabitants of the historic center, it would often seem that the Vomero simply does not exist), is a quarter that developed at the end of the 19th c. on a hill that was once famous for its panoramic views and its healthy setting, where the city plans of the mid-19th c. show practically only the star-shaped layout of Castel S. Elmo, the Certosa (or charterhouse), a large villa like the Villa Floridiana, which stood alongside the many villas that patricians and magistrates had built here from the 17th and 18th c. Sadly, the chaotic development of this area has not only destroyed the rural houses, but even virtually the entire complex of "Liberty," or Art Nouveau villas that once distinguished this hillside settlement.

Dating back a little earlier is the expansion onto the beach of Chiaia, where, as early as the 16th c., there was a little village, and where, logically enough, there were many houses of fishermen and many religious foundations; along the beach was a fair number of villas, suf-

A fisherman mends his nets in the little tourist port of Mergellina

ficient in number to make it necessary, in order to defend against pirate raids, to build a tower. Further to the west, stands the church of Piedigrotta and the fishing village of Mergellina; still further along are the villas of Posillipo, which can only be reached – from Palazzo Donn'Anna on – by water.

The expansion took place especially during the late 19th c. and later, following the construction of the large thoroughfares running midway up the slope; on the hill, or Collina di Posillipo, only after WWII. Nowadays, all of the streets that at various elevations wind across the face of Posillipo feature splendid panoramas and numerous houses; only the oldest one, Via Posillipo, built by Murat in 1812, bears traces of its former splendor, wending its way through the greenery of many true parks, or "parchi."

4.1 The expansion to the north: from the Museo Nazionale to Capodimonte

This itinerary (see plan on pp. 74-75) runs from the Museo up to Capodimonte, a small village near which was created the "royal site" of Capodimonte, and where the renowned porcelain manufactory was founded (the building still stands in the park). Established (1739) by Charles of Bourbon, who was the direct proprietor of it, it was then shut down (1759) because he – leaving for Spain, where he was to become king – took with him tools, patterns, and artists, even ordering the destruction of the kilns and workshops. His son Ferdinand refounded the factory in another site, far away, and yet another in 1771, in which products were made until 1805. In the area, in any case, there are still workshops and retail outlets.

At the beginning of the itinerary are two important churches (S. Teresa and S. Agostino); this first stretch of the road to Capodimonte, built during the decade of French occupation, required the leveling of the hill, so that the buildings dating back earlier on either side stand at a considerably higher elevation while, after the intersection at the same elevation with the road linking the Stella and Mater Dei, other buildings stand at a lower elevation. You will cross over the quarter, or Quartiere della Sanità, on a bridge, with a fine view of what survives of the green hills and the majolica dome of S. Maria della Sanità, and then you will reach the Tondo di Capodimonte (where there begins a stairway designed by Niccolini and begun in 1836 on a line with the long straight thoroughfare begun under Napoleon) and, near the church of the Buon Consiglio, at the modern entrance to the catacombs, or Catacombe di S. Gennaro.

S. Teresa degli Scalzi (also known as the Studi; I, A1; III, B4). This important Carmelite church was built at the beginning of the 17th c. by Di Conforto; it is decorated in the transept by two large *paintings** by G. del Po depicting the *Flight into Egypt* (on the right) and *Domenico di Gesù Maria at the Battle of Prague*, both of them done at the beginning of Austrian rule, a period which also produced sculptures and epigraphs concerning the emperor and a prince Spinelli. In the apse, note the main altar by Sanmartino (from the church of the Divino Amore) which replaces the altar that is now in the chapel, or Cappella del Palazzo Reale; at the

far end, note a painting by De Matteis. On the left side, the chapel, or Cappella di S. Teresa* by Fanzago. Frescoes by Battistello (with the exception of the modern ovals) in the 2nd chapel on the left.

In Via S. Teresa, at nos. 88-94 is the house in which Leopardi died (14 June 1837, plaque). Facing it, and partly hidden by houses is the high facade of S. Maria della Verità, better known as *S. Agostino degli Scalzi**, a splendid church built in the early 17th c., also by Di Conforto, and wholly sheathed in its vaulted ceilings by a singular, rare, and handsome array of stuccoes; for the paintings of the altars, this is practically a gallery of 17th-c. Neapolitan art; note the handsome marble inlays. It has been closed for restoration since 1980.

Further along in the hemicycle, or *Emiciclo di Capodimonte*, note a *commemorative stele for Humbert I* bearing the words of the king who, in 1884, upon learning of the outbreak of cholera as he was about to leave for the Friuli region, said: "In Pordenone, people are celebrating, in Naples people are dying. I leave for Naples."

Madre del Buon Consiglio (III, A4). This church was built (1920-60) in imitation of St. Peter's in the Vatican, and it contains numerous artworks taken from churches that have been destroyed or abandoned: 18th-c. altars, sculptures by M. Naccherino (*Apostles*), and a full-fledged art gallery, with paintings from the 16th to the 19th c.

Catacombe di S. Gennaro* (III, A3), or Catacombs of St. Januarius. These are the most important catacombs in southern Italy, with exquisite frescoes (second to the tenth centuries). The cemetery, the original core of which dates back to the 2nd c., reached its current state of development in the 4th c., with two levels of galleries. It was used until the ducal era, and this span of use is unrivaled in similar complexes; among those buried here were St. Agrippinus (bishop in the 3rd c.), and then St. Januarius (turn of the 5th c., his relics were stolen in A.D. 831 by Sicone of Benevento), the occasional duke, many bishops, and Cesario Console (died in A.D. 878). The catacombs, near which a sort of early-Christian basilica had been built, were repeatedly and continually devastated, between the 13th and 18th c. The tour begins on the upper floor where, in the deambulatory on the right

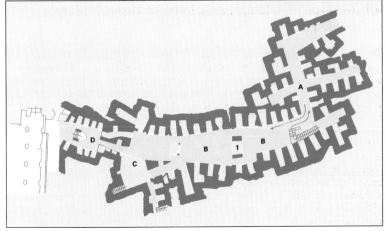

Plan of the Catacombe di S. Gennaro, upper level

(A) there are frescoed arcosolia, including one, right at the beginning, with the earliest depiction known of *St. Januarius* (5th c.). If you retrace your steps, you can enter the main deambulatory (B; at the beginning on the left, cubicles with frescoed arcosolia). Three arches (1) lead into a large hall bounded, on the other side, by three more arches, set on columns carved out of tufa stone. Further along, on the right, cubicles, frescoed and decorated with architectural elements carved into the tufa. You then enter a room (C) in the vault of which, there were once paintings of the *first 14 bishops of Naples* (scanty traces); nearby is the crypt of the bishops, with arcosolia adorned with *mosaics** dating from the 5th c., depicting busts of bishops (including a bust of Quodvultdeus, bishop of Carthage, who died in Naples in A.D. 454, recognizable by the dark skin of his face). A corridor leads to a room (D), adjoining the basilica of S. Gennaro; before the modern entrance had been built, this was the true vestibule of the upper floor; in the vaulted ceiling, note the almost vanished traces of major frescoes dating from the 2nd/3rd centuries (*Adam and Eve, David and Goliath, Construction of the Tower*, this last being a true iconographic *unicum*, based on two passages from a Greek work, the "Shepherd" by Hermas).

A road skirts the right side of the basilica (p. 76) and leads to the lower floor. This is the *basilica of S. Agrippino* (A) with a large conical decorated skylight; on the altar (1) is the "fenestella confessionis" through which it was possible to touch the tomb of the saint; behind the episcopal throne carved out of tufa-stone, on the right side, arcosolia and loculi with frescoes and mosaics. On

the left is the loveliest room (B) in the catacombs, certainly built as an aristocratic hypogeum, and later handed over to the Christian community. On either side are sarcophagi carved into the tufa, and on the ceiling are paintings from the 2nd c.; in the floor, amidst tombs from the later period, a baptismal basin (2; certainly the baptistery built in 762-64). At the center of the far wall is an aedicule (3) with paintings from the 9th c. depicting Christ and saints, who have crowns in hand, as seen in other frescoes, symbolizing the attainment of their eternal reward.

On either side of the aedicule, note the entrances to the two deambulatories. In the cubicles of the larger deambulatory (C, on the left) there are still a number of lovely paintings depicting a *Beardless Christ* (4), the *Good Shepherd, Moses Causing Water to Flow from the Rock* (5), *Jonah* (7), a *peacock between vases* (8), a *vase with a grapevine*, and, on the floor, the only *marble epigraph*

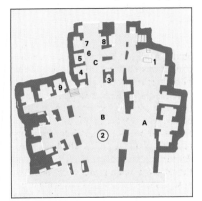

Plan of the Catacombe di S. Gennaro, lower level

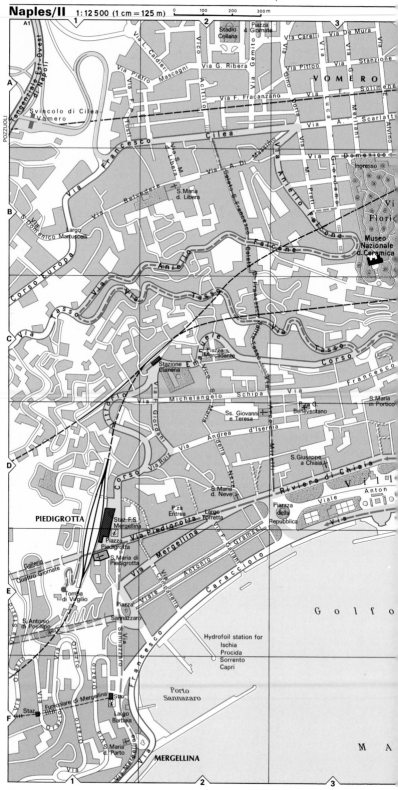

VOMERO

Museo
Nazionale
d. Ceramica

PIEDIGROTTA

Hydrofoil station for
Ischia
Procida
Sorrento
Capri

Porto
Sannazaro

MERGELLINA

Golfo

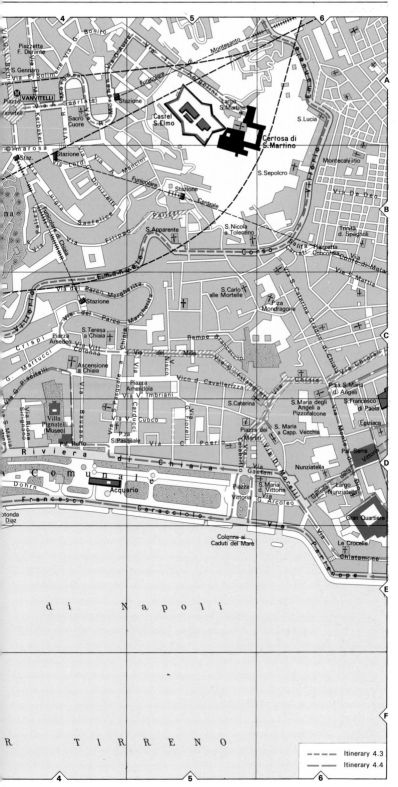

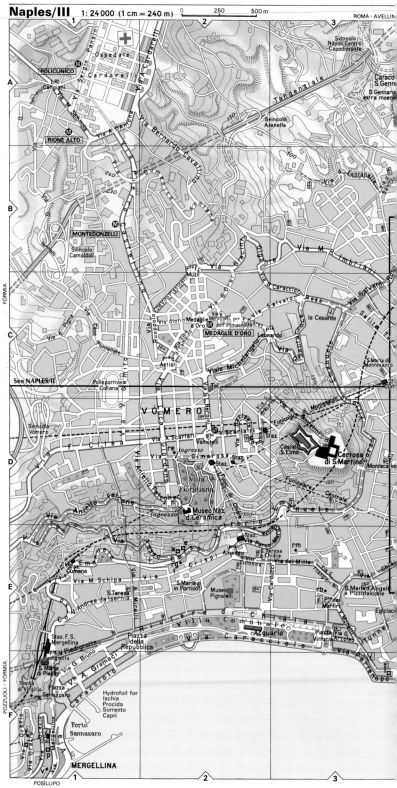

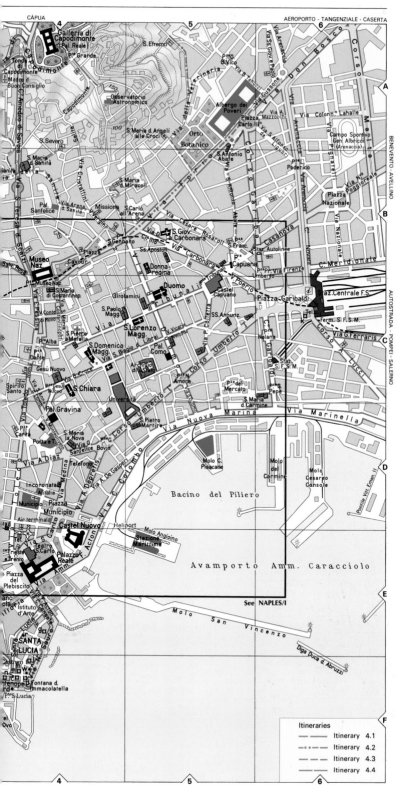

Galleria di Capodimonte (Pal. Reale)
Pal. Grande
S. Efremo
Tondo di Capodimonte
Madre d. Buon Consiglio
Osservatorio Astronomico
S. Maria d. Angeli alle Croci
Orto Botanico
S. Severo
S. Maria d. Sanità
S. Cristallini
Missione
S. Carlo all' Arena
S. Gennaro
Pal. Sanfelice
Museo Naz.
Cavour
Pal. Museo Naz.
S. Maria di Costantinop.
Donna Regina
Duomo
Girolamini
S. Paolo Magg.
S. Pietro a Maiella
S. Lorenzo Magg.
S. Domenico Magg.
Pal. Como
Archivio
Dante
Gesù Nuovo
Spirito Santo
S. Chiara
Università
Pal. Gravina
S. Maria la Nova
Posta e T.
Sanfelice
Telefono
Incoronata
Alitalia
Municipio Piazza Municipio
Air terminal
Castel Nuovo
Heliport
Teatro S. Carlo
Palazzo Reale
Piazza del Plebiscito
Istituto d'Arte
SANTA LUCIA
Tenope e Fontana d. Immacolatella
Pta. S. Lucia
Ovo

Albergo dei Poveri
Piazza Carlo III
Via S. Antonio Abate
S. Antonio Abate
Poderico
Piazza Nazionale
S. Giov. a Carbonara
SS. Apostoli
Castel Capuano
Piazza Garibaldi
SS. Annunz.
Naiana
Pta. del Mercato
S. Maria d. Carmine
Pta. del Carmine

Campo Sportivo Gen. Albricci (Arenaccia)

Staz. Autolinee
Staz. Centrale F.S.
Ferm. S.F.S.M.
Via A. Ferraris
Staz. S.F.S.M.

Via Nuova Marina
Via Marinella

Molo C. Pisacane
Molo del Carmine
Molo Cesareo Console

Bacino del Piliero

Molo Angioino
Stazione Marittima

Avamporto Amm. Caracciolo

Molo San Vincenzo

Diga Duca d. Abruzzi

See NAPLES/I

Itineraries

— · — · — Itinerary 4.1
— · · — · · — Itinerary 4.2
— — — Itinerary 4.3
——— Itinerary 4.4

still in place (6) with the legend, "Hic requiescit Babulius."

In the deambulatory on the right, note the marble column (not part of the Christian cemetery) that bears, in Greek, the name of Priapus (another reference to the pagan world can be found in the *ithyphallic goat*, skipping and bounding in the painting on the wall at the entrance to the deambulatories). On the same column, you can see an inscription in Hebrew, one of the few surviving pieces of medieval evidence left by the Jews of Naples (the expulsion of the flourishing Jewish communities of the kingdom occurred a few years after the expulsion ordered in Spain in 1492).

You may then return to the hall in the baptistery where (now on the right, 9) you will find the crypt, or *Cripta di S. Gennaro*, supposedly containing the relics of St. Januarius and the saints who were martyred with him at Pozzuoli, with three layers of plaster on the walls (the oldest one dates back to the 3rd c.; on the latest one note the depictions of St. Januarius and his companions).

Palazzo Reale di Capodimonte* (III, A4). Until the 18th c., this was just a small village; then Charles of Bourbon decided to establish in 1739 the celebrated manufactory of porcelain and to erect a building that could contain the art collections that he had inherited through his mother, Elisabetta Farnese. The palazzo – the design and construction of which was assigned in 1734 to G. A. Medrano and Antonio Canevari – housed the collections until the Restoration, and, donated by the House of Savoy to the Italian State in 1920, it became the home of the Dukes of Aosta until 1946; from 1957 on it has housed the Museo and the Gallerie Nazionali di Capodimonte (see below). The facade, in particular, is noteworthy for the

The Sala delle Feste, Capodimonte

two arms at the extremities, which reach out to embrace the central section, and is punctuated by twin pilaster strips that frame two orders of windows, above them is a mezzanine and a crowning balcony.

To complete the building, the **Parco** was laid out by Ferdinando Sanfelice along five avenues, running radially from the gate, or Porta di Mezzo and crossing an area of 120 hectares; one relic of the "industrial" past of this place is the building of the porcelain manufactory, or Manifattura di Porcellane. Note the splendid views of the gulf.

Museo and Gallerie Nazionali di Capodimonte**. The reopening of this museum, at the end of 1995, was quite an event, and since then, the number of visitors that have been touring the rooms of this residence had not been seen in years in a comparable Neapolitan institution. And yet, the collections had been closed to the public only one year previous, for necessary projects of modernization. Whether because of the unusual speed with which the projects were completed or because of the interest in the new installation of the collections, tourists from Naples and from around the world have come in great numbers to see the Farnese masterpieces. The installation on the main floor ("piano nobile") features the same arrangement ordered by Charles of Bourbon: the paintings – no fewer than 213 – are arranged chronologically and by schools; the objets-d'art, linked to the furnishing of the historic apartments, or Appartamento Storico, are arranged as a "gallery of rare objects"; the entire fourth floor, from the end of 1996, has been devoted to contemporary art.

The historic nucleus of the collections of Capodimonte bears the name of the Farnese family, and in fact those collections originated with the arrival in Naples, by inheritance, of the rich collections begun by Pope Paul III in Rome, and were originally intended as decorations for the palazzo by Michelangelo in the Eternal City. Over the course of the 18th c., these collections were expanded with the addition of new acquisitions and material taken from suppressed monasteries, and with the addition of the Borgia collection in the 19th c., followed in the 20th c. by the De Ciccio collection, and a greater presence of Neapolitan paintings. In the Museum, moreover, there are canvases and paintings taken from other churches, still used as such, for considerations of security.

The Farnese collection includes some of the most important artworks present in the Museo: the *portrait of Cardinal Gonzaga* by Andrea Mantegna; the **Transfiguration**** by Giovanni Bellini; a *portrait of Bernardo de' Rossi** by Lorenzo Lotto; *portraits of Paul III and other members of the Farnese family*, by Titian; the **Zingarella (Gypsy Girl)**** and the *Mystic Wedding of St. Catherine* by Correggio; the *Anthaea* by Parmigianino; *Pietà* and the *Vision of St. Eustace*, by Annibale Carracci; *Jesus Served by the Angels* and the *Assumption of Mary Magdalene*, by Giovanni Lanfranco; the *Charity* of Bartolomeo Schedoni; the *Parable of the Blind* and the *Misanthrope* by Pieter Bruegel the Elder; the *Farnese coffer** (1548-61), in gilt silver with cut crystal, by Giovanni Bernardi.

Other acquisitions resulted in the addition of the *Atalanta and Hippomenes* by Guido Reni, the fragments of the altarpiece, or **Pala di Città di Castello****, the work of Raphael and Evangelista di Pian di Meleto, the *Annunciation** by Filippo Lippi, the *St. Euphemia* by Mantegna – which, along with panels by Bernardo Daddi (*Virgin Mary with Christ Child*) and Bartolo di Fredi, formed part of the Borgia collection – the *Sacred Conversation* by Jacopo Palma the Elder, the **Crucifixion**** by Masaccio, and the *Drunken Silenus* by Jusepe de Ribera; of various origin are the *Calvary* by Polidoro da Caravaggio and the *Adoration of the Magi* by Cesare da Sesto.

Originally hanging in Neapolitan monasteries and churches were: *Our Lady of the Assumption*, by Pinturicchio; *St. Louis Crowning King Robert*, by Simone Martini; *St. Francis Giving the Rule to St. Jerome*, by Colantonio; the *Annunciation** by Titian; the **Flagellation**** by Caravaggio; the *Slaughter of the Innocents*, by Matteo di Giovanni; the *Deposition from the Cross*, by Pietro Befulco. There is a lavish panorama of Neapolitan painting, especially from the 17th to 18th c., with masterpieces by Luca Giordano, Massimo Stanzione, Mattia Preti, Francesco De Mura, Paolo De Matteis, and Corrado Giaquinto.

Authentic "unicums" are the panel, or **Tavola Strozzi****, which depicts the Naples

of the 15th c., the *panel from S. Maria de Flumine* (13th c.), cartoons by Raphael (**Moses****) and Michelangelo (**Three soldiers****); also note the copy of the *Last Judgment*, by Marcello Venusti.

Of no less importance and size is the collection of 19th-c. painting and sculpture, originally assembled to furnish the palazzo and integrated by other collections; of particular note are the creations of Giacinto Gigante, Domenico Morelli, Giuseppe De Nittis, Vincenzo Gemito, and Francesco

Crucifixion, by Masaccio (purchased by the Museo and Gallerie Nazionali di Capodimonte in 1901)

Paolo Michetti.

Under the heading of the so-called applied arts ("arti minori") we find the seven large **tapestries** (Episodes of the Battle of Pavia) woven by the manufactory of Brussels in the 16th c. to a design by Bernart van Orley, the *porcelain* – with splendid examples of "biscuit" work, by Filippo Tagliolini, *weapons and armor*, and *bronze figurines*, as well as a *Roman floor*, uncovered on Capri. Belonging to the De Ciccio collection are more than 1,300 items, including *majolica* dating from the 15th to the 18th c., Chinese and European *porcelain*, *enamel objects*, *ivories*, *watches* from French and Swiss manufactories, and glass from Murano. A great many objects have to do with the Bourbons, from the *portraits of members of* the family to the *sedan chairs*, the collections of *porcelain* and *majolica* produced in the most important manufactories of Europe, the little **porcelain drawing room****, created for Maria Amalia in the Palazzo Reale of Portici in 1757-59, and transferred here in 1867: more than 3,000 pieces of porcelain cover the walls, and the legends in Chinese refer to the establishment (1732) of a Chinese college intended to train young Asians as missionaries.

The "Olympus" of contemporary art is assembled on the fourth floor, emblematic of the interest that Naples has always had for avant-garde art, encouraged by its gallery owners and its patrons of the arts. From the exhibition of Alberto Burri's work comes the

Grande Cretto Nero, along with the jars by Jannis Kounellis set amidst heavy iron panels, the *Onda d'Urto* by Mario Merz (a nave made of industrial re-bar, filled with stacks of newspaper), the slabs by Enzo Cucchi, the series of white *bas-reliefs* by Michelangelo Pistoletto. And there are also installations and works by Sol Lewitt, Mimmo Paladino, and Andy Warhol.

If you leave the park by the Porta Grande, you will reach the astronomical observatory, or *Osservatorio Astronomico* (III, A4) through an incredibly pristine stretch of cultivated countryside. Founded in 1819 on the hill of Miradois, the observatory occupies a handsome neoclassical building by the brothers Gasse; in several of the building's rooms is a *Museum*.

4.2 From the Museo Nazionale to the Albergo dei Poveri, and the Sanità

The itinerary (see plan on pp. 74-75) can be divided into two sections. The 1st route runs along the axis from Piazza Cavour along Via Foria to the Piazza Carlo III; three detours lead to S. Maria della Stella, S. Maria dei Miracoli, and S. Efremo Vecchio.

Despite the modern transformations and the violent character that the city has begun to acquire in the 1980s, in the wake of the earthquake, many of the streets on the left of Via Foria still preserve – and not only in their names (Vico dei Miracoli, Vico delle Fate a Foria, Miradois which derives from the Spanish "mira todos," or more likely, from the name of the Regent Miradois, who had a palazzo there) – some sense of the clear air and the miraculous light that, in the "belle giornate," or beautiful days of the 17th c., pushed the Neapolitans to stroll up toward S. Maria degli Angeli alle Croci, one of the loveliest places in the city. Even today, despite all the unpleasant aspects of a stroll through an isolated street in a modern city (syringes and drug addicts going about their activities, to be perfectly clear), the Salita del Moiarello, around the observatory, or Osservatorio Astronomico (better if you are on your way down, for the fine views of the city) and on a fine day, is an experience not to be missed.

The second route begins opposite the Porta S. Gennaro and leads through the quarters of the Vergini and the Sanità to the hospital, or Ospedale di S. Gennaro dei Poveri and to the Fontanelle, through one of the most crowded and distinctive quarters (practically a city unto itself, with an entirely autonomous life), which has developed along the roads that led to the Christian cemeteries.

From the Museo Nazionale to the Albergo dei Poveri

Piazza Cavour (I, A2; III, B4). Formerly Largo delle Pigne, this square lies alongside the Museo; overlooking it is the *Rosariello alle Pigne* (with a fretwork facade built by A. Guglielmelli and interior staircase; major canvas by Giordano on the main altar).

Via Stella climbs up toward the church of S. Maria della Stella, from which an entire working-class quarter takes its name. Built high atop the hill at the end of the 16th c., and burnt down in 1944, the church was rebuilt on the original plan, and was decorated with artworks taken from other churches that had been destroyed; for example, the marble inlaid pilaster strips and the main altar (from S. Sebastiano) and the canvases in the ceiling of the transept which form part of the cycle by Pietro del Po that once adorned the Palatine chapel, or Cappella Palatina of Castel Nuovo. Among the paintings, only the *Our Lady of the Immaculate Conception and Saints** by Battistello was originally housed in this church, and survived the fire because it was in the sacristy, a handsome 18th-c. room that was spared by the flames.

Porta S. Gennaro (I, A2-3; III, B4). This gate opens in the enclosure walls, near the point at which the walls built under the viceroys began, and only a few meters away from the site of the Greek gate. This is the only gate that is still surmounted by one of the aedicules that frescoed by M. Preti over all of the gates, as a votive offering of the city following the plague of 1656. Another recurrent votive offering, which was more commonly preserved, was the *bust of St. Cajetan* on the interior facade.

Gesù delle Monache* (I, A3). On the interior of the enclosure wall, just after the door, one has an angled view of the high facade of the church that was founded at the turn of the 16th c., which, according to the intentions of Queen Joan, the widow of Ferrante I, was to become the "pantheon" of the royal family of Aragón, by now pushed aside with establishment of the viceroys. The project was never accomplished, and the church was not completed until 1582. The facade, a fretwork diaphragm behind which stands the entrance, is the oldest example of a type of structure that was to become much more common in the 17th c. and in many churches by Fanzago. On the interior, the 16th-c. layout is faced with a sumptuous Baroque decoration on which A. Guglielmelli (ca. 1680; little dome over the presbytery), L. Vaccaro (stuccoes in the chapels), L. Giordano and F. Solimena (frescoes and paintings) all worked. Of particular note is the main altar by Enrico Pini with the splendid little door of the tabernacle.

Succulents and cacti in the Orto Botanico

At the beginning of Via Foria is Via dei Miracoli, which climbs up to the square (built in the 18th c.), which is overlooked by the church of *S. Maria dei Miracoli*, renovated in 1662-75 by F. A. Picchiatti. The interior, with a single nave, with four chapels on either side and a transept, abounds in paintings (by Giordano, A. Malinconico, and A. Vaccaro) and marble inlays (done by D. Lazzari, G. D. Vinaccia, V. d'Adamo, and B. and P. Ghetti; the latter two did the handsome holy *water stoup**).

S. Maria degli Angeli alle Croci* (III, A5). This church stands at the top of an ascent,

or "salita," along which, according to the customs of the Osservanti, there were once wooden crosses, though they have since been eliminated. Founded in 1581, it was entirely rebuilt by Fanzago during the rule of the viceroy Medina de las Torres; Fanzago, in the refinement of the decorations, maintained the rigor and the "poverty" of the order of the Osservanti, using white and gray marble on the interior as well; the only note of color was given by the wooden statues on the altars, the work of Fra' Diego da Careri; only a few survive. By Cosimo Fanzago, note the *statue of St. Francis* in the facade and the very handsome *pulpit**; by his son Carlo, on the other hand, note the remarkable altar frontal on the main altar, with a depiction of *Dead Christ**.

Orto Botanico* (III, A-B5), or botanical gardens. Among the most important botanical gardens in Italy, it was founded in Napoleonic times (1807). Because of the remarkable climate, it is possible to cultivate nearly every sort of flowers here. Among the collections, of particular note are the collections of desert plants, the collections of *Cycadinae* (among the richest on earth), of fern trees (unique in Europe), and the old collection of citrus trees.

Albergo dei Poveri (III, A5). This poor house stands on the Piazza Carlo III, which commemorates the name of the most important sovereign of the Bourbon dynasty (he was Charles III, as the king of Spain), founder of the immense building, which was intended as a haven for the "poor of the entire kingdom," as the Latin epigraph over the entrance indicates. The enormous construction, begun in 1751 to plans by Fuga (which called for an even larger construction) and left unfinished, housed charitable institutions until the earthquake of 1980.

From Piazza Cavour to the Sanità and to the Fontanelle

Largo dei Vergini (I, A2; III, B4). This square is characterized by a remarkable double-Y plan, and is one of the most organic 18th-c. settings in the city; on the left is the church of *S. Maria Succure Miseris*, built, to plans by Sanfelice, on the ruins of an Angevin church (S. Antoniello, buried under the flooding and silt of the "Lava dei Vergini"). Next, on the left (no. 19), is the *Palazzo dello Spagnolo* (so-called because it belonged in the 19th c. to a Spanish nobleman), built by Sanfelice, and characterized by an open staircase in the courtyard, one of the most

Festivities in the Rione Sanità

distinctive and charming staircases of the Neapolitan 18th c.

Church of the Padri della Missione* (III, B4). Behind the anonymous facade is one of the most interesting architectural complexes of the Neapolitan 18th c., attributed to L. Vanvitelli. You will enter an atrium set on a line with a long corridor that leads to the monastic complex; on the left is a room that served as the pronaos of the church, laid out to an elliptical plan, set between two rectangles, and covered by a large dome without tambour, and with eight large windows at the base. On the main altar, in marble inlay, note the canvas by De Mura.

Palazzo Sanfelice (III, B4). Built by Sanfelice as his own home (1728). In the long facade you may note two identical portals: the 1st leads into a courtyard at the end of which is one of the most singular staircases designed by the architect, the shape of which can be understood only by climbing it; in the 2nd, you will instead see a typical Sanfelice staircase, made even more enchanting by the presence of the garden in the back.

S. Maria della Sanità* (III, B4). This church stands at the center of a quarter that is one of the most populous and characteristic; it is better known among the inhabitants of the zone as the church of S. Vincenzo, for the worship of the statue of S. Vincenzo Ferreri (St. Vincent Ferrer, also known as *'o munacone* in local dialect) that is kept in the church. The church was built to plans by

Fra' Nuvolo (1602-13) over the catacombs, or Catacombe di S. Gaudioso, a 5th-c. cemetery that was used in later centuries as well. With a tall campanile and a majolica-covered dome, the church's interior is characterized by its great simplicity, with moldings and a general absence of polychrome decorations, but complex in the articulation of its volumes, because, corresponding to the division of the arms of the cross into a nave and two side aisles there are no fewer than twelve small domes. Making the structure still more original is the idea of raising the main altar over the chapel that stands before the entrance to the catacombs, so that it is thus incorporated – as in a giant reliquary – in the zone of the presbytery, toward which climb two staircases sheathed in marble inlay. The main altar dates from the 18th c., and has a 17th-c. ciborium; the handsome pulpit with marble inlay is by D. Lazzari (1678). Among the paintings, we should mention works by G. V. Forli, G. B. Azzolino, A. Beltrano, A. Vaccaro, P. De Rosa, and L. Giordano. Dating from the early-Christian period is the stone pulpit (chapel in the left transept); according to tradition women about to give birth can sit in it to obtain grace and protection.

A gate under the presbytery leads down into the *crypt*, where you will find the entrance to the *catacomb** where St. Gaudiosus is buried. In the various *cuniculi*, or passageways, are frescoes and mosaics dating from the 5th and 6th c.; the cemetery continued to be used in modern times, and a number of unusually macabre depictions date back to the 17th c. Corresponding to a number of wall tombs, upon which a standing skeleton is painted, and adorned only with a "symbol" indicating some aspect of the deceased (spade, gown, toga), there emerges the actual skull; one singular "funerary relic" is a room – once quite common in many Neapolitan churches – known as the "camera delle cantarelle," where cadavers were seated on a hollow chair and left there to desiccate.

Not far off is the church of *S. Severo*, built by D. Lazzari (1680-90), which stands on the structures of an older early-Christian basilica, founded near the catacombs, or Catacomba di S. Severo. The interior is partially carved out of the tufa-stone wall of the hill above; in the apse, note the altarpiece by Teodoro d'Errico. From the church you can enter the catacombs, or *Catacomba di S. Severo*, comprising a tripartite *cella* and a cubicle in which there are a number of arcosolia painted in the 5th c.

4.3 The Vomero district

The itinerary (see plans on pp. 74 and 75) runs along Via Salvator Rosa (with suggested detours toward the streets that run into it on the left side). You will walk through moderns quarters until you reach the charterhouse, or Certosa, and from here you will continue to the Piazza Vanvitelli and on to the Floridiana. Along Via Aniello Falcone, which descends with broad curves, running around the old Villa Belvedere, which appears, high up, on the right, and you thus leave the Vomero; the street then runs into Via Tasso, which in turn intersects the Corso Vittorio Emanuele. The Castello and the Certosa can be reached via the funicular, or Funicolare di Montesanto (III, C3).

Via Salvator Rosa (III, C2-3; B3). Called the "Infrascata" until 1869, this road is named after the painter who was born in the Arenella, toward which it runs. It runs up the hill with broad curves past buildings that date back to the 17th and 18th c., including the monastery of S. Maria Maddalena de' Pazzi on the right; this monastery was built in the 17th c., making use, like many other new monasteries, of the structures of palazzi left in bequest. Along the left side, you will find many of the streets that ran up the hill in great numbers, between Montesanto and Piazza Dante.

The most singular – nowadays, we might say picturesque – and humid, so that it was actually rejected as a site of monasteries, was the *Cavone*, now Via Correra, which runs steeply down toward Piazza Dante. There are other, more monumental streets that still lead toward churches, many of them now shut down, but illustrious, such as the church of *Gesù e Maria* or the many churches along the *Salita Pontecorvo*, once a splendid monastic street, and then there are *S. Potito* and *S. Giuseppe dei Nudi* ....

After Piazza Mazzini, in a broad area to the left stands the church of S. Maria della Pazienza, also known as "La Cesarea" because it was founded in 1601 by a magistrate, Annibale Cesareo, who is portrayed in the handsome *tomb** by M. Naccherino.

Castel S. Elmo* (II, A5; III, D3). Built (1537-46) by P. L. Scrivà at the behest of the viceroy Toledo on the site of the old Angevin Belforte which had been built in 1329; it was built as part of the general reinforcement of defensive works, and it crowned the new ring of enclosure walls. It was erected – to an elongated, six-pointed star-shaped plan – with tufa stone dug up during the construction of the deep moats. It was used more against the city of Naples than to defend it; the viceroy took shelter here during the revolt of Masaniello; it was

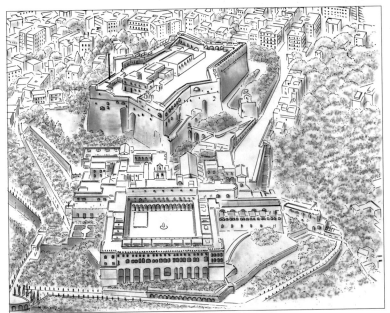

Castel S. Elmo, and the Certosa di S. Martino

used to imprison many of the revolutionaries of 1799 who had raised the first Liberty Tree here. A ramp leads up to the entrance, adorned by a large heraldic crest of Charles V and a handsome epigraph, and it continues into the interior until it reaches the parade ground ("piazza d'armi") where the little church of S. Erasmo also stands (*tombs of the chatelains,* a *model of the castle and of the charterhouse,* or Certosa, dating from the 18th c.). Used for centuries as a prison, it has housed such illustrious prisoners as T. Campanella a many of the patriots of the Italian Risorgimento. From the ramparts, you can enjoy a *panoramic vista*** of the city and the gulf, from Mt. Vesuvius to Ischia and to the Camaldoli.

Certosa and Museo Nazionale di S. Martino** (II, A5; III, D3; see plan on p. 83). The charterhouse, or Certosa, was founded in

complex of the Certosa, at that point in the city's history when the religious orders were being suppressed, not only should be preserved intact in its monumental nucleus, but that the Certosa could best serve, given its prestige and location, to document every aspect of the history of Naples and Neapolitan society. And a museum of Neapolitan history, from 1900 and for many decades, it truly was; anyone who has seen the intelligent arrangement of works and souvenirs, or who studies its organization through its catalogues, realizes that the museum was, in its very criteria of exhibition, already a monument. Seemingly endless restoration projects, made necessary by the earthquake of 1980, still make it impossible (1997) to tour the entire array of collections and rooms.

On the large square, or "piazzale" (from which you can enjoy a panoramic view of the city; note "Spaccanapoli") is the small *church for women* (who were forbidden to enter the area of the Certosa, or charterhouse); on the right is the entrance: in the courtyard is the facade of the church, whose 14th-c. pronaos was "masked" by a Serlian window, by Fanzago. The splendid *interior**, with a single nave and chapels (derived from the side aisles of the Gothic church), is the setting that best shows the exceptional level attained in terms of decorative renewal. Between the end of the 16th c. and the first two decades of the 18th c., the construction yards of S. Martino were the site in which much of what was new in Neapolitan art was developed, in models that were later used elsewhere. The dominant personality in the years 1623-56 was that

One of the exhibits in the Museo Nazionale di S. Martino

1325 by Charles, the Duke of Calabria, who assigned the job to Francesco De Vito and Tino di Camaino; the building was renovated and decorated in the 17th and 18th c., and it constitutes, with the treasure, or Tesoro di S. Gennaro, the most spectacular testimonial of Neapolitan civilization of the 17th c. In its rooms, moreover, there is a remarkable museum created by G. Fiorelli, just after 1866; Fiorelli perceived that the

of Fanzago, architect and sculptor, who was responsible for the overall "direction" of the decoration, glittering with marble inlay, first undertaken earlier by Dosio. Fanzago played a crucial role in the selection of the artists who decorated the various rooms, and as a result, the monastery still preserves some of the most noteworthy products of the Neapolitan arts of the period.

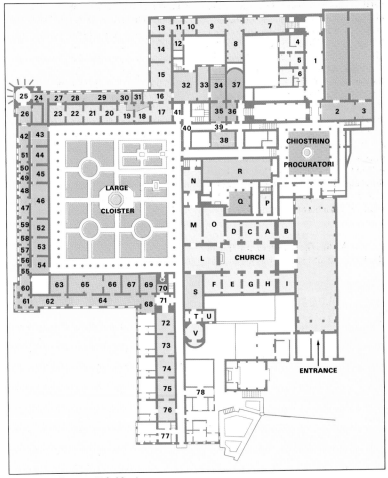

Plan of the Certosa di S. Martino

Fanzago built the transennas of the chapels, the distinctive festoons of fruit and flowers, almost all of the putti on the fornices, and the large "flowers" on the pillars, as well as designing the flooring. In the vaulted ceiling the pattern of the Gothic cross vaults, which can just be made out, is masked by the brilliant composition by Lanfranco which joins them in a depiction of the *Ascension of Jesus*.

In the counterfacade, note the *Pietà* by Stanzione, on either side, *Moses and Elijah*, by Ribera, who did the *Prophets* above the arches of each chapel. And we must stop here. For the chapels and the other monumental spaces here, as is the case with the treasury, or Tesoro di S. Gennaro, it would be impossible to list all the works of the artists who worked here, without slighting some, or worse, directing the reader's attention to one work at the expense of another. Suffice it to mention, aside from

those already mentioned, the names of Battistello, B. Corenzio, Giuseppe Cesari (the Cavalier d'Arpino), Micco Spadaro, P. Finoglia, A. Vaccaro, S. Vouet, Guido Reni, C. Maratta, F. Solimena, L. and D. A. Vaccaro, G. Sanmartino, M. Bottigliero, F. De Mura, P. De Matteis, and N. Tagliacozzi Canale: as well as wood-carvers, marble-workers, and stucco-artists. An exceptional ensemble creation, the complex is remarkably homogeneous, maintains a consistently elevated level, and it is fair to say that all, literally all, of the great Neapolitan artists of the 17th and 18th c. worked, culminating in the *Triumph of Judith*, by Luca Giordano, then in his seventies (1704) in the vault of the chapel, or Cappella del Tesoro (A): a sunny fresco that seems to be a forerunner of the Rococo and even of Fragonard, rivaled only by the solemn *Deposition* by Ribera on the main altar.

From the church, you walk out once again

83

into the courtyard, over which loom the tufa-stone walls of the Castel S. Elmo; on the left is the cloisters, or *Chiostro dei Procuratori*, by Dosio, linked with the large cloisters by a corridor along which structures from the 14th c. have been uncovered. The *large cloisters** – built by Dosio on existing Angevin cloisters, is set at the center of the enormous artificial platform built in the 14th c. (Gothic underground chambers, not always open) to set the convent complex at the same elevation – was reinvented by Fanzago, with half pilasters set on columns, portals at the corners of the deambulatory, with busts of the *Carthusian Saints** (two are by D. A. Vaccaro), the statues on the loggia and the balustrade of the little *cemetery of the monks**. At the center is a "false" well, a source of light for the immense cistern below.

From the Chiostro dei Procuratori, you can follow an entryway (1) that leads into the gardens* – a rare array of pergolas, gardens, and olive groves preserved in the heart of the city – and to the halls of the Museo.

The **crèche sections**, the product of a tradition that is pretty well unrivaled in Italy, is composed of figurines created by the most renowned modelers of 18th-c. Naples, and two exceptional complexes: the crèche, or *Presepe Cuciniello**, named after the donor, with more than 180 shepherds, 10 horses, eight dogs, a rabbit, and no fewer than 309 details; the wooden statues* of the 15th-c. crèche of the church of S. Giovanni a Carbonara. Accompanying this section is the section installed in the halls, or Sale del

The Presepe Cuciniello, an 18th-c. crèche (Museo Nazionale di S. Martino)

Quarto del Priore, featuring the old art gallery, and the recomposed 16th-c. tomb, or *Sepolcro di Carlo Gesualdo*; the section of the sculptures, which range from 1300 to the 20th c.; the section, or *Sezione Orilia* – boiseries, porcelain, "biscuit," ceramics, sculptures and paintings from the Middle Ages to the 18th c. – and the *pharmacy*, with glass work from Burano (15th to 19th c.) on display, from the Bonghi collection.

Piazza Vanvitelli (II, A3; III, D2). This center, from which all the streets of the Vomero radiate out, with the destruction of the environment, the villas, and the structures that once characterized it (for example, the funicular stations) has come to resemble any other middle-class quarter. Some of its churches still preserve the artworks (and some even have the dedication) of other, historic churches that have been destroyed.

The Floridiana* (II, B3; III, D2). This is the largest and the best preserved of all of the villas of the Vomero. It existed already in the 18th c., and was given by Ferdinand I as a gift to the Duchessa di Floridia, whom he wed in a morganatic marriage, and whom, it would appear, left behind her more memories than a queen. The "palazzina," or mansion, named after its new proprietor, was rebuilt in the neoclassical style by A. Niccolini (1817-19) who also designed the lovely park.

Purchased by the Italian state in 1919, it was meant to house the collections of the **Museo Nazionale della Ceramica "Duca di Martina."** * The main nucleus of the collection comprises, in fact, the collections donated (1911) to the Italian state by the heirs of Placido De Sangro, Duke of Martina, a com-petent and generous collector of items of the applied arts, especially ceramics. Among those items, particular note should be paid to the porcelain from various Italian, European, and Asian manufactories, majolica, glass, tooled leather, Gothic ivory, enamels; among the paintings, we should mentioned the sketches by Neapolitan painters of the 18th c.

Corso Vittorio Emanuele (II, C1-2-3-4; B4-5-6; III, E2-D-C3). Built in 1853-60 (with the name of Corso Maria Teresa), this road runs from Piedigrotta to Piazza Mazzini where, joining Via Salvator Rosa, it descends toward the Museo, forming a large uphill ring road ("circonvallazione a monte"). Along its route, there are also older buildings, linked up by the winding thoroughfare. At the intersection with Via del Parco Margherita, on the left, you will find the *Castello Aselmeyer*, built (1902-1904) by Lamont Young, an English architect who was active for years in the area owned by the Grifeo family (now, in part, the park, or *Parco Grifeo*), set between the Vomero and Via Crispi. At a curve, also on the left, is the church of *S. Maria Apparente*, 1581; following it is the enormous monastery, or *Monastero di Suor Orsola Benincasa*, founded in the 16th c., and the headquarters of the university institute with the same name (note the handsome cloister, and graffiti decorations inside the chapel, or Cappella degli Angeli), then on the right, note the *Palazzo Spinelli di Cariati*, dating from the 18th c.; on the left, the church of *S. Lucia al Monte* and, just a bit before Piazza Mazzini, the imposing *Palazzo Tocco di Montemiletto*, dating from the 17th c., but extensively restored in the 19th c.

4.4 Chiaia and Posillipo

The initial part of the itinerary (see plans on pp. 72-75) is divided into three sections. The 1st explores the hill, or Collina di Pizzofalcone; the 2nd runs around the foot of the hill as far as Piazza Vittoria along the waterfront, or Lungomare, or make that plural – the Lungomari, the new and the old waterfronts, or the Nuovo Lungomare and the "Old" Lungomare, which lost its waterfront exposed with the creation of the landfill, on which many of the most important hotels were built; the 3rd runs along Via Chiaia (with a long detour toward the elegant roads built in the 19th c.) and joins up again with the 2nd part at Piazza Vittoria, then continuing on to explore the Riviera di Chiaia, with a detour into Via dell'Arco Mirelli. The itinerary (with a detour to Fuorigrotta) then continues to Posillipo. This itinerary, more than any other, allows the visitor to enjoy the sweeping and panoramic vistas of the splendid natural setting of the city, but it is not without historic and artistic interest as well.

Pizzofalcone

S. Maria degli Angeli a Pizzofalcone* (II, C-D6; III, E3). The name "Pizzofalcone" is of uncertain significance and was used, from the 13th c. on, to describe the Monte Echia, the mount upon which was founded the ancient town of Palepolis, a fundamental element in the Neapolitan landscape because, with the Castel S. Elmo, the charterhouse, or Certosa, and the Castel dell'Ovo it marks the "watershed" dividing the older part of the city and Chiaia and between the views from the west and from the east. Running up to it is Via G. Serra, which leads to the Baroque Theatine church of S. Maria degli Angeli (1600-10), one of the masterpieces of Francesco Grimaldi. The church has a nave and two side aisles, with transept and dome, and with little domes over the side aisles, and it is punctuated on the interior by a dense and lively array of ribbings. It was decorated in the 17th c. with works by F. M. Caselli (canvases of the choir and the transept) and Beinaschi (frescoes in the vaulted ceilings and in the dome).

Via Monte di Dio (III, E3). This street began to be lined with villas and palazzi beginning in the 16th c., becoming by the 18th c. one of the most monumental residential streets in Naples. Despite the damages of war, it is still lined with notable palazzi, including the *Palazzo Carafa di Noja* (no. 66) and the *Palazzo Serra di Cassano* (no. 14-15), one of the loveliest and the best preserved; it now houses the Istituto Italiano di Studi Filosofici, and is renowned for an imposing *staircase** by Sanfelice which does not fit into the the more common typologies found in 18th c. Naples; it is made more monumental and solemn by its placement inside the atrium overlooking the courtyard (the staircase appears reversed with respect to the entrance, because it was designed for another entrance, on Via Egiziaca, closed in mourning by the dukes, or Duchi Serra di Cassano, because it was through this entrance that their son Gennaro was dragged away in the repression of the Revolution of 1799; it was not reopened until 1995) in one hall, note paintings by G. Diano. The street ends in the *Gran Quartiere di Pizzofalcone* (now the barracks, or Caserma "Nino Bixio") built in the 17th c. to house the Spanish troops, who thus abandoned their quarters on Via Toledo.

Nunziatella* (III, E3). This was a Jesuit institution, or Noviziato dei Gesuiti, and has been the headquarters, since 1787, of one of the best known military schools in Italy. The church, radically renovated by Sanfelice, has one of the most interesting and homogeneous *interiors** with frescoes and paintings by De Mura, canvases by L. Mazzanti, De Matteis, and G. Mastroleo, and a splendid main altar by Sanmartino, who

also did the two *tombs of the brothers Giovene*.

Castrum Lucullanum (III, E-F4). On the tufa-stone crag atop the hill (views of the gulf), near the Renaissance *Villa Carafa di Santaseverina*, site of the military section of the state archives, or Archivio di Stato, are the scanty ruins of the *Castrum Lucullanum*, a late imperial structure incorporating a renowned and sumptuous villa that belonged to Lucullus. In A.D. 476, Romulus Augustulus, the last emperor of the West, was imprisoned here; the fortress and the surrounding village were the site, until A.D. 902 of monastic settlements.

The Lungomare, S. Lucia, and the Chiatamone

S. Lucia and the Lungomare* (Via N. Sauro and Via Partenope; II, E6; III, E-F4). S. Lucia was one of the most famous places in Naples, with hotels that were renowned in the 18th c. and the early 19th c., until the great landfill moved the waterfront away. The first stretch of the modern waterfront, or Lungomare, corresponding to Via N. Sauro and Via Partenope, is therefore quite distant from the old one (consisting of Via S. Lucia and Via Chiatamone). Along it, you may note the monument to Humbert I and the fountain, or *Fontana dell'Immacolatella* by M. Naccherino and P. Bernini (1601), formerly in the Palazzo Reale, and many of the most luxurious hotels and various yacht and sailing clubs. At the beginning of the "interior" route, on the left, you will see the church, once isolated on the water, of *S. Lucia a Mare*, which gives its name to the entire quarter, or "rione"; existing as far back as the 9th c., this church has been destroyed and rebuilt repeatedly, for the last time after 1943. Next, on the right, is the church of S. Maria della Catena, in which is buried the admiral F. Caracciolo, hero of the revolution, or Rivoluzione del 1799.

Via Chiatamone (III, F3-4). This street begins immediately after a curve over which looms the high rocky face of the Monte Echia which, although it is studded with barbicans, still gives one some idea of the appearance of the hill on which the oldest nucleus of the city was built, as it must have appeared to its founders. The term Chiatamone derives from the Greek word *platamon*, which means a "cliff studded with caves"; it was these caves, at the base of the hill and overlooking the sea, that had been inhabited from prehistoric times until the classical period, and they housed cenobites in the Middle Ages, and were the site of scandalous orgies in the 16th c., to the point that the viceroys felt compelled to seal them up. Forming part of the circuit of bastions of the new walls, the Chiatamone was a favorite spot for promenades, resulting in a singular mixture of commoners, soldiers, and travelers, and preserving the "scandalous" nature that so impressed travelers of all periods. Nearly at the beginning of the street are the ramps, or *Rampe di Pizzofalcone*, built at the behest of the Spanish viceroys to link the Castel dell'Ovo with the Gran Quartiere on the hill; next, at nos. 26 and 27 is the palazzo that once housed the hotel, or *Albergo delle Crocelle*, which had many illustrious guests in the 18th and 19th centuries. Another famous place of the 18th-/19th-c. city was the *Reale Casino del Chiatamone* (formerly the Casino del Principe di Francavilla, a

with an entrance from Via Morelli, just after the tunnel of the *Galleria della Vittoria*. Most of these cavities – which can be found everywhere and are generally subterranean – have lost over time, or never had, the characteristics of natural grottoes, because they originated as quarries (and were also used as shelters during the last war).

Castel dell'Ovo* (III, F4). This castle stands on the islet of "Megaris," upon which stood part of the villa of Lucullus; in the 17th c., the island took the name of the Salvatore (Savior), due to the presence of a Basilian cenobium; it appears to have been already fortified in pre-Norman times. This is the oldest castle in Naples, the result of continual expansions, done at the behest of the Normans and Frederick II; under Frederick and under the later Angevin rules, this was the headquarters of the royal treasury, and served also as the royal resi-

Castel dell'Ovo, a fortified complex built on the little island of Megaris

prince who held parties there that became famous), built on the side toward the sea; the building still exists (no. 55); it was at first transformed into a hotel and heavily remodeled, though it still preserves a number of handsome neoclassical rooms on the ground floor. Next comes the church of the *Concezione al Chiatamone*, known as "Le Crocelle," with a facade dating from the 18th c., and, in the interior, paintings by Paolo De Matteis, who is buried here. In many of the courtyards of the adjoining palazzi it is possible to observe the yellow tufa-stone wall of the Monte Echia; in order to have some idea of the characteristics of the grottoes that punctuate its base, we would suggest visiting a particularly large one that is used as a parking structure,

dence. The name of Castel dell'Ovo (literally, "castle of the egg") began to enter into common use during the 14th c., perhaps due to the elongated elliptical plan, but at the same time there began to develop one of the many legends linked to the fame of Vergil as a wizard, according to which the destiny of the castle itself was linked to the fate of an egg that was guarded by it. The medieval characteristics of the fortified citadel complex – which original documents show as bristling with towers and opening out to the sea with a large arch that joined the two parts of the islet – were eliminated in the 16th c. The castle, badly damaged during the siege of 1503, was renovated in accordance with the then-modern techniques of military defense, and underwent further transformations in the 17th c. (done by F. di Grünemberg) and in the 18th c., right up to the recent radical restructuring undertaken following the termination of its use as a military installation (1975). It is flanked and crossed throughout its length by a road that climbs steadily uphill; aside from the spectacular and impressive views of the curtain walls, the sea, and the city, we should also point out a number of structures that clearly reveal the dense stratification of the monumental complex: the so-called hall of columns, or *Sala delle Colonne*, divided into four aisles by arches set on shafts of columns that may well have come from the villa of Lucullus; the Basilian settlements; the *church of the Salvatore*; the towers, or *Torre Maestra* and the *Torre di Normandia*; the loggias from the Gothic and from the Aragonese period.

To the east of the castle, once isolated in the sea, on a landfill, the "picturesque" *Borgo Marinaro* has been built, originally intended as housing for the families of fishermen and sailors of S. Lucia.

From Via Chiaia to Piazza Vittoria

Via Chiaia (II, C6; III, E3). This street follows the line of the large valley that separated the hill on which stood *Partenope* from the hill, of Collina delle Mortelle (upon which, near Via Nicotera, stood the necropolis). Lined with shop windows, it correspond to the central stretch of an ideal "shopping promenade" that begins with Via Toledo and continues along Via Calabritto, Via Filangieri, and Via dei Mille, and which, in the topographic successions, follows a chronological sequence that had its beginnings in the 16th c. and comes up to the present day, making these streets the most elegant commercial thoroughfare. Running over it, just after the intersection with the bustling *Gradoni di Chiaia* (a street, once made up of stairways, leading up to the church of *S. Caterina da Siena* by Gioffredo), is the bridge, or *Ponte di Chiaia*, built in 1636 to link the two hills. On the right, note the church of *S. Orsola a Chiaia* and the theater, or *Teatro Sannazzaro* (1875); at the point where the road curves, note the *Palazzo Cellamare*, built up against the old viceroyal walls in the 16th c., and restored and enlarged in 1722 for the Giudice family, and renowned in the 18th c. because – after being rented to the Principe di Francavilla and later to the sovereign himself – it was the site, with the prince, of memorable entertainment, and later was destined to house part of the royal collections and to

house painters who were in the favor of the court, such as Kauffmann and Hackert. The portal by Fuga is all that a tourist can admire; beyond it is a silent courtyard, a large garden, and frescoed vaults from the 18th c. After this, in a small opening in the road, is the church of *S. Caterina a Chiaia*, dating from the early years of the 17th c. and restored repeatedly over the years; inside, the queen of Sardinia, Maria Clotilde, is buried; she was the sister of no fewer than three kings of France (Louis XVI, Louis XVIII, and Charles X) and the wife of Charles Emmanuel IV; she died in Naples in 1802.

On the right, with Via Filangieri, you will begin a detour along the elegant and aristocratic streets built in the late 19th c., with a number of interesting buildings by Giulio Ulisse Arata, an architect who was quite active in the quarter, including the noteworthy store/home at no. 61 and the *Palazzo Mannajuolo* (at no. 36, with a beautiful staircase, 1912), closing off at the intersection with the steps, or Gradini F. D'Andrea, the view along the intersecting Via dei Mille, in which, after a series of other palazzi by Arata, on the right you can see two older buildings: at no. 48 note the 16th-c. *Palazzo d'Avalos del Vasto*, rebuilt by Gioffredo with neoclassical interiors and a lovely garden, and at no. 66 note the *Palazzo Carafa di Roccella*, dating from the 18th c., partially demolished to make way for the new street, and badly damaged by an attempt at demolition in the 1950s. Next comes the church of *S. Teresa a Chiaia*, rebuilt by Fanzago; in the interior, built on a central plan, note the handsome canvases by L. Giordano. You will then reach the *Piazza Amedeo*, heart of one of the most elegant quarters built in the city between the end of the 19th c. and the early years of the 20th c. On the right is the beginning of *Via del Parco Margherita*, built from 1886 on to link the center of the Rione Amedeo with the Corso Vittorio Emanuele. You will find here a vast array of the Art Nouveau architecture (Liberty) of Naples; midway up the hill is *S. Maria dell'Anima*, church of the German Catholics, built after the demolition (1890) of an older church, which stood in Via Sedile di Porto, and from which come the altars dating from the 18th c. and canvases by the Austrian painter M. Knoller (1758).

Piazza dei Martiri (II, D5; III, E3). At the center is the column, or *Colonna dei Martiri*, built to a design by Alvino (1866-68) in commemoration of the anti-Bourbon revolts (1799, 1820, 1848, 1860) symbolized, in their various outcomes, by the attitudes of each of the four lions at the base.

S. Maria della Vittoria (II, D5; III, E3). This church is dedicated to the Virgin Mary, protectress of the victors of the Battle of Lepanto (7 October 1571); founded (1628) by none other than the daughter of Don

John of Austria, who commended the Christian fleet, and completed (1646) by her niece. On the interior – which has a central plan, a dome, and four handsome ancient columns – note the epigraphs and paintings concerning the foundation of the church and the battle. Near the sea, isolated, stands a column made of cipollino marble, found near the campanile of the cathedral and placed here in 1914 in commemoration of the Caduti del Mare, or those who died at sea, on an existing base (1867), part of a monument to the Caduti di Lissa.

Villa Comunale (II, D3-4-5; III, E2-3). Extending for over 1 km, between Via Caracciolo and the Riviera di Chiaia. Built at the order of the king, as a public garden, between the years of 1778-80 by C. Vanvitelli and the gardener F. Abate, it was enlarged repeatedly. In it is the *Casina Pompeiana*, the large *Cassa Armonica* (bandstand) in cast-iron and glass (designed by Alvino, 1877) and the zoo, or Stazione Zoologica. It is decorated with neoclassical sculptures and fountains, including the fountain known as the *Fontana delle Papa-relle*, formed of a large porphyry tazza found in Paestum, which stood for centuries in the atrium of the cathedral of Salerno, the *Fontana di S. Lucia* by M. Naccherino and T. Montani (1607, until 1898 in Via S. Lucia); the *Fontana d'Europa* by A. Viva (1798, until 1807 in Via della Marinella) as well as busts and monuments by interesting sculptors of the 19th c. and the early 20th c., especially from the south; over all looms the *monument to Armando Diaz* (1936).

The villa is separated from the sea by *Via Caracciolo**, a splendid road which offers sweeping vistas of the gulf and the city.

Stazione Zoologica and Acquario* (II, D4; III, E2). This zoo and aquarium was founded – to encourage the study of the underwater world – by the German Anton Dohrn in 1872-74 (enlarged in 1888, 1904, and again in 1957), and is one of the oldest and most prestigious institutes of its kind in the world. The building was constructed by A. von Hildebrandt. It houses the oldest aquarium in Europe, built to house only species present in the Gulf of Naples. The old reading room of the library, or Biblioteca, is decorated with *frescoes** by Hans von

Marées (1873; amidst decorations by Hilde-brandt, who also did the busts of Darwin and Von Baer), depicting rural and marine settings, an important documentation of the sway held over the minds of men from northern Europe by the landscape and people of southern Italy.

Riviera di Chiaia* (II, D3-4-5; III, E2-3). Here, again, this is an "old" waterfront, or "vecchio" Lungomare, famous for its concave structure, with more sweeping and spectacular vistas than those offered by the modern Lungomare, which extends into the sea with a convex structure. Along it, you will still find traces of the street grid of the Borgo di Chiaia and its older buildings; in the first stretch of the Lungomare, there are many palazzi built between the 17th and 19th c.

Villa Pignatelli* (II, D4; III, E2). This villa was built in the neoclassical style by P. Valente (1826) and G. Bechi for the Acton family; purchased in 1841 by the Roth-schilds, it was remodeled on the interior,

View of the neoclassical Villa Pignatelli

with the contributions of G. Genovese and an anonymous Parisian architect who gave it the Second Empire appearance that so distinguishes it. It then passed into the hands (1867) of the Pignatelli di Monteleone family, and was donated by the Principessa Rosina to the Italian State (1952). The garden (to plans attributed to Bechi) is noteworthy also because it is the only one left on the Riviera. Overlooking it is a loggia with Doric columns; on the interior, note the *Toilette delle Dame*, which still has the decorations done by Bechi; Genovese did the red room, or *Sala Rossa* and the smoking room, or Fumoir (now the library, or *Biblioteca*) while the anonymous French architect did the ballroom, or *Sala da Ballo* (now used for conferences and lectures), the little green room, or *Salottino Verde* and the sky-blue room, or *Sala Azzurra*. Located here is the museum, or *Museo "Principe Diego Aragóna Pignatelli Cortes,"* comprising the furnishings, artworks, and the library and collection of records of the villa. In a pavilion in the garden is the carriage museum, or Museo delle Carrozze, founded in 1975, with a collection of carriages and accessories dating from the end of the 19th c. and the early 20th c., established with private donations. The villa also presents exhibitions and concerts.

Ascensione a Chiaia (II, C4; III, E2). This church was founded as early as the 14th c., and was entirely rebuilt at the behest of the Conte di Mola, Michele Vaaz, who lived in the adjoining palazzo beginning in 1626. The church, with a central plan, was designed by Fanzago, and is preceded by a portico, and preserves on the interior, rich with marble inlay, *canvases** by Luca Giordano.

S. Maria in Portico (II, C3; III, E2). this church stands at the center of a working-class neighborhood, and is made picturesque in part by the polychrome facade and the dome. Founded in 1632 by the Duchessa di Gravina, Felice Maria Orsini, on her new estates, and intended for the Padri Lucchesi, it was nicknamed "in Portico" in commemoration of that order's Roman headquarters in the Portico d'Ottavia. The facade is by A. Guglielmelli; on the interior, canvases dating from the 18th c., altar, and stuccoes by D. A. Vaccaro.

Piazza della Repubblica (II, D2; III, E1). In the final extension of the Riviera di Chiaia which, in the Piazza della Repubblica, joins up with Via Caracciolo, you may note, at no. 72, the *Palazzo Guevara di Bovino*, built in the 19th c. in imitation of the original nucleus of Palazzo Pitti and, at no. 66, the *Palazzo Barile di Caivano*, with surviving relics of the architecture by Fanzago and frescoed rooms on the main floor ("piano nobile"). At the center is the monument, or *Monumento alle Quattro Giornate* (26-30 September 1943) with four large panels carved by M. Mazzacurati.

Toward Posillipo

Via Mergellina and Via Piedigrotta (II, E-F1; III, E-F1). These two streets fork on a line with the Fascist building that replaced the Torretta (which gave its name to this part of the city), which had been built in 1564 as protection of the coastal residences, in the wake of a raid by Turkish pirates. Via Mergellina preserves, along its entire right side, the old front of buildings that overlooked the sea prior to the 19th-c. landfill. The terms Piedigrotta and Fuorigrotta derive from the fact that the two places are located, respectively, east and west of the grotto, or "Grotta," the tunnel dug in the 1st c. B.C. under the hill, or Collina di Posillipo in order to ease travel from Naples to Pozzuoli. This same function is now served by the *Galleria Quattro Giornate* (1940, which uses the structure of the "Grotta Nuova" dug in 1882-85) and by the *Galleria Laziale* (1925, beginning from Piazza Sannazaro) which leads into the modern quarter of Fuorigrotta. On the right is the train station, or *Stazione di Mergellina* of the state railways, or Ferrovie dello Stato.

S. Maria di Piedigrotta (II, E1; III, F1). Founded, according to tradition, in 1353, in place of an older church that existed at least as far back as 1207. Its entrance faced the grotto, or Grotta; it was rebuilt in 1452 (note the handsome columned *cloisters* of the monastery, now the Ospedale della Marina) and then again at the turn of the 16th c., until it was restructured in the 17th c., when its orientation was changed. This is one of the most important shrines to the Virgin Mary, the center of a well-known celebration (7 September) – it has almost become proverbial – that is inevitably quite popular, and which in centuries past usually had the solemn participation of the royal family in the procession. At the behest of the Bourbons, then, it was restored and decorated in a 19th-c. style. Alvino designed a new facade (1853) and Gaetano Gigante decorated the interior with paintings in the vaulted ceiling (1818-22). On the interior, which reveals in its anomalous plans the various events of the construction process, you may note a *Deposition of Christ**, a panel (ca. 1480) by an anonymous Neapolitan painter who shows French and Flemish influence, and who is known as the Maestro della Pietà di Piedigrotta (2nd chapel on the right); *Virgin Mary with Christ Child*, a wooden statue from the workshop of Tino di Camaino; various panels from the 16th c., the choir, also dating back to the 16th c., and the imposing monument, or *Monumento Filangieri* by N. Renda.

Parco Virgiliano* (II, E1; III, F1). Beyond the viaduct, on the left, is the entrance to one of the places particularly popular with those on the Grand Tour. In the setting of a small park, created in 1930, are the so-called tomb of Vergil, or Tomba di Virgilio (a Roman columbarium dating back to the reign of Augustus, traditionally said to have been the tomb of the poet, who wished to be buried in his villa in Posillipo), the entrance to the "Grotta Vecchia," the *Crypta Neapolitana*, carved out in the first c. B.C. (more than 700 meters in length; 4-6 meters in width; blocked by collapses in the 1920s, it is closed to the public because of restoration that should have been done after WWII), in which there are medieval frescoes and *epigraphs*, as well as a large epigraph ordered by the viceroy Pietro d'Aragona (1668) to proclaim the efficacy of the Phlegrean mineral waters (moved because of work done on the road). Midway along the route is the *tomb of Giacomo Leopardi*, who died in Naples in 1837, buried at first in the demolished church of S. Vitale a Fuorigrotta, and moved here in 1939.

this church was built at the behest of Jacopo Sannazaro, not far from his home (protected by a tower, still standing, behind the church) on land given to him by Frederick of Aragón, in 1497. The poet, who was born in Naples of a noble family of Lombard origins in 1455, and died in Naples in 1530, composed his *De partu Virginis* in Mergellina, donated his property to the Servites, and expressed the wish to be buried there, as he was. In a room behind the altar, in fact, is the *Tomba di Iacopo Sannazaro**, the work of G. A. Montorsoli, B. Ammannati, and F. Ferrucci known as the Tadda (1537), with a complex iconography, almost certainly the brainchild of Sannazaro himself; on either side of the tomb, upon which the poet himself is portrayed, are the figures of Apollo and Minerva (trans-

View of Naples from Chiaia, looking toward Mergellina, by Gaspare Vanvitelli (Florence, Galleria Palatina)

Mergellina (II, F1; III, F1). Once an outlying town clustering around its port (once a fishing port and now a tourist marina) and S. Maria del Parto. Of the original landscape, celebrated over the centuries for its loveliness, little now survives, after the landfills that have extended the coastline into the sea. At the far boundaries of the Piazza Sannazaro, toward Piedigrotta, you may note the old ramps, or *Rampe di S. Antonio a Posillipo*, which climb up to the 17th-c. church of S. Antonio a Posillipo (from a terrace, fine panoramic view of the city). Nearby is the crowded *Porto Sannazaro*, along whose waterfront the Neapolitans love to stroll in the evening in the summer, just as their forebears did for centuries along the Molo Grande.

S. Maria del Parto (II, F1). Set high on a terrace, which you can reach along a stairway,

formed by the monks, with a legend on the base, into David and Judith); the bas-relief on the front is reminiscent of the setting of Arcadia (described by the poet in his work, called *Arcadia*, in the Italian vernacular) depicting Neptune, Pan, Marsyas, and the Nymphs; the epigraph with a commemoration of the nearby tomb of Vergil was dictated by Cardinal Bembo. At the foot of the tomb note the 16th-c. funerary slabs of the young Fabrizio Manlio and Bishop Diomede Carafa, a figure to which is linked the depiction of *St. Michael Overthrowing Lucifer*, by Leonardo da Pistoia, in the 1st chapel on the right; a painting that is widely known, because the "Devil of Mergellina" has a woman's face, widely and long said to have been the face of a woman who tempted, unsuccessfully, the pious Carafa, depicted as the Archangel. Among the other works, we should mention the statues (linked to the tomb) of Sts. Jacob and Nazarius (whose names are clearly reminiscent of the poet) set on either side of the main altar, and the figures of a crèche, by Giovanni da Nola.

Via di Posillipo* (off map; see pp. 94-95). Built at the behest of Murat, this road was constructed between 1812 and 1823. At its beginning, near the sea, is the 17th-c. fountain, or *Fontana del Sebeto*; next, high up, on the right, is the neoclassical *Villa Doria d'Angri*, with a little pagoda in the style of the "chinoiserie"; then, on the left, Palazzo Donn'Anna. Climbing higher and higher over the sea, amidst villas and gardens (on the right, note the *Parco della Rimembranza*, with its votive altar, or Ara Votiva), the road runs up to the crossroads, or *Quadrivio del Capo*, where ancient roads begin, to Marechiaro and to Gaiola, and from which one can reach the Parco di Posillipo. From the road, Naples appears silhouetted against the distinctive profile of Mt. Vesuvius; this recurring view from Posillipo (Via Petrarca; Piazzale di S. Antonio…) has become, often with a Mediterranean pine in the foreground, the symbolic image, the *topos*, of Naples. The success of this view dates back to the 18th c., when the expansion of Naples toward Chiaia, and its inclusion in the Grand Tour, along with the general interest in Mt. Vesuvius (which resumed its volcanic activity, after centuries of dormancy, in 1631, and continued it until 1944) served to codify it, while paintings and engravings helped to propagate it.

Palazzo Donn'Anna (off map; see pp. 94-95). This is one of the best known palazzi of the city, because of its remarkable setting and unusual structures; it appears in many view paintings. Built by Fanzago (1642) for Donn'Anna Carafa, the powerful wife of the Viceroy Medina, it remained unfinished and acquired the charm of an ancient ruin, almost fitting in with the natural grottoes and the remains of the Roman villas along the coast of Posillipo. There is no basis for the rumor, slow to die, that this was used as a trysting house by the queen, Joan II. Not far away, along the beach, badly deteriorated by still recognizable, is the *villa di Sir William Hamilton* (the English ambassador mentioned above), with a distinctive semicircular terrace overlooking the sea.

Ara Votiva per i Caduti per la Patria (off map; see p. 94-95). This votive altar for those who died for the fatherland, literally, is a remarkable and astonishing building, begun in a neo-Egyptian style in 1883 to plans by A. Guerra, and built by Matteo Schilizzi; it was intended as a mausoleum for his brother, Marco. Work on the immense monument, interrupted in 1889, was resumed in 1923 when the city purchased it as a final resting place for the Italian war dead.

Parco di Posillipo* (off map; see pp. 94-95). Situated on the crag, or Rupe di Coroglio, this park offers extraordinary panoramic views of the gulfs of Naples, Pozzuoli, and Baia. Nearby is Nisida, an island but also the crater of an ancient volcano, like all the others (Posillipo itself is nothing more than the edge of an enormous underwater crater) which "built" the Phlegrean Fields, or Campi Flegrei. Of course, there are splendid views of Ischia at sunset.

Marechiaro* (off map; see pp. 94-95). A road runs down here, passing by *S. Maria del Faro*, a church that is documented as early as the 13th c.; it was probably built on the site of an ancient lighthouse, and was then restored in the 18th c. by Sanfelice by commission from the owners, the family Mazza, whose heraldic crest recurs throughout the church, appearing even on a late-Roman strigil sarcophagus. Marechiaro was originally a fishing village in the little square of which, amidst many restaurants, you can still see some Roman remains and traces of buildings dating back to the 18th c. You may then climb down a little stairway to reach the sea, where you may enjoy a renowned panoramic view of Mt. Vesuvius, beneath the *finestrella*, or window, that a plaque indicates is the one mentioned in the song "O Sole Mio," by S. Di Giacomo and F. P. Tosti.

Gaiola* (off map; see pp. 94-95). This is the name of an island and a fishing village where you may see the ruins of the *Villa of Vedius Pollio*, known as *Pausilipon* – in Greek, "painsoothing" – whence the place name of Posillipo. The ruins, extending over a surface of 9 hectares, belonged to a theater and an odeon as well; connected to it is the grotto, or *Grotta di Seiano*, a manmade Roman tunnel. Perhaps only a boat tour, from Mergellina to the Gaiola and beyond, will allow one to sense and enjoy fully – despite the ravages of the last few decades – the beauty and charm of these places.

5 The Campi Flegrei, Procida, and Ischia

The Phlegrean Fields, or Campi Flegrei (from the ancient Greek word *phlegraios*, or burning) is the name of the volcanic region (which also includes Naples) to the west of Mt. Vesuvius, a fundamental part of any trip to Italy, because of its mountainous features, lakes, the remarkable variety of the coastlines, the fertility of the soil, the delightful mildness of the climate, the views, the accumulation of ancient myths, the heritage and the literary descriptions, from Vergil to the travelers of the Grand Tour, and beyond.

The splendor of the setting – summed up in a celebrated verse by Horace: "Nullus in orbis sinus Bais praelucit amoenis," meaning, there is no gulf on earth as lovely as the pleasant Baiae – and the thermal features of this area encouraged, in Roman times, the development of many towns and villages here, the imposing ruins of which still stand. The coasts of the Gulf of Naples and the Gulf of Pozzuoli had, however, already experienced a complex history of small settlements, known as the *epineia*, which in the archaic age were directly ruled by Cumae, the oldest Greek colony on the mainland.

We would recommend that you begin your tour of Pozzuoli by exploring its topography and studying the various historic phases of expansion, because its continual settlement, along with the volcanic and "slow" seismic activity ("bradisismo"), has greatly affected the

Capo Miseno, the hill mentioned by Vergil in the Aeneid

ancient configuration of the site. The Roman structures survive, isolated in small archaeological areas, and incorporated into modern structures. The imperial city was organized on terraces sloping down toward the sea; transverse communications were assured by roads running perpendicular to the coastline (*clivi*), spanning the differences in elevation. A remarkable piece of evidence that allows us to reconstruct the ancient topography are the little glass flasks, produced between the 3rd and 4th c. A.D., depicting views of the *Sinus Puteolanus*, or bay of Pozzuoli, with a schematic plan of the main buildings.

At Baiae, or Baia, too, the progressive extension of the coastline has made it impossible to glimpse the original lay of the landscape here. The roads – i.e., the waters where ships would anchor – had a more enclosed form, and most of the structures extended out over the sea, where they now lie underwater. "To own a villa at Baiae, during the last century of the Roman Republic, constituted at once an exhibition of power and wealth, a mark of prestige and social standing, a social obligation that the duties associated with rank made it hard to avoid. There is not a single name, among the great figures of ancient Rome during the period of the Social Wars (or civil wars), that does not appear in the list of the guests and residents of Baiae, from Marius, Sulla, Lucullus, Caesar, Pompey, and Cicero to Mark Antony. It is impossible to list the vast array of myths, literary references, and historical events that clustered in this area: Capo Miseno, with its cairn-shape, took its

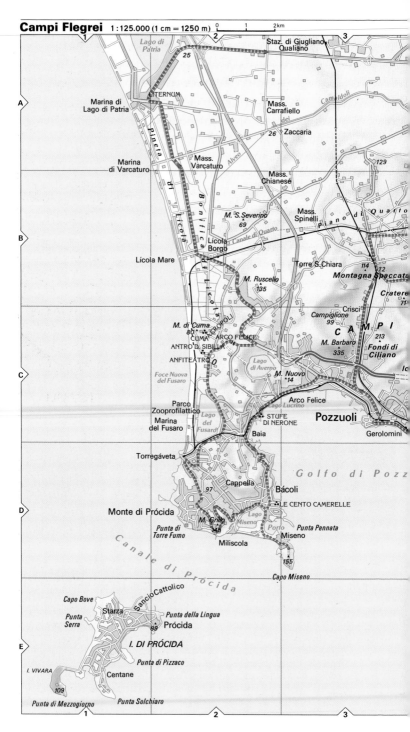

Campi Flegrei 1:125.000 (1 cm = 1250 m)

name from the herald of Aeneas, who was supposedly buried there; at Cumae, or Cuma is
the so-called cave of the Sibyl, or Antro della Sibilla.

Ischia and Procida, too, were formed by Phlegrean volcanic activity; there are numerous craters (many of them underwater; the chief crater is formed by the Monte Epomeo,
a tectonic volcano standing 788 m high). At Ischia, a series of eruptions, beginning in

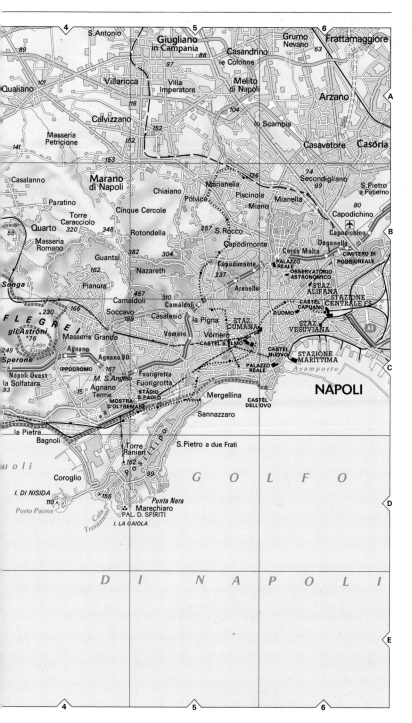

the third millennium B.C. and continuing until 1302, gave rise to new topographic reliefs, profoundly affecting the patterns of development and settlement, forcing the inhabitants to flee; in some cases earthquakes destroyed the towns and villages entirely. The volcanic activity created numerous springs and fumaroles, which were used from antiquity on for thermal spas and baths; moreover the soil is exceedingly fertile, and yields particularly lush vegetation (citrus groves, pine forests, chestnut groves, but especially vineyards), giving rise to the nickname of "Isola Verde," or Green Island. It was inhabited as early as prehistoric times, and was colonized by Greeks of Euboean origin (8th c. B.C.) who settled to the north, on the promontory of Monte Vico. The reasons for Greek colonization in such an early period can be found in the quest for metals; the *emporion* here was, in fact, an outpost and bridgehead for trade with Etruria. In 474 B.C., it was occupied by the tyrant Hiero I of Syracuse, now Siracusa; successively it entered the sphere of influence of Neapolis, where it remained until the reign of Sulla. Under Augustus, it returned definitively as part of the territory of Naples, as compensation for the seizure of Capri. Following the barbarian and Saracen invasions, which devastated it repeatedly, it shared the fortunes of Naples. In 1495 the castle was given in deed by the king to Innico d'Avalos, whose heirs governed Ischia and Procida until 1729. Over the course of the 16th c., Ischia was the target of new pirate raids; to ward them off, numerous towers were built, some of which are still visible. In 1799, the English, allies of the House of Bourbon, established a garrison here; the French seized it in 1806. The economy is based on agriculture and fishing, as well as some trade and, especially, tourism, encouraged by the loveliness of the place, the pleasant climate, and the abundance of natural hot springs. The many hotels are almost all equipped to provide thermal cures (baths, muds, and inhalations).

Procida is located between Capo Miseno and Ischia and is formed by the edge of four craters just breaking the surface (they are recognizable: they correspond to four bays); it has a highly irregular morphology, although it is flat and might seem fairly uniform; the high and jagged coast alternates with broad sandy beaches and bays. The volcanic soil makes the vegetation quite lush; farming, along with sailing and fishing and, for many years now, tourism, are the main economic activities. The island has been inhabited since prehistoric times (the nearby islet, or Isolotto di Vivara, a protected area, has also yielded Mycenaean ceramics), and from the 11th c. on it housed various Benedictine settlements, around which there developed over the course of the 18th c., a number of villages. From the 12th c. until the 18th c., it was governed by three families: the Da Procida, then the Cossa and, lastly, the d'Avalos. In the 18th c., the House of Bourbon made this a hunting preserve, using as their "royal residence" the building that was once Palazzo d'Avalos. The place is charming, the island preserves an image of exclusivity, but not of high society; it is popular with those who like quiet holidays.

5.1 From Naples to Pozzuoli

The itinerary (18 km plus detours) has in Camaldoli an ideal point of departure, outside of the itinerary, but a fundamental element because, from there, you can enjoy the most complete panoramic vista of the Phlegrean Fields, or Campi Flegrei, and the neighboring islands.

You will reach Pozzuoli along the coastal route from Bagnoli or else along Via Domiziana, from which a detour will allow you to visit Agnano and the Astroni; also along Via Domiziana is the entrance to the Solfatara. In Pozzuoli, you should head toward the amphitheater, or Anfiteatro; on the left, in Viale Capomazza, there are remains of structures, perhaps the *collegia* of the guilds of flautists and musicians, associations that were intimately linked with the life of the theater which, probably, stood not far away. Near the crossroads of Via Rosini and Via del Carmine was the zone of the new *forum* built under Augustus, who structures have since been canceled by modern buildings (you can still see faint reflections of the decorations). Then you will visit the Villa Avellino and, returning to Via Rosini, you will make a slight detour, turning to the right, into Via Vecchia S. Gennaro, where, on the left, in the garden, or Giardino Sardo, you will see the Piscina Cardito. After touring the amphitheater, or Anfiteatro, you may continue along Via Terracciano where, set in a private park, are the baths, or Terme di Nettuno. You will then reach the crossroads, or Quadrivio dell'Annunziata; just shortly before, on the left, you can see remains of *tabernae*, and, uphill, close to another private park, the ruins of a residential building, built on terracing. There are also *tabernae* at the beginning of Via Luciano. A short detour leads to the remains of the stadium. You may then return to the crossroads ("quadrivio") and continue along Via Celle and, after passing the railroad bridge, you can head for Quarto along Via Campana.

The Camaldoli*
The climb up to the hermitage, which

stands at the highest point (elev. 458 m) of the Phlegrean Fields, or Campi Flegrei, is an obligatory experience, given the sweeping *panoramic views** to be enjoyed from the plaza before the entrance and from the two belvederes, the Belvedere dei Camaldoli (the most extensive and best known, inside the hermitage, which ranges from Mt. Vesuvius to the Gulf of Gaeta and inland toward the Matese) and the Belvedere Pagliarella. In the church (1585), paintings by A. Gramatica with Camaldolese Saints.

Agnano

Celebrated even in antiquity for its hot springs and baths, caused by volcanic activity, this town was mentioned by travelers on the Grand Tour as well for the grotto of the dog, or Grotta del Cane (closed to the public) where the carbonic acid that was released would asphyxiate a dog thrust into the cave to demonstrate the phenomenon (and then recovered, to repeat the "show" for the next set of visitors). Of the handsome Liberty, or Art Nouveau baths built to plans by Arata, and then demolished in the 1950s for the construction of new ones, there remain only traces. Further north is the race track, or *Ippodromo*; to the west is the zone of the Pisciarelli, celebrated in Roman times for an aluminum-bearing spring.

Astroni*

This lovely crater is completely covered with vegetation, and is one of the few protected areas of the Phlegrean Fields, or Campi Flegrei; it owes its remarkably pristine state to the fact that, for centuries, it was a royal game preserve, from the times of King Alfonso of Aragón to the reign of Humbert I; today it is operated by the WWF.

Solfatara*

This is certainly one of the best known sites in the Phlegrean Fields, or Campi Flegrei. Called the Forum Vulcani in Roman times, it has a perimeter of 2.3 km, and it presents perfectly the distinctive phenomena of a dormant volcano.

Pozzuoli

Of this city (elev. 28 m, pop. 75,142) scanty archaeological sources indicate human set-

tlement in the Rione Terra as early as the 7th c. B.C.; literary sources mention the foundation of Dicearchia (ca. 530 B.C.), "the city of good government," by a group of Samian exiles. In 194 B.C. a Roman colony was founded here, a bridgehead for trade with the eastern Mediterranean and, above all, the landing facility for wheat for the city of Rome. This important role in the Roman policy of distribution of bread explains the strategic value of the city and the size and elaborate design of the port where the Alexandrian fleet – the *classis alexandrina* – landed (bringing wheat from Egypt) and in which there were imposing infrastructures used in the storage of foodstuffs.

Volcanic activity at the Solfatara, Pozzuoli

From the Rione Terra, a point extending into the gulf, the town expanded along the coast. The western sector and the littoral strip nearly all the way to Lake Lucrino accommodated the structures of the harbor; the broad upper terrace, the point of arrival of the roads from Naples and Capua, became a residential area and the site of public buildings in later expansions. Under the rule of Augustus, the town burgeoned, and was subdivided, like Rome herself, into *regiones*. Under the rule of Nero, the new amphitheater was built, along with the wharf; plans were also made for a large navigable canal, which was meant to link the port of Ostia with Pozzuoli; the emperor ordered it built, but it never was completed. The city's decision to back Vespasian in the struggle for the succession to the imperial throne, won it the favor of the Flavians. As a result, the city's territory was enlarged, and Via Domiziana was built, a more direct link to Rome. There are numerous ruins of public buildings, clear evidence of the city's vitality throughout the 2nd c., and even later. The history of Pozzuoli ends as it began: the absence of fortifications in an unstable period and the silting up of the coasts, which became marshy, once again shrank the town, in the 5th c. A.D., to the promontory of Rione Terra, a new fortified citadel on the gulf.

The Rione Terra* (B1), one of the most picturesque historic centers of Campania, with its panoramic vistas of the gulf, was evacuated in 1970 because of "bradisismo," a combination of volcanic and slow seismic activity, and currently (1997) it is inaccessible. It preserves, even in its urban layout, traces of the earliest Roman settlement; a long stretch of road paved in volcanic slabs was unearthed under Via Duomo, the *decumanus maximus*; along which is the *Capitolium**, later transformed into the cathedral. A bad fire (1964) uncovered the structures from the time of Augustus, which had previously been visible only in part. The temple, erroneously thought to be dedicated to the cult of Augustus, is pseudo-peripterous, Corinthian, and has its walls in fake *opus quadratum*; it has always attracted scholars and antiquarians; an inscription informs us of the name of the architect: L. Cocceius Auctus. G. B. Pergolesi is buried in the cathedral (died 1736).

The **port** (A-B1) is the site of a fish market, particularly exciting when the fishing boats return. The modern wharf incorporates the structures of the ancient Roman wharves. If you continue along Via Colombo and Via Roma, you will enter the center of the emporium. Because of the "bradisismo," or slow seismic and volcanic activity, there has been a notable regression of the coastline; the "ripa puteolana," or Pozzuoli shore, whose colonnaded buildings were visible until the 19th c., has disappeared. In the emporium stood the *horrea* (silos) and the *stationes* (headquarters of the guilds of merchants).

You then reach the **Macellum*** (Serapaeum, or Serapeo, A1), the best-known building in Pozzuoli, emblem of the ancient commercial vocation of the area. For may years it was considered to be a temple of Serapis, due to the discovery of a statue of the god, and later it was thought to have been a bath house; it was not until 1907 that its actual function was understood. Subjected, by the seismic and volcanic activity ("bradisismo") to sinkings and risings, in the first half of the 19th c. a public bathhouse was installed here, making use of the ancient structures as modern infrastructure. The traces of the lithodomes, mollusks that live at the waterline and which have long been present on the columns, indicate the various levels at which the structures were immersed, and have always been subjects of considerable

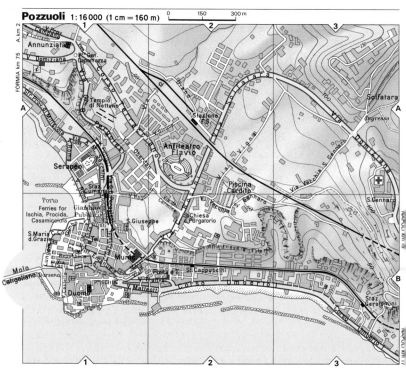

interest and the source of studies on the Phlegrean geological phenomena.

The Macellum was the public market of the Roman city and was laid out according to a customary plan that, in Campania, can also be found in Naples and at Pompeii. Its form and ornamentation are indications of a magnificence that was to be found only in the Eternal City. Over a porticoed courtyard extended rows of *tabernae* (shops) which could be entered either from the square or from the roads running around the market and linking it with the urban grid. The main entrance, overlooking the sea, consisted of a large vestibule; across from it was a large apse with a religious function, sumptuously decorated. The sequence of columns of the portico, in African marble, was interrupted on this side by four columns of a larger size (11.78 m tall) in cipollino marble; three of them, still in place, bounded the pronaos of the sacellum, covered by a half-dome. In the apse, there are three niches for statues; on the sides, there stand four halls for the sale of meat and fish. The two rectangular rooms at the corners were luxurious latrines. The central *tholos*, set on a podium, with a fountain in the center, was bounded by 16 Corinthian columns made of African marble. Marble sculptures and puteals emphasized the external circuit of the circular structure and the access stairways. The plan, which dates back to the period between the end of the 1st c. and the 2nd c. A.D. underwent major renovations during the reign of Severus.

In the eastern sector of the terraced city is the **Piscina Cardito*** (A-B2), a large cistern, probably dating from the 2nd c. A.D., with a square plan and a vaulted ceiling supported by 30 pillars, faced in *opus signinum* to make the walls waterproof.

Not far away is the amphitheater, or **Anfiteatro*** (A2), the second amphitheater built in Pozzuoli, and third in size only to the Colosseum and the amphitheater of Capua. It still has, over the entrances in clearly legible letters, the inscription "Colonia Flavia Augusta Puteolana Pecunia Sua." The attribution to the reign of Vespasian is questionable, because the sources record a great spectacle held at the orders of Nero in Puteoli in honor of Tiridates. The higher parts of the structure, which can still be seen, were systematically stripped of all their decorative elements; the covering of earth, on the other hand, has helped to preserve the systems and services of the arena, providing a documentation that is unrivaled almost anywhere else on earth. On the exterior, facing the southern entrance,

is an apsed fountain. The crowds entered the amphitheater along an elliptical portico based on a *platea* made of blocks of travertine. The elevation was articulated in three architectural orders, and was crowned by an attic. The *cavea* was subdivided into numbers *cunei*, or wedges, and into three "precincts," which reflected distinctions of social standing and honor among the spectators, who entered through twenty entryways. To keep up with the technical de-

An archaeologist at work at the Pozzuoli excavations

mands of the *venationes*, or hunting spectacles, and the games, which were increasingly complex and articulated in theatrical terms, there was a considerable development in the underground chambers of arenas, which in Pozzuoli were arranged around two central axes, which intersected, subdividing the area into four sectors. The two entrances, which could be used by rolling stock, at either extremity of the ellipse, and thus corresponding to the two main entrances, were closed with boards, allowing the public to pass over them. Along the elliptical corridor and the shorter axes, there were trapdoors connecting with the arena, so that cages could be hoisted up, containing the wild beasts. The great central ditch was used in the preparation of the backdrops and scenic devices, raised in the center of the arena during the games.

In the western sector of the terraced city are the immense baths, or **Terme di Nettuno** (A1), which occupied a number of different terraces that sloped down toward the sea (first half of the 2nd c. A.D.). You can make out the ruins of the area devoted to cold baths, with a central apsed hall and side rooms. As you return to Via Terracciano, at the same elevation as the baths, but on the opposite slope, you will see the ruins of the nymphaeum, or Ninfeo di Diana, a circular structure inscribed in a rectangle (end of the 2nd c./beginning of the 3rd c. A.D.), which may once have been linked with the lower baths.

The tour ends along **Via Campana*** (A1), the ancient road between Capua and Pozzuoli, which still preserves notable stretches with the ancient paving. Along the sides of the road were clustered the *tabernae*, *stationes* and, above all, mausoleums, for the most part columbaria, family tombs or the tombs of guilds, with one or more chambers. Inscriptions and sculptures reminded the passerby of the presence of the dead, providing information about the families who contributed to the history of the city that the wayfarer was now approaching, and the merits of those families. At the point where the road entered the city, the mausoleums clustered on either side in considerable numbers. Of the structures that stood along the right side, there survives only one example of the many that once existed.

The **mausoleums of Via Celle*** attracted the attention of travelers as early as the 18th c.; amidst the *cellai*, the huts of shepherds, and the undergrowth and bushes, these travelers sensed the charm and allure of the silent stones and bricks. There are now 14 buildings that can be dated back to the period between the 1st c. B.C. and the 2nd c. A.D. The spaces that extend between those buildings have been, in time, filled in with other buildings, creating the sense of a continuum of structures and buildings that you can still see along the left side of Via Celle. The entrance is near the northern boundary of the complex, on a line with the crossroads, or Quadrivio di S. Stefano. Many of the buildings were equipped with an underground chamber and an upper story. The niches of the columbaria, which held the marble or terracotta urns of ashes, were accompanied by *formae*, sepulchers that were constructed by digging a ditch in the flooring, in accordance with the rites of inhumation. In a number of the rooms, we can see remains of the original decorations, in stucco and paint. There is an alternation between structures with a relatively simple plan and mausoleums with greater articulation, with an exedra elevation, and of considerable size. Once you emerge from the enclosed area, you can continue, along the ancient route of Via Campana, toward Quarto. Shortly thereafter, on a line with the overpass of the beltway ("tangenziale"), there is another cluster of *mausoleums**. Located on private property (Fondo di Fraia) – and despite the modern renovations that have transformed the entrances and opened breaches between the structures – they are of particular interest because of the excellent state of preservation of the *stucco decorations**. Along with the geometric and plant repertories, which are reminiscent of the decorative patterns of the so-called IV style of painting, there are figures that clearly hearken back to the Dionysian world and the symbologies of salvation and funerals. The complex, which also shows signs of a late rehabilitation and reuse, can be dated back between the 1st and 2nd c. A.D.

Follow Via Nuova Campana and you will reach the *Montagna Spaccata*, an artificial cut in the mountain, done in ancient times to allow the road to cross through, and to the plain, or Piana di Quarto. The town takes its name from the *mansio* (stopping place) that stood at the fourth mile marker from Puteoli along Via Campana. The plain is scattered with prehistoric artifacts and the remains of Roman villas and mausoleums. Here too the best preserved and most interesting complex to tour is a funerary monument; from Via Campana you turn off onto Via Brindisi, where there is a necropolis. An enclosure wall surrounds an area in which there are three mausoleums; the largest one has a pyramid shape atop a cylindrical drum. The area in the back is further subdivided into enclosed lots; in the largest lot there are the ruins of two more mausoleums and other rooms for celebrations honoring the deceased – of particular interest is the *triclinium* preserved near the northwest corner. A smaller room – due to the presence of a raised bench reminiscent of the cooking surfaces in the houses of Pompeii – has been hypothesized as a kitchen for the preparation of sacred meals.

5.2 From Pozzuoli to Cuma

From Pozzuoli the itinerary (30 km plus detours) runs toward the Monte Nuovo (a regularly shaped volcanic cone that was formed with the eruption of 1538) and Lake Lucrino, from which a short detour leads to Lake Averno (visible also from a panoramic terrace near the intersection of the beltway, or "tangenziale"); you can then continue toward Baia, Bacoli, and Miseno. From here, you may head north toward the Lake Fusaro and Cuma with possible (and recommended) detours toward Monte di Procida and Acquamorta, which offer fine vistas of Procida and Ischia. A broad curve in the road running around Lake Fusaro indicates that you are now close to the excavations of Cuma, ancient Cumae.

Lake Lucrino and Lake Averno*

The twofold nature of the two coastal lakes still survives over the centuries, despite the neglect and decay. On the banks of the silent Averno, surrounded by vineyards and fields, there are ruins of Roman buildings, traditionally described as temples; the mystery and the sacred atmosphere, bound up with the idea of the underworld and the afterlife, still seem to prevail here, in contrast with the livelier Lake Lucrino which, surrounded as it is by restaurants, and in more direct contact with traffic, still seems to emanate a sociable atmosphere, as it must have in antiquity as well: it was famous for its cultivation of shellfish, and was proverbially a source of great wealth.

links to the interior. Following the Civil Wars and the transfer of the military port to Miseno, the Averno returned to its tranquil silence, while the Lucrino was affected by the expansion of Pozzuoli. The many hot springs, the natural steam vents (*Stufe di Nerone*), and the lovely setting made the place popular, and there were many villas between the lakes and the coast.

We suggest you stroll around the Lake Averno, enjoying some of the remarkable and dramatic views: it is still eminently possible to detect the volcanic origins of the lake, which occupied the structure of a crater; in the slopes are the entrances to the *Roman tunnels*, or galleries. In the grotto, or *Grotta della Sibilla*, which stands near ancient Roman port structures (*Navali di Agrippa*) tradition had it, implausibly, that the Sibyl had once lived, with her *lavacra*, or washing facilities, in the smaller rooms leading off of the tunnel. The passageway, instead, formed part of the infrastructures of the military port. On the opposite shore is the grotto, or Grotta di *Cocceio* or *Grotta della Pace* – a straight walkway

The gulf of Baia, dominated by the Aragonese castle

Most of the ancient structures are underwater, and have been detected through aerial photography; at a distance of about 400 meters from the coast, it is possible to see the road, the old Via Erculea, which ran along the spit of land that in ancient times separated Lake Lucrino from the sea. Vergil immortalized the learned traditions according to which, from Greek times on, Lake Averno was thought to be the site of the entrance to the underworld and the afterlife. The sacred nature of the place was in part violated in the years of the late Republic, when Agrippa took advantage of the fine setting to install a military port here. A navigable canal linked Lake Lucrino with the sea, and the lake became the anchorage of the port; the calmer, inland Lake Averno was the site of the shipyards and other infrastructures. Another canal linked the lakes and the galleries, creating easy

about 1 km in length, lit by light shafts, and flanked by an aqueduct – which made it possible to enter directly into Cumae and its port. To the right of the access road to the lake is the so-called temple, or *Tempio di Apollo*, perhaps a large hall from a bathhouse (2nd c. A.D.).

Baia

This small village (elev. 3 m) is famous for the pleasant climate and landscape and the sumptuous imperial residences. The ruins, which are visible and form part of the archaeological park, come from the terraced constructions of the hill and the lower coastal area, because many other ruins are now underwater. The architectural typology is that of the large leisure villa, built in imitation of the palaces of the eastern dynasties, with lavish use of space and with areas for leisure activities (promenades, gardens, panoramic terraces). As evidence of the buildings now underwater, submarine archaeologists found a set of ruins at the Punta Epitaffio, where, alongside structures from a bathhouse and a large villa, there was a *triclinium*/nymphaeum (part of the imperial palace; see page 5) in which was found, still in place, part of the sculptural decoration depicting Ulysses in the act of offering the goblet to Polyphemus, with his companion holding a wineskin, and other statues (now being installed in the Castello di Baia). Immediately after you enter the archaeological park, or **Parco Archeologico*** you will see the large promenade, or *ambulatio* that gave its name to the entire complex of buildings linked to it, once part of a villa that dates from the Republic (end of the 2nd c.-beginning of the 1st c. B.C., with later reconstructions), set on several levels. Later constructions have in part deformed the original layout, which finds counterparts in the large leisure villas (*villae otiorum*) built along the coast, with spectacular views over the sea. Similar constructions dotted the entire Phlegrean littoral strip and, at Baiae in particular, characterized the image of the landscape, which was gradually transformed with the appearance of imperial estates which, with additions and renovations, modified the original layout. The *ambulatio* was covered with vaulted ceilings set along a line of central pillars and walls running lengthwise, serving as a foundation for the upper terrace, beneath which were also a series of cisterns and service chambers, visible behind the long western wall of the covered walkway. An apsed rectangular hall opens at the center of the west side. A pair of stairways at the end of the walkway provide access to the upper terrace, which bounds the excavated area, and contains the residential rooms (apsed hall, peristyle…). The southern stairway leads back down to the lower terraces, which connect all the various sections of the villa. A new walkway opened on the 3rd level, framed by a terracing wall that was in turn covered by vaulted roofs set on pillars. The 4th and 5th terrace presents parallel rows of rooms linked by intermediate hallways; the rooms of the 4th terrace are smaller, and used for service functions, while the rooms of the 5th terrace are quite large, and were bedrooms and living rooms. The last level, which was the most extensive, was used as a garden area, and was probably surrounded by a peristyle. A walkway buttressed by arches led to the so-called baths of Mercury, or **Terme di Mercurio***. The current ground level does not correspond to the ancient one, which as early as the 18th c. was described as being flooded with water, which

almost reached the levels of the vaulted ceilings. The entrance, even now, runs through a breach in the walls, while the original entrance was to the east. The dome, which dates from the late Republic or the reign of Augustus (end of the 1st c. B.C.), constitutes an innovation for the period. It is built in cement structure with radial blocks of tufa stone that converge on the great central oculus which, with four other openings, provided the natural lighting. In the walls, there were eight niches; the walls were faced with slabs of marble, while the vaulted ceiling, probably in a later phase, was covered with *mosaics*. The room, perhaps a *frigidarium* or a *natatio*, formed part of a bath complex, of which a number of rooms survive, some from the same period and others probably added during the reign of Severus (first half of the 3rd c. A.D.).

Returning backward, along the buttressed walkway, you will reach the *sector of the Sosandra*, on a line with the lower terrace, which presents the same orientation as the villa of the *ambulatio*, and a complex structural history. The first phase dates back to the Republican period (2nd/1st c. B.C.) and, probably, the complex was founded as a villa which, over the course of the years, took on increasingly spectacular and complex forms. In the 2nd c. A.D., there was a radical transformation, which probably also modified the functional purpose of the complex: according to one hypothesis, the complex was converted into an *hospitalia* (hotel) for the visitors to the nearby thermal spas; according to other scholars, the renovation dates back to the age of Nero, when the emperor donated facilities for rest and recreation to the sailors of the fleet of Misenum, or *classis misenensis*. The lower sector comprises a large terrace, bounded by a portico, overlooking which are various residential rooms (remains of frescoes). Overlooking the peristyle and the sea are the structures of the upper terrace, occupied by a nymphaeum/theater, while other rooms, arranged in a circular plan, overlook a portico and hemicycle. The upper sector was articulated around a covered space, probably occupied by open-air *triclinia*, surrounded by a portico with three wings. To the west were residential rooms (*triclinia*, *cubicula*), and in one of them is an interesting mosaic with masks and scenes, probably for theatrical use. This sector also had a *balneum* which still preserves part of its stucco decorations (middle of the 2nd c. A.D.). The name of this sector came from the discovery of a statue of Aphrodite Sosandra, a Roman copy of a Greek original dating from the first half of the 5th c. B.C. (now in the Museo di Napoli). The entire area immediately to the south of the sector of the Sosandra was occupied, from the very foundation, by thermal installations, perhaps for the specific qualities of the ground here, and for the possibility thus offered of capturing hot steam, which was useful for the operation of the *laconica* (sweat rooms, used for *sudationes*), which were built partly underground. The area can be divided into three sectors, which reflect the various phases of expansion. The first constructions (1st c. B.C.-Age of Augustus) occupied two zones, uphill and downhill, leaving unoccupied an intermediate strip. The entire area was subjected to thorough-going renovations under Hadrian; the first sector, which lay on higher ground, was equipped with a square-plan *frigidarium*, an *apodyterium* (or dressing room), rooms for ablutions and for hot baths, a *laconicum* (or sweat room), carved into the hillside and covered with a domed vault, with a central oculus.

The intermediate sector (2nd c. A.D., with late renovations) presents a bath house (set on a massive substructure, which evened out elevations and sharp slopes) in which there emerges an apsed hall, around which were arrayed smaller rooms. To the north, there are three rooms, traditionally known to antiquarians as the three "rooms of Venus," or "Stanze di Venere", the destination of many visitors in years gone by for the excellent conservation of the stuccoes, which have now almost all been lost.

A room in the Museo Archeologico dei Campi Flegrei, Baia

Outside of the park, but linked to the complex, and clearly visible from the station, or Stazione della Cumana, is the so-called temple, or **Tempio di Diana***, a large hall, about whose function there is much debate. Dating from the reign of Severus, it has been suggested that it served to celebrate and worship the members of the imperial family. Built to a circular plan, inscribed in an octagon, it consists of rows of tufa and brick. In the upper fascia, which was meant to support the roofing, the masonry is all brickwork. The roof, which some have reconstructed as a simple half-dome, presents a pointed-arch section, and was built with considerable skill, using heavier materials in the upright sections at the base, and using a porous tufa-stone in the higher sections. Outside of the park, and beyond the road, is the temple of Venus, or **Tempio di Venere***, part of the renovations ordered by Hadrian of the sector of the Sosandra; with a circular plan on the interior and octagonal on the exterior, it is partially buried; it was covered with an umbrella-vault roof, which has since collapsed.

The splendid gulf culminates theatrically in the castle, or **Castello di Baia***: built in the Aragonese era on the ruins of a Roman villa, traditionally said to have belonged to Caesar, it was modernized during the rule of the viceroys. It now houses the archaeological museum of the Phlegrean Fields, or **Museo Archeologico dei Campi Flegrei*** (currently, 1997, undergoing installation), in which a theoretical restoration of the layout of the sacellum, or *Sacello degli Augustali* in Miseno has been created (the tetrastyle pronaos, with a dedicatory inscription, and, above it, a pediment with relief and, behind the columns, the imperial statues); accompanying this are the so-called plaster casts, or *Gessi di Baia*, which were used to replicate Greek originals from the classical age. Soon, the *statues of members of the Claudian clan*, or Gens Claudia, which adorned the hall, or Sala del Ninfeo di Punta Epitaffio (Claudian age) will be on exhibit.

Bacoli

This small town (elev. 12 m., pop. 27,628) corresponds to the ancient *Bauli*; in it, numerous Roman ruins attest to the proliferation of coastal villas. Near the sea, is the so-called tomb, or **Sepolcro di Agrippina**, in reality, an *odeon* that was transformed into a nymphaeum, part of the structures for leisure activities at a large villa. Three concentric deambulatories, set at various levels, supported the steps. Access stairways linked the orchestra to the galleries. The earliest layout can be dated back to the Julian/Claudian period. The traditional name comes from the contrived combination of the surviving structures with the sad story, taken from the sources, of the assassination of Agrippina on the Phlegrean coasts, and her burial there in a large tomb. A further testimonial to the proliferation, beginning in the time of the Republic, of villas along the coastline can be had from the complex, or Complesso delle **Cento Camerelle** (Via delle Cento Camerelle 165): this complex comprised two water reservoirs, at different elevations, that were functional to the needs of a large villa that has been only partly excavated. The upper cistern is subdivided into four aisles by three lines of pillar; the lower cistern consists of a network of elongated rooms that intercommunicate.

The celebrated **Piscina Mirabile*** was built on the promontory that dominates the port of Miseno. This is one of the largest Roman

The Casino Reale on Lake Fusaro

cisterns still in existence; it was the terminus of the aqueduct, or Acquedotto del Serino, dating from Augustan times, and served the needs of the port facilities of Misenum, with a total capacity of 12,600 cubic meters. With a rectangular plan and a vaulted roof, it is divided into five aisles by four rows of cruciform pillars. Access, for necessary maintenance work, was through two arched staircases, located at the northwest and southeast corners. At the center a basin served as a distillation tank; the intake main still exists; the outflow, on the other hand, took place from above, with a special hydraulic machinery.

Miseno

Miseno is now a small town (elev. 6 m) in whose harbor, between the Battle of Actium (31 B.C.) and the death of Agrippa (12 B.C.), there was once stationed one of the main imperial fleets, directly at the orders of the emperor and commanded by a praefect of equestrian rank. The natural configuration of the site encouraged the installation of a well articulated port complex, because an open bay was followed by an enclosed basin (Maremorto), both connected by a navigable canal, that has since been filled in. The entrance to the roads, or anchorage, was bounded by a double mole, or wharf; galleries and tunnels carved into the promontories (Punta Pennata, Punta Sarparella) served to create an interplay of marine currents designed to prevent the silting up of the port, whose double structure made it possible to place the shipyard in the calmer waters of the Maremorto and to place the harbor in the open basin. All around there developed the infrastructures necessary to the life of the military base. On the promontory stand the ruins of a villa thought to have belonged to the praefect of the fleet; at the foot of the hill is the chapel, or *Sacello degli Augustali*; dedicated to the emperor cult, this building was partially carved out of the living rock, and is subdivided into three rooms. The central room, apsed and set on a podium, is preceded by a tetrastyle, or four-pillar pronaos; numerous elements of the artistic and architectural decorations are now in the castle, or Castello di Baia. Dating from the Julian/Claudian age, the building underwent numerous modifications under the Antonines. We recommend the walk up to the Monte di Miseno (from which you can enjoy a splendid panoramic view); but perhaps only an excursion in a boat in the port, preferably in the hours just before sunset in the late spring, will allow the visitor to appreciate the colors of the Phlegrean area, as you sail between modern mussel farms and Roman ruins.

Lake Fusaro

On its banks, if you follow the road that runs around it, inland, to the east, you can still see ruins of Roman structures, of various era and purpose. The entire area, which was densely inhabited and exploited in earlier times, became in the 18th c. a hunting preserve of the king; Ferdinand IV ordered the construction of the elegant *Casino*

Reale, with a central plan, in the lake, just a short distance from the east bank, and to plans by C. Vanvitelli.

Cuma

Founded in the third quarter of the 8th c. B.C., this town is described by the sources as the oldest Greek colonial settlement in the west, a Euboean foundation that followed an earlier *emporion* on Ischia, the ancient Pithecusa. It extends across a plateau that rises slightly toward the sea and culminates, in the northwestern corner, with the rise of the Monte di Cuma, the ancient acropolis. The city walls, made of blocks of tufa stone, ran along ridges and crests, and linked a square area with the fortress, the so-called lower city, or "città bassa," which was distinguished from the monumental area of the acropolis, the site of the chief city sanctuaries. The sea, due to the progressive silting up which had already begun in Roman times, has actually receded perceptibly: it originally lapped at the edge of the acropolis and the southern coast, and it was in this area that the ports were located. The Greek city supplanted an aboriginal settlement, evidence of which has been provided by the discovery of tombs and of strata of artifacts and debris on the acropolis. Governed for many years by a wealthy landed aristocracy, it underwent a period of profound transformation in the late-Archaic age (end of the 6th c./beginning of the 5th c. B.C.). In 474 B.C., not far from here, a major battle was fought between Greeks and Etruscans; the superiority of Cumae was assured by the reinforcements provided by Syracuse, or Siracusa. Conquered by the Samnites in 421 B.C., during Roman times its administrative status was linked to that of Capua.

During the Byzantine era, the fortress of Cuma was considered to be an impregnable citadel, and was subjected to a tough siege during the Gothic-Greek war.

In 1205 the city was definitively destroyed and abandoned. Today the ruins occupy a landscape that, despite the unbridled spread of illegal construction, can still be described as agricultural.

Once you have entered the archaeological park, or **Parco Archeologico***, you will climb up toward the acropolis through a passageway carved into the tufa (possibly derived from a Bourbon quarry). Immediately after there are two galleries, to the right the Roman crypt, and to the left the so-called grotto of the Sibyl, or **Antro della Sibilla*** (B1-2) badly damaged, in its first stretch, by the collapse of the roof. With a trapezoidal cross-section, the floor was lat-er lowered, creating straight walls running perpendicular to the ground. On the right side extended secondary branch tunnels that were largely open onto the sea. Roughly midway along the length, on the left side, there extended a further branching out, articulated into three chambers, used in Roman times as cisterns and, in early-Christian times, to contain sepulchers. To the south, the cave ends in a large vaulted chamber that gives access, on the left, to a tripartite cubicle with doors or transennae, documented by the holes for fastening still visible on the jambs. This place, particularly secluded and secret, was identified as the cave from which the Sibyl made her prophecies. The Sibyl was a prophetess who offered her services to the pilgrims who frequented the sanctuaries of antiquity; her sayings were collected in books, and her fame as a soothsayer endured, and even found its way into the Hebrew and Christian traditions. The search for the sites of the Sibyl began as early as the late-Roman age, and then as now, the prime source in the quest for the cave was the poetry of Vergil who, in turn, drew upon traditions that were centuries old. The traditional interpretation has recently been re-explored; the gallery runs parallel to the coastline, beyond the walls that linked the acropolis to the southwestern corner of the city, and this has led to a hypothesis of an original military function. The final chamber, which some believe dates from Hellenistic times, is – in the opinion of others – a funerary chamber of the late-Roman era.

As you exit the grotto, ignoring for the moment the Roman crypt, you will climb up along a modern ramp (along the route, you may note stretches of the Greco-Roman walls) verso the acropolis, the entrance to which (during Roman times) was marked by a *tower*, with a Roman layout. An access ramp on the left led directly to the lower terrace, occupied by the sanctuary, or Santuario di Apollo, and later obstructed by the construction of a group of cisterns.

Continuing along the "Via Sacra," you will encounter on the left a **panoramic terrace**, from which you can see the broad littoral strip of Cuma, Capo Miseno, the gulf of Pozzuoli, and the Neapolitan area to the south. The sandy littoral was formed only recently, and hides the original inlets and lagoons of the ports of Cumae.

If you return to the "Via Sacra," you may turn left and reach the lower terrace, occupied by the sanctuary, or **Santuario di Apollo*** (A1-2). On the left are the ruins of a building (6th/5th c. B.C.) built in blocks of tufa stone, a large cistern that was in all probability linked to a monumental fountain. To the south is the temple, or Tempio di Apollo. From the Greco-Samnite phase, there remain only faint traces, including the foundation *platea*, while most of the evidence has to do with the restructuring that was done during the reign of Augustus, when the temple was embellished with the addition of a colonnaded terrace, open toward the lower city, or "città bassa." The cella was divided into three aisles by pillars; of the peristasis there still stand some of the columns, built in brickwork and subsequently stuccoed. In early-Christian times, the temple was transformed into a basilica, and in the ancient *platea* burial ditches were dug.

Near its eastern edge, the terrace overlooking the lower city, or "città bassa": opposite, the horizon is closed off by the Monte Grillo, one of the natural boundaries of the town of Cuma, in which you can distinguish perfectly the artificial pass, probably cut as early as the Greek period, and monumentalized in imperial times with the arch, or Arco Felice (see plan below). Through that passageway, Via Domiziana exited the city. Shifted slightly westward, you can make out a further depression on the slopes of the mountain: this is the entrance to the grotto, or Grotta di Cocceio. At the base of the acropolis extended the forum, recognizable by the mass of the public buildings: the *Capitolium*, the Masseria del Gigante, and slightly off to one side, a bath complex. Behind these buildings and on the slope of the hill is the entrance to the Roman crypt. In the plain extending toward Lìcola, outside

of the enclosure wall, extended the most important Cumaean necropolises.

After you leave the sanctuary of Apollo, you may continue along Via Sacra, climbing up to the upper terrace, where you will find the so-called *Temple of Jove* (A1). While there is reliable evidence linking the name of Apollo to the lower sanctuary, there is no such certainty for this temple which, oriented on an east–west axis, was profoundly remodeled in Roman times and later transformed into a church (note the ruins of the altar and the baptistery, of which the basin with its marble facing still remains). If you climb back down Via Sacra, you will return to the entrance of the cave of the Sibyl, or Antro della Sibilla, and the Roman crypt, or **Cripta Romana*** (A1-2), which can be observed from above due to the collapse of the vault, which probably had already happened by the time of the war between the Greeks and the Goths. The first stretch was visible for a long time, to the point that an ancient tradition identified it as the famous grotto of the oracle. The visible part is in fact the last stretch of a tunnel that, starting from the lower city ("città bassa") near the Forum, or Foro (A2), cut through the mountain toward the port. The construction of this tunnel was part of a larger and more complex project of military and urban renovation of the Phlegrean area in the late Republic, and was completed with the construction of the grotto, or Grotta di Cocceio (B2-3) which, with the tunnel through the Monte Grillo, linked Lake Averno to Cumae, or Cuma: in this way, there was a direct alternative route between the military port built at the behest

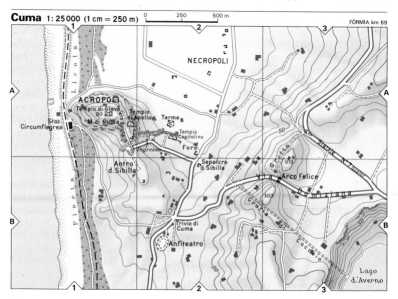

Cuma 1: 25 000 (1 cm = 250 m)

of Agrippa – between the lakes of Lucrino and Averno (*Portus Iulius*) – and the port of Cumae. From up high, you can see a large vestibule with four niches for statues. After you leave the park, or Parco, you can tour (also with a permit) other parts of the lower city, or "città bassa." Set in an outlying location is a *thermal complex*, built at the end of the 1st c. A.D.; the forum has been only partly explored. The square was bounded by a double-order portico. The discovery of a frieze of arms, the architectural decoration of the epistyle, allows us to date the construction of this area to the period between the 2nd and the 1st c. B.C. The shorter, western side is occupied by the *Capitolium*. The foundation of this building dates back to the 3rd c. B.C., when the temple was probably dedicated to Jove alone. An inscription in mosaics, inserted into the *opus signinum* flooring, stated that the temple was the result of the munificence of the family of the Heii.

As you emerge from the Forum, if you take Via Monte di Cuma until you reach the intersection with Via Vecchia Licola, you will encounter the ruins of another bath house, known as the tomb of the Sibyl, or *Tomba della Sibilla*, of considerable interest for its plan that dates from the Samnite period.

If you request permission and directions from the employee of the local office of the archaeological commission, or Soprintendenza Archeologica, you can reach a raised platform from which you will have a good vantage point on the ruins of the amphitheater, or *Anfiteatro*, the original construction of which can be dated to the end of the 2nd c. B.C.; the interior is occupied by crops growing on terraces that follow the curves of the ancient *platea*. Continuing along Via Provinciale, you will reach the **Arco Felice*** (end of the 1st c. A.D.), a monumental entrance to the city and a passage of Via Domiziana, probably built with a view to establishing

A corner of the excavations at Cuma

a more direct connection between Rome and the port of Pozzuoli (remains of the original volcanic slab pavement). A majestic fornix, built of brickwork, buttressed by lesser arches, and embellished along its flanks by niches for statues, monumentalized a passageway that may have existed as early as the Greek period.

5.3 Procida and Ischia

You can get to these two islands by ferryboat or hydrofoil, from Naples (in 90 or 100 minutes) and Pozzuoli (in 60 minutes). Procida, small and flat, is crossed by a complex and panoramic road; Ischia, large and mountainous, is girded by a road that links – with many spectacular vistas – all of the island's towns and villages. To tour it, you may hire one of the charming little micro-taxis, brightly color motor-carriages that have replaced the old horse-drawn carriages. If you start from the Port, and head north, the road will climb up, skirting the sea, until you reach Casamicciola Terme, a spa and beach town. Continuing from there you will reach the elegant and tranquil town of Lacco Ameno, set on an inlet at the foot of the Epomeo; here are some of the most exclusive hotel complexes. From Piazza Girardi you have a choice: if you turn left, you will reach the ring road, or "circumvallazione," or else you can continue along the waterfront road, or "lungomare," passing through the Piazza S. Restituta, with the sanctuary of the same name. Once you return to the state road, or "statale," you will run inland for a way, returning to the coast on a line with Forio, a charming little town with white houses, over which juts the round tower of the old fortress, a fine vacation spot. After passing through the village, the road, which is panoramic in certain stretches, continues uphill amidst vineyards as far as Panza, a small farming town (elev. 155 m), from which a road runs, with many broad vistas of the sea, as far as Sant'Angelo, a charming fishing village. From Panza on, as you continue, you will reach the most scenic stretch; the coast, in fact, in this area, is particularly jagged, with high cliffs looming over the sea, and the road offers a number of spectacular views. After Serrara, center of the township of Serrara-Fontana, you will pass a series of ravines, the best known of which is the Cava Scura (see below). You will then reach Fontana, the highest village (elev. 452 m); from here, you can climb up to the Epomeo in just over an hour on foot or by mule (the "ciucciari," or mule drivers, offer their services at the foot of the ascent). You will then continue downhill (past Buonopane, a little village famous for the "'ndrezzata," a popular dance of ancient origin) as far as Barano (elev. 224 m), situated in a handsome location, from which it is possible to descend to the beach, or Lido dei Maronti, a broad sandy beach characterized by the presence of fumaroles (from Maronti you can tour the Cava Scura: rudimentary hot baths carved into the tufa stone, consisting of basins of hot water, associated with the "fumarole," geysers of boiling steam). Further along, past the crossroads and after passing under the arches of a 16th-c. aqueduct, you will follow a straight road running through the lava from the eruptions of 1301-02, and, after passing through the pine forest, you will reach a square crossed by the avenue that leads back to the port of Ischia.

Procida

You will land at the picturesque *Marina di Sancio Cattolico* (or the Marina Grande, village in the township; elev. 36 m, pop. 10,837), which is overlooked by an unbroken curtain of houses with bright colors (pink, yellow, light blue), and then you will climb up toward the Piazza dei Martiri, with a view over the sea; from here you will continue uphill toward the castle, or *Castel-*lo, now a penitentiary. The large square that lies before it overlooks, with a splendid vista, the eastern side of the island and the *Marina della Corricella*, a picturesque little fishing village set high on the coast, and linked to the beach by many stairways, along which loom the houses. From the penitentiary you can reach the Terra Murata, the most elevated area on the island (elev. 91 m). This area, originally known as the Terra Casata, was until the early 16th c. the only settlement on the island, because it could easily be defended against Saracen attack. Beginning in 1563, at the behest of Innico d'Avalos, it underwent a vast transformation, which radically altered its structure: the large palazzo was built, along with a road that linked it to the marina, or harbor, and town walls were built, leading to the present name (*Terra Murata* means walled town). In the town is the abbey church of *S. Michele Arcangelo*, built in ca. 1026, destroyed repeatedly and then rebuilt toward the end of the 16th c. The decoration of the interior was the work of artists influenced by Giordano: in the wooden ceiling, note a canvas "signed" by Luca Giordano but actually executed by a pupil of his, during the master's stay in Spain (1699); a number of the canvases between the windows are by Simonelli, on the main altar, note the *St. Michael* by N. Rossi (with a fine view of the island); also noteworthy is the main altar, in marble inlay. From the confraternity church to the lower level, there are fine panoramic views. After you return to the Marina Grande, you can reach the southeasternmost point of the island, where you will find the Marina della

The picturesque fishing port of Marina della Corricella, Procida

Chiaiolella, built in an ancient crater, and the beach, or Lido di Procida, favorite spots for swimming and sunbathing, separated by a spit of land. Across from the Chiaiolella is the islet, or **Isolotto di Vivara**, shaped like a crescent moon, and entirely covered with Mediterranean maquis, or scrub, and populated with rabbits and other animals (nature reserve of the WWF); it is linked by a wharf/aqueduct, but you can only visit from the sea, with permission from the regional government of Campania. At a distance of 2 km stands the belvedere of Centane, which overlooks the bay, which is enclosed by two points, or Punta Solchiaro on the right and Punta Pizzaco on the left; along the way back, if you turn off toward the Punta Serra, there is a haunting little cemetery overlooking the sea.

A characteristic terracotta relief from Ischia

Ischia

The largest and most important town on the island (elev. 14 m, pop. 16,737) is made up of an older section (Ischia Ponte) and a modern part (Ischia Porto). The earliest inhabited settlement here arose in Roman times, to the east, not far from Carta Romana, and was called Aenaria (this was a major metal-working center). Around the 5th c. A.D., the first settlement was established on the crag of the castle, or Castello, which developed until it became a fortified citadel. From the 13th c. on, the "borgo" of Celsa (the present-day Ischia Ponte) began to develop; inhabited by fishermen and sailors, it grew considerably in the 17th c., when the citadel of the Castello was abandoned. The present-day Ischia Porto developed in the 18th c., and has grown in terms of its economy and its structure over the past fifty years in particular. The *port* originated from a little lake that formed in a volcanic crater; in 1854, Ferdinand II had the lake opened to the sea by the excavation of a canal. After the port, on the right, note the town baths, or *Terme Comunali* (B1), built in 1845, rebuilt in 1880, and completely modernized in 1953. Further along, on the left, you will reach Via Roma and the Corso Colonna, lined with numerous stores, restaurants, and cafes – this is a favorite spot for strolling and promenades. Further on, on the left, note the church of *S. Maria*

delle Grazie (18th c.), with a majolica dome. You then continue on toward Ischia Ponte, passing along the little beach of the fishermen, with its handsome colorful houses with arches, and you will reach Via del Seminario, where, immediately to the right, is the bishopric, or Vescovado; inside are the front of an early-Christian sarcophagus and a number of fragments of funerary monuments taken from the old cathedral, or Cattedrale. In Via L. Mazzella, on the left, stands the *church of the Assunta* (D2) founded in early times (12th c.), rebuilt in the Baroque style, and since 1810, the town cathedral. Inside are a noteworthy baptismal font with a late-Renaissance basin supported by three Virtues that date back to the 14th c., large canvases by G. Diano and, in the apse, a wooden *Crucifix* from the 13th c.; in the transept, and in the sacristy, note two panel paintings dating from the early 16th c. The campanile was, originally, a defensive tower built in the 14th c. At the edge of the town stands the castle, or *Castello di Ischia** (E2). This was a Byzantine military garrison in the 5th c., and under Charles I of Anjou, a fortress was erected at the summit, while below there had already developed a village that, between the fourteenth and 16th c. grew to became the main inhabited center of the island. In 1438 Alfonso V had the islet linked to the land by a masonry bridge, ordered an access ramp cut into the rock, and had the castle fortified with bastions. From 1495 it was inhabited by the family of d'Avalos, the governors of the island; over the course of the 16th c. the island lost its population, and was definitively abandoned in 1809, following a bombardment ordered by Murat against the British, who had occupied it. Today, all that remains are a few ruins and the castle, which was sold to a private citizen, but which is open to the public. After you cross the bridge you climb up the ramp and you will then reach the cathedral, or *Cattedrale* (where Vittoria Colonna and Ferrante d'Avalos were wed in 1509), which dates back to 1301 and was rebuilt in the 18th c.; what survives is a part of the roof, the 16th-c. flooring, and, in the crypt, a number of frescoes of the school of Giotto. Further along, on the left, is the *church of the*

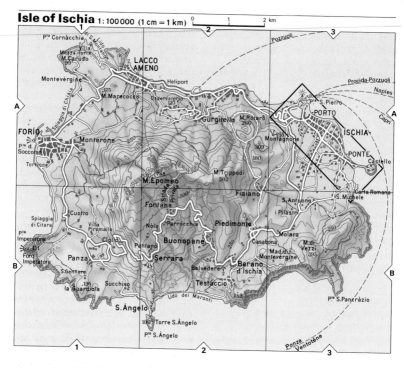

Isle of Ischia 1:100 000 (1 cm = 1 km)

Immacolata (18th c.), covered with a dome and entirely restored, in which exhibitions of painting are now held; alongside it stands the Clarissan convent, or *Convento delle Clarisse*, with a cloisters and a notable, if macabre, cemetery of the nuns; continuing along, on the right, you will see the little *church of S. Pietro a Pantaniello* (16th c.), with an hexagonal plan; finally, you will reach the bastions of the castle, used from 1823 on as a prison (from 1851 until 1874, political prisoners were held here, including C. Poerio and S. Spaventa). From the various terraces, one can enjoy – need we say it? – splendid panoramic views* of Ischia and the gulf.

Once you return to the island, you can go, nearby (1.5 km), to the *belvedere of Carta Romana* (E1).

Casamìcciola Terme

Famous in antiquity, along with Lacco, for its springs. In 1604 the Governatori del Pio Monte della Misericordia of Naples founded a spa here for the separate use of the members of religious orders and the poor and sick of the city. Because of the loveliness of the place, the mildness of the climate, and the excellent hotels, it became in the 18th and 19th c., celebrated throughout Europe, and was regularly visited by many aristocratic families, while famous artists enjoyed long stays here. In 1883, the town

was destroyed by a violent earthquake and was rebuilt toward the sea (elev. 3 m, pop. 6,780). Two squares now constitute the center of the little town: Piazza Bagni, uphill, and Piazza Marina, on the coast. In the Piazza Bagni, with the building of the Pio Monte della Misericordia, there are many bathhouses; the Piazza Marina, which is always bustling with activity, is situated across from the port, built in 1969-70, for ferryboats to dock.

On one of the hills behind it, the Sentinella (elev. 123 m), stands the Osservatorio Geofisico, founded in 1891, from which you can admire a lovely panoramic view*.

Lacco Ameno

Situated at the far north end of the island (elev. 2 m, pop. 4,073), at the foot of the Monte Epomeo, this was where, in the first half of the 8th c. B.C., the first Greek colonists in southern Italy landed. They took up residence on the promontory of the Monte Vico, which dominates two bays; this settlement is mentioned in the sources as Pithecusa.

The city was famous for its trade in metals and for its excellent clay (and in fact this island supplied Naples with clay until the 19th c.). From 1863 on, due to the lovely landscape and the curative properties of its hot springs, the town of Lacco was dubbed Ameno ("pleasant"). Jutting up out of the sea is the distinctive shoal with its mushroom shape, a symbol of the town. Beginning in the 1950s, Lacco developed intensely, in part due to the decision of the powerful publisher Angelo Rizzoli, who made it his "feudal land holding"; it was he, in fact, who decided to transform the old spa, or Terme Regina Isabella, into a luxury hotel/spa complex, followed by the construction of other hotels which, even today, are the most elegant and exclusive on the island. Several of those hotels overlook the central square, which takes its name from the sanctuary, or *Santuario di S. Restituta*, comprising one modern church, rebuilt in 1886, and an older church, dating from 1036, but rebuilt in the 14th and 18th c. In the newer church, there are a 16th-c. panel painting and ten canvases depicting the martyrdom of St. Restituta; the smaller, older church was built on the site of a 4th/5th-c. basilica, the ruins of which can still be seen in the crypt. In the underground chambers and in adjoining rooms there is a museum, featuring finds taking from local digs, and holy furnishings. Nearby, in a vast park, is the 18th-c. Villa Arbusto, renovated by Ignazio Gardella as the residence of Angelo Rizzoli; it contains a museum and a major center for archaeological studies. The **Museo Archeologico*** (now being installed) is important for its information and documentation on the early period of Greek colonization in the west; among the finds are materials from the necropolis of San Montano (*Nestor's Cup*, with one of the earliest known inscriptions in Greek meter) and from the settlement of Monte Vico. From Lacco Ameno you can reach (1.5 km) the bay, or Baia di San Montano, a lovely beach set between the promontories of Monte Vico (elev. 116 m) to the east, and the Monte della Guardiola (elev. 106 m) to the west.

Forio

In an area that was a favorite with the ancient Romans there lies a beach that the Romans named after Venus of Cythera (Venere Citerea), a beach abounding in hot springs, the present-day beach, or Spiaggia di Citara. Situated in the westernmost area, far from the main harbor, and unequipped with spa facilities until recently, the town

(elev. 18 m, pop. 12,607) has undergone an urban development unlike that experienced by other towns, and has made the best use possible of its close links with the surrounding countryside and the sea, basing its economy on agriculture and trade. Overlooking the open sea, it was particularly vulnerable to pirate raids; over the course of the centuries, therefore, no fewer than 16 coastal watch towers were built, all linked one with another, and nearly all still in existence. Of them, the most important one is the round tower that looms over the settlement, the *Torrione*, built in 1480, from the terrace of which once can enjoy a fine overall view of the town, with its picturesque white houses with small courtyards, with a grid of narrow, winding lanes. At the center of the town is the church of *S. Maria di Loreto* (16th c., rebuilt in the Baroque style), flanked by two bell towers. On the interior, note the rich decorations in marble inlay and stuccoes; in particular, note the handsome pulpit and the balustrade of the main altar, 1710; from the church you can enter the Baroque oratory, or *Oratorio dell'Assunta*. In the town square, or Piazza del Municipio there stand

The picturesque Santuario del Soccorso, Forio

two churches side by side: *S. Francesco*, with a handsome wooden choir and a number of canvases from the school of Giordano, and *S. Maria Visitapoveri* (rebuilt in the 18th c.) with a series of paintings by Alfonso Di Spiagna, a majolica floor, and a broad wooden choir. In the upper part of the town is the *church of S. Vito*, founded in the 10th/11th c., rebuilt entirely in 1745. The layout with a nave and two side-aisles is surmounted by a dome; there are lovely paintings from the 17th and 18th c. and, in the sacristy, a silver statue of the saint (St. Vitus), done to a model by Sammartino. Outside of the town, on a point, is the sanctu-

Sant'Angelo

Until 1948, the year of the construction of the road that linked it to Succhivo, this little fishing village (elev. 8 m) could be reached only by a mule track and from the beach, or Spiaggia dei Maronti by a trail. Set high on the coast, with colorful houses and narrow lanes, the whole town overlooks the sea. A spit of land links to the islet, or Isolotto di Sant'Angelo, composed of lava (elev. 106 m), surmounted by the ruins of a tower, forming two bays that contribute to the singular beauty of the site. Attracting tourists with its swimming and spa, in the evening it is lively, thanks to the many bars, restaurants, and lovely little shops scattered through the pedestrian lanes. A trail leading eastward will take you on the handsome beach, or Spiaggia dei Maronti.

Monte Epomeo

You will follow the road that branches off to the left from the state road ("statale"), after the little village of Fontana, for roughly 1.4 km; then you can continue on foot, along a mule path, until you reach a little level (elev. 767 m) where you will find the church of *S. Nicola* and the *hermitage*, both carved out of tufa-stone. The little church dates back to 1459 and until recently attracted frequent and folkloristic pilgrimages; in the chapel, or Cappella del Crocifisso is buried one of the governors of the island who, in 1754, after narrowly surviving a brush with death, decided to dedicate his life to St. Nicholas and to become a hermit. The hermitage is linked with the church and, in a corridor running parallel to the vestibule, which leads to a belvedere, are the cells; next to the vestibule were the kitchen and the refectory, transformed a few years ago into a pleasant trattoria. Continuing along, you will reach the summit, and from here you may enjoy a panoramic vista* of nearly all of the island (with all its towns, bays, and promontories, the other craters, and, above all, the impressive lava flows) and the gulfs of Naples and Pozzuoli; if it is a clear day, your view will range from the Isole Pontine to the Cilento. In many boulders that tumbled off the mountain, distinctive "houses of stone" have been carved out, a "timeless" form of rural architecture: many rock-cut houses date back at least to the 17th c. and some are still inhabited. It is also possible to climb up from Casamicciola or Forìo, crossing the handsome chestnut forest of the highland of the Falanga.

ary, or Santuario del Soccorso (16th c.), very picturesque, in white plaster, with an exterior balustrade in majolica, in which there are a 16th-c. *Crucifix* and numerous votive offerings from sailors and emigrants. The square that lies before it juts out over the sea and offers a splendid panoramic view, especially at sunset. On the hill of Zaro, there are many modern villas, including the Villa Walton with a lovely *garden**. On the state road, or Statale Pansa, adjoining the plant of the "D'Ambra Vini," is the museum of peasant culture, or *Museo Contadino*.

6 Mount Vesuvius, Herculaneum, and Pompeii

"On Sunday, we went to Pompeii. Many disasters have occurred in the world, but few have provided as much joy for posterity. I believe that it would be difficult to imagine anything more interesting. [...] We met there a cheerful and pleasant group of Neapolitans, very straightforward people of a happy disposition. We dined at Torre Annunziata, at a table arranged at the edge of the sea. It was a beautiful day, and we had a good view of the delightful panorama of Castellammare and Sorrento. All of the people there were happy to dwell in such places; some of them said that without a view of the sea, it would be impossible to live. All that I require is that this image remain in my spirit, and I will return happily, when the time comes, to my mountainous homeland." (Goethe, 1787)

Once you reach the crowd of strolling peddlers and the restaurants clustered before the entrance to the excavations of Pompeii, it will be difficult for you to recognize the destination of so many travelers of the Grand Tour. A visitor, even before he or she enters the digs, must have considerable powers of imagination to succeed in perceiving, under the present-day appearance of things, the aspect that these places must have had up until a few decades ago. What you now see is the product of cultural models which, since the end of World War II, with responses and interventions tied to various places and times, have created the physiognomy and image of the chief monuments of Italy.

Frescoes of herms and fountains in the Casa del Bracciale d'Oro, Pompeii

The "star" of this route is Mt. Vesuvius, in part because it was due to its eruption that the cities of Pompeii, Herculaneum, Oplonti, and Stabiae were preserved, unrivaled anywhere on earth. The drive around the volcano presents considerable interest in terms of landscape and environment (the area, horribly devastated by recent fires, should soon be transformed into a protected park) and in terms of the history of art, for the many villas built, especially along the coast, between the 18th and 19th c., for the early-Christian monuments of Cimitile and Nocera, for the architecture of the 15th and early-16th c. in Somma Vesuviana and Nola, and for the sanctuary, or Santuario della Madonna dell'Arco, of considerable importance, along with the renowned festival, or Festa dei Gigli of Nola, for its aspects of folklore.

Among the obligatory destinations, however, are also Pompeii and Herculaneum, ancient cities that are unique for the ways in which they were destroyed yet preserved; here too the history of the excavations themselves is a phenomenon to be considered as epochal events in their own right, both because of the vast European repercussions and because of the clear ties between politics and culture, which allow us to reconstruct a slice of Italian and European history from the 18th c. to the present day. While digging a well in 1709, the Prince d'Elboeuf happened upon the *scaena* of the theater of Herculaneum; this

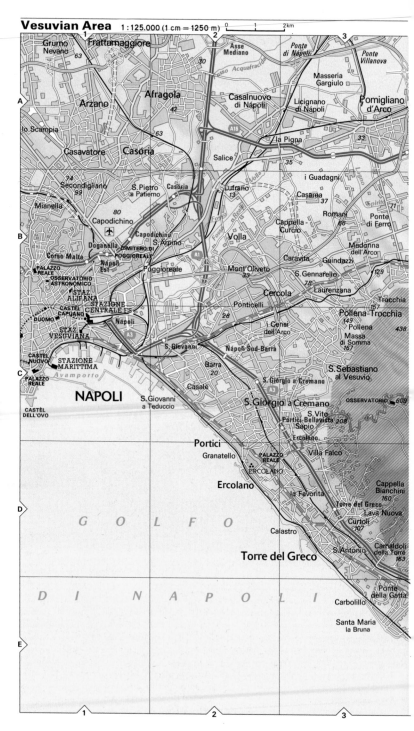

Vesuvian Area   1:125.000 (1 cm = 1250 m)

marked the beginning of a series of excavations by shafts and tunnels, in search of artworks and ancient marble to enrich the royal collections or for reuse in new buildings. This period culminated with the discovery of the Villa dei Papiri, which is still buried, and which was explored and despoiled through the "cunicoli." This was the first important period of Bourbon excavations, linked to the creation (1755) of the Accademia Ercolanese, an

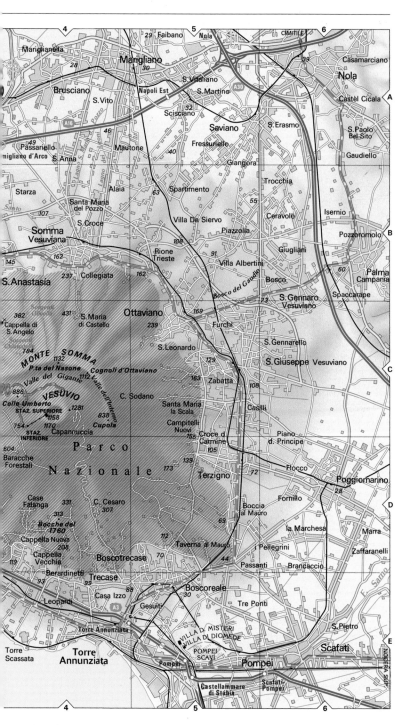

academy founded for scientific purposes and for the protection of the image of the new excavations. In the same period, there began the excavations of Pompeii, recollections of which, as various sources demonstrate, had survived. The circulation of prints and publications was linked to the birth of phenomena that were, in appearance, different, but which tended to the same final goals, such as, for instance, the production, in the porcelain man-

115

ufactories, of services of china which, donated to the principal courts of Europe, imitated the styles and iconography of an ancient world. These were the years of the first great collections, of a burgeoning market in antiquities, and of the earliest legislation to protect ancient sites and artifacts. The revolution, or Rivoluzione del 1799, and the arrival of the French occupying forces produced new enthusiasm for archaeological research. Despite the purges that ensued following the restoration, many of the bureaucratic innovations that were introduced remained. Excavations resumed in Herculaneum (1828-37), as if in defiance of the earlier French policy of concentrating on Pompeii, with the well-tested technique by this point of open-pit excavation which, in Herculaneum, clashed with the different ways in which the city was buried: Herculaneum was, in fact, buried under a wall of mud and volcanic detritus. Once this wall of ashy mud had solidified, the tufa-rich earth, be-

Aerial view of the crater of Mt. Vesuvius, inactive since 1943

coming hard and compact, protected buildings and furnishings from the molestation of thieves and created ideal conditions for the preservation of organic substances, especially wood, and – as a result – of the structures of the roofs and the supports of the upper floors. What emerges is a particularly detailed image of everyday life in ancient times, as well as complex and costly problems of conservation. Atop the ancient Campanian town – of which the memory had never entirely been lost – a modern town grew up, which, then as now, hindered the continuation of the digs. The Savoy monarchy could not fail to focus its attention on issues of such worldwide interest as the excavation of the Vesuvian cities and, after the purchase of new land, in 1869, in almost perfect synchronousness with the birth of a united Italy, under the supervision of Fiorelli, the excavation of Herculaneum was resumed, with the emergence of old and new problems of planning and, above all, conservation. The same operation was undertaken under the new Fascist government, and, from 1927 on, under the supervision of Maiuri, the excavations proceeded apace: it was that particular campaign that, for the most part, brought the archaeological area to its present configuration. Nowadays, many of the problems of the archaeological exploration of the Vesuvian cities remain unchanged, and especially the question of land management and the necessity of preserving structures that, protected for centuries by their snug volcanic blankets, began to decay much more rapidly once they were exposed to the light of day and to the air. As a result, there was a radically different idea of how to use these monumental areas and of just what their significance should be, and the new requirements, which require the preservation "on the site" of the furnishings of the homes, led to new efforts in planning and preservation. The chief efforts of the present day, therefore, are not so much focused on the quest for new residences in the context of the urban enclosures, as much as efforts to improve the conservation of these sites, with special explorations in the area of historical reconstruction, the protection of the environment, and an understanding of the ancient ecosystem.

6.1 The area around Mount Vesuvius

The itinerary begins in the eastern outskirts of Naples, and then continues, along the state road, or Statale 18, toward San Giorgio a Cremano, Portici, Herculaneum, and Torre del Greco, along a line of 24 km, without an interruption in the urban build-up. This first stretch, in which you will tour the excavations of Herculaneum, is marked by the presence of the Vesuvian villas, revolving around the royal residence in Portici, and culminates, between Herculaneum and Torre del Greco, in the so-called Miglio d'Oro, or golden mile, where many of the most important villas stand. From Herculaneum begins the easiest road for the excursion up to the crater of Mt. Vesuvius.

From Torre Annunziata you will leave the coast, and head toward Pompeii, and from there you may choose to take a detour (we recommend using the highway, or "autostrada") toward Nocera.

The state road, or Statale 268, on the slopes of Mt. Vesuvius, runs through towns, overlooking the plain of the Sarno, in which there is a less overwhelming sense of development. After 2 km you reach Boscoreale, where you can see the ruins of a Roman villa, whose rooms were largely intended for the production and storage of wine, an activity that is still important in this area, especially in the adjoining town of Boscotrecase and in Terzigno (where there are ruins of five Roman villas), where, in the 18th-c. Villa Bifulco, there is a well preserved vintner's cellar, or "cellaio." You will then pass through San Giuseppe Vesuviano and Ottaviano, flourishing industrial towns (textiles industry) on the slopes of the Monte Somma, and, with a detour onto the Statale 367, you will reach Nola and Cimitile.

Portici

This town, largely modern in appearance, has a particularly high population density (elev. 29 m, pop. 65,319) and has been greatly developed over the past few decades. Founded in the Middle Ages, it preserves only a few structures that date back prior to the terrible eruption of 1631, while the majority of its historical and artistic heritage dates from the Bourbon era.

From the Croce del Lagno a little road, on the right, runs down toward the sea where, on a lava-stone platform that extends out beyond the coastline, there stand the industrial sheds of the former locomotive factory established at the behest of Ferdinand II of Bourbon in 1840, a year after the inauguration of the railroad that

united Naples with the Villa Reale di Portici. In this factory, which remained operative until a few decades ago, you may now visit (since 1982) the railroad museum, or Museo Ferroviario di Pietrarsa* which features locomotives, exhibition panels, and old tools that illustrate the history of the Reale Opificio Meccanico of Pietrarsa. At the end of the central boulevard, note a cast-iron statue of King Ferdinand II.

You will then return to the state road, or Statale (in Portici, Corso Garibaldi) which is lined by villas that have been devastated, more savagely than elsewhere, by wildcat development, the break-up and sale of gardens, and neglect. At no. 129 is the Villa Lauro-Lancellotti, by Schiantarelli (1776); the large square, at the intersection with Via Diaz – bounded by an exedra that culminates in decorated pillars – is all that remains of the Palazzo dei Principi della Riccia; not far away (no. 115), is the 19th-c. elevation of the Villa Menna, built in the 18th c.; as you continue along, you will go by (nos. 61-85) the long facade of Palazzo Ruffo di Bagnara (1720), at the end of which stands the solemn, austere Epitaffio di Portici, erected just a few months after the terrible eruption of 1631 along Via Regia at the point in which the damage caused by the catastrophe begin to appear most evident. If you turn in to Via Gianturco you will then head down to the marina, or Porticciolo del Granatello, where, overlooking the sea, stands the Villa d'Elboeuf, to which two stories have been added, and with two exterior stairways leading up to the main floor; it was built (1711) by Sanfelice for the prince who began the excavation of Herculaneum. The center of Portici is the Piazza S. Ciro, at the end of Via Garibaldi, or else, if you start at the Granatello, along the Corso Umberto I, built in 1881 through the lower park of the Reggia. Overlooking the square is the church of S. Ciro, consecrated in 1642 and enlarged in the 18th c. (paintings by L. Giordano and G. Bonito); facing it are the ruins of the Palazzo dei Principi di Stigliano (16th c.). The area behind the church corresponds to the oldest part of the city, with small and winding lanes, in which the popular market, or "mercatino," is held. Among these lanes, at Via Marconi 49, is the Villa Meola (1724), attributed to D. A. Vaccaro, a delightful example of Neapolitan Rococo, with a theatrical open staircase over the green garden in the rear; in Via Arlotta (n. 42) you may note the Palazzo Perrelli, one of the oldest buildings, renovated in the neoclassical style.

After you pass the Palazzo Reale (on the right, note the *Villa Maltese* by D. A. Vaccaro, redecorated in the 19th c.), the road enters the township of Herculaneum. In Via Università (nos. 48-54) is the *Palazzo Mascabruno*, incorporated (1740-54) into the complex of the Reggia, or palace, much in the same way that, at no. 93, the *Palazzo Valle* was transformed in 1787 into a barracks, or Caserma della Guardia Reale; note the portal, adorned with equine protoma. All of these structures are linked to the **Palazzo Reale**, and line the road that, after crossing through the large courtyard with the appearance and functions of a "place royale," continues toward Herculaneum. Its construction was closely bound up with the intentions of King Charles and Queen Maria Amalia to pursue the tendency of the Neapolitan aristocracy of building their suburban residences at the foot of the great volcano, increasing, with this decision of

Entrance to the Parco della Reggia, Portici

theirs, the concentration at Portici of many the villas that were built thereafter. This decision was encouraged, as well, by the resumption of excavations at Herculaneum, under the patronage of the king himself, who established a museum for the finds in the Palazzo Caramanico, a building that was later incorporated into the "reggia," or palace. The work, begun in 1738 by Medrano, was carried out, from 1741 on, according to the plans of Canevari, and was completed with the subsequent contributions of L. Vanvitelli and F. Fuga. Currently this is the building of the agrarian studies department, or Facoltà di Agraria, of the Università di Napoli. The building is structured around the courtyard-qua-square, and is set in a park, divided by the palace itself, into two sectors, one lying toward Vesuvius, the other toward the sea. Beneath the first viaduct is the portal of the royal chapel, or *Cappella Reale*, built in 1749 with the transformation of the existing little court theater, or Teatrino di Corte,

that was called for in the design by Canevari. From the courtyard, it is possible to glimpse the idea that inspired the design of the entire complex, defined by long visual perspectives in accordance with the principle of "infinite perspective," which can also be found in the design of the palace, or Reggia di Caserta. At Portici there is an intersection of two principal axes of perspective: the first, running through the two opposing viaducts, is formed by the very direction of the road itself which, at the center of the courtyard, extends toward the parks with a new view, from Vesuvius toward the sea, filtered through the diaphragm of the porticoed atriums. From the atrium on the right, one can enter the lower sector, with the facade facing the sea, preceded by a broad semicircular terrace, from which two "pinzer" ramps run down toward the park, built by F. Geri. In the atrium, a large staircase with architectural perspectives by V. Re (1750) leads to the main floor, where the first two halls have decorations by the same artist, and, in the vaults, frescoes by C. Gamba; the following rooms were redecorated under the rule of Murat. In the setting of the university department, or Facoltà di Agraria, there is a Chinese cabinet, with mosaic flooring taken from Herculaneum, and the *Chinese hall* ("sala cinese"), now used as the main lecture hall, or Aula Magna. In the uphill wing, one can observe, from the loggias toward Vesuvius, the radial design of the avenues that make up the *garden*, just before the *upper park*; at the intersection of the avenues is the fountain of swans, or *Fontana dei Cigni*, by G. Canart, with statues taken from the excavations of Herculaneum. Beyond the garden extends the upper park, planted in the lava flow of 1631. In the dense grove of holm oaks, Ferdinand IV ordered the construction of a ball court, with bleachers and a pavilion, now little more than a ruin, and a castle, a small-scale reproduction of the fortress, or Fortezza di Capua, used in feigned military exercises.

Herculaneum

As it crosses the little city (elev. 44 m, pop. 61,233) the street takes the name of Corso Resina (the name of the town built on the lava that buried Herculaneum, still in use until a few years ago). Along this "corso" are a number of other 18th-c. villas; at no. 11 is the *Palazzo Granito di Belmonte*, with a theatrical open stairway overlooking the garden behind the villa and the sea; at no. 61 is the *Palazzo Correale* and, across the way (no. 68), *Palazzo Tarascone*, with an unusual octagonal courtyard.

As you continue, you will reach the excavations of the city buried in the eruption of A.D. 79 (see itinerary 6.2 on p. 123). Immediately afterward begins the stretch of the old Via Regia that, between Resina and Torre del Greco, was known as the Miglio d'Oro, or golden mile, for the beauty of the setting and the presence of lovely villas set in large parks (partly preserved).

At no. 296 is the Villa Aprile, dating from the early 18th c., and renovated, with respect for the original layout, during the early 19th c.; the splendid park, which was already lavishly decorated with statues and fountains, was embellished in the typical Romantic style with a little open-air theater (transformed into fish pond at the turn of the 20th c.), a fake ruin of a Doric temple, a wooden chalet, and a little manmade lake, with a waterfall that tumbles down from a fake ruined medieval tower.

Across the way is (no. 283) the *Villa Campolieto**, the most famous of all the Vesuvian villas. Begun in 1755 by Gioffredo for the Sangro di Casacalenda and completed by Luigi and Carlo Vanvitelli, it suffered serious damage during World War II and the long successive abandonment. Restored in 1982, it now houses various cultural events. Beyond the entrance (often the entrance is from the garden on the right) is the luminous vestibule opening onto the courtyard and the garden. On the left is a stairway designed by L. Vanvitelli which, as at the Reggia di Caserta, leads to the upper vestibule, covered by an elliptical dome. Many of the rooms in the villa are frescoed, by F. Fischetti, the Magri, and J. Cestaro. The handsome circular courtyard is bounded by a colonnaded portico atop which is a terrace-belvedere; on the left are the 18th-c. stables.

Not far away, at no. 291, is *La Favorita**, a villa built (1768) by F. Fuga for the prince, or Principe di Jaci, later part of the royal estates. The queen Maria Carolina describe it as "Favorita" in commemoration of her favorite villa of Schönbrunn and, as the royal residence, it was sumptuously furnished and enriched with new buildings and pavilions arranged in the large park. The facade is a variation from the usual scheme, since it does not feature a central main entrance, but rather two simple side doors, beyond which extend the boulevards that lead to the foot of the imposing semicircular staircase set on the front overlooking the garden.

The climb up to Mt. Vesuvius

The activity of the volcano, the "youngest" one in Campania, began roughly 12,000 years ago and, according to reconstructions offered by geologists, the original crater must have been simply huge, comprising a single mountainous formation with just one peak, the Monte Somma. A long period of dormancy transformed the Somma into a quiet mountain (which may have risen as high as 2,000 m), covered with forests and vineyards, which must not have caused excessive concern to the population that in the meanwhile had set up housekeeping at the foot of the volcano. The calm was brusquely interrupted by the tremendous eruption of A.D. 79 which buried Herculaneum, Pompeii, and Stabiae; on that occasion the violent explosions that accompanied the eruption cause the walls of the Somma to collapse, revealing a second cone that had formed on the base of the ancient crater. A series of minor eruptions, which dragged out until the 14th c., were followed by roughly three centuries of complete dormancy, to the point that the

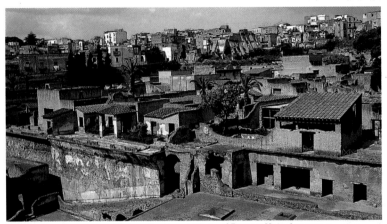

Modern housing encroaching on the excavations of Roman Herculaneum

mountain was once again covered with vegetation; but in 1631 the activity of the volcano resumed, with considerable violence. Since then, there have been numerous other eruptions, including the eruption of 1794, which destroyed Torre del Greco, as well as the long activity of effusion, which began in 1871 and culminated in the eruption of 1906, which halted only at Boscotrecase and Torre Annunziata, and the most recent, in 1944, in where there was a collapse of the upper walls of the crater, and the disappearance of the distinctive sharp smoking cone. The volcanic complex today possesses two peaks, separated by a little saddle at an elevation of roughly 700 m, the Somma (elev. 1,132 m), a surviving portion of the original volcano, and Vesuvio, or Vesuvius (elev. 1,281 m). The fumaroles, which emerge both on the interior and the exterior of the crater, constitute the only trace of present-day volcanic activity, but the dangers of a new eruption are today considerably aggravated by the high concentration of urban centers on the slopes of the volcano.

The easiest way up to the summit begins near the highway exit ("casello autostradale") for Herculaneum. Drive over the highway and you will intersect with Via Cozzolino, an easy road running midway up the slope, with fine views of the Gulf of Naples, and then you will continue along with steep switchback curves until you reach the *Osservatorio Vesuviano* (elev. 609 m), built in 1845 at the behest of Ferdinand II, from the large square in front of which you have a fine view over the dense development below, and of the looming flank of the volcano. Once you return to the road, which runs up through the lava of the most recent eruptions, you will reach a fork in the road (elev. 831 m): turn to the left, and you will reach elevation 1,017 m (a vast esplanade with a wonderful panoramic view), and from here you can climb up to the crater on foot; the crater is about 200 meters deep, and has a maximum diameter of about 600 meters. The immense *vista** embraces the entire coastline, from the Gulf of Gaeta to the Sorrento peninsula.

Torre del Greco

Repeatedly destroyed by eruptions of Mt. Vesuvius (particularly savage were the eruptions of 1631 and 1794), the city (elev. 43 m, pop. 99,556) was always rebuilt, and grew primarily along the coast, while in the more modern part, on the slopes of the neighboring volcano, a considerable number of villas have been built, partially hidden by the dense vegetation of the parks. The town takes its name from one of the watchtowers built at the behest of Frederick II along the littoral strip and from the cultivation of wine grapes, which in this area, produce the so-called "vino greco," or Greek wine. It is renowned for its coral craftsmen, who follow a tradition that dates back centuries, and in the past brought the city such wealth the Ferdinand IV called it the "golden sponge" of the kingdom.

On *Corso Vittorio Emanuele* – taken from the old Via Regia – note (nos. 92-96) the *Palazzo Vallelonga*, dating back to the turn of the 18th c.; facing it, Via C. Battisti runs down, among modern constructions, to the sea and the port, cutting through the oldest part of the city, very picturesque but sadly neglected. When you return to the Corso Vittorio Emanuele you will come to the intersection with Via Vittorio Veneto, central axis of the modern expansion; after you cross the Piazza Palomba where, adjoining the art institute, or Istituto d'Arte, is the museum of coral, or *Museo del Corallo*, you will turn into Via del Purgatorio; in this street (no. 122) stands the *Villa del Cardinale*, built in 1746 and deed to Cardinal Spinelli, archbishop of Naples, who made it his summer residence, a tradition which his successors found agreeable and preserved; on the interior, frescoes attributed to the Gamba family.

Torre Annunziata

The city (elev. 10 m, pop. 50,744), which stands on the ruins of the ancient city of Oplonti, destroyed by the eruption of A.D. 79, acquired its present name about the middle of the 15th c., due to the presence of a chapel dedicated to Our Lady of the Annunciation, or Cappella dell'Annunziata, around which the two towns expanded, like Torre del Greco, due to the construction of a watchtower to warn of the arrival of Saracen raids.

In 1758 Charles of Bourbon built a weapons factory here (the ruins of it can still be seen in the Piazza Morrone). The construction, entrusted to F. Sabatini, a pupil of Vanvitelli, was completed by Fuga. The energy needed to run this industrial complex was provided by a manmade canal, dating from the end of the 16th c., which brought water from the springs of the Sarno to the edge of the city, driving numerous mills as well, another traditional activity – that of milling – that was closely linked to the flourishing food industry that developed in Torre Annunziata in the 18th and 19th c. Today, there are only a few pasta mills surviving, as compared to the 150 that were counted in the period immediately following World War II. Near the sea are the *Terme Vesuviane Nunziante*, spas named after a general who, in 1831, unearthed the ruins of a Roman bath complex, and who ordered the construction of the spa that still operates here. We should also point out the church of Carmine (Corso Vittorio Emanuele), with an early-16th-c. panel painting; the sanctuary, or *Santuario di Maria SS. della Neve* (Via Alfonso De Simone), dedicated to the protectress of the city, with a panel of the Annunciation, in the apse, and a 16th-c. basin, as well as the church of the SS. *Giuseppe e Teresa* (Piazza Cesaro), with a canvas depicting *St. Theresa Imploring Holy Intervention for the End of the Eruption of 1631.*

Of greater interest are certainly the **excavations of Oplonti***. In the center of the city, excavations have unearthed two villas, said to have belonged to Poppea and Crassus. The first villa is an immense complex (the central nucleus of which dates back to the 1st c. B.C.) that was uninhabited at the time of its destruction, probably by the earthquake of A.D. 62; it presents a splendid *pictorial decoration** in the so-called second style, large loggias, and an immense pool, adorned with marble sculptures. The second villa would seem to be, given the vast number of amphorae found here, an aristocratic residence that was converted into an emporium or warehouse for the storage of wine.

Plaster cast of a resident of Pompeii smothered by ash in A.D. 79

Pompeii

Even following the eruption in A.D. 79, which destroyed the ancient Roman city (see itinerary 6.3 on p. 127), this site was not entirely abandoned, and was repopulated with the formation of a new village, known as the Valle Casale, which was a feudal holding of the Caracciolo and Piccolomini families. In the 17th c., the marshes created by the waters of the Sarno forced the inhabitants to abandon the city, which did not revive until many years later, around the excavations and the sanctuary, or *Santuario della Madonna del Rosario*, a renowned site for pilgrimages, built from 1876 on (completed in 1939), and now in the center of the city (elev. 14 m, pop. 26,118), in a vast square, with a monument to the founder, the Avvocato Bartolo Longo.

We would advise detouring toward a major town of ancient Roman Campania, Nuceria Alfaterna. The Longobards of Benevento elevated it to the status of a county ("contea"), but in 1137 it was devastated by the troops of Roger the Norman; it was a feudal land holding of the Carafa family until 1648, and, beginning in 1850, it was divided into the two towns of Nocera Inferiore and Nocera Superiore.

At **Nocera Superiore** (elev. 70 m, pop. 23,072) is the church of *S. Maria Maggiore**, an early-Christian baptistery, probably dating back to the end of the 6th c., with a circular plan and three apses (of which only one survives) and a deambulatory, covered with a barrel vault, and marked off by a line of monolithic twin columns that support the arches on which rests the central dome, rebuilt after the collapse, caused by the eruption of 1944. The baptismal font is surrounded by a ring of eight columns, only five of which survive, set on a small wall at the edge of the basin. The importance of the monument is increased by the vast array of stylistic references (North African, Roman, Palestinian, Syriac, and even Gallic).

Boscoreale

From Torre Annunziata via Boscotrecase you will reach Boscoreale (elev. 55 m, pop. 27,831), famous for the villas discovered – and stripped of silver and frescoes, which are now in the Louvre and other foreign museums – between 1897 and 1900. The *rustic villa**, one of the largest in the Vesuvian area, is known as "La Pisanella"; documentation and finds linked to the villa are contained in the new archaeological museum, or **Museo Archeologico***.

Nola

A feudal holding of the Orsini family until 1528, Nola (elev. 34 m, pop. 32,613) was one of the most important cities in Campania under the Roman empire. Its name comes from the foundation (5th c. B.C.) of the new Samnite city, Novla, on the site of an older settlement of Ausonian origin. It declined following its destruction by the Vandals (A.D. 455). To St. Paul the Lesser, the bishop of the city from A.D. 409 on, who is said to have invented bells, the "Festa dei Gigli" is dedicated; this is one of the best known and most spectacular celebrations in Campania, and commemorates the return of the bishop from Africa and the lilies tossed by the people of Nola along his path: on the Sunday after 22 June, enormous wooden spires, some 30 meters tall, are borne in procession through the streets of the city.

At the center of the city stands the *Duomo*, or cathedral, founded at the end of the 14th c. and rebuilt, following a fire in 1861. In the vast interior, with a nave and two side aisles, separated by monolithic columns made of granite, there is a *pulpit* with reliefs attributed to Giovanni da Nola, whose tomb is in the chapel, or Cappella di S. Paolino, where the relics of the saint are also preserved. In the ancient crypt, supposedly consecrated by St. Felix, the first bishop and the patron saint of Nola, with the relics of the saint there are also numerous marbles and reliefs from the Middle Ages and the Renaissance.

The square dedicated to Giordano Bruno, who was born in Nola, is dominated by the white mass of the *Palazzo Orsini**, built in 1461 with the use of recycled material from one of the city's two amphitheaters (very few traces of which survive); the long facade, covered with its whole length with an inscription, presents an elegant portal and lavish carved decorations in the cornices of the windows. Alongside, on the left, is the 16th-c. *church of the Gesù*, the work of G. de Rosis; on the interior are paintings by M. Pino and G. Imparato and a 15th-c. *Crucifix*. Facing it from across the way is the *church of the Misericordia*, or of *S. Biagio*, dating from the 14th c., with a noteworthy Gothic portal; it may prove interesting to enter the lane, or "vicolo" along the side of the church (note the marble fragments set in the walls of the houses that stand on either side) where you can observe the exterior of the apse; also worthy of note is the small campanile. On the interior, note the 14th-c. frescoes and the Renaissance tombs attributed to G. da Nola and A. Caccavello. In the base of the *Palazzo Covoni*, built in the Renaissance, in Via G. Bruno, you may see fragments of Roman decorations. Overlooking the vast Piazza d'Armi (literally, parade ground) are the Bourbon barracks built to plans by L. Vanvitelli.

Cimitile

Farming town not far from Nola (elev. 40 m, pop. 6,874), formed in the wake of the many pilgrimages to the tomb of St. Felix (or San Felice).

Adjoining the parish church of S. Felice in Pincis is the entrance to the important **complex of early-Christian basilicas***,

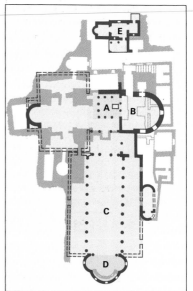

Plan of the basilicas of Cimitile

presently closed (for restoration work that has been going on for decades now) despite the fact that it represents, in terms of complexity and importance of the ruins, the most illustrious piece of 5th-c. architecture in all of southern Italy, linked to the prestigious figure of St. Paul the Lesser, who worked (A.D. 401-402) on the structures built a few decades earlier atop the *martyrium* of St. Felix and in the funerary area surrounding it, probably built over the course of the 2nd c., and both presenting the variety of characteristics that could be expected in a cemetery center and place of pilgrimage dating back prior to the reign of Constantine. The tomb of the martyr was marked by columns and standing around it was a small basilica with two apses on the short side, differing in size and chronology. In the cemetery area there are also two chapels, one of which was obtained by recycling Roman structures. St. Paul the Lesser arranged to enlarge, order, and monumentalize the sanctuary of Felix, which already had a large hall of worship, along with the site of other smaller buildings. The *martyrium* then was enclosed by a square-plan aedicule, with recycled columns supporting round-head arches, adorned on interior and exterior by mosaics (A); facing it, with an orthogonal orientation with respect to that of the little twin-apsed basilica (B), a larger basilica was built, and was probably already finished in A.D. 403. This basilica, linked to the aedicule – which thus came to constitute in every sense the center of the sanctuary – with a double triforium, had a nave and two side aisles, separated by columns (C) and ending in a raised apse with a triconch plan (D). On both sides of the new basilica with a single plan, there are two rooms, almost as if they were two chapels; the four cell were to be used for more secluded prayer, and were meant to offer a place – as St. Paul the Lesser himself puts it in the epistles – "*ad pacis aeternae requiem.*" Unlike the layout, which is reminiscent of models found in northern Africa, the masonry technique is that typical of local tradition, and makes use of the *opus listatum*.

Of the complex, which was later covered by stuccoes in the Baroque period, partially buried and then excavated and restored, the following elements have been uncovered: the *Basilica di S. Felice in Pincis*, of which survive the bases of the columns that supported the nave, while the apse was transformed in the 14th c., with a conversion into a chapel dedicated to St. John; the quadriporticus that lies before the basilica, with mosaic decorations, to which an apsed hall is linked, part of the older construction; the *Basilica dei SS. Martiri* (E), with a frescoed interior, is preceded by a porch (8th c.) with carved pillars.

6.2 The excavations of Herculaneum

The city occupied a promontory set between two streams, along a road that linked Naples with the Sorrento peninsula, and also served Pompeii. The morphology of the soil here was radically altered by the eruption of A.D. 79 and by subsequent volcanic events. Only a small section of the city has been explored and any final conclusions concerning its layout and specific aspects are premature. If we combine the information provided by the open-pit excavations with the information that we can gather from the documentation provided by the Bourbon-sponsored excavations done by shaft and tunnel ("cunicoli"), we can reconstruct a partial image of a city subdivided into regular *insulae*. To the north of the area excavated are a theater and what would seem to be a temple building; across the mountain stream is the Villa dei Papiri. Based on the sources as well, we can safely say that the city, smaller than Pompeii, was also less autonomous in political terms, even though it shared most of the major events. We know very little of early times here: we have none of the rich array of epigraphic and monumental documentation that allows us, in the case of Pompeii, to reconstruct an image of the pre-Roman city. Dionysius of Halicarnassus recalls that it was founded by Heracles, and that it was because of this origin that it took its name. Probably inhabited by an aboriginal population, it experienced in the 5th c. B.C. the same degree of instability and unrest that swept the rest of the region, and underwent Samnite occupation. It took an active part in the Social Wars, and was besieged and expunged by a representative of Sulla (89 B.C.). It became a *municipium*, and in the Roman era it acquired "residential" status. Under the rule of Augustus, of particular note was the munificence of M. Nonius Balbus, boss of the city. The earthquake of A.D. 62 damaged the city, just as it did Pompeii.

The city is organized into streets running parallel with the coast (*decumani*) which in-

Interior of the Casa di Nettuno e Anfitrite

tersect at right angles with *cardines*, or streets running toward the fortified southernmost boundary where, for each of them, there is an open gate leading down to the sea. The area of the forum must have stood close to the *decumanus maximus* (northernmost boundary of the area that has been excavated). The city walls, traces of which remain to the south, were soon demolished by the new and patrician villas of Roman times that sprang up between the city walls and the port. The city's houses have long attracted the interest of scholars, who have

Excavations of Herculaneum

1:2000 (1 cm = 20 m)

A3 km 1

Corso Ercolano

Entrance

Via Cortili

Decumano Massimo

Aula Superiore

Loggia

Casa del Salone Nero

Casa del Bicentenario

Casa d. Bel Cortile

Casa dei due Atri

Casa d. Atrio Corinzio

Casa d. Nettuno

Casa d. Sacello di legno

Palestra

Piscina

Casa del Mobilio carbonizzato

Aula Absidata

Casa di Galba

Casa d. Telaio

Casa con giardino

Pistrinum

Terme

Casa d. Gran Portale

Casa Sannitica

Vestibolo d. Palestra

Decumano Inferiore

Casa del Tramezzo di legno

Pistrinum

Casa a Graticcio

Vicolo

Giardino

Casa d. Genio

Casa d. Scheletro

Casa d. Erma di bronzo

Casa d. Alcova

Casa del Rilievo di Telefo

Casa d. Gemma

Casa d'Argo

Casa dell'Albergo

Casa dell'Atrio a mosaico

Casa dei Cervi

Casa di Aristide

Sacra Marina

Sepolcro di M. Nonio Balbo

Terme Suburbane

Sacelli

Area Sacra

124

noted patterns of plan and architecture that are particularly articulated and modern. More than is the case in Pompeii, there are cases of stacked stories, which transform the original concept of the aristocratic home, arranged along a horizontal plane, opening onto an open-air porticoed courtyard, the property of a single family. In Pompeii, as well, the latest phases clearly showed signs of the fragmentation of the original homes into several apartments,

but at Herculaneum the phenomenon seemed to lead fairly rapidly as well to new architectural forms, described in sources and documented by archaeological finds in Rome and Ostia, resulting in houses subdivided into several apartments, on several stories, replacing the peristyle and atrium with the central courtyard.

The southern insulae. From the entrance, you can reach the southern sector, which offers a broad elevation consisting of homes of the well-to-do which, looming over the for-tifications, extended down toward the wa-terfront area, opening out theatrically to-ward the sea, which is now further away than it was in ancient times. You will im-mediately encounter the *Casa dell'Albergo* (D1), badly damaged by ancient and modern occurrences. It is one of the largest houses, with a private bathroom with a decoration in the second style. Note, behind the peri-style, the terrace supported by vaults, and extending toward the sea. Gardens and rooms with panoramic views can also be found in the neighboring house with a **mosaic atrium*** (D2), in which the standard se-quence of *atrium-tablinum* is accompanied by the residential and reception area, with rooms arranged around a porticoed gar-den with intercolumnar masonry, ending to the south in a large *triclinium* and a loggia. If you return to the Cardo IV, you can visit the Casa a Graticcio and the Casa del Tramezzo di Legno, which expand the array of typologies of houses in Herculaneum. The **Casa a Graticcio*** (C1-2) offers an ex-ample of a multi-family dwelling on two sto-ries, characterized by the rational use of the available space, clear intended for rental. The balcony, which overlooks the street, was supported by columns based on the sidewalk, a distinctive characteristic of the private dwellings of Herculaneum. Its name comes from the style of masonry employed: wooden load-bearing frames filled in with masonry in *opus incertum*. The **Casa del Tramezzo di Legno*** (C1-2), with an an-cient layout, preserves its elevation right up to the level of the third floor, as well as the flooring of the atrium in *opus signinum*, and the rigid and almost austere articulation of the rooms around the central axis of atrium-tablinum. It takes its name from the "ac-cordion" partition (or "tramezzo") that served to separate the two rooms. Behind it was a porticoed garden.

Insula V*. After the intersection with the lower *decumanus*, you can tour the **Casa Sannitica*** (C2), with a pre-Roman layout which preserves, in the entryway, the dec-oration in the first style and a fine specimen of a colonnaded atrium. In the context of the Insula V, there are various sorts of houses; we would point out the *Casa del Mobilio Carbonizzato* (B2), the *Casa di Nettuno e Anfitrite** (B2, a summer *triclinium* with mar-ble and mosaic decorations), the *Casa del Bel Cortile* (B2), the *Casa del Bicentenario** (B2, paintings in the fourth style), the *Casa dell'Atrio Corinzio* (B2), the *Casa del Sacel-lo di Legno* (B2), and the *Casa del Grande Portale* (C2).

The baths. Facing the Casa Sannitica is the Insula VI, occupied, in the southern sector, by the **baths*** (C1-2). The complex was sub-divided into a men's sector and a women's sector. From the Cardo IV one reaches vestibule of the women's baths, and from here to the *apodyterium* (dressing room, G) with mosaic flooring, depicting, in the cen-ter, a triton with a marine entourage. Next, in line, are the *tepidarium* (H) and the *cali-darium* (I). On the Cardo III was the entrance to the men's sector, flanked by a latrine. A narrow, elongated dressing room allowed visitors to head either for the *frigidarium* on the left (with around plan, and a dome paint-ed with a light blue background, with fish, C) or toward the succession of *tepidarium* (mo-saic floors with a replica of the triton found in the women's *apodyterium*, D) and *cali-darium* (E). The complex ended in an open porticoed area used as a gymnasium (A).

The *decumanus maximus** (A1-2). This sector has long aroused considerable in-terest, due to the high concentration of public buildings that surround it. One thing that we do know is that the forum was not far away. The large *plateia* (over 12 me-ters across) was reserved to foot traffic

Plan of the thermal baths, Herculaneum

alone. Along the north side there was a large porticoed building with *tabernae* and shops. The sector under exploration is closed off to the east by a large *apsed hall* (hypothetically interpreted as the temple of the Mater Deum; an inscription notes that it was restored at the direct command of Vespasian, and, like the Temple of Isis, it must have been located in this area) and by a *fountain* with the emblem of Heracles; to the west is an *arch* with four fornices, which must have supported a bronze quadriga, or chariot, of which numerous fragments have emerged from the excavations. Uphill, on the north elevation of the *decumanus*, in the 18th c., excavations were done, with the shaft and tunnel method ("cunicoli"), of a large public complex known as the *Basilica*; the building was stripped. Its function is anything but clear: the similarities in layout cause scholars to link it to the Building of Eumachia in Pompeii; the structure – of which, in modern times, the *chalcidicum* (the porticoed atrium) has been excavated – is known in its layout thanks to old prints and drawings. A large rectangular porticoed hall culminated in a wall with double apse. On the interior of this hall equestrian and honorary statues were found (two marble equestrian statues of M. Nonius Balbus and one in bronze; portrait statues of members of the imperial family) with pertinent inscriptions. Part of the sculptures and paintings that decorated the two apses and the smaller niches (Heracles and Telephus, Theseus, Achilles and Chiron, Marsyas and Olympus) are now in the Museo di Napoli.

Insula VII. In the northeast sector of the Insula VII, overlooking the *decumanus maximus* is a building that had already been thoroughly explored and stripped of its marble furnishings during the reign of the Bourbons. Probably, according to epigraphic evidence, this was the site of the college, or *Collegio degli Augustali*. On the opposite side of this same *cardo* is another public building, of questionable interpretation. With a nearly square plan and with a flat roof supported by four columns, the interior was later transformed, resulting in a smaller room (paintings with mythical depictions) set against the far wall. Probably, this was the site of the *curia* or else a place of worship. You may then walk down along the Cardo V where, on the left, through a monumental vestibule, you may enter the gymnasium, or *palaestra** (B-C3), used by the guilds of the young; at the center of the area, which was discovered and only partially excavated, is a cross-shaped pool, decorated in its center by a bronze fountain depicting a Hydra, the mythical monster vanquished by Heracles, twisting around a tree. The rectangular room, apsed at the center of the western side, was probably used in the worship of the Julian-Claudian family.

Toward the end of the Cardo V is the **Casa dei Cervi** (D2) which is articulated along a central axis which offers a view down toward the sea. It is named ("house of stags") after the discovery in the garden of two marble groups of stags attacked by dogs. In the house, there is also a statue of a *Satyr with a Wineskin* and another statue of a *Drunken Hercules* and, of special note, the decoration of the corridor with windows, in which it is possible to see a number of little figural paintings that survived the strippings of the Bourbon era. A *pergula* led onto the open-air terrace (*solarium*).

Insula Orientalis I. The entire Insula Orientalis I, to the left of the *cardo*, was subdivided into just two houses which, making best use of the differences in elevation, are structured on several different floors, some of them underground. Beyond the *Casa della Gemma* (D3), you should note in particular the **Casa del Rilievo di Telefo*** (D3). This house is built on two levels, in accordance with two contrasting axes, in order to accommodate the difference in elevation and to obtain the best possible exposure. From the entrance on the Cardo V one entered directly into the atrium, which took on elaborate forms through the addition of a peristyle to the customary Tuscan order. A corridor linked it with the lower terrace, upon which extended the porticoed garden. In the reception rooms, richly decorated with marble flooring and facings, the neo-Attic relief ("rilievo") was uncovered which gave this house its name. Outside of the walls, the **suburban area** extended. Set on a broad square, in a reserved area, was a statue of M. Nonius Balbus, proconsul and patron of the city during the rule of Augustus, and a funerary altar preserving a long inscription that recalls the merits and honors attributed by the city to the munificent patron. To the east extends the complex of the **suburban baths*** (D-E3). Through an atrium (to the right of which was one of the *praefurnia* meant for the heating of the rooms through the circulation of hot air in interstices in the floors, the walls, and the ceilings) one entered the *frigidarium*, with decorations in the fourth style. Then a waiting room, with fine stucco reliefs, led into the *calidarium* (apsed, with *labrum*, a basin for the splashing on of cold water, and a rectangular basin for hot baths) and the heated pool (*natatio*). A circular room with a conical ceiling was used as the sweat room, or *sudationes* (*laconicum*).

The theater. Outside of the enclosure walls surrounding the excavations, still buried, but accessible through the Bourbon "cunicoli," is the **theater** (entrance on the Corso Ercolano). The rich array of decorations was stripped in the 18th c. The theater was either built or restored by L. Annius Mammianus Rufus (reign of Augustus), whose name appears on the inscriptions set on the entrances, along with that of the architect Numisius. It has a semicircular buttressed *cavea*, with straight vaulted entrances (*parodoi*); also commemorated here was the munificence of M. Nonius Balbus.

6.3 The excavations of Pompeii

Pompeii stands on a sort of lava plateau, overlooking the port at the mouth of the River Sarno. In ancient times, the coastline was closer in and the river flowed nearer than it does now; volcanic events have partially shifted the river's course, eliminating the broad oxbow curve near which the city originally stood, and moving the river's mouth. The site is of considerable strategic importance; it was a point of passage for roads of regional importance, and it was a natural port for the towns further inland. The foundation of Pompeii seems to have been the result of a joint effort of the farming towns which, at the end of the 7th c. B.C., permanently occupied the coastal site best suited to trading and commerce. The first urban agglomerations date from the beginning of the 6th c. B.C. In archaic times, the city already occupied the entire surface of the future Roman town, integrating green areas and more built up areas within the city walls. The 5th c. B.C., a period of extreme instability in the history of southern Italy, has left very little documentation. This was a period of numerous and profound transformations, during which the most important coastal cities of Campanian fell into the hands of the Samnites. Something of the sort befell Pompeii and the subsequent documentation (4th/1st c. B.C.)

we have evidence in the so-called "campaign posters," inscriptions that were generally painted on walls, indicating the name of the candidate for office and his qualifications. The city received colony of veterans from the army of Sulla and the integration of these new elements into the social fabric took place without major trauma. In A.D. 62 the town was badly damaged in the earthquake: when, seventeen years later, it was buried in lava and lapilli (a rain of lava stones), it had the appearance of a large

Mosaic decorations in the Casa della Fontana Grande, Pompeii

offers exceedingly valuable epigraphic and monumental evidence that is useful in the reconstruction of the political and social life of a Samnite town. At the beginning of the 1st c. B.C., during the Social Wars it rose against the Romans and, in 89 B.C., capitulated. From 80 B.C. on it was governed by the magistracies typically found in Italic *municipia*. Of the lively political life of Pompeii,

construction yard: the main public and sacred buildings, in fact, had not yet been completely restored. The eruption froze the reconstruction and the new social transformations that the city was beginning to experience and to reflect in its material structure.

This itinerary is made up of four sections: the first illustrates the forum area, or Quartiere del Foro and the oldest parts of Pompeii; the second, Via dell'Abbondanza, the quarter of theaters and the amphitheater; the third, the large residences of the northern region; the fourth, the suburban area, with Via dei Sepolcri and the Villa dei Misteri.

The Quartiere del Foro, or quarter of the forum. After the ticket window, you may skirt the **city walls** and the southwestern suburbs. The city, from its foundation in the 6th c. B.C., extended over the entire hill (66 ha), and was fortified with an enclosure wall made of blocks of soft lava stone that, in the course of the 5th c. B.C., was modernized and replaced by a ring of walls built of limestone from the River Sarno, which was likewise used in the Samnite rebuilding of the walls, which added a large earth bas-

tion as well. During the age of Sulla, reconstructions and restorations were undertaken along the walls, with towers built in *opus incertum*. Along the stretch of wall near the gate, or Porta Marina, following the age of Sulla, villas were built that in part made use of the artificial terracing of the fortifications, and they expanded into the suburbs. In a location overlooking the sea, the room opened out onto one of the finest vistas available in the city. To the right of Porta Marina is an ample terrace, upon which stood the temple, or *Tempio di Venere*; set upon a buttressing stood the podium, surrounded on three sides by a portico. Subsequent work has modified its layout, but the sanctuary conserves its similarities to models that were common in Italy during the time of Sulla. The temple was built at the

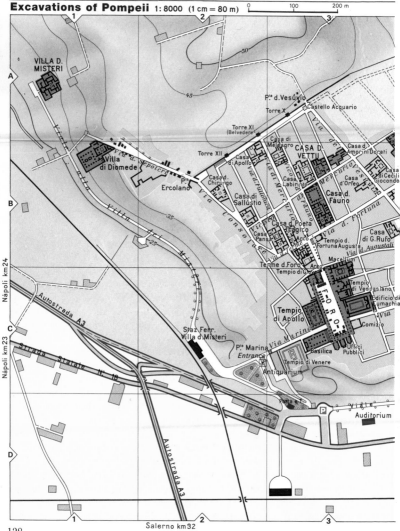

Excavations of Pompeii 1:8000 (1 cm = 80 m)

orders of Sulla; Venus was his tutelary deity, and the construction of a sanctuary dedicated to the goddess that had encouraged the rise and continued power of the dictator's family, in a prominent location near one of the entrances, must have taken on enormous significance for the city, which in those years received a colony of Roman veterans. The gate of **Porta Marina*** (C2-3), with a double fornix and vaulted walkways for pedestrians and for carriages, led into the oldest quarter of the city, the area of the Forum, or Zona del Foro.

The arrangement of the street grid which defines it, unusual in comparison with the more regular layout of other quarters, speaks clearly of a different history. The area bounded to the north by Via della Fortuna and to the east by Via Stabiana – one of the oldest roads running along the hill, naturally defined by angles of slope, and the urban section of a major road that linked the cities along the gulf to the Sorrento peninsula – was immediately studied as the earliest settlement, and defined with the German term of "Altstadt" (old city). Internally, it proved to be organized along a north–south axis that ran, along the eastern edge, through the area of the forum. Streets with a distinctive fish-bone layout ran along the sides, assuring that rainwater would run off, given their carefully calibrated slope. This was the most heavily urbanized area of the city which, for the most part, at this point, had an agrarian appearance and relatively few buildings. In Samnite times (beginning of the 3rd c. B.C.) new thoroughfare were built through the rest of

the city. The ancient Via Stabiana was re-aligned and straightened, and along it were built streets running west-east to assure the subdivision, through a network of smaller streets, into *insulae*, or blocks, and the interconnection of the various city gates.

Near the area of the forum is the **Sanctuary of Apollo** (C3). Its present-day arrangement is the result of restorations done in the wake of the earthquake of A.D. 62, but the general layout is still that of the Hellenistic period (2nd c. B.C.). Its size, which was larger in the archaic age, was reduced for the construction of the forum. A wall en-

Aerial view of the Forum, Pompeii, with the main causeway, Via dell'Abbondanza

closed the surface of the sanctuary, and a colonnaded portico enclosed a courtyard. The original tufa-stone columns, with Ionic capitals, were modernized with stucco, which altered their proportions and transformed the capitals into Corinthian capitals. The east face of the peribolus displays important features for the reconstruction of the history of the sanctuary. The old orientation of the temple fit badly in the new forum, and in order to mask this discrepancy, the sanctuary was linked with its area with a series of pillars of progressively greater thickness. Originally, on this side there were ten gates, a clear indicator of the

importance of the sanctuary in the life of the city. Along the porticoes were statues, including an Apollo the Archer and a bronze Artemis (the originals are in the Museo di Napoli). At the center of the courtyard, on a high podium, is the temple. Of particular interest is the floor of the cella, which still preserves the dedicatory inscription in Oscan. The podium was built with blocks of stone and elements of cut stone from older structures (6th c. B.C.). On the front of the podium is the altar. Interesting dedication, in Latin, which commemorates magistrates of the period of the colony founded by Sulla, among whom is M. Porcius, who also contributed to the construction of the odeon and the amphitheater. On the left, a marble column, part of a sundial arrangement, a votive gift of the *duumvires*, as the inscription tells us.

Of the **Forum*** (B-C3), the commercial, economic, and political heart of the city, we know only the latest history, while we know very little about its earliest versions (6th/3rd c. B.C.). Between the 2nd and 1st c. B.C. is when the earliest monumental structures known appear to have been built. A Latin inscription commemorates the erection of porticoes; the square, in fact, was partly bounded by tufa-stone colonnades, on two levels and in a double order (Doric and Ionic); the inscription, which probably dates back to the third decade of the 1st c. B.C., referred to these structures or part of them. In this same phase, the flooring consisted of slabs of tufa stone and, was, at a lower level, linked with the porticoes by three steps. At the far end was the temple, later transformed into a *Capitolium*, but in origin, perhaps dedicated to Jove alone. On the long eastern side, there were modest structures (perhaps *tabernae*), later replaced by buildings of worship and of Eumachia. Perhaps as early as this phase, the short southern side was occupied by *comitium* and by the public buildings linked to political activities. On the long western side were the basilica and the sanctuary of Apollo. In the Julian-Claudian period, in accordance with principles based on the models used in Rome and on imperial munificence, the square was sheathed in white travertine. The floor level was raised and paved in a new material, and the porticoes were redone: both projects were left unfinished. The square was endowed with a podium for orators and, to the south, with bases for statues and *donarii* (donations), modifying a system of decorations that may already have existed in part during the Republican period. The northern elevation of the forum was closed off by the bulk of the *Capitolium* and framed between two arches possibly dedicated to Nero and Drusus. A further arch to the north linked the forum to Via di Mercurio (B2-3).

The **Basilica***, used for the administration of justice and the exercise of trade, was built as early as the second half of the 2nd c. B.C. After you pass through the *chalcidicum* (entry portico), there are five doors leading into a large colonnaded setting, with a high podium surmounted by Corinthian columns at the far end, flanked by symmetrical rooms; in this sector was the *tribunal*.

If you return to the forum, you can tour the southern sector of it, occupied by three rooms which were the offices of the chief magistracies and, perhaps, housed the archives; like the *comitium*, located near the intersection with Via dell'Abbondanza, they were thoroughly restored and renovated after A.D 62. Along the eastern side you will find the **Building of Eumachia***. On the architrave of the porticoes of the forum, corresponding to the entrance, was the dedicatory inscription, repeated near the lesser entrance on Via dell'Abbondanza, mentioning the main architectural articulations of the complex, built at the behest of the priestess Eumachia. The *chalcidicum*, or porticoed entrance, was identified in the portico of the forum overlooking the building, closed on its sides by transennae and adorned with statues. On the facade were niches, including two which could be reached by steps, and were probably used by auctioneers during public auctions. On the interior, around a courtyard, there ran a portico that was further enclosed by a covered corridor; on the far end there stood a large niche with a statue of the *Concordia Augusta*, now headless, but which must have had the features of Livia. On a line with it, but not immediately visible, in the covered corridor, is a statue of Eumachia, dedicated by the *fullones*, the workers in wool (original now in the Museo di Napoli). The complex can be dat-

ed to the reign of Tiberius, with later remodeling. Note in particular the *marble frieze** which frames the entrance, belonging to the original phase and showing signs of recycling. The building, which bore on its main elevation statues and *elogia* of the forefathers of the *Gens Julia*, with clear reference to the public buildings of Augustan Rome, probably served a commercial and economic function.

Next come buildings of worship; the first, perhaps dedicated to the Genius of Vespasian, presents – at the far end of the courtyard – a sacellum preceded by a carved altar; the second, built during the reign of Nero, was probably dedicated to the public Lares.

The northeast corner is occupied by the **macellum**, or marketplace that, in accordance with the most common typology, features regular rows of *tabernae*, set around a porticoed courtyard. Opposite the entrance are three rooms: the central room was destined to the honors of supplying the imperial household, while rooms for the sale of meat and fish stood on either side. At the center was an area for the cleaning and sale of fish. This building already existed in the 2nd c. B.C., but it acquired its present appearance following renovations in the Julian-Claudian era, and after A.D. 62. On the northwestern wall of the courtyard, there are pictorial decorations in the fourth style, with mythological depictions.

The true perspectival vanishing point of the forum was the **Capitolium**; founded in the second half of the 2nd c. B.C., at the beginning of the 1st c., it underwent partial reconstruction, and the cult of the Capitoline Triad was introduced (Jove, Juno, and Minerva). Set on a tall podium, accessible by a flight of stairs along which stood the altar in the new layout, was the temple, with columns only on the facade (prostyle) and preceded by a large vestibule (pronaos). In the cella, with three aisles, is the base for the statues of the cult. On the sides of the stairway, note the bases of equestrian statues.

After you pass through the honorary arches, you will reach the intersection between Via del Foro and Via della Fortuna, where, on the right, is the temple, or *Tempio della Fortuna Augusta* and, on the left, the baths, or **Terme del Foro** which, built as they were in the early years of the colony founded by Sulla, were surely part of the campaign of construction intended to give a new appearance to the rebuilt city (baths, temple of Venus, *odeon*, amphitheater...). The building was designed and constructed with the use of traditional systems of heating, with movable heat sources (braziers); the sophisticated system whereby, through interstices in the flooring and along the walls, the heating was done with the spread of hot steam, boiled in a furnace, was another innovation that came just slightly later, and only a few of the rooms were modernized. The complex had a men's sector and a women's sector; its plan imitates the older baths of Stabiae. The entrance from Via delle Terme leads into the *apodyterium* (dressing room) of the men's sector, on the walls of which were wooden cabinets for the clothing. At the far end was the *frigidarium*, a circular room with a dome, for cold baths. A corridor leads to the service rooms and the boiler, while a door led into the *tepidarium*, in which were preserved the rich stucco decoration of the vault, a number of objects of furnishing and, of particular interest, niches on the walls, framed by telamones in terracotta. The last room was the *calidarium* with a basin for hot baths and a large marble *labrum* (basin for ablutions) with a dedicatory inscription on the rim. The women's sector presented a more intimate form and the succession of *apodyterium*, *tepidarium*, and *calidarium*. To the south was a porticoed courtyard.

The Via dell'Abbondanza, the Quartiere dei Teatri, and the Amphitheater. From the Forum began the long **Via dell'Abbondanza** (C3,4-B4,5) along which stood the baths, or **Terme Stabiane*** (B-C4), the oldest public baths in Pompeii. The early layout seems to date back to the end of the 4th c. B.C. The baths took on their present form over the course of the 2nd c. B.C. and were later subjected to gradual modifications. In the earliest period, the complex also including a simple porticoed courtyard (actually a gymnasium, or *palaestra*) and a row of small rooms arranged to the north, near a well. It is probable that these rooms were used for individual baths. Actual thermal rooms, artificially heated, were only added at a later date, and they occupied the eastern sector. The rooms needed for the creation of steam through combustion (*praefurnia*) were located in the center, and separated the eastern wing into two sectors, used for men's and women's baths. From the southeastern corner of the portico was the entrance to a room leading into the men's baths, linking up with the round hall of the *frigidarium* and the *apodyterium*. Next came the *tepidarium* and the *calidarium*, a large apsed rectangular hall with a basin for hot baths to the east, and with a *labrum* for rapid splashings of cold water. The layout is repeated in the women's sector, devoid, however, of a *frigidarium*. To the west of the courtyard, on the open side of the portico, was the pool (*natatio*).

The little lane that bounds the baths to the west leads to the *lupanarium*, or brothel.

The quarter of the theaters, along with the forum, was one of the main public centers. In the appearance it now presents, it was the product of a reconstruction done in the 2nd c. B.C., by the Samnite city government and its powerful families, whose fealty was directed to the area near the **triangular forum** (C4; page 128), where most of the public buildings for leisure activities and assembly were concentrated. Set on a highland and looking south toward the sea, in the 6th c. B. C. a *Doric temple* was built here (ruins badly renovated, and nearly destroyed), with reconstructions and renovations in the 4th and 2nd c. B.C., when it was adapted to the new layout of the area and surrounded by portico with three branches, in the Doric order. Near the short northern side was the entrance, rendered monumental by *propylaea*. In front of the temple are three altars, an enigmatic double enclosure, and a well, monumentalized by a Doric *tholos*.

From the portico to the south, you entered the Samnite gymnasium, the theater, and the large lower portico. Behind the *cavea* of the large theater were the gymnasium (*palaestra*) and the temple of Isis. The **Samnite gymnasium**, originally a quadriporticus that was cut down due to the renovation of the adjoining temple, was built with money left by bequest to the *vereia* of the people of Pompeii, a military association dating from the Samnite period. In it was found the finest copy of the famous *Doriphorus* by Polycletus (now in Naples).

The neighboring **Temple of Isis***, founded as early as the 2nd c. B.C., was one of the few public buildings of Pompeii to have been entirely repaired from the damage suffered in the earthquake (A.D. 62) that preceded the eruption in A.D. 79. The plan of this sanctuary is strongly linked to a number of particular features of the cult. At the center of the porticoes, set on a base, was the sacellum of the goddess. Near the southeastern corner, note a small enclosure that led into an underground chamber, in which were preserved the sacred waters of the Nile, needed for rites of purification. Behind the western porticoes were large rooms used for gatherings and ceremonies. The temple was discovered during the Bourbon excavations with all its furnishings and pictorial decorations. A complete illustration of the monument with a history of its discovery can be seen in the Museo di Napoli.

The **large theater*** (3rd/2nd c. B.C., with renovations during the rule of Augustus) was still built in accordance with the Greek system, taking advantage of a natural slope for the creation of the *cavea*. The *parodoi*, entrances to the orchestra, arranged along a single axis, were roofed over during the age of Sulla. The *cavea* was subdivided, with corridors, into *summa cavea*, *media cavea*, and *ima cavea*; the first two sectors were further divided into five wedges. The *summa cavea*, set atop a crypt, dating from the age

rection. The *cavea*, divided into five wedge shapes, or *cunei*, is arranged in two sectors, separated by a ring corridor and a balustrade. The lower sector was, as in the theater, destined for use by important spectators. There is no *summa cavea*. There was a secondary array of decorations of considerable effect and refinement. The retaining walls of the *cavea* (the *analemmata*) were concluded at their tops by shaped cornices, at their sides by telamones carved out of tufa stone, reminiscent of the terracotta statues of the baths of the Forum ("terme del Foro").

After you return to Via dell'Abbondanza,

The Roman amphitheater, erected alongside the walls of Pompeii

of Augustus. Decurions and notables were given seats in the *ima cavea* and the *tribunalia*, the boxes located upon the roofs of the *parodoi* and mentioned in an inscription. The *scaena* formed, after the renovation during the rule of Sulla, a single unit with the *cavea*. Set on a podium was the actual stage. The rear elevation (*frons scenae*) reproduced in masonry the facade of a princely palace, embellished with statues and columns, and presenting three doors: the current arrangement is clearly subsequent to A.D. 62.

Behind the theater is a large quadriporticus, used by spectators to stroll and converse. During the last period, the quadriporticus was transformed into a barracks for gladiators.

The **odeon*** (or small theater) was intended for musical performances and, as a theater, for political assemblies. The building was erected in the age of Sulla and dedicated by M. Porcius and C. Quinctius Valgus, the *duumvires* of the city, representing the renewal of the age of Sulla. The semicircular *cavea* is inscribed in a square. Two straight, covered passages, or *parodoi*, led into the semicircular orchestra. The structures of the *scaena* have a rectilinear di-

you will continue through the area of the **new excavations*** begun in 1911 which, because of the preservation on site of many of the finds, offer a virtually complete image of every aspect of the city's everyday life. You may note the *Officina di Verecundus* (B4), a workshop for the production of wool cloth, the **Fullonica Stephani*** (dyer/dry cleaner), the handsome **Casa del Criptoportico*** (B-C4,5) behind which, on the southern lane, is the large **Casa del Menandro*** (C4,5) which was the source of the silver work now in the Museum at Naples.

Quite near to the area of the amphitheater, by now, are the **Casa di Loreio Tiburtino*** (B5), with a splendid garden; a residence in which there is a clear love of illusionism with the recreation, in miniature, of elevations and settings typical of the large extra-urban villas, and the **Villa di Giulia Felice*** (B5,6).

Behind it is the **large gymnasium**, or *palaestra* (B5,6), dating from the age of Augustus and used by the associations of young people; it faces the **amphitheater*** (B6), one of the first constructions of a place for spectacles, solidly built in masonry. The local tradition of gladiatorial games and the distance from the rigid regulations in effect in

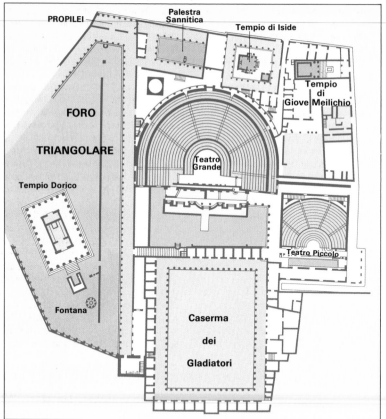

The triangular forum and the theater quarter, Pompeii

Rome, put Campania in the vanguard in terms of construction of public and private buildings in new architectural styles. The building – erected at their own expense by M. Porcius and C. Quinctius, the same magistrates who supervised the work on the *odeon* – stands near the southeastern corner of the fortifications, making use of those structures as retaining walls for the *cavea* on the southern and eastern sides. The site, in a peripheral position, was selected as a way of preventing the great crowds of eager spectators from blocking traffic in the city and interfering with everyday life. The outer retaining wall featured buttresses ending in arches. Above it was an open-air corridor, and it was on this level that was based an elliptical tambour crowned by a walkway. This last structure, which was not buried by the eruption, is badly damaged. The upper story of the open-air deambulatory, an entryway to the *summa cavea*, was accessible along exterior stairways that ran along the retaining wall. From the exterior, corridors led to the *crypta*, the interior deambulatory upon which opened

the entrances to the *media cavea* and *ima cavea*. Two of the radial passageways to the arena had flooring made of paving stones that allowed the passage of carts and carriages. Not all of the places in the upper sectors were sheathed in stone from the very beginning, because the construction was evidently gradual, and some of the sectors were equipped with wooden structures. Along the building you can see evident traces of the technical facilities used in raising the *velarium*, a system of awnings extended over the *cavea*, so as to protect the spectators from the sunlight.

The Regio VI and private housing. In the Regio VI, even in the 1st c. A.D., there was a strong atmosphere of tradition, emanating from the architectural style and forms of the main private residences. This is a sector, built up as early as the 3rd c. B.C., in which were found the homes of the leading families of Pompeii during the age of the Samnites. On Via delle Terme and Via della Fortuna you may note high portal built of tufa stone, entrances to homes that, despite the extensive renovations that ensued, still preserved their ancient plans and wall decorations. The contrast with the more recent construction techniques and the modern style of decoration was evident, and this operation of conservation proves, to the modern visitor, even more noteworthy. To maintain unaltered forms that had become outdated, and in some cases restoring them, meant attributing dignity and worth to tradition, in the belief that it ennobled the origins and history of one's family, in the eye of one's fellow townsfolk. The most notable example is represented by the **Casa del Fauno*** (B3). It occupied the area of an entire block, or *insula* (roughly 3,000 sq. m), dimensions that were comparable only with the palaces of Hellenistic dynastic rulers. The layout developed over the course of the 2nd c. B.C., on the existing structures of a smaller home. Beyond the high portal of tufa-stone, decorated with the distinctive "sofa-shaped," you entered the *fauci*, or entrance, embellished with a stucco decoration depicting the facade of a small sacellum. The floor, in *opus sectile*, was accompanied by a mosaic fascia, with tragic masks. The entire decoration of the house, announced right from the entrance, reflected an eastern style of high craftsmanship. These were the years of an opening of the Italic world toward the basin of the Mediterranean. The military successes of Rome were opening the main ports of the Mediterranean to Italic trade. The artistic and cultural models reflected this fortunate social and political situation. The mosaics – made of fine minute tiles, or *tesserae* so as to reproduce the smallest chromatic nuances, and generally based on a terracotta substrate (*emblemata*) and then inserted into the center of mosaic floors composed of tiles in a larger module, reproducing motifs of eastern influence – alternated with flooring in marble slabs (*opus sectile*) with designs in perspective, utilized at the same time in the main public places of the city. Most of the flooring has been detached, and is now in the Museo di Napoli. Of particular interest are the decorations in the first style, imitating with stucco and colors, false masonry and architectural partitions, in a few points enriched with figurative motifs (monochromatic scenes, friezes). The

house is arranged around two atriums. Opening onto the main atrium, in the Tuscan order, i.e., devoid of columns supporting the *compluvium*, were the *cubicula* (bedrooms: in the first room on the right, note the remains of decorations in the second style, an emblem with satyr and bacchante on the floor) and, at the far end, the *alae*. At the center of the north side was the *tablinum*, a living area, with flooring in *opus sectile* with cubes in perspective. At the center of the *impluvium* is a copy of the bronze Faun that gave the houses its name (Casa del Fauno), a remarkable Hellenistic sculpture (the original is in Naples); on the sides are two *triclinia*. The secondary sector was articulated around a colonnaded atrium (women's quarters or service area). Along the corridor linking up with the second peristyle (once used for the garden) there stood, in a row, a stable, bath areas, the kitchen, and a *triclinium*. At the end of the first peristyle is an exedra, framed by a pair of columns and with pillars "in antis," whose flooring, the high point of the decoration of the house, was the celebrated mosaic of the Battle of Alexander the Great

Detail of painted masks in a lunette in the Casa del Bracciale d'Oro, Pompeii

(now in Naples, and perhaps derived from a painting by Philoxenus of Eretreia), preceded, at the threshold, by mosaics with Nilotic depictions.

Among the most interesting houses in the Regio VI are, in Via di Mercurio, the *Casa dell'Ancora*, the *Casa di Castore e Polluce*, the *Casa di Meleagro* (B3), the *Casa di Apollo* (B2). At the far end of the street is the tower, or Torre XI (A2) of the city walls, from which you may enjoy a splendid panoramic view* of the city; along the Vicolo di Mercurio is a tavern (*osteria*) with counters (*caupona*) and the *Casa del Labi-*

rinto (B3). Nearly at the beginning of two streets that run into the Vicolo di Mercurio are the Casa dei Vettii (Vicolo dei Vettii) and the Casa degli Amorini Dorati (Via Stabiana), which are two of the most famous and exquisite examples of Pompeiian residence.

The **Casa dei Vettii*** (B3) is one of the most popular and often visited places in Pompeii; with a double atrium of ancient design, renovated over the course of the 1st c. A.D., it belonged to a family of freed slaves, and it preserves virtually intact its *painted decorations** with a rich array of figures, the service rooms, and the arrangement of the peristyle. Immediately in the vestibule is a painted Priapus, to ward off the evil eye; you then pass into the atrium, with *impluvium* (on the right is a little courtyard with the kitchens), and then you step out into the handsome garden, rebuilt in its original form, overlooked by the main rooms of the house. The **Casa degli Amorini Dorati*** (B3) offers a excellent example of the unbridled passion for gardens that swept the high society of Pompeii in the last decades of its existence.

In the nearby Regio V we would point out the *Casa di Lucio Cecilio Giocondo* (B3) and the *Casa delle Nozze d'Argento* (A-B4). Along Via delle Terme stand the *Casa del Poeta Tragico* (B3, the Casa di Glauco in the novel, *The Last Days of Pompeii*, by Bulwer Lytton), the *Casa di Pansa* (B2,3), beyond which you will continue along Via Consolare, where there is a *pastry shop* (*pistrinum*), the **Casa di Sallustio** (B2), and the **Casa del Chirurgo** (B2, house of the surgeon, so named for the discovery of surgical instruments, now in the Museo di Napoli) in which you can perceive traces of the even older houses that extended over a relatively small surface area, with a rectangular plan occupied, crosswise, by a covered atrium, and with a small vegetable patch behind it. The former was, at a late date, transformed into a hotel, while the latter originally had a covered atrium.

The Via dei Sepolcri and the Villa dei Misteri. After you enter the gate, or *Porta Ercolanese*, you will take **Via dei Sepolcri*** (B1,2). In accordance with a custom that was common in the Roman world, along the main thoroughfares leaving a city, there were a series of funerary monuments. The preeminent location was considered a source of honor, and the explicatory inscriptions presented wayfarers with the main families of the city to which they were traveling. Immediately after the gate, on the right, for example, is the *tomb of Marcus Porcius*, who was one of the most influential personalities in Pompeii under Sulla. Continuing among a series of handsome tombs, you will reach an area occupied by villas, including the Villa di Diomede (B1). After you emerge from the enclosure of the excavations, you may head for the **Villa dei Misteri*** (A1) which was built in accordance with a well-known typology of the Roman world. Founded in the first half of the 2nd c. B.C., it underwent a major renovation around 60 B.C.: most of the decorative elements that survive, which can be classified as belonging to the second style, are a result of that intervention. Over the course of the 1st c. A.D. a part of the villa was transformed into a rustic quarter. It overlooked the sea, with a terrace supported by a cryptoporticus. The old entrance stood on the opposite side. Once you pass the entrance, you will find yourself in the peristyle, corresponding to which, on the same axis, was the sequence of atrium and *tablinum*. On the southern side of the peristyle were a small bath, the service area (kitchens), and a smaller atrium. The peristyle became the center of the rustic sector of the villa. On the northern side, in fact, were the *torcularium* for pressing grapes and other service rooms that have yielded many tools and farming utensils. In this sector, you will find the remains of decorations in the fourth style, dating from the same period as the functional reconstruction of the peristyle. Of particular interest are the landscape-based decorations of the atrium, the cunning command of perspective found in the fake architecture of the *cubicula*, and the fine decoration in a mature third style of the *tablinum*. But the villa is especially famous for the **series of paintings*** of the southwestern *triclinium*, the largest such array (17 x 3 m) surviving from antiquity. In these "megalographies" we see the depiction of Dionysian-Orphic rites. The focal point of the depiction was the couple, partially preserved, of Dionysus and Ariadne, enthroned. The lateral scenes were variously interpreted, and there exists no single accepted interpretation of the frieze. The scenes of ladies at their toilet would seem to allude to women's initiation rituals and, consequently, to the rite of passage par excellence: matrimony. Other interpretations attribute the entire meaning of the depiction to a celebration of the birth of Dionysus and his unsettling powers, intimately linked to the powers of nature.

7 The Sorrento peninsula and Capri

Sorrento and Capri: two mythical names, made famous by the splendid landscape and by a relatively recent body of travel literature, especially if we compare it with the truly imposing mass of writings left by the travelers of the Grand Tour, concerning the Phlegrean Fields, or Campi Flegrei, and Mt. Vesuvius.

Relatively overlooked in the 18th c. (Capri appeared to Goethe, who observed it in passing on his way to Palermo, as nothing more than an unattractive and rocky little island) they were those "islands of the sirens" that the 19th c. and especially the early 20th c. were to transform into obligatory stops for international tourists.

The western side of the Sorrento peninsula, extending as far as the Punta della Campanella, is bounded to the east by the Monte Faìto, to the south by the chain of the Monti Lattari. Because of its morphological features, it can be divided into two areas: the territory of Vico Equense, with scattered isolated towns and villages, characterized by limestone out-

The Isle of Capri, one of the best-loved resorts in the world

croppings dense with vegetation, and the Sorrento plain, comprising a tufa-stone bastion over the sea that runs gently up toward the surrounding hills.

Typical of the territory are intense cultivation of vineyards along the coast and olive groves on the interior; despite frequent fires and a devastating speculation in real estate development, there are wonderful forests.

Aside from its evident environmental value, the peninsula also has major historical and artistic importance. Dating back to the 6th c. B.C. was the foundation of a Greek colony at Sorrento. During the reign of Augustus, it was selected by the Roman aristocracy as a "place of delights," and its coastlines were punctuated with luxurious villas by the seaside. Between the 14th and 15th c. the predilection of the Angevins for the peninsula and the timid development of the agrarian economy favored the development of small new towns (Meta, Piano) in the plain and of the village of Vico Equense.

The luxuriant plain, or Piano di Sorrento, extends over a tufa-stone platform overlooking the sea; once it was abounded in forests and olive and citrus groves, but now is studded with buildings. On the plain in the Angevin period, there formed the earliest "casali," or villages, which under the viceroys, even though the demands for independence and the revolts against the rule of Sorrento showed no signs of abating, continued to grow rapidly, in part due to the growth in trade and communications; since these activities took place only by sea, necessarily there followed the foundation of the shipyards.

One indicator of the social and economic prosperity that the peninsula had attained are the large and wealthy religious foundations and the civil architecture that enriched the many villages with villas, prestigious palazzi, large farmhouses that belonged to noble landowners, ship owners, or sea captains.

Many of the towns of the peninsula present an irregular and twisting grid, with many blind alleys that were useful in defending against Turkish raids. In Sorrento, Vico, and Castellammare it is still possible to make out the original regular layout.

Capri is an island formed by a single compact limestone block, detached from the Sorrento peninsula and subject to phenomena of "bradisismo" (slow seismic activity) of which traces remain in the Roman structures now immersed in the waters of the Blue Grotto, or Grotta Azzurra, and the baths of Tiberius. Its appearance is characterized primarily by the presence of two highlands: the western highland of Anacapri with the summit of the Monte Solaro (elev. 589 m) which is also the highest peak on the island; and the eastern summit of the Monte Tiberio (elev. 334 m) jutting out into the sea with exceedingly sheer cliffs. Between the two highlands, almost corresponding to the center of the island, is a depression at the foot of which are the Marina Grande and the Marina Piccola.

The island was already inhabited in the Paleolithic, and at that time it was still an extension of the Sorrento peninsula; colonized by the Greeks, it experienced a phase of considerable splendor during the early years of the Roman empire, becoming the permanent site of Tiberius's court, who spent the last years of his life encouraging the construction of numerous villa-palaces. In the high Middle Ages it became a dependency of Amalfi, and shared its fortunes. A moment of some interest came in the 18th c., with the undertaking of the first archaeological excavations, encouraged by Charles of Bourbon, but the true rebirth of the island came with the "rediscovery" of the Blue Grotto, or Grotta Azzurra, which took place in the 19th c. From that point on, Capri became part of the major international tourist circuit, favored by the remarkable natural setting and the pleasant climate, and its myth, handed down by the artists and intellectuals of the 19th c. who stayed there – through all of the natural changes of custom and culture – continues to flourish today.

7.1 The Sorrento peninsula

After touring Castellammare di Stabia, you will get back on the state road, or Statale 145 which winds up along the slopes of the Faito, offering views of the Gulf of Naples. After about 1 km you will reach the Angevin castle, or Castello Angioino; on the opposite side of it, a little lane leads up to the sanctuary, or Santuario di S. Maria della Libera. Continuing along, the road doubles around the crag, or Sperone di S. Maria di Pozzano – where the church of the same name adjoining the little village of Pozzano – descending steeply along the coast until you reach the Punta Orlando, beyond which is the spa, or Terme Lo Scrajo.

Here begins the winding route of the Bourbon thoroughfare (1834) which, after running through Vico, passes Punta Scutolo, where you have a fine view of the entire Sorrento plain, then crosses the main square of Meta, marked by the church of the Lauro.

Then, after forking into the state road, or Statale 163, which leads to Positano and to the Colli, you will continue through Meta, Piano, and Sant'Agnello, which by this point are linked by an uninterrupted series of buildings to Sorrento. From here, after passing through the Marina di Puolo, you will reach Massalubrense (14 km). Since 1952 the towns of the peninsula, as far as Sorrento, have been linked with Naples by the railroad, or Ferrovia Circumvesuviana.

Castellammare di Stabia

This was a Samnite *oppidum*, or stronghold in the 6th and 5th c. B.C., and was involved in the Samnite Wars. Destroyed in 89 B.C. by Sulla, it was rebuilt on the plateau of Varano and then annihilated by the eruption of A.D. 79. Castellammare (elev. 6 m, pop. 67,267) was soon rebuilt because of the importance of the springs, to the degree that in the 9th c., a castle was built to guard the most important spring. In the Angevin period, Charles I built walls and enlarged the castle and the port. In 1740 Charles of Bourbon began systematic excavations in the territory and established a crystal manufactory here; his son Ferdinand enlarged the port and founded shipyards there, which were further enlarged by Ferdinand II, who also equipped the area with a paved road to Naples and the carriageway to Sorrento. These initiatives were positive factors in the development of Castellammare, which still preserves, though to a lesser degree, the characteristics of an industrial town.

There are 28 springs, used in a wide variety of treatments, making this a major spa; there are two facilities: the old, or *Antiche Terme* in Piazza Amendola (the earliest springs, now renovated, were founded by Ferdinand IV) and the *Nuove Terme* on the hill of Solaro along the scenic road.

In the Piazza Giovanni XXIII note the town hall, or *Palazzo Municipale* (formerly the Palazzo dei Farnese, feudal lords since 1541) and the 16th-c. *cathedral*, enlarged and decorated in the 19th c.; on the interior, paintings by G. Bonito, G. Diano, and the workshop of Lanfranco, a statue of *St. Michael* from the 6th c., and a 13th-c. urn (chapel, or Cappella del Patrono S. Catello).

On the opposite side is the *church of the Gesù*, 1615; single nave, and features artworks by De Matteis and Giordano.

Between the square and the sea extends the Villa Comunale where, among tall palm trees, is the Cassa Armonica, or bandstand, in cast-iron with slender tortile columns supporting the glassed-in roof (1898-1911). From the villa you head toward the harbor, one of the most important in southern Italy, near which are the shipyards *Cantiere Navale* (Italcantieri), with a glorious tradition: founded by Ferdinand IV in 1783, the first Italian steam ships were built here in 1835, as well as the first Italian armored warship (1876), and the school ship Vespucci.

The *Antiquarium Stabiano* contains Italic, Greek, Samnite, and Roman archaeological finds from Stabiae and its villas (of particular importance are the *detached frescoes*), and many medieval works in marble.

The castle at Castellammare di Stabia

The uphill ring road, or Circonvallazione a Monte (*Strada Panoramica*) would allow the visitor to visit a number of the most important monuments and sites in the surrounding area, if they were open in any regular fashion. You reach the crossroads for Gragnano where you will immediately turn off to the left. A few meters later, a narrow lane off to the left leads to the Villa Arianna, located on the hill, or Collina del Varano, and comprising 13 rooms overlooking the gulf, and decorated with notable frescoes, especially the frescoes of the Sala d'Arianna. Beneath them, in the hill itself, is the grotto, or *Grotta di S. Biagio* (not open to the public), which can be reached

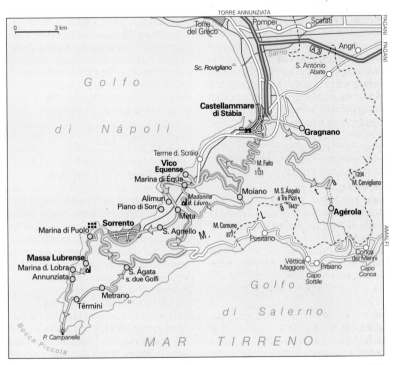

from Via Nocera: perhaps this was originally a pagan crypt, transformed in the 10th c. into a small Christian basilica, dedicated to the worship of St. Michael, which was quite common throughout southern Italy under the Longobards. If you drive for another kilometer or so, and then turn left, you will reach the *Villa Romana (S. Marco)* comprising two large peristyles at different levels, around which are the living quarters. The upper peristyle conserved on the left side 17 columns, decorated at the base of the shaft and with spiral fluting on the rest of the column (destroyed in the earthquake of 1980). A ramp leads down to the lower peristyle, with 30 columns on three sides and, at the center, a large umbrella basin. Along the scenic road, at less than 1 km from the town of Scanzano, you can turn off to the left onto the road that leads to the *Villa Quisisana*, built by King Robert in 1310 and later renovated, a royal residence until the arrival of the Bourbons, converted into a hospital at the orders of Garibaldi and then into a hotel. The villa is now closed, but you may visit the upper park.

Also overlooking the scenic road are the bulk of the castle, or *Castello* (the Castrum ad Mare de Stabiis which gave its name to the city), built in the early Middle Ages, enlarged and reinforced by Frederick II and Charles I, with round towers and enclosure walls running down toward the sea.

Castellammare is the point of departure for excursions on the **Monte Faito** (elev. 1103 m), the furthermost mountain in the chain of the Monti Lattari, where forests of conifers, ash, and chestnuts give way, midway up the slope, to rough expanses of meadow, used as pasturage. Along the slopes, there are olive and citrus groves and vineyards. The excursions can be taken either by cableway ("funivia," starting from the station, or Stazione della Circumvesuviana; open from April to October) or else along the road (16 km) which, after the Villa Quisisana, reaches the *Belvedere del Faito*, where you may enjoy one of the most renowned panoramic vistas of the Gulf of Naples. If you climb up along the left you will reach the upper station of the cableway; continuing along the ridge of the mountain toward the southeast, you will reach the Porta del Faito (elev. 1,222 m) and, along a trail just under the ridge, you will reach – after several hours of hiking – the summit of the Monte S. Angelo ai Tre Pizzi (elev. 1,443 m), and from there the view is splendid*.

Vico Equense

Even though the site had been inhabited previously, it was not until Roman times that conditions become adequate for the formation of the little village of Aequa. Devastated during the wars of Sulla, it was damaged by the eruption of A.D. 79. Rebuilt, it was once again razed by the Goths. The rebirth of Vico Equense (elev. 90 m, pop. 19,912) came in the 14th c., when Charles II founded the new village, or "borgo," enclosed by walls and laid out on the earlier, regular grid; it also included the summer residence of the sovereign and the cathedral, or Cattedrale. All that survives of the old town are a few traces, including portals and windows along the little lanes of the historic center.

Hand-crafted coral jewelry from the Sorrento peninsula

The cathedral, or *Cattedrale*, founded in the 14th c., is the only example of a Gothic church on the peninsula. The facade, rebuilt in the 17th c., is flanked by the 16th-c. campanile with three orders; through the lower order, with an arcade, you reach the church courtyard, high over the sea. It has been renovated repeatedly, and the interior has a nave and two side aisles, divided by pillars; the nave culminates in the original 14th-c. apse; among other artworks, the church contains canvases by G. Bonito, the tomb of Gaetano Filangieri, and the 14th-c. sarcophagus, or *Sarcofago Cimmino*. Nearby is the castle, or Castello Giusso (formerly Castello Carafa, Castello di Capua, and Castello Ravaschieri), looming high over the sea. The oldest core of the town, founded by Charles of Anjou, with 15th-c. elements in the present-day "terrace," was renovated between the 17th and 19th c. The main building consists of a C-shaped structure that is the result of an enlargement – through the addition of two side arms – of the central structure, back in 1535.

We should also mention the medieval gate, or *Porta di Vico*, the bishopric, or *Vescovado*, the *church of SS. Ciro e Giovanni*, with majolica dome, the Museo Mineralogico della Fondazione Discepolo, the *Antiquari-*

um Equano, with some of the archaeological finds uncovered at Vico on exhibit (archaic Doric capitals, furnishings from the necropolis) and lastly *S. Maria del Toro* which, built in the first half of the 16th c. and later enlarged, stands with its campanile atop a small hill at the outskirts of Vico; on the interior is a lacunar ceiling and the 17th-c. frescoes in the dome.

Meta

This small town (elev. 111 m, pop. 7,521), situated on a short slope that runs down toward the sea, is dominated by the *church of the Madonna del Lauro*, traditionally said to have been founded on the site of a temple of Minerva. The church was rebuilt in the 16th c., and underwent modifications and restorations in the 18th and 19th c.; we would point out the wooden door with carved panels dating back to the 16th c., the chapel, or *Cappella della Madonna del Lauro*, with an old wooden statue of the Virgin Mary, intarsias and frescoes from the 18th c., the period when the wooden statues in the presbytery and the furnishings of the sacristy were also made. If you walk down along Via del Lauro, you will reach the center of Meta, and then if you continue along Via Vocale, Via Caracciolo, Via Liguori, Via Lama, and Via S. Lucia, lined by a homogeneous series of buildings (15th/19th c.), you will reach the Marina di Meta.

Piano di Sorrento

This important market town (elev. 96 m, pop. 12,640) preserves, surprisingly and despite the wildcat development, a number of pristine pieces of its original structure, in the area between the Piazza Cota and the *Basilica di S. Michele*, which was founded between the 9th and 10th c. and rebuilt repeatedly. On the interior, there are paintings by G. Imparato (1587, in the ceiling), Andrea da Salerno, M. Pino, F. Santafede, and I. Borghese. In the transept, on a marble balustrade that surrounds the presbytery by the Roman architect G. B. Antonelli, note four candle-holding angels of the school of Bernini and *Stories of Christ* from the school of Solimena, who is also thought to have done the *Madonna del Rosario* on an altar in the transept. As you walk down Via S. Margherita, you will pass through the old "casali" or farmhouses, of Gottola, Cassano, and S. Giovanni which, virtually intact, still reveal features dating back to the 14th, 15th, and 18th c.

Sant'Agnello

This small town (elev. 67 m, pop. 8,465) stands practically at the gates of Sorrento. In the main square, atop a high staircase, is the church of the *SS. Prisco e Agnello*; on the interior are paintings from the 17th c. Behind the station stands the old center of S. Agnello, the Rione Angri. If you continue along Via Cappuccini – which, flanked by 18th-c. *villas*, runs to the church of the Cappuccini – and Via Crawford (with the hotel, or *Albergo Cocumella*, set in an old monastery and old villas and homes) you will reach Sorrento in an atmosphere that preserves many traces of the splendid settings that made the fortune of this peninsula in terms of tourism.

Sorrento

The Greek foundation of the city (elev. 50 m, pop. 17,004) in an area that was already inhabited in the Neolithic Age, is colored with legend and poetry; the very name of *Surrentum* is linked to the worship of the Sirens, common in the peninsula. The city, set high atop its tufa bastion, and defended by three high valleys, submitted to Rome, becoming a *municipium* at the end of the Republic; the original settlement was newly fortified and the territory was divided among veterans. The amenity of the site and the proximity of Capri, the favorite residence of Tiberius, contributed to the for-

Lemon liqueur, a local specialty

tune of the city. Following the domination of the Goths, Sorrento was reconquered by Byzantium, to which it was tied as well during its centuries as an autonomous dukedom. Dating from this phase is an interesting artistic testimony in the series of carved slabs, in the Sassanid style (Museo Correale, Cathedral). In 1133, conquered by the Normans, Sorrento lost its independence; destroyed in 1558 by the Turks, it was soon protected by a new set of walls (1561) and watch towers were built along the coast. The 17th c. witnessed the renewed prosperity of Sorrento, which between the 19th c. and the early 20th c. became one of the most popular tourist spots on earth. Sadly, the lovely environmental conditions of the Piano di Sorrento, which in the past encouraged communications and settlements, in comparison with the impervious Amalfi side of the peninsula, have also been the cause of an uncontrolled and savage real estate development.

The original settlement almost seems to coincide with the area that is now enclosed between the Piazza Tasso and Viale degli Aranci, once encompassed by the ancient fortified enclosure, only slightly smaller than the ring of walls of the age of the viceroys. It is still possible to see the early regular layout of *cardines* and *decumani*, where the *decumanus maximus* coincided with the present-day Via S. Cesareo and Via Fuoro (this place name may have a link with the Forum) and the *cardo maximus* was what is now Via Tasso.

The tour begins in the **Piazza Tasso** (C3), set at the edge of the historical center (fine view of the high valley, through which runs the little lane that leads down to the Marina Piccola), and adorned by the statue of *St. Anthony the Lesser* and by a *monument to Torquato Tasso*, who was born in Sorrento in 1544. Overlooking the square is the *church of S. Maria del Carmine* (on the interior, decorated with late-Baroque stuccoes, is a *Virgin Mary* by O. Avellino, on the ceiling), the hotel, or *Albergo Vittoria*, with interesting Liberty, or Art-Nouveau, rooms, and the *Casa Correale*, rebuilt in 1768 with a majolica courtyard. From the square, you may reach the center of the city by following the modern Corso Italia or, preferably, Via Pietà (ancient *decumanus*) along which you may note the 13th-c. *Palazzo Veniero* (no. 14) and the 14th-c. *Palazzo Correale* (no. 24), transformed in 1610 into the Ritiro di S. Maria della Pietà. The street ends at the foot of the *campanile of the cathedral* open in its base by arcades, and decorated with recycled columns. Overlooking the Largo Arcivescovado is the **cathedral** (C3), of ancient origin, rebuilt in the 15th c., and repeatedly restored (facade dates from 1924). In the pronaos are two recycled columns; on the right side, note a marble portal, 1478. The interior, built to a Latin-cross plan, with a nave and two side aisles, is adorned in the ceiling with canvases by N. and O. Malinconico (nave) and G. del Po (transept). Among the other artworks, we should mention, in the nave, the episcopal throne (1573), composed of heterogeneous elements and, facing it, the marble pulpit from the same period, beneath which is a *Virgin*

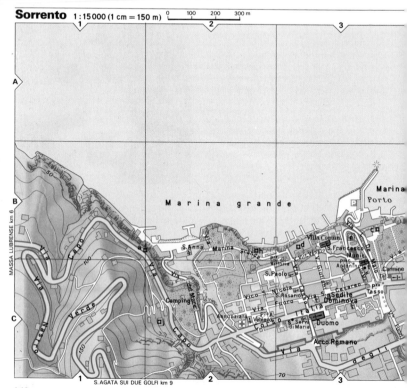

Sorrento 1:15 000 (1 cm = 150 m)

Mary with Christ Child and the *two St. Johns** by Silvestro Buono (1580). In the 1st chapel on the right, note carved marble work, including a marble altar frontal of the *Savior* (1522) and an *Annunciation* (14th/15th c.); in the presbytery is the choir, which should be noted as a particularly fine example of wooden intarsia work, which, from the middle of the 19th c. on, has distinguished the local craft tradition, and finally (at the head of the right side aisle) a fragmentary *marble slab* dating from the 10th c., with a lioness, reutilized a number of centuries later as a funerary slab (on the back is a depiction of the deceased).

Follow, across from the campanile, Via Giuliani, and immediately on the right you will note the **Sedile Dominova*** (C3) in the Largo Dominova. Built in the second half of the 15th c., this is a rare specimen of a typology now common in the region and linked to the Sedili Nobiliari, institutions that as early as the Angevin period administered the cities (ruins of the other "sedile" of Sorrento, the Sedile di Porta, stand at the end of Via S. Cesareo near the Piazza Tasso). The little square construction appears now as a loggia with arcades, enclosed by balustrades on two sides; the walls of the other two sides are frescoed with perspective paintings. The structure culminates in

a majolica dome dating from the 17th c.

Lining **Via S. Cesareo** (C3), the ancient *decumanus* that leads back to the Piazza Tasso, are many interesting buildings, dating especially from the 17th c. and the 18th c.; among them note the *church of the Addolorata* with elegant interior (1722), the portal at no. 81, and the house at no. 61.

From the Piazza Tasso you will reach the square that takes its name from the *church of S. Antonino* (Piazza di S. Antonino, B-C3), founded between the 10th and 11th c., with an interior featuring a nave and two side-aisles, divided by recycled columns (other ancient columns can be seen in the main portal; on the right side, note the portal dating from the 11th c.). In the homogeneous Baroque interior, we should mention the painting in the ceiling of the nave, by Giovan Battista Lama (1734), canvases by G. del Po (*The Siege of Sorrento in 1648 and the Plague of 1656*) on the walls of the transept, the lower structure, and, in the sacristy, a crèche dating from the 18th c. Across from the church is the town hall, or Municipio (B3), which is located in the former monastery, or *Monastero di S. Maria delle Grazie*, of which you can see the courtyard – once the cloister – and, on the side, the church, on the interior of which is a notable array of 17th-c. decorations. Along

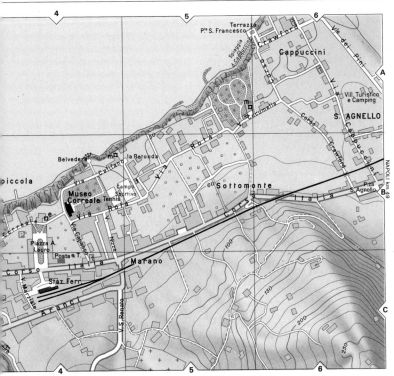

the route leading to the church of S. Francesco (B3), along Via S. Maria delle Grazie and Via B. Donnorso, you may note one of the loveliest Durazzo portals of the coast. In the church of *S. Francesco* (B3), with a 17th-c. interior, we should point out the 16th-c. intarsiated door and the adjoining little 14th-c. *cloisters** in which the intrinsic artistic interest is enhanced by the lovely array of plants and flowers.

Adjoining is the entrance to the *Villa Comunale* (B3), whose pleasant features, as is typical of public gardens in tourist towns between the 19th c. and the 20th c., are enhanced by the choice of location, which here offers a spectacular panoramic view* of the Gulf of Naples. There is another sweeping panorama from the neighboring Piazza Vittoria where the Hotel Tramontano (B3) incorporates what survives of the *birthplace of Tasso*. From here, you can head toward the village, or "borgo," of the Marina Grande by exiting the walls near the old Greek gate ("porta greca"). The tour of the city then continues along Via Tasso, an

A fine excavated bust from the Museo Correale di Terranova

ancient *cardo maximus*, where you may note the Baroque churches of *S. Paolo* and of the *Rosario* (C3). In the westernmost sector of the city, you should note the handsome house of Cornelia Tasso, the Baroque church of the *Annunziata* (C2) and the *Congrega dei Servi di Maria* (C3).

You will return to the Piazza Tasso and you may then take Via Correale to reach the **Museo Correale di Terranova*** (B4), housed in an 18th-c. villa built in an area donated to the family of the Correale by Joan of Aragón in 1428. The museum preserves its character as a patrician collection. Reorganized following the earthquake of 1980, it contains Greek and Roman archaeological finds from the Sorrento peninsula (including an *Artemis on a Deer*, a Greek original from the 4th c. B.C., and the celebrated *Base of Sorrento**, with bas-reliefs linked to the religious policies of Augustus), medieval marble work (*plutei and slabs** from Sorrento with abstract and zoomorphic motifs of Sassanid origin, dating from the 10th and 11th c.), Neapolitan and Sicilian furniture from the 17th/19th c., inlaid furniture from 19th-c. Sorrento (Donazione Gargiulo), a major collection of Italian, European, and Oriental

porcelain, Venetian glass, Bohemian crystal, clocks, Neapolitan and non-Italian paintings from the 17th and 18th c.: of special note is the collection of paintings of the School of Posillipo (Pitloo, Duclère, Gigante).

As you leave the city you will head toward the Capo di Sorrento, where you should note the ruins, known as the Bagni della Regina Giovanna (first half of the 1st c. A.D.), of the **Villa of Pollius Felix***, praised by Statius, the most interesting of the many ruins of Roman villas along the coast.

Massa Lubrense

This township comprises a number of centers (elev. 121 m, pop. 12,467), and was founded in the 10th c. In 1210 the church of S. Maria della Lobra was built, at the constitution of the diocese. In 1389 it was rebuilt as a fortified citadel and queen Joan stayed here. Always faithful to the Anjou, it was made a duchy, and was destroyed in 1451 by Ferrante of Aragón, for the frequent uprisings. After the great Turkish raid of 1558, the system of defensive works was reinforced; in the 17th c. the Jesuits founded a college here, and Massa become a flourishing cultural center. The French, in 1807, reinforced the fortifications in order to hold out against the English, who had established a garrison on Capri.

In the village, or Frazione di Massa Centro, the cathedral of *S. Maria delle Grazie* dominates the square, or Largo del Vescovado; built in 1512-36 and rebuilt in 1760, it preserves in the apse a painting of the Virgin Mary, the *Madonna delle Grazie*, by Andrea da Salerno.

Continuing in Via Marina, you will reach the *church of S. Maria della Lobra*, with a portal dating from the 16th c.; on the interior, with a 17th-c. ceiling, are wooden sculptures, marble altars, and majolica floors dating back to the 18th c.

From the Largo del Vescovado you will continue on the left and climb for 1.6 km, then detouring to the right through the village, or *Frazione Annunziata*. The town of the Annunziata lies at the foot of the Castello di Massa (1389), of which a round tower survives. In the square, the church of the same name, the old cathedral of Massa (demolished in 1465 and rebuilt in 1590); in the 18th-c. interior, we would point out a polychrome marble altar and a majolica floor.

7.2 The Isle of Capri

The itinerary begins from the port of Marina Grande, where hydrofoils and ferryboats arrive, and where you will find the lower station of the funicular to Capri. The port is the point of departure for excursions, by rowboat or motorboat, among which we would recommend those to the Blue Grotto, or Grotta Azzurra (90 minutes or 25 minutes) and the tour around the island (in motorboat, about 2 hours).

The most direct access to the town of Capri is by the funicular. If you wish to drive (3 km), then take Via Colombo, which continues uphill among trees, villas, and gardens. On the right, you can see the stepped road that leads to Anacapri, known as the *Scala Fenicia*, or Phoenician stairs, a steep and ancient path with more than 500 steps carved out during the time of the Greek colonists, and restructured by the Romans, and which – until the construction of the existing road (1877) – constituted the only link between Anacapri and the coast. Not far away stands the *church of S. Costanzo*, founded in the year 1000 and enlarged in 1300, which contains the relics of the saint, Constantine, patriarch of Constantinople, and patron saint of Capri. The interior is basilican, but in it you can recognize the original Greek-cross plan, inscribed in a square with recycled columns, supporting the dome and the vaults of the side-aisles (four columns were moved into the Palatine chapel, or Cappella Palatina of the Reggia di Caserta and replaced), has undergone a radical restoration.

The road, which runs through vineyards and citrus groves, offers a sweeping and panoramic view of the Marina Grande, the Sorrento peninsula, and the town of Capri, with the highlands, in the background, of the Monte di S. Michele and the Madonna del Soccorso, near which you can see bits of buildings of the Villa Jovis. After you pass the two picturesque cemeteries of Capri (Catholic and non-Catholic), you will reach the crossroads, or Quadrivio di Capri, from which you can either climb up, on the right, to Anacapri (3.8 km from Capri; bus) or else descend, straight ahead, to the Marina Piccola (2.6 km). If you turn to the left into Via Roma, with a broad view of the sea, you will reach the panoramic terrace across from the upper station of the funicular.

After the tour of the center of Capri, the itinerary branches off toward Castiglione and Marina Piccola to the west and Villa Jovis to the east; from the latter, you will return to Capri along a trail (45 minutes) on the eastern side of the island.

After you return to the Quadrivio you will climb up among vineyards, with a fine view of Capri and, below, to the right, the Marina Grande. The road, which runs steeply uphill, presents a stretch carved right into the steep rock face, forming an exceptional belvedere (elev. 250-280 m) over the Gulf of Naples and the Sorrento peninsula, dominated by the ruins of the castle, or Castello Barbarossa. At the end of the climb, you will reach the highland of Anacapri, covered by a luxuriant vegetation and fine vineyards.

After touring Anacapri, the itinerary branches off toward the Monte Solaro and the Blue Grotto, or Grotta Azzurra.

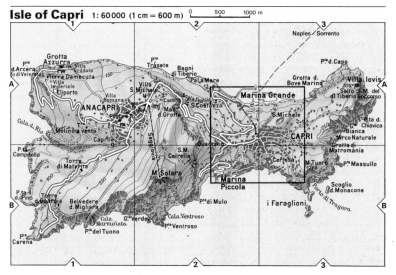

Isle of Capri 1: 60 000 (1 cm = 600 m)

Marina Grande

This is the most frequently used port on the island, and is also a noted beach and swimming spot. The town (elev. 2 m; page 145, A2 and 148, A1-2), extending along the little port, is set at the center of a broad inlet overlooking the Gulf of Naples, at the western edge of which extends the beach, while just a bit further along you can see the ruins of the so-called Palazzo a Mare, or seaside palace, probably Augustus's favorite residence on the island, stripped during excavations done at the end of the 18th c. and seriously damaged between 1806 and 1815 – when Capri was fought over between the French and English, allies of Ferdinand IV – with the creation of the parade ground, or Piazza d'Armi (now a playing field). The more monumental ruins of the Roman era are the so-called baths of Tiberius, or *Bagni di Tiberio*. The large Roman villa was meant to extend over a vast area, including a number of different rooms and structures set in a park.

Grotta Azzurra*, or the Blue Grotto

The famous grotto (p. 145, A1) was already known to the ancients, as we can see from the ruins of Roman structures inside and outside the grotto (Villa Gradola, see p. 145), but the true discovery, which gave the grotto its international renown, came during the 19th c. (1822), during a chance exploration by a fisherman from the island.

The large cavity has undergone, in the past geological eras, a slow sinking of about 20 meters due to "bradisimo," a mixed volcanic and seismic phenomenon, which led to the total blockage of all direct light sources, save through a large aperture, beneath sea level, from which the light gives the interior of the grotto its famous light-blue coloring, swathing all the walls of the grotto. The aperture is about two meters across and just over a meter high; the interior, which can be reached with special boats, measures some 54 x 15 meters, and is 30 meters tall, while the depth of the sea ranges from 14 to 22 meters. The lighting effect produced by the sunlight filtering through the water, aside from the distinctive and lovely bluish reflections from the rock, give objects in the water a silvery color. In a corner of the cavern is the so-called gallery, or *Galleria dei Pilastri*, an underwater tunnel with three branches flowing into a gallery that penetrates into underground cavities punctuated with stalactites. The entrance of one of these grottoes has traces of a Roman quay.

Capri*

Capital of the island and, traditionally, a busy center of tourism and high society (elev. 142 m, pop. 7,220). The town, nestled among the slopes of the hills of S. Michele and the Castiglione, is formed of little houses, in tufa and limestone, covered with terraces and extrados vaults, which make up a dense and intricate grid work of lanes. Elegant boutiques and refined clubs fill the winding lanes that surround the central Piazza Umberto I, creating a bizarre mixture of picturesque local Mediterranean houses and the refined international style of hotels, shops, and restaurants.

Piazza Umberto I (B2). This small square, known here simply as the "piazzetta," is always bustling and crowded, and is the heart of Capri – and has been for centuries, given the remarkable archaeological finds that have been dug up here. Enclosed by low buildings, with the clock tower, or *Torre dell'Orologio*, looming over all, it almost has the cozy appearance of a courtyard, often packed with the little tables of the cafes that overlook it, and opened on one side by the stairway that leads up to the *church of S. Stefano*, rebuilt at the end of the 17th c., to plans by Francesco Antonio Picchiatti, by Marziano Desiderio, in fanciful Baroque style, with dome and little "cupolettas," while on the interior are the tombs, or *Sepolcri di Giacomo e Vincenzo Arcucci*, by Michele Naccherino (formerly in the charterhouse, or Certosa) and, in the presbytery, a noteworthy ancient Roman floor in marble inlay, from the Villa Jovis.

Facing the church is the *Palazzo Cerio*, a renovated version of the castle of Joan I of Anjou (Castello di Giovanna I d'Angiò); it now houses the *Centro Caprense*, dedicated to the history of the island.

Certosa di S. Giacomo* (C2). This charterhouse was built in 1371-74 at the behest of Giacomo Arcucci who, following the confiscation of his property, retired here and died; the structure suffered serious damage following the incursions of Turkish pirates (1553, 1563) which led the monks to build a watch tower, which was destroyed during the last century. With the suppression of the orders, during the decade of French occupation, the structure was converted for use as a penitentiary, and then as a military installation. Currently, it is being used as a multifunctional center, for exhibitions, conferences, congresses, and musical events. Even though it has been heavily renovated, it remains one of the most important pieces of architecture on the island, and it is distinguished by typical extrados vaults in the roofing. The church opens with a pointed-arch portal, adorned with bas-reliefs and a 14th-c. fresco in the lunette. On the interior, with a single nave, with cross-vaults, there are still traces of 17th-c. frescoes. In the monastery there are two cloisters: the smaller cloisters, dating from the 15th c., has small columns with Roman and Byzantine capitals; the larger cloisters, dating from the late 16th c., is formed of arches on pillars, and is bounded by the main service halls of the monastery. The apartment of the prior is set at the edge of the precipice, and from the belvedere, you can enjoy a splendid view of the sea, toward Tragara, the Faraglioni, and the Marina Piccola. In the refectory, you will find the *Museo Diefenbach*, a museum that features a collection of the works of the German painting Karl Wilhelm Diefenbach, four Roman statues of marine deities found in the Blue Grotto, or Grotta Azzurra, between 1964 and 1970, while in the rectory, which has been restored, note the memorabilia, souvenirs of Capri, and drawings of G. Gigante, a celebrated painter and member of the School of Posillipo.

Parco Augusto* and Via Krupp* (C1-2). Via Matteotti, with a fine view of the charterhouse, or Certosa, leads to the Parco Augusto, a public garden that overlooks the sea, with scenic terraces offering panoramic views of Capri, the Faraglioni, and the Marina Piccola. In one of the most secluded corners is a *monument to Lenin*, who spent time on the island, when it was a haven for many Russian intellectuals and revolutionaries, including Maxim Gorky. You will pass under the overpass of the park and then you will enter Via Krupp, a celebrated road, built at the behest of the German steel tycoon; the road adapts cunningly to the rocky ridge, with switchback curves (fine view of the whole road from above), and climbs steeply down to the sea, offering lovely views of the coast, and then intersects with the road to Marina Piccola.

Castiglione and Belvedere Cannone* (C2). From Piazza Umberto I along Via Madre Serafina, which, like many other streets in Capri, alternates roofed-over sections, running under houses, with open-air stretches, offering views of the Marina Grande and Capri itself, you will reach the Belvedere Cannone, from which you can survey the eastern part of the island, with the Faraglioni and the inlet of Marina Piccola. Just before the Belvedere Cannone, a stairway leads up to the medieval *castle of the Castiglione*, which has been completely renovated.

Excursions

Villa Jovis*. If you begin from the Piazza Umberto I, you will cross the eastern side

Via Krupp, carved into the cliff face at Capri

of the settlement, until you reach Via Tiberio, which runs uphill among villas and olive groves, offering lovely views. The road passes near the little fourteenth-c. *church of S. Michele* and continues along the plain, flanked by small enclosure walls around vegetable patches and orchards, olive and citrus groves. After passing the tower, or *Torre del Faro* – a construction dating back to the reign of Tiberius, square at the base, with a cylindrical structure

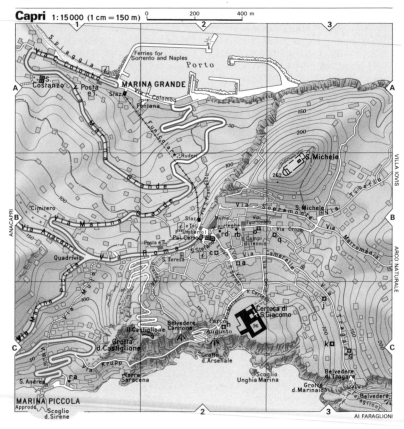

set atop the square base – the road leads to the excavations of the isolated imperial villa, which cover the summit of the eastern promontory of the island, known as Monte Tiberio (p. 145, A3).

The large villa, built at the behest of Tiberius, was the object of an early exploration, under the rule of the House of Bourbon, an exploration which really amounted to little more than a ransacking and plunder of the ornamental features, the most important remains of which are in part collected in the Villa S. Michele of Anacapri, in the Palazzo Cerio, and in the Museo di Napoli (one of the inlaid-marble floors is in the church of S. Stefano). A campaign of excavations, complete and systematic, was undertaken in the 1930s by Amedeo Maiuri, who thus unearthed one of the finest examples of a palace/villa from the imperial period.

The complex extends over a surface area of over 7,000 sq.m, with platforms and terraces that follow the sharp slope (40 m) upon which the villa stands.

Immediately after the entrance is the so-called Tiberius's leap, or *Salto di Tiberio*, a belvedere at the edge of a rocky precipice, from which, according to an erroneous and bloody-minded popular tradition, the emperor would have his chosen victims hurled. A stepped ramp leads up to the imperial complex, in which the various quarters are arranged around a large central structure, occupied by four cisterns, used to collect and store rainwater: to the south is the entrance and the rooms used as the bathhouse; to the west are the lodgings of the service staff; to the east is the quarters used in receptions and entertainment with six rooms arranged around a hemicycle; to the north extended the residence of the emperor, where you can still make out traces of marble flooring; adjoining the imperial residence was an immense *loggia/belvedere*, 92 m long, used by the emperor for his strolls.

If you return to the ramp, climbing up along the ruins of the villa, you will climb up to the esplanade that looms over the excavations (elev. 354 m) and where you will find the chapel, or *Cappella di S. Maria del Soccorso* and a statue of the Virgin Mary (1901); from here you may enjoy a spectacular view of the entire Gulf of Naples and part of the Gulf of Salerno.

From the Arco Naturale to Tragara. From the crossroads already mentioned in the route toward the Villa Jovis, you should turn into Via Matromania, at the end of which you will head toward the natural arch, or *Arco Naturale** (p. 145, A3), a spectacular product of the erosion of the limestone rock of which the entire island is formed, set high above the western coast of the island. If you head back to a small plaza, you can climb down a steep stepped path, presently very badly maintained and thus difficult to use, which leads to the grotto, or *Grotta di Matromania* (B3), dedicated in antiquity to the cult of Cybele, the goddess after whom the grotto was named, and transformed in Roman times, with masonry work, and decorations in stucco and mosaic. From here you can continue, climbing along a little road, often consisting of steps, that leads up, with a continual series of views of the sea, to the Belvedere di Tragara. Along the route, on the Punta Masullo (B3), you can see the *Villa Malaparte**, one of the most renowned and interesting works of modern architecture in Campania; with the sharp clarity of its shape and the color of its plaster work, the villa contrasts with the harsh surface of the rocky promontory on which it stands; it was built by Adalberto Libera in 1938-40 for the writer Curzio Malaparte. You will then reach, along Via Pizzolungo, the *Belvedere di Tragara** (elev. 130 m.), which opens out over the Faraglioni below (p. 145, B3; 148, C3). Continuing along a small and steep lane, you will reach the sea at the little *port of Tragara*, with the ruins of a Roman port, opposite the shoals, or Scoglio del Monacone, which also has Roman ruins, while on the right, rise the *three*

Faraglioni, which loom dozens of meters straight out of the sea. The first of these three rocks (elev. 109 m) is known as the *Stella* and is joined to the coast, the second one is the lowest of the three (elev. 81 m) while the third (elev. 104 m), known as the Scopolo, is inhabited by a rare type of light-blue lizard.

Marina Piccola

Beach resort, as well as the island's southern landing point. The little town (p. 148, C1) extends to the foot of the Monte Solaro, between the Marina di Mulo and the Marina di Pennauto, divided by the shoal, or Scoglio delle Sirene which, extending into the sea with its picturesque natural arch, reveals the ruins of a wharf dating from Roman times. The port of Marina Piccola is a point of departure for interesting excursions to the Grotta Verde, the Faraglioni, and the other marine grottoes of the southern side of the island.

Anacapri

Set on the slopes of the Monte Solaro, is the second center (elev. 275 m, pop. 5,593; p. 145, A1-2) of the island; largely composed of white houses, it extends in a lush esplanade. From the Piazza della Vittoria, which features the lower station of the chairlift to the Monte Solaro, if you follow the picturesque Via Capodimonte, crowded with stores working the mass tourism trade, you will reach the *Villa S. Michele* (A2), which belonged to Axel Munthe, a Swedish physician and a popular author. The building, erected near a chapel dedicated to St. Michael, and on the site of a Roman villa, contains furnishings and artworks dating from the 17th

The famous Faraglioni sentinels guard a brilliant blue sea, Capri

to the 19th c., as well as a number of ancient works in marble; note the lovely garden and splendid panoramic view* over the northern side of the island.

You will return toward the Piazza della Vittoria and from there you may head toward the central Piazza S. Nicola where there stands the Baroque *church of S. Michele*, built in 1719 to plans by D. A. Vaccaro. On the octagonal interior, note a remarkable *majolica flooring**, depicting the Garden of Eden, or Paradiso Terrestre, executed in

The renowned Piazzetta at Capri

1761 and designed by Solimena; on the altars, canvases by De Matteis and G. del Po; in the apse, *St. Michael*, by N. Malinconico; in order to observe the pattern of the floor as a whole, you should climb up to the organ loft, at the entrance of the church.

Further along, in the Piazza Diaz, is the *church of S. Sofia*, founded in the Middle Ages but heavily renovated, and devoid of a single coherent program, as can be seen in the unusual asymmetrical and diverse appearance of the five smaller domes that crown the building.

Excursions

Monte Solaro. The peak (elev. 589 m, p. 145, B2) can be reached by a cableway (departure from the Piazza della Vittoria) which runs up the green northern slope of the mountain, to within a few meters from the summit, where you can see the ruins of a fortification built in the 19th c. by the English, atop a medieval structure, and from which you can enjoy a vast panoramic view of the island and the gulfs of Naples and Salerno.

Santuario di S. Maria Cetrella. If you follow the trail that runs up the northern slope of the Monte Solaro, you will reach a crossroads, with a small chapel, where you will turn to the left toward the sanctuary, or Santuario di S. Maria Cetrella (elev. 434 m, p. 145 B2), a 14th-c. construction, isolated on the edge of the rocky face that overlooks the Marina Piccola with a splendid panoramic view of Capri.

Belvedere di Migliara. As you leave Caprile, you will take the road, or Strada di Migliara, that runs into the farmland of the countryside, with fine views of Anacapri and Ischia, until you reach the Belvedere di Migliara (elev. 292 m., page 145, B1), set at the beginning of the southwestern promontory of the island, at the tip of which (Punta Carena) there stands a lighthouse. If you climb the rocky ridge on the left and look out over the Punta del Tuono, you can see the entire southern coast of the island, as far as the Faraglioni. On your way back, if you take a trail that runs just to the left, along the sheer rock face, you will reach the tower, or *Torre della Guardia*, and then you will continue along to the tower, or *Torre Materita*, part of the defensive works against pirate raids, erected (16th c.) by the monks of the charterhouse, or Certosa, and later transformed into a home for Axel Munthe, who lived there from 1910 until 1943.

The Punta di Vetereto and the Blue Grotto, or Grotta Azzurra. If, from Anacapri, you take the road that runs along the western side of the island, you will reach a crossroads that leads, on the right, to the ruins of an impressive *Roman imperial villa* (p. 145, A1). Despite the devastations that have been inflicted over the centuries, it still has a long loggia/belvedere, supported by arches and pillars, extending along the edge of the rocky face, in every way similar to the Villa Jovis. Just a bit further along, at the eastern extremity, stands the tower, or *Torre di Damecuta*, another defensive structure erected against the incursions of pirates, where other rooms of the villa were found, and which offers a splendid view of the sea. Continuing, the road winds its way to the plaza that stands over the narrow entrance to the Blue Grotto, or *Grotta Azzurra* (see above), where you can still see the few surviving ruins of the little *Roman Villa Gradola*.

8 Campania Felix or Terra di Lavoro

The slow work of the watercourses, combined with the action of the volcanoes (Roccamonfina, Campi Flegrei) filled in the shallow sea bed, which extended out from the foot of the Apennines. It was precisely the volcanic nature of the soil, encouraged by the mild climate, that made this land remarkably fertile, to the point that it certainly deserved the nicknames it was given and which came to identify it over time: Campania Felix (i.e., blessed) and Terra di Lavoro (land of labor), but here the etymology involves the Latin *Terra Leboriae*, which has nothing to do with labor, and everything to do with the tribe of the Leborini, who lived here in ancient times. Crossed by the River Volturno, this area helped for centuries to meet the nutritional requirements of Rome, and later of the Kingdom of Naples. The favorable conditions allowed the development of numerous settlements of different peoples. The Greek settlements along the coasts had their counterparts on the interior in the small towns inhabited by Italic tribesmen: in the plains, the Oscans, on the pre-Apennine foothills, the Samnites. The expansionist ambitions of the Samnites for the control of the rich plain soon clashed with the burgeoning Roman power. The long series of clashes

Statues and water displays enliven the vast park of the Palazzo Reale, Caserta

over this part of Campania began at this time; too important to too many, for economic, commercial, and military reasons, this land became the theater of decisive battles and final clashes in the conquest of the south of Italy, or Mezzogiorno. In this way, it witnessed the wanderings of Hannibal, and the revolt of Spartacus, the consolidation of Longobard power, and the dawning of Norman domination. In the meanwhile there arose new cities and major monastic settlements, which contributed to the reorganization of the territory following the devastation in the wake of the fall of Rome. This was the case with Capua, one of the largest cities in the empire, which came back to life atop the ruins of its former self, but with the name of Santa Maria Capua Vetere, while the present-day Capua was refounded by the Longobards in a curve of the River Volturno; or Norman Aversa, the first step in the conquest of the kingdom; or even one of the filiations of the abbey, or Abbazia di Montecassino, the monastery, or Monastero di Sant'Angelo in Formis, built on the ruins of the sanctuary, or Santuario di Diana Tifatina. Following the Norman conquest, the plain came to be situated on the edge of the newly founded Kingdom of Sicily, with Capua for centuries as its main stronghold.

Today the destruction of farming, replaced by buildings that are more-or-less in violation of the building code, linked to the speculation in development, have profoundly modified the environment and the features of the landscape. Despite the general devastation, a number of features of the ancient human presence that are specific to these areas and that appear as constants, such as the unusual way in which grape-vines are cultivated as "maritata," or wedded to poplar trees – a system used by the ancient Romans – so as to form high-hanging festoons between the trees, in the fields, between the houses, and long the roads. Another is the system of centuriation which still underlies much of the network of roads and which is clearly at play in the layout of many of the towns.

8.1 Caserta

From Naples by highway you will quickly reach the tollbooth and exit of Caserta Nord (24.7 km), from which Via Appia (Statale 1) will quickly take you to the entrance to the Palazzo Reale. The visit to Caserta can be completed with at tour of San Leucio (3 km) and the Ponti della Valle, along the state road, or Statale 265, between Maddaloni and Valle di Maddaloni.

A must in completing this tour is a climb up to Casertavecchia (10 km from Caserta), one of the most interesting medieval towns in Campania.

Caserta

The city (elev. 68 m, pop. 71,281) was built at the edge of the plain, following the construction of the Reggia, on the site of what had been until 1752 a little village, known as La Torre (from a feudal tower of the family of the Acquaviva d'Aragona), named Caserta after the old nearby town, which thereafter became known as Casertavecchia. The true urban development did not come until the second half of the 19th c., but its prevalently modern appearance is a result of the intense and chaotic construction activity that went on here in the years just after WWII.

The **Palazzo Reale***, or royal palace, of exceptional size and uncommon beauty, is the most monumental and one of the most splendid complexes of the sort in Italy. Its construction came about at the behest of its founder, Charles of Bourbon (who purchased this feudal land holding for 489,348 ducats), who wished to emulate the splendor of the French court of Versailles, raising the kingdom to a European level and, at the same time, offering the Neapolitan government a headquarters that was less exposed to possible attack by enemy artillery; a risk that became frighteningly real in 1742 when an English naval squadron had seriously threatened the vulnerable capital. The design of the monument, entrusted to Luigi Vanvitelli, was approved in 1751, and work began at the start of the following year, and were finally completed in 1774 under the supervision of Carlo Vanvitelli, who had taken over the project following the death of his father (1773). The project, which should also be considered in terms of urban planning, is based on an exceedingly long perspective view that, from the large avenue, or "viale" (once lined with trees) coming from Naples, through the su-

perb atrium that runs the length of the building, frames the glittering waterfall at the far end of the park. Even if today this immense view is interrupted by the railroad, the "perspectival telescope" preserves all of its spectacular majesty.

This building, with a rectangular plan (247 x 184 m), is articulated around four large courtyards, and includes five floors and has a total of 1,200 rooms (among them are the rooms of the royal apartments on the second floor, which constitute a full-fledged museum of furnishing and decoration, with collections that document the passage from the Rococo style to the neoclassical). The facade is majestically defined by the rhythm of a solemn cadenza of semicolumns alternating with fluted pilaster strips set on a rusticated base; the rear elevation, entirely similar but richer and more elegant, can be considered the true "facade of honor," counterbalancing the immense park.

The interior is characterized by a vast and monumental *atrium* divided into a nave and two side-aisles, and opening on the sides onto the four courtyards. As you walk through it, you will reach the *lower vestibule**

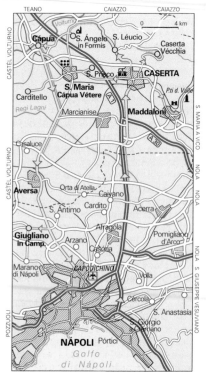

The Palazzo Reale, Caserta, with its huge French-style gardens behind

bounded by eight large pillars; to the left is the ancient *statue of Hercules**, originally from the Farnese collection; from the center of the vestibule, you have a glimpse of the courtyards and a view of the park. To the right extends the spectacular *staircase of honor**, the central ramp of which frames the statue of Charles of Bourbon on the back of a lion (personification of royal highness, or *Maestà Regia*), flanked by *statues of Merit and Truth*; the elliptical vaulted ceiling has a double structure so that the musicians can be housed without being seen, for either solemn or festive occasions. The artists who worked in the palace, or Reggia were selected by Vanvitelli as particularly well suited to fit into a homogeneous array of decoration. Aside from the painters G. Starace (vaulted ceiling of the staircase), F. Fischetti, and D. Mondo, we should mention the sculptors A. Violani, P. and T. Solari, P. Persico, and G. Salomone.

The stairway then continues with two parallel flights of steps, which lead to the elegant *upper vestibule**, similar in form and structure to the lower vestibule, and singular in its unusual vortex effect, produced by the caissons in the lacunar vaulted ceiling. Facing it is the entrance to the Palatine chapel, or **Cappella Palatina*** (normally closed), the only element of the palazzo that shows a clear derivation from Versailles: the rectangular plan is covered with a barrel vault and a semicircular apse.

On the left, you enter the **royal apartments***. The first room is the great hall, or *Salone degli Alabardieri* with a fresco by Mondo in the vaulted ceiling, exalting the

Bourbons, and stuccoes by T. Bucciano. Next come the *Salone delle Guardie*, embellished with stuccoes and bas-reliefs (by T. Bucciano, G. Salomone, P. Persico), frescoes (G. Starace), and sculptures extolling the glories of the Farnese family (since king Charles was the son of the last Farnese, Elisabetta). You will then pass into the great hall, or *Salone di Alessandro* (in the vaulted ceiling, fresco by M. Rossi), with Empire-style furnishings and with a large clock, made in 1828, with a remarkable 24-hour dial; from the window, which corresponds to the central balcony of the facade, there is broad view of the avenue running to Naples.

If you continue to the right you will reach the rooms of the new apartment, or *Appartamento Nuovo* (1807-45), in which the halls, or *Sala di Marte* and *Sala di Astrea*, are followed by the *Sala del Trono* (throne room, designed by G. Genovese), with depictions of the kings of Naples and the provinces of the kingdom. You enter the apartment of the king, or *Appartamento del Re*, which included the council chamber, or Sala del Consiglio, the bedroom, or Camera da Letto di Francesco II, and various facilities and services; beyond is the bedroom, or Camera da Letto di Murat, in pure Empire style, and, after a passageway, the oratory, or Oratorio.

You will then return to the hall, or Salone di Alessandro, and from there you will pass into the old apartment, or *Appartamento Vecchio**, decorated with fabrics and wallpaper from the manufactories of San Leucio. This wing of the palace was inhabited by Ferdinand IV (1780) and Ferdinand II, who died here in 1859. The first four rooms, dedicated to the seasons, have vaulted ceilings frescoed with mythological allegories; two other rooms precede the private rooms of the sovereigns, set at the end of the apartment; among the paintings, note the *temperas** by Hackert. To the left of the hall, or Sala delle Dame is the library, or *Biblioteca* with over 10,000 volumes; next comes a large hall that features a magnificent crèche, or *presepe** dating from 18th-c. Naples, with more than 1,200 figures. In the halls that follow is the art gallery, or *Pinacoteca*, with paintings by Italian and non-Italian artists from the 18th c., and early 19th c., including the *Ports** by Hackert, and other view paintings and paintings celebrating the houses of Farnese and Bourbon.

In the second courtyard on the left, is the little theater, or **Teatrino di Corte*** (1769) with five orders of boxes and broad openings behind the stage, which allowed the use of the park behind as a striking theatrical backdrop.

In the second courtyard on the right is the **Museo dell'Opera**, or museum of the construction, in which, among other things, are displayed the *models** by Vanvitelli of the Reggia; in an underground chamber, with entrance between the 2nd and the 1st courtyard on the right, you may see tombs dating from the second half of the 4th c. B.C. and their furnishings.

The **park***, the creation of the creative genius Vanvitelli, strikes at first glance with the remarkable theatrical effect produced by the long central axis (ca. 3 km) comprising a sequence of basins, fountains (not always in operation), and waterfalls, enriched with large sculptural groups, and sloping down from the hill to the plain.

If you follow the central avenue, or "viale," you will reach the fountain, or *Fontana Margherita*, also known as the *Fontana del Canestro* (see plan on p. 150, C1); you will then climb up to the bridge, or *Ponte di Ercole* (C1) which then takes you to most spectacular area. This is the beginning of the upper fish pond, or *Peschiera Superiore* (475 x 29 m), fed by the waterfall, or *Cascata dei Delfini* (C1); after this, there is a higher stretch of land, with a long meadow ending at the fountain, or *Fontana di Eolo* (B1), a large basin with 29 statues of the Winds, arranged on artificial shoals, which serve to gather the water, which then flows under the meadow and reappears in the waterfall, or Cascata dei Delfini. You will then continue to climb up, among balustrades upon which stand statues of slaves, and then

you will reach another level, where there is a long basin in which the water runs, tumbling through seven sets of rapids; at the end of the basin is the fountain, or *Fontana di Cerere*, or else *Zampilleria* (A-B1), characterized by statues of dolphins, tritons, and the rivers Simeto and Oreto, from which gush powerful sprays of water; in the center is the group of Ceres (Cerere in Italian, hence the name of the fountain) and Nymphs. Alongside runs another basin, with 12 sets of rapids, which then flows into the fountain, or *Fontana di Venere e Adone* (A1). After a stairway, with balustrades and statues, you will reach the basin into which flows, from on high (elev. 78 m) the great waterfall, or **Grande Cascata**, also known as the *Fontana di Diana* because of the group of Diana and Acteon; on the sides, two sets of steps lead up to the grotto (elev. 204 m), from which the water originally spills out, after having flowed downhill for 40 kilometers.

The aqueduct, or *Acquedotto Carolino*, an imposing piece of engineering by Vanvitelli, was begun in 1753 and inaugurated in 1769; to reach the Reggia, it was necessary to tunnel through five mountains and build three large viaducts, the most important of which, known as the *Ponti della Valle**, 529 m long and 56 m high, crosses the broad valleys between the Monte Longano and Monte Calvi (we recommend visiting it, to complete your tour of the park, along the state road, or Statale 265, just after Maddaloni). At the top of the waterfall is a view of the enormous expanse of the park and the plain and, beyond, on clear days, as far as the Phlegrean Fields and Ischia.

Beside the fountain, or Fontana di Diana is the English garden, or **Giardino Inglese*** (A-B2), laid out in 1782 by the Englishman, G. A. Graefer, under the supervision of Carlo Vanvitelli. The place was made particularly charming by its avenues, or "viali," which, by adapting to the irregular lie of the land, wind up terminating unexpectedly in copses with fake ancient ruins. In one of these copses you will find a statue of Venus (A2) kneeling on a rock in the middle of a little lake and, in the background, artificial ruins in which statues from Pompeii have been set up. If you follow the little stream that runs out of the lake, you will reach another small and charming pond, at the center of which is a shoal, with a little fake Roman temple.

You will return to the fountain, or Fontana Margherita, where you will take the avenue on the right that leads into the woods, or Bosco Vecchio, as far as the large fish pond, or *Peschiera Grande* (270 x 105 m; C1). Toward the center of the woods is the *Castelluccia* (D1), with an octagonal plan, conceived as a place of leisure for the young Bourbon princes.

San Leucio

This town, like Carditello (see p. 163), was part of the vast project of territorial reorganization, undertaken in the wake of the construction of Reggia, around which a new city was meant to spring up, linked by long tree-lined boulevards with Naples and the other royal estates in the area around Caserta. Once it became clear that the city would not be built, attention focused on the suburban residences. At San Leucio (elev. 112 m) the hunting lodge, or Casino di Caccia del Belvedere came to find itself at the center of one of the most remarkable undertakings of 18th-c. Naples, a silk manufactory built at the command of Ferdinand IV, who did more than simply to establish the factory. The sovereign, in fact, intended to establish a colony, with a statute of its own, housed in a new city that would be personally linked with its founder, even in its name, Ferdinandopoli. The colony of

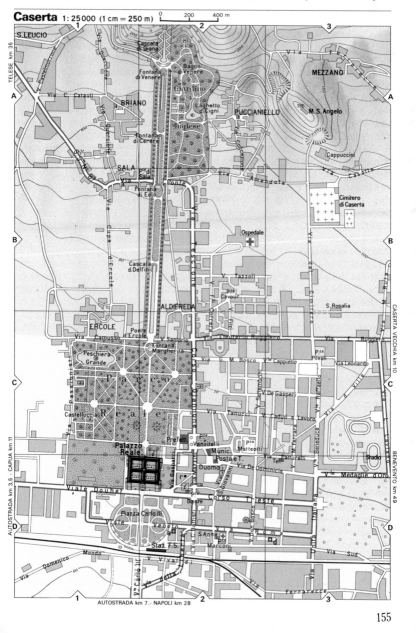

Caserta 1:25 000 (1 cm = 250 m)

San Leucio received its "constitution" in 1789; the fundamental principles of its statute predicate equality among the residents of the new city, an idea that, actually, in the larger context of European cultural progress, seemed to anticipate the theories concerning socialist communities of Owen and Fourier.

The colony was in fact established, but once again, the new city failed to materialize; plans for it were drawn up by Collecini, who designed it according to a regular geometric grid with a central square and a network of radial and concentric streets, lined by homes, divided up into the two quarters of San Carlo and San Ferdinando, while the factory, the school, and the royal apartment would be installed in the Belvedere, in a location dominating the slope of the hill. The part of the project that was in fact implemented, and which can still be seen today, concerns the houses near the entrance of the Belvedere, and this is the part that best reflects the "communitarian" nature of the initiative: two lines of row houses which, if it had been completed, would have enclosed a courtyard in which each member of the colony would have established their own little vegetable patch. It is possible to tour a number of private textile manufactories with 19th-c. looms.

Casertavecchia

This picturesque medieval village, or "borgo," (elev. 401 m) was founded in the 8th c. by the Longobards of the principality of Capua; it experienced a considerable increase in population, becoming an episcopal see, following the raids of the Saracens in the plains of Campania.

Its decline began with the construction of the Reggia, which led to the foundation of the Nuova Caserta and the abandonment of the old village, or "borgo."

On the slopes of the hill is the church of *S. Pietro ad Montes**, dating from the 12th c., with an isolated campanile.

Today Casertavecchia is one of the most interesting and best preserved villages of southern Italy, and has managed to preserve its original appearance, not only in its noteworthy monumental buildings, but also in many of its houses and streets.

The settlement of Casertavecchia clusters around the cathedral, or **Cattedrale*** (1113-53), clearly inspired by the model of the cathedral of Sessa Aurunca, mingling elements taken from the Romanesque architecture of Apulia, Sicilian/Moorish architecture, and the Benedictine architecture of Montecassino. The facade, in tufa, presents three marble portals; corresponding to the largest of the three is a triangular pediment, beneath which runs a cornice of small hanging arches, running the entire perimeter of the building; in the pediment is a sequence of little intertwined blind arches, which we also find in the *drum**, a masterpiece of chromatic refinement, rich colors, and varied motifs. On the side of the cathedral are horseshoe arches, which might derive from the four-light mullioned windows of the cloister, or Chiostro di S. Sofia in Benevento, or, like many Muslim motifs, through a direct Spanish or Sicilian adaptation. On the right is the *campanile** (1234) which spans the street, with a large pointed arch, some 32 m high, and culminates in an octagonal cross sections, in which we find again the motif of the intertwined blind arches, which extends to the four little corner towers.

The interior is divided by recycled columns with a nave and two side-aisles terminating in apses: alongside the semicircular central apse, there are two smaller apses in the same shape. Pointed arches with hanging ribbing, as in certain Sicilian examples, of Moorish derivation, support the dome, which is elliptical and set on "trumpet" pendentives, and conclude the long procession of arches set on columns; the transept features ribbed cross-vaults, added later. At the end of the nave is the *pulpit*, set on five columns, recomposed in the 17th c. with pieces of medieval ambos, adorned with mosaics. Similar decoration is found in the altar and the flooring before it; in the transept, two 14th-c. tombs, based on the funerary typology developed by Tino da Camaino and, in the sacristy, a wooden *Crucifix* from the same period.

Beyond the right side of the cathedral is the little church of the *Annunziata*, built at the end of the 13th c., with a rich marble portal, preceded by an 18th-c. portico; the interior, with a single nave, is lit by high mullioned windows.

Particularly charming is a promenade along the streets lined with numerous medieval houses; in the eastern sector, note the ruins of the castle, or *Castello*, the only noteworthy surviving element of which is a powerful *tower** standing 30 m tall, with a polygonal base of 16 sides, faced in light stone atop which rises a cylindrical shaft made of dark tufa-stone, built as a residence by Richard – count of Caserta from 1231 on, and as of 1246 the son-in-law of Frederick II – in the context of an existing castle. Work on its construction is thought to have occurred in the decade 1240-50.

8.2 The Two Capuas

Not far away from Caserta, now the chief town of the Terra di Lavoro, stand the two cities that in various periods have each worn the name of Capua, constituting the history of this plain for centuries. The itinerary begins from the older of the two towns, Santa Maria Capua Vetere (7 km from Caserta), and continues north along the Appian Way, or Via Appia, toward Capua (4 km). An indispensable complement to a tour of the two cities are those to San Prisco, not far from the older city (on Via Appia, 2 km), and at Sant'Angelo in Formis (5 km from Capua), celebrated for the presence of the ruins of the Benedictine abbey, from which it takes its name. The trip back to Naples runs through Aversa with a detour to Carditello.

Santa Maria Capua Vetere

This city (elev. 36 m, pop. 30,796), is on the site of the ancient Capua, an important center of Etruscan culture, conquered by the Samnites, and later an ally of Rome. It always maintained a certain autonomy and staged repeated revolts against the Romans (it was at Capua that the famous slave revolt broke out, under the leadership of Spartacus); in the 5th c., it was considered to be the 8th city in the empire, and the largest one in southern Italy. Because of its location, isolated in a plain, it was particularly vulnerable to the attacks of barbarians; the worst raid, which led to the city being abandoned, came in A.D. 841, when the town was burned by the Saracens. The surviving inhabitants, after taking refuge on the Monti Tifatini, and founded the new Capua on the ruins of ancient *Casilinum*, a place on the River Volturno that could be better defended. In the old city, around the church of S. Maria Maggiore, there grew up a small "casale" or hamlet, which, in the 14th c., was indicated by the dedication of its church, and then took on the more complete name of Santa Maria Capua Vetere, in commemoration of the ancient city, of which imposing archaeological digs and ruins still survive. The cathedral, or **Duomo*** (C2), is a vast basilica with a nave and four side-aisles, all of remarkable breadth; the original layout dates back to the 5th c. Built, according to tradition by St. Symmachus, bishop of the city from A.D. 424 to 439, on the cemetery of S. Prisco, some believe that it was enlarged in the two outer aisles by Arechi II, the Longobard duke of Benevento, in A.D. 787; the apse was built in 1666; further restorations were done in the

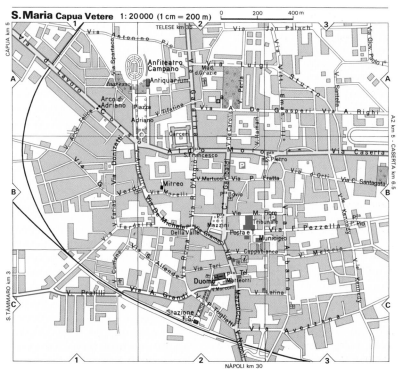

S. Maria Capua Vetere   1: 20000 (1 cm = 200 m)

18th c. and at the end of the 19th c., as is shown by the long neoclassical facade and the lavish Baroque decoration of the interior. The sole surviving relic of the original structure is the array of 51 columns that punctuate the nave and four aisles, taken from monuments of ancient Capua. We should mention, among the many artworks that adorn it, canvases by G. Diano and F. De Mura; on the left side, handsome view of the 16th-c. dome of the chapel, or Cappella di S. Maria Suricorum.

The **Museo Archeologico dell'Antica Capua** (B2) displays in chronological order the

end of the first and the beginning of the 2nd c. A.D., replacing a prior structure, it was then restored by Hadrian; further work was undertaken at the behest of Antoninus Pius. The amphitheater measured 169 x 139 m, and with its four stories, rose to a height of 46 m; the first three stories were formed of 80 arches in travertine, with keystones comprising busts of deities (some of which are now in the Museo Campano, while seven adorn the facade of the town hall, or Palazzo Municipale, of Capua), while the fourth floor was faced with blind arches, with pilaster strips; the arches on the second and

The archaeological site at S. M. Capua Vetere, showing the Anfiteatro Campano

materials discovered over the last 40 years in the territory of ancient "Capua." The Bronze Age is documented by discoveries made between the River Volturno and the canal of Agnena. Next come copious materials (tomb furnishings with Etruscan-Corinthian bronzes and ceramics) from the orientalizing period, the archaic period – to which we should refer traces of the settlement – and the classical period, from which the tomb furnishings reveal elements of Greek importations and Campanian origin. The Samnite domination relives through finds from painted tombs (one of these has been reconstructed), while the centuries between the wars of Hannibal and the conquest of the colony by Caesar in 59 B.C are treated in a special room. Of considerable note are the collections of terracottas and materials from the sanctuaries of Diana Tifatina and from the Fondo Patturelli.

The Amphitheater of Campania, or **Anfiteatro Campano*** (A1-2), second in size only to the Colosseum. Founded between the

third level were embellished with statues, of which there remain *Eros*, *Venus*, and the so-called *Psyche of Capua* (now at the Museo di Napoli). On the interior, above the steps or bleachers, was a monumental colonnade built by Hadrian, and, on a higher cornice, there stood the poles which held up the *velarium* (it would seem that the use of the *velarium* in Rome was introduced in imitation of this arena).

The monument underwent serious damage in A.D. 456 and in A.D. 841; it was reused as a fortress by the Longobards and underwent centuries of ransacking and plunder. You can see the ruins of the first level – with two arches, which preserve the busts of Ceres and Juno in the keystone – and part of the second level; there is no longer a trace of the steps of the *cavea*, but it is possible to walk the length of the corridors below, where there are several fragments of mural paintings.

Alongside it stands the **Antiquarium** (A2). It contains materials found in the city and in the surrounding territory, including inscriptions of the *magistri campani* from the 2nd/1st c. B.C., which refer to public works executed in ancient Capua.

As you return toward the Piazza Mazzini you may visit, in Via Morelli, the **Mitreo*** (B2), or Mithraeum, a monument dating from imperial Rome, discovered in 1922 (guided tour, inquire with the custodians of the amphitheater) dedicated to the cult of the Persian god Mithras. It is particularly interesting because of the excellent because of the excellent state of preservation in which it has survived; it is composed of a large underground chamber (23 x 3 m) with benches for the faithful, arranged along the long sides. The vaulted ceiling is frescoed with six-pointed stars and the far wall has a rare fresco showing *Mithras Killing the Bull* (2nd c.), flanked by other paintings, badly damaged, with scenes having to do with the initiation of the faithful; this is the most complete cycle known concerning the Mithras cult.

Between the Corso Moro and Via del Lavoro is the arch of Hadrian, or **Arco di Adriano** (A1), also known as the *Archi di Capua*, in all probability dedicated to the emperor who was most attentive to this city. Built in brickwork, with a marble facing, had three fornices set on pillars, in which there were niches for statues now lost; there remain three pillars and one of the side arches.

Along the current Via Caserta (which follows the route of the ancient Appian Way, or Via Appia) are two major and renowned Roman tomb.

The so-called **Carceri Vecchie***, or old prisons, are the largest funerary structure in the region, and are laid out in a way that is distinctive of mausoleums, and comprise two stacked cylindrical structures, with semi-columns alternating with niches in the lower structure. The other tomb, better preserved and already restored under Ferdinand IV, is known as the **Conocchia***, and consists of a square structure with curvilinear sides and corner turrets, upon which stands a tambour.

At a distance of 2 km to the east of the city, you will reach **San Prisco**, a small town (elev. 48 m, pop. 8,941) founded in early times. The feature of greatest interest is the parish church, where you can still see, following the renovations done in the 18th c. – the sole surviving early relic – the chapel, or *Cappella di S. Matrona**, named for the Roman patrician woman who, in the 6th c., ordered the construction of a basilica in honor of St. Priscus: a sacellum with a square plan and four corner columns detached from the wall and still adorned with *mosaics** in the vaulted ceiling and in the lunettes with palms, golden vases, doves, and the symbols of the Evangelists.

Capua

This city (elev. 25 m, pop. 19,576), which spreads out in an oxbow curve of the River Volturno, and enclosed by 16th-c. bastion, has always been of major strategic importance. The Longobards of Capua, after the burning of the old city in A.D. 841, decided to found the new Capua on the ruins of ancient *Casilinum*, a small town linked to the older Capua, constituting its river port. In A.D. 856, the survivors, led by Lando I, populated the new city, which, because of its important strategic position, played a new role, as the capital of an independent principality (900-1134), the product of a secession from the principality of Salerno. Over the following centuries, it became increasingly a model of a fortress town. Set along the Appian Way, or Via Appia, controlling the ancient Roman bridge that ran across the River Volturno (this is the only large river town in the south of Italy, or Mezzogiorno), it represented, until the Unification of Italy, an ideal entry port to the south of Italy, and one of the last bulwarks for the dynasties that ruled there: its conquest was decisive if one wished to attempt to occupy the kingdom.

The center of the city is the **Piazza dei Giudici*** (B2), lying athwart the *Corso Appio* (the main road which follows the route of the old Appian Way, or Via Appia), with the town hall, or *Palazzo Municipale* (1561) which bears on its facade seven busts taken from the amphitheater of ancient Capua. Alongside is the medieval *church of S. Eligio*, rebuilt in Baroque form in 1747. Next comes the 15th-c. arch, or *Arco di S. Eligio*, with broad cross-vaults and, above them, a little loggia. On the southern side, is the little 17th-c. *Seggio*, with a statue of Charles II. The Via Duomo leads to the cathedral, or **Cattedrale** (B2), founded in A.D. 856, rebuilt in the 12th c., renovated in 1724 and again in 1850, nearly entirely destroyed in the bombing of 1943 and rebuilt again in a modern style. It was clearly reminiscent of the abbey, or Abbazia di Montecassino, as well in the porticoed atrium, renovated or built (1072-86) by Archbishop Erveo, and then rebuilt again after that. On the right side is the *campanile** dating from the 9th or 11th c., restored frequently, three stories tall, with twin-light mullioned windows, and with ancient columns in the base. The modern interior, with a nave and two aisles, set on columns, still preserves numerous relics of the old church: the *candelabrum with*

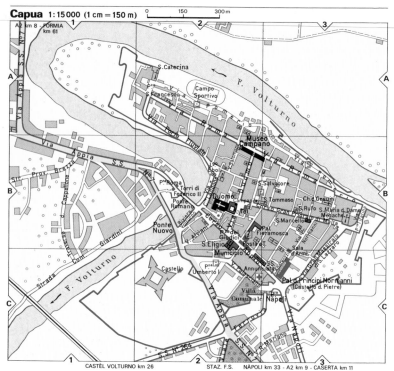

CASTÈL VOLTURNO km 26   STAZ. F.S.   NÁPOLI km 33 - A2 km 9 - CASERTA km 11

the Paschal taper* (13th c.), in the chapel, or Cappella del Sacramento, a Virgin Mary with Christ Child, by P. Alamanno; in the apse, *Our Lady of the Assumption*, by Solimena; in the crypt (18th c.), with 24 columns, there is a chapel (adorned on the exterior with medieval pilaster strips and capitals) in which you should note a marble *Dead Christ** by Bottigliero (1724) and an *Addolorata* dating from the 18th c.

Near the right side of the church (side portal from the 12th c.) you can enter the former chapel, or Ex Cappella del Sacramento, site of the *Museo Diocesano*, established in 1993, where there are artworks dating from Roman times to the 19th c. (including Longobard and Norman work in marble and a panel by Antoniazzo Romano).

You will then follow Via Duomo which leads to the museum, or Museo Campano, installed in the monastery, or Convento della Concezione and the *Palazzo Antignano**, dating from the 15th c., with an original Catalonian portal; also of interest are the handsome open staircase in the courtyard and the large cross-vault set on ancient columns and Longobard capitals, which from Via Duomo leads to Via Roma.

Inaugurated in 1874, the **Museo Campano*** (B2-3) contains work which help to document the history of civilization in Terra di Lavoro; adjoining it are an important library, or Biblioteca, with 10th-c. parchments, incunabula, and an archives, or Archivio, of fundamental importance for the history of Capua.

Among the collections are the *Lapidario Mommsen*, the second-most important collection of Roman epigraphs found in the countryside of Campania ("agro campano"), after the collection of the Museo di Napoli, a rich series of *Roman funerary steles* from Capua and Casilinum; sculptures (*Volturnus*) and inscriptions taken from the Amphitheater; among the inscriptions is the famous one concerning the establishment of the *Colonia Julia* by Augustus. The most singular and prestigious collection of the museum comprise the *votive hoard** taken from the sanctuary dedicated to the Italic goddess of fertility, Matuta, found near the Fondo Patturelli at Santa Maria Capua Vetere in 1845. The finds comprise the remains of the podium and of a step of the altar of the temple, and an endless array of coroplastic works and architectural terracottas, as well as a considerable number of statues (ca. 200) of Mothers, or *Madri**, in gray tufa, seated with one or two children in their arms. These are votive statuettes which, in their rudimentary and geometric composition, are among the most precious documents of the popular art of Campania between the 5th and 1st c. B.C.

In the medieval section, you should note the statues from the gate, or *Porta di Capua**, taken from the demolished gate built by Frederick II, among the most important works of 13th-c. Italian sculpture (*busts of Pier delle Vigne and Taddeo da Sessa*, counselors of the emperor, the colossal head, known as the Testa di *Capua Fidelis*, a head of Jove, and a headless statue of *Frederick II*, enthroned). Among the artworks from the 15th to 18th c. are sculptures by A. Caccavello, G. D. D'Auria, M. Naccherino, G. da Nola, and paintings by B. Vivarini, G. del Po, and a large fresco of the *Ascension* (1290-95).

After you leave the museum, you turn to the right, in Via Principi Longobardi, you will enter the area of the place, the memory of which survives in the names of the **Longobard churches*** of *S. Giovanni a Corte, S. Michele a Corte*, and *S. Salvatore Maggiore a Corte* (B2-3) devastated in part by recent restorations. The first two churches preserve traces of the early construction in the fragments of frescoes in the crypt (the lowered dome of S. Michele clearly shows eastern influences); the church of S. Salvatore presents, on the other hand, greater relics of the Longobard foundation (10th c.), in particular note the little campanile with two levels of twin-light mullioned windows and the three arches in the facade, formerly overlooking the portico. On the sides of the nearby *church of S. Domenico*, the large Gothic windows have been exposed. You will then follow the Corso Gran Priorato, where you may note the church of the *SS. Rufo e Carponio** (B3), with a campanile dating from the 13th c.; further along is the church of *S. Marcello Maggiore* (B3), dating from the 12th c. (but rebuilt in the 19th c.), with an interesting side *portal** made up of items taken from various sources: the architrave is formed from the funerary inscription of one of the earliest counts of Capua.

You will turn to the right, in Via dei Principi Normanni, where you may note the *church di S. Salvatore Piccolo*, with a Longobard inscription in the architrave of the portal; you will reach the castle, or *Castello delle Pietre*, the residence of the Norman princes (11th c.; C3); built with large blocks of stone taken from the

amphitheater, or Anfiteatro Campano, it preserves a massive tower, which has been extensively renovated.

Once you return to the Corso Appio, you will proceed on your left until you reach the elegant, late-16th-c. gate, or *Porta Napoli** (C3), beyond which, once you cross the moat, you can make out the bastions of the Renaissance **enclosure walls***; if you turn to the right, you can observe the 16th-c. castle, known as the Castello degli Spagnoli (C2).

You will return through the gate, and then you may continue to follow the Corso Appio; on the right you will skirt the side of the **church of the Annunziata*** (C2-3). Founded at the end of the 12th c., it was rebuilt in the years of 1531-74 and completed in the Baroque period; it is dominated by a soaring, elegant dome designed by D. Fontana. The right side has a base – formed of large stone blocks taken from the amphitheater, or Anfiteatro Campano – crowned by Corinthian pilaster strips and by a cornice. The interior, restored after the serious damage inflicted in 1943, has a single nave, with side chapels and a handsome gilt wooden ceiling, with paintings by F. Vitale. In the chapels, canvases by Conca, Mondo, and

One of the mother figures in the Museo Campano, Capua

others; in the transept and apse, *canvases** by De Mura; the carved wooden and inlaid choir (scenes from the *Life of Christ*) dates back to 1519.

Once you reach the Piazza dei Giudici you will turn to the right into the street where the Palazzo Fieramosca (B2-3) stands; it already existed in the 13th c., and was the home in 1447 of Rinaldo Fieramosca, the father of Ettore Fieramosca, the hero of the duel, or Disfida di Barletta. The palazzo earlier had belonged to Bartolomeo di Capua (14th c.), a great dignitary of the Angevin court, and then to Ludovico of Durazzo, the father of Charles III, king of Naples, and known in fact as "Il Capuano," that is, "the Capuan." It is possible to make out in the construction the various characters accumulated by its centuries of stratification: on the facade, medieval and Renaissance windows overlap; the pointed-arch portal is adorned with Angevin lilies while in the courtyard you may note two 11th-c. Longobard capitals.

Along the Corso Appio, you will return toward the River Volturno and the modern bridge, called the *Ponte Romano*, in commemoration of the ancient bridge, destroyed in 1943, at the beginning of which stand the ruins of the gate, or **Porta di Capua** (B2). Frederick II had ordered the restoration of the Roman bridge and, at the point where the Appian Way, or Via Appia, entered Capua, he ordered the construction of a monumental gate, in accordance with a project that involved him as more than a mere client; indeed, Frederick too active part, working almost as an architect, in what are still known as "Frederician architecture," of which this gate is one of the most important examples. Begun in 1233 and completed in 1239-40, it was demolished (1557) in the context of the reconstruction of the city walls ordered by the Spanish. There survive the bases of the two towers that flanked it and the sculptures that are now in the Museo Campano.

Sant'Angelo in Formis

At a distance of roughly 4 km from Capua stands this small town (elev. 50 m) which, on the slopes of the Monte Tifata, has taken the name of the basilica that stands there, one of the most important medieval monuments of Campania. After you cross the village, you will reach a gate, known as the *Arco di Diana*, which leads into an enormous plaza overlooking the plains. Here, in a location that is nearly isolated from the town, stands the **Basilica*** of S. Michele Arcangelo, built on the ruins of the temple, or Tempio di Diana Tifatina. The interest of this monument is considerable, both in terms of the architecture, and for the important series of frescoes, and, above all, because, following the total destruction of the abbey, or Abbazia di Montecassino,

during WWII, here, perhaps more than anywhere else, it is possible find traces of the original model.

As early as the 10th c. there existed a church, known as "ad arcum Dianae," which, having fallen out of use, was ceded to the Benedictines of Montecassino, and was rebuilt (1072-87) in its present-day form by the Abbot Desiderius, who endowed it with a monastery of considerable size, now almost wholly vanished. The facade is preceded by a portico with five arches, supported by four recycled columns with Corinthian capitals; the central arcade, which is higher, has a round head, while the side arches feature a pointed arch of Islamic style. In the central arch is set a classical-style portal, and in the architrave is an epigraph commemorating the foundation promoted by Desiderius; in the lunette is a fresco with a depiction of *St. Michael*; above the portal is the *Virgin Mary with Two Angels* (the one on the right was repainted); in the lunettes of the other arches, frescoes with stories of *St. Anthony Abbot* and *St. Paul the Hermit*. This series of external frescoes can be dated to the end of the 12th century.

To the right of the facade is the massive *campanile** (in the construction of which, recycled material for the temple of Diana was used abundantly), with a square plan, set on two levels in lively chromatic contrast. The lower fascia, in blocks of travertine, culminates in a classical style cornice; next comes the second level in terracotta, with twin-light mullioned windows. The interior, basilican, without transept, is subdivided into a nave and two side-aisled, with Corinthian columns upon which stand round arches, ending in three apses. You can see traces of the medieval mosaic floor, similar in the decorative schemes to those used in the prototype of Montecassino, while the wooden ceiling of the nave is a reconstruction dating from 1927. Near the entrance are two holy-water stoups and baptismal fonts, obtained from the readaptation of various architectural elements; to the left of the altar is the simple marble pulpit (12th c.).

The *frescoes** are the most important cycle in terms of extension and completeness ever to survive, of their sort, in all of southern Italy, especially because they allow us to measure the degree to which the artists had escaped the hieratic Byzantine style, and the degree of vernacular art that entered into it. These date from the period of Desiderius because the abbot (who became Pope Victor III in 1084, and died in

1087) is depicted in the apse, during his lifetime, as is shown by the square halo, instead of a circular one. The cycle proceeds in accordance with the customary styles of Byzantine painting: in the nave, three stacked registers narrate *Episodes from the New Testament* – the scenes are in order from the highest register of the right wall, near the altar, and they are arranged as if in a book, so that the eye should survey the entire perimeter of the church before starting over on the next register down; on the pendentives between the arches, *Prophets and Sibyls*; on the entrance wall is the *Last Judgement* (the figure of Christ has been repainted); in the vault of the apse stands the powerful figure of *Christ Enthroned, Giving Benediction Amidst the Symbols of the Evangelists*; in the lower fascia, note the Archangels, with the figure of the *Abbot Desiderius in the Act of Offering the Model of the Church* and (repainted) *St. Benedict*. In the right apse (the left apse has been lost), there is a *Virgin Mary with Christ Child and Two Angels*, and, in the lower band, *Martyred Female Saints*. The walls of the side aisles contain, on two registers, *Episodes from the Old Testament*, while on the pendentives are depictions of *Male and Female Benedictine Saints*.

Along the road to Aversa, you may take a detour to the left, and you will reach the royal site of **Carditello**, built in 1787 by Collecini at the behest of Ferdinand IV, who wished to restructure the royal estate, where, as early as 1745, construction of a hunting lodge had been started, and then left incomplete. In the intentions of the monarch, the complex, aside from serving the usual functions of a court retreat, linked to the presence of the hunting lodge, was actually to work as a farming operation, arranged around the royal residence. The project, thus, involved the construction of two lower structures, slightly set back, so as to highlight the central building, flanked by two vestibules offering passageways to the courtyard in the back and to the stairs; the chapel, set beneath the royal apartment, has a central plan and a dome. Four other courtyards, behind the long curtain wall, were to be used to raise cattle and for other agricultural activities. The space lying before the complex was organized with a beaten-earth track, inspired in shape by ancient Roman circuses, and used for horse racing. At the center is a little circular temple, topped by a dome, which served as the royal box, while on the sides were two fountains with obelisks.

Aversa

After Caserta the most populous town of the province (elev. 39 m, pop. 54,276), the town was founded in 1030 by the Norman prince Rainulfo Drengot, whose political skill soon (1038) led to the recognition of the independent county ("contea") of Aversa and the establishment, in 1050, of the episcopal see. This was the first territory obtained by the Normans in the south, and a bridgehead for further conquests. The medieval characteristics of the foundation can still be identified in the particular grid of the historical center, which is elliptical, with concentric and radial streets extending around the cathedral and the lost castle, or Castello di Rainulfo.

The entrance is marked by the monumental gate, or *Porta Napoli*, built in the 18th c. by G. Gentile, at the boundary of the 16th-/17th-c. expansion. Next to the gate is the *campanile of the church of the Annunziata*, begun in 1477, with work continuing until the 17th c., and from that point on left unfinished. After you enter the door, on the right, you will see the entrance to the complex of the **Annunziata***, founded during the period of Angevin rule and endowed with a hospital beginning in the 15th c. Af-

The 18th-century residence of the Bourbons, Carditello

ter you cross through the handsome *marble portal*, the work of J. Mormile (1518), you will enter a courtyard overlooked by the church, with a Baroque facade, preceded by a pronaos with three arches set on four slender Corinthian columns. The interior, seriously damaged by bombing and by decades of neglect, presents a single majestic nave, on a Latin-cross plan, covered with a barrel vault. The dome, which collapsed in 1823, was rebuilt, but on a smaller scale. The church still preserves many artworks, including two panels by A. Arcuccio and M. Pino (1571) and, on the altar of the left transept, an *Adoration of the Shepherds*, by Solimena (1698).

The heart of the medieval city is the cathedral, or **Cattedrale*** (S. Paolo), begun in 1053 by the prince of Capua, Riccardo (Richard). It has suffered considerable damage, from fires and earthquakes, which led to the reconstruction of many parts of the cathedral, until the reconstruction of the longer section of the building in the 18th c. An arch links the church with the massive *campanile*, rebuilt following the earthquake of 1456, which features, cemented into the walls, columns and pieces of marble, recycled from the ruins of Atella. Despite the numerous reconstructions, it still preserves important elements of the medieval construction, which place it among the most important examples of Romanesque architecture in Campania. From the Piazza Normanna you can clearly see the *octagonal drum**, adorned with two orders of blind arches set on little marble columns and crowned by a singular little lantern, supported by four tortile columns. On the same side, you can also see, cemented into the foot of the transept, a *portal*, with an inscription in which mention is made of the prince Giordano, son of Riccardo, who, from 1078 on, continued the work that was interrupted by the death of his father. The entire zone of the *apse** belongs to the Norman construction: the deambulatory, in which there are three semicircular apses, is punctuated by seven bays with cross-vaults supported by ribbings with a large, square cross-section, and may date from the end of the 11th c.

On the interior are a *St. Sebastian*, by A. Arcuccio (15th c.), interesting for its depiction of the city in the background, in the deambulatory are two *bas-reliefs** and other sculptures from the 9th-10th c.; Catalonian wooden *Crucifix* (ca. 1250), *Virgin Mary and Saints** by Solimena, *main altar* designed by L. Vanvitelli, a 17th-c. reproduction in stucco of the Santa Casa, or holy house, or Loreto, and a *panel* painting by C. Smet.

In Piazza Trieste e Trento is the old *church of S. Maria a Piazza,* which was built, perhaps in a period prior to the very foundation of the city, near the Norman fortress, from the "piazza d'armi," or parade grounds from which it supposedly took its name; with Gothic facade and, on the interior, frescoes from the school of Giotto (1335-40).

Not far away is the former monastery, or *Ex Convento di S. Lorenzo*, founded in the 11th c. and suppressed in the 19th c. The monastery (now a university building) was among the largest Benedictine settlements, and finally rivaled even the episcopal see of Aversa. Still surviving are a lovely Renaissance cloisters, with columns and an upper loggia. A handsome *Romanesque portal*, with two lions supporting tortile columns on either side, adorns the facade of the large church.

Returning toward Porta Napoli you will reach the Piazza Principe Amedeo, where you can detour to the church of *S. Francesco* (13th c.). The original convent complex derived from the transformation of a castle, confiscated by the Angevins from the Rebursa family, which housed the first headquarters of the Clarissans in the city. Extensively renovated in 1645 and again in the 19th c., it preserves medieval relics, in the base of the church and in two surviving arches of the cloister. The interior, with a single nave, and transept and side chapels, features a lavish Baroque decoration in polychrome marble: in the second chapel on the left, *Adoration of the Shepherds*, by Pietro da Cortona; in the choir, *Ecstasy of St. Francis*, a canvas by Ribera, in terrible condition, and two large canvases attributed to the school of De Mura. In the lower choir of the nuns is a fragment of a fresco depicting a *Virgin Mary with Christ Child* (13th/14th c.).

9 Salerno and the Amalfi coast

Salerno, lying between the hills and the sea, in the northernmost point of the broad gulf that bears its name (Golfo di Salerno), is the second-largest city in Campania, in terms of population, expanse, and economic activity, an obligatory point of departure for tourists heading for the Amalfi coast and Paestum. A town that is rich in historical and artistic heritage, but also an agricultural and industrial center.

The gulf is bounded to the north by the southern slope of the Sorrento peninsula, featuring a rocky bastion that is frequently cut across by broad high valleys; this stretch of land takes the name of the Amalfi coast, or Costiera Amalfitana, one of the most famous and enchanting settings in Italy, both because of the spectacular landscape and because of the artistic and historic heritage of the place. The topography makes its different from the northern slope of the peninsula, which is characterized by terraces along a slight slope; this leads

Festivities for St. Joseph's day in the streets of Amalfi

to differences in the agricultural landscape because, while on the Sorrento slope, there are citrus and olive groves, stretching out as far as the eye can see (which is nowadays also allowed for rampant development), on the Costiera Amalfitana the same crops, the vegetable patches and the gardens, are all contained in terracing, the product of centuries of backbreaking labor. The formidable nature of the coastline has also made land communications difficult (the road, now marked as Statale 163, was not even built until 1840) and has imposed the construction of urban concentrations that adapt to the topography, much like the terracing for agriculture. These little towns are nearly all located near little beaches, where deep high valleys run down to the sea, confirming the traditional interplay between sea, land, and trade and agriculture, so peculiar to the history of Amalfi.

The coast, which was inhabited in the Paleolithic era (grotto near Positano), but not in the classical period, if we leave aside the various Roman villas built when Capri was a favorite residence of Augustus and Tiberius, began to be populated in the early Middle Ages. The oldest and the largest of these settlements was Amalfi, which gives its name to the entire coastline, since it was also the chief political and economic center. Amalfi's dominion extended along the coast from Cetara to Positano, and inland. Defense was provided by a single system of castles (especially inland). The multi-center articulation of the territory that was typical of the Amalfitan Middle Ages can be clearly seen in the roles that each town played in the context of the dukedom: at Atrani, the investiture of the duke took place, at Minori was preserved the body of St. Trophimus, the patron saint prior to the arrival of the relics of St. Andrew; Ravello and Scala constituted the chosen residence of the noble families.

The need to adapt to such a challenging landscape has engendered a particular sort of housing, still evident in nearly all of the towns, and especially in Amalfi and Atrani, where, in an intricate system of streets, consisting of narrow twisting lanes and steep stairways, the houses are built against the slopes, and are often built one practically atop the other, and in some cases covering the roads themselves. The labyrinthine construction made the towns easier to defend against invaders, and protected the residents from sun and wind. The most common type of house along the coast, in some cases isolated, is the cubic structure, covered with a vaulted roof, and known as a "lamia," and generally whitewashed. Dating back to the ducal period came the introduction of the system of farming by terracing the mountain slopes, which till then had been covered by forests; terracing is still typical of the area, and there are citrus groves, vineyards, and olive groves mixed in with the Mediterranean brush and scrub. The cultivation of citrus fruit – along with tourism and the making of ceramics – is one of the leading activities here. Another feature of the landscape is the series of coastal towers, commonly known as the "torri saracene," even though they were built by the Spanish viceroys as protection against the Saracens.

Aside from the exceptional naturalistic and environmental interest of this itinerary, it is noteworthy for the remarkable concentration of medieval monuments and works of art (from the cathedrals of Salerno and Amalfi to the Abbey, or Badia di Cava, and the ambos of Salerno and Ravello), as well as of later periods.

9.1 Salerno

Salerno (elev. 4 m, pop. 144,956) is prevalently a modern city that developed over the last one hundred years, particularly after the last war. Its historic center, relatively intact, spreads down the hillside toward the water, its upper section dominated by the Castello di Arechi, and the lower section by the cathedral and its campanile. Of fair-

ly uncertain origins (in the little village of Fratte, to the north of the city, there are the ruins of a necropolis dating back to the 6th/3rd c. B.C. and an inhabited settlement), Salerno accepted in 194 B.C. a Roman colony, and soon acquired an important political and commercial role in the surrounding territory, especially in the wake of the decline of Paestum. In A.D. 646 it was conquered by the Longobards and in A.D. 839 it became the capital of a principality, independent of *Beneventum* (Benevento), and the southernmost outpost of the Longobard possessions. A prince named Arechi II fortified the town and built an aqueduct; in 1077 it was besieged and taken by Robert Guiscard, who made it the capital (for about 50 years) of the dukedom of Puglia, elevating it to its greatest splendor, to the point that, even later, Salerno continued to be one of the most important cities in the continental kingdom of Sicily. During this period, the city built its cathedral, or Duomo (one of the most important examples of Romanesque architecture in the region); this was also the time of the expansion of the famous and illustrious Medical School, the

oldest such institution in Europe, encouraging the study and diffusion of medicine; this school – which existed as early as the 9th c. – was particularly renowned in the 12th and 13th c. In this School, where women were also welcome, law, philosophy, and theology were also studied. With the foundation and development of the university of Naples, or Università di Napoli, the school of Salerno began to decline, and was finally suppressed by Murat in 1812. The decline of Salerno began in the Swabian era, and from 1419 on it was a feudal holding and a state-owned township. For several months in 1944, following the Allied landing, this was the capital of the Italian government.

When you enter Salerno, you have the sensation that you are entering an entirely modern city, and in reality much of the urban center that coincides with the focus of commercial and administrative activity does date back to the end of the 19th c. The historical center, on the other hand, is high on the slopes of the hill, and indeed preserves its nature as a seafaring town, enclosed in its intricate medieval layout, made up of narrow winding lanes, the site of crafts concentrations and small trade. Dating from the 1950s and 1960s, lastly, is the most modern part of the town, a disorderly and chaotic expansion of buildings, in the easternmost section of the city.

The tour of the city is divided into two itineraries: the first explores the central core of the medieval city, while the second focuses on the zone of the ancient quarter of the *Planum montis*.

The medieval center

This itinerary runs from Piazza Amendola (C2), which is the center of the city, although not in strictly topographic terms. Overlooking it is the *Villa Comunale* to the west, beyond which is the theater, or *Teatro Verdi* (1870-80). Across from the Villa Comunale is Piazza Luciani, overlooked by picturesque loggias and flower-covered terraces, which form the boundaries of the medieval quarter.

Via Portacatena (B2). This street, which is narrow and winding, begins at Piazza Luciani. Nearly at the beginning, on the right, is the campanile of the Baroque *church of the SS. Annunziata*, by Sanfelice (handsome altar in inlaid marble); another interesting work dating back to the 18th c. is the *Palazzo Genovesi* by M. Gioffredo, at no. 3 of the little Piazza Sedile del Campo. Nearby are the remains of the gate, or Porta Roteprand-

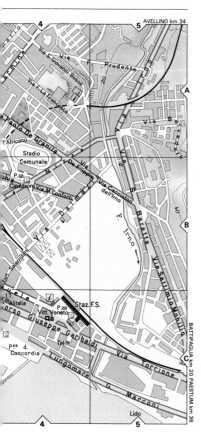

Via dei Mercanti, Salerno

di and the churches of *S. Andrea*, with 12th-c. campanile, and *S. Alfonso* (S. Maria de Laula) from the 10th/11th c. At the end of the street is the arch, or Arco di Arechi (8th c.), once the portal of the Palazzo del Principe (princely palace).

Via dei Mercanti* (C3). This bustling street, which begins after the arch, is the main thoroughfare of the old quarter, and it still displays numerous features of medieval architecture. In the lanes immediately after the arch, there are a number of interesting churches and the *Palazzo Fruscione* which, like several of the churches, preserves fragments of medieval structures and decorations.

S. Giorgio (C3). This is one of the loveliest Baroque churches (1674) in the city, preceded by an atrium, and with an interesting *portal*. The interior* features rich decorations with gilt stuccoes and numerous paintings, some of which are by Andrea da Salerno (1st and 2nd altar on the right and apse), others by Angelo Solimena, del 1675 (dome, transept, and pendentives of the chapels), and others still by Francesco Solimena (4th altar on the right). The last-named artist also did the *frescoes** (1680) in the chapel on the left. Also of interest is the wooden Baroque pulpit.

Duomo* (B3). This cathedral constitutes one of the most noteworthy medieval monuments in the region, and was begun in 1080 at the behest of Robert Guiscard (Roberto il Guiscardo) and the archbishop, Alphanus (Alfano), a Longobard who admired Greek

culture, an adherent of the Gregorian reforms, abbot of Montecassino in 1057, and, in 1058, named archbishop of Salerno. He immediately set about promoting – in concomitance with the discovery of the relics of the Apostle Matthew and the elevation of Salerno to the status of capital of the Norman dominions – the construction of a new cathedral, consecrated in 1085 by Pope Gregory VII, who was in exile in Salerno.

It is a basilica with a nave and two side-aisles, preceded by an atrium (almost square) that opens toward the interior through a portico – in which the stilted arches set on columns and decoration in stone inlay are reminiscent of Byzantine and Islamic models – and with a high transept and a raised presbytery. The transept preserves the same sort of windows (six single-light mullioned windows and two oculi), but unlike the basilica of Desiderius, it juts slightly in the central structure; the raised section became in fact one of the distinctive features in the architecture of the churches of the Norman period throughout the territory of the southern kingdom.

The reference to ancient models can be found again at Salerno in the recovery of a monumental legend of Roman origin, in which there is mention, in a colossal epigraph, set high on the facade of the church, of the names of the Apostle Matthew and of Robert Guiscard; and in the mosaic decoration of the apses.

In the 18th c. it was redecorated in the Baroque style, but in the last c., restoration projects have uncovered part of the original structure, especially resulting in the restoration of the facade. The church is preceded by a porticoed **atrium*** which one reaches along a 17th-c. stairway and a large Romanesque portal (11th c.), known as the *Porta dei Leoni**, with marble friezes and fresco (18th c.) of *St. Matthew* in the lunette. To the right of the stairway is the hall, or *Sala S. Lazzaro* (two naves, divided by pillars) believed to have been a hall of the medical school, or Scuola Medica. The quadriporticus comprises granite columns upon which rest stilted arches, showing Moorish influence, above which, on two sides, extends a loggia with twin-light and five-light mullioned windows, decorated with polychrome intarsias, again with round arches. The side in front of the church culminates in a Baroque marble balustrade and statues dating from the 18th c. (*St. Matthew*, in the center, by M. Bottigliero). Beneath the portico there are a number of Roman and medieval *sarcophagi**. At the center of the atrium there is a basin dating from the classical age, taken from Paestum. On the right, note the imposing Romanesque **campanile*** (1137-45), it too showing Moorish influence, and comprising three orders of twin-light mullioned windows (the first two floors are make of large blocks of travertine, while the upper floors are made of rows of bricks) culminating in a cylindrical structure, decorated with intertwined arches, in tufa and brick, and polychrome intarsias. In the facade, which mirrors the interior basilican layout, there are three portals; the central portal, Romanesque, features in its jambs and in the architrave lavish decorations with animal and floral motifs, culminating in a lunette with fresco (11th c. and 18th c.) depicting *St. Matthew and St. John*. The *bronze doors** were cast in 1099 at Constantinople.

The interior preserves, in the farthest area, much of its original decoration, which survived the renovations of the 18th c., including the two **ambos*** and the **iconostasis*** with splendid mosaic and sculptural decorations. The main ambo (13th c.), on the right, is supported by twelve columns; in front of it stands a particularly tall (5.3 m) **candelabrum for the Paschal candle*** (13th c.) decorated with mosaics, and set upon a group of carved animals. The ambo to the left, which is older (1181) than the first one, is supported atop four columns with finely carved capitals and basket arches, in the pendentives of which are depictions of the symbols of the Evangelists and the prophets. Also quite old are the floors of the choir and right transept and the right apse. There are numerous funerary monuments, especially in the transept, almost all of them made of ancient Roman sarcophagi, but the most important is the tomb, or *Sepolcro della Regina Margherita di Durazzo** (a queen, and the wife of Charles III), set at the end of the left side aisle, by Antonio Baboccio. In the far walls of the side aisles and in the pillars that separate those aisles you may note traces of the old Romanesque construction (columns and arches). Opening onto the side aisles, there are twelve chapels; in the 1st chapel on the right and in the 4th chapel on the left, there are artworks by Francesco Solimena. In the transept, aside from various sarcophagi, you may note (to the left) a marble polyptych by an anonymous artist of the 14th c., possibly from the Medical School of Salerno. Set against the pillars of the nave are, to the right, the *pulpit* (17th c.), supported by four small tortile columns atop column-bearing lions, and, to the left, the *throne of the archbishop*, in Baroque style. In the right apse, beneath the altar, you may note the relics of St. Gregory VII, a pope who died in exile in Salerno in 1085. The apse is adorned – like the other two apses – by mosaics in the Byzantine style, executed between 1258 and 1266; restored at the behest of Pope Pius IX, it has been called the chapel, or Cappella di Gregorio VII or the Cappella delle Crociate, because it was here that the weapons of the Crusaders were blessed before they set off for the Holy Land.

The Baroque crypt in the Duomo, Salerno

Along the sides of the side-aisles, at the far end, are the entrances to the vast **crypt*** which was rebuilt in Baroque style in the 17th c. by Philip III, at his own expenses, in honor of the Apostle, patron saint of the city. The space, which appears to be divided into a nave and two side-aisles, is entirely faced in polychrome marble by Domenico and Giulio Cesare Fontana; the vault was frescoed in 1643 by Corenzio; on the double altar are two bronze *statues of St. Matthew*, by M. Naccherino (1622).

The sea front and hilltop castle of Arechi II, Salerno

Museo del Duomo (B3). Established in 1935, it features four halls, each concerning a different century, with numerous paintings dating from the 13th to the 18th c., including works by Roberto d'Oderisio, Stanzione, Giordano, Andrea Vaccaro, Francesco Solimena, and Sebastiano Conca; a cross with gems, possibly once the property of Robert Guiscard; a collection of degrees from the Medical School; illuminated codices from the 13th and 14th c; an *Exultet**, a fundamental work of illumination from 13th-c. Campania, and an exceptional, famous complex of sculptures in ivory (possibly an altar frontal) dating from the 12th c., one of the largest from the period, depicting 54 *Scenes from the Old and New Testaments**.

Episcopio (B3). Founded in the 13th c., it features in its restored facade broad arches, supported by recycled columns.
On the interior is an interesting oval hall, divided into two aisles by large Roman columns, with capitals adorned with carved heads of women.

Museo Archeologico Provinciale (C3), or archaeological museum of the province. Behind the cathedral, or Duomo, begins the quiet *Via S. Benedetto*, lined with a succession of ancient courtyards and old crafts workshops, which leads to the monumental complex of the former abbey, or Ex Abbazia di S. Benedetto, which incorporates the remains of the Norman palace (Reggia Normanna). In the little square, on the left, stands a Romanesque church, restored, which originally was preceded by an atrium, of which there now survives only the side facing the church, and the opposite side. This last side is incorporated into the structure of the Reale Castelnuovo which contains the Museo Archeologico Provinciale, and which has

been brought to light, along with the Renaissance loggia, by restorations.
Established in 1927, the Museo, or museum, contains archaeological materials from excavations throughout the large territory of the province, displayed in accordance with chronological and topographic criteria. On the ground floor is an exhibition of prehistoric and early historic materials (as late as the 6th c. B.C.) from the Agro Picentino and from Lucania; funerary furnishings from the archaic necropolises of Pontecagnano, Arenosola, Oliveto Citra, Sala Consilina, and Palinuro (9th/7th c. B.C.: objects in bronze and pottery of the Villanovan culture, painted ceramics with geometric patterns). On the upper story, composite collections document life in Salerno under the Romans; among these artifacts, you may note a lovely *head of Apollo* (a Campanian bronze from the 1st c. B.C.) discovered in the waters of the gulf in 1930. A sector houses the permanent exhibition, or Mostra Permanente, dedicated to the Campanian Etruscan town of Fratte (materials from the settlement, archaic and Hellenistic architectural terracottas, including a disk-shaped acroterion, dating from the 4th c. B.C., with a depiction in relief of *Hercules Battling the Nemaean lion*, materials from the necropolis).

Via S. Benedetto ends in Via Velia, which continues to the left as far as the spectacular, monumental ruins of the medieval aqueduct, or **Acquedotto Medievale** (B4), comprising several stories, in pointed-arch arcades.
Built by the Longobards (8th c.), it was restored by the Normans to serve the abbey, or Abbazia di S. Benedetto.
In the Vicolo Adalberga, is the old Palatine church of *S. Pietro a Corte*, of Longobard origin, in which important frescoes dating from the 11th c. have been uncovered. The church, with

a Romanesque basilican layout, is flanked by a little campanile of the same age, and is preceded by a portico dating from 1576.

Crocifisso (B2). This old church (10th/11th c.; rebuilt in the 17th c.) stands in the Piazza Matteotti, overlooking Via dei Mercanti. The Romanesque plan of the interior is basilican in style: a nave and two side aisles, with broad arches supported on recycled columns and three apses. In the vault of the apse, a modern mosaic reproduces a fresco from the crypt depicting *St. Sixtus, St. Lawrence, and another saint*, the work of a master of Catalonian and Rossillon influence, from the 13th c.

In the crypt, supported by two pillars incorporating the original columns, you may note, also by the same anonymous master, another fresco with the *Crucifixion*.

The "Planum Montis"

Via Duomo, beyond the cathedral, climbs up to Via Alfano I, in the heart of the old quarter of "Planum Montis." Turning left into Via Alfano I you reach Via Abate Conforti

(B3; at no. 7 stands the *Archivio di Stato*, or State Archives); from here you can follow Via Trotula De Ruggero to the *church of S. Maria delle Grazie*, built at the end of the 15th c., and which contains an interesting panel painting (1493) of the *Madonna delle Grazie** by Cristoforo Scacco. The old sacristy (known as the Sala Scacco-Vaccaro) has been set up as a museum and art gallery ("pinacoteca") of the parish church; it contains, among reliquaries and various sacred furnishings, a number of canvases that have been attributed to Andrea Vaccaro. From a terrace before it you can enjoy a fine panoramic view of the city and the gulf.

Castello di Arechi II (A2). This castle was founded by Byzantines, enlarged by the Longobard prince Arechi, and reinforced by the Normans and Aragonese; it stands high (elev. 263 m) over the city, and was long in a state of ruin. For the past few years, it has been undergoing restoration, and there are plans to make it the site of the Museo Storico Salernitano; it currently contains a library, a collection of ceramics (8th/19th c.), and halls for temporary exhibitions.

9.2 The Amalfi coast

The Amalfi coast, or Costiera Amalfitana, is served by a single road, the state road, or Statale 163, Amalfitana, which largely runs through cuts in the living rock. It follows the line of the coast, passing through a number of towns in succession, sometimes at sea level and sometimes at elevations of up to 200 meters. These characteristics allow the traveler to admire a panoramic vista that is, in certain stretches, breathtaking.

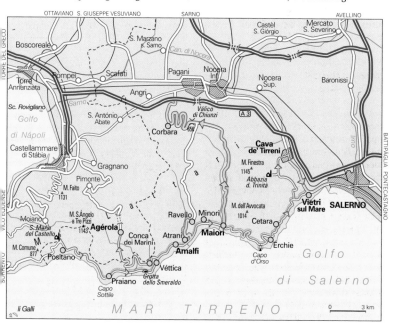

The itinerary begins from Vietri (exit from the highway, or Autostrada A3) and, following a possible detour toward Cava de' Tirreni (3.5 km) and the abbey, or Abbazia della SS. Trinità (3.7 km), and continues as far as Positano (40.6 km). Among the first towns it reaches are Cetara and Erchie, a small and tranquil village (elev. 4 m), that originated around a Benedictine abbey (S. Maria de Erchi) of the 10th c., suppressed in 1451, and endowed with a fine beach (*Marina di Erchie*). You will soon reach *Capo d'Orso*, beyond which extend the fine beaches of the Costiera; from the belvedere you can enjoy an unbroken view as far as Punta Campanella and Capri.

You will then pass through Maiori and Minori; toward Ravello you will climb sharply, as you pass through the Valle del Dragone. You will continue toward Atrani, which you will cross on a viaduct, and Amalfi. Along the middle of the slope, you will cross a series of little towns set high on the rocks. After Conca dei Marini, the landscape of the coast becomes more arid. After you pass through a tunnel, you will cross a viaduct over the valley, or *Vallone di Furore**, crossed by the mountain stream, or Torrente Schiato (almost always dry) which runs down from the highland, or Altopiano di Agerola. The spectacle offered by the sheer rocks, in some cases covered with vegetation, by the group of bare houses, and the sea that penetrates into the fjord, is quite impressive. In a succession of crags and high valleys you will reach Positano; beyond you will continue in the direction of Sorrento. The state road, or Statale, which runs for 8 km at an elevation of 200 meters, runs toward the interior, and leaves the coast, with a steep climb and broad curves. The views of the Amalfi coast, or Costiera (*Belvedere di Positano**) from this stretch, are truly fantastic. Once you reach Colli di S. Pietro, you will take the extension of the state road, or Statale 145, known as the Nastro Azzurro, which offers splendid views, of both the Amalfi coast, or Costiera, and of the Sorrento peninsula, and after 7 km, reaches Sant'Agata sui Due Golfi.

Vietri sul Mare

Overlooking the Gulf of Salerno is this town, famous (elev. 80 m, pop. 9,267) for its production of artistic and building ceramics. In the high section of the old town is the parish church of *S. Giovanni Battista* (1732), with majolica dome and campanile, on the interior of which is a polyptych dating from the 16th c.

At a distance of 2.2 km, toward the interior, in the village of Raito, in the tower, or Torre del Parco della Villa Guariglia, there is now a *Museo della Ceramica*, which includes a documentation on the production of ceramics from the 17th c. to the 1950s.

As you follow the state road, or Statale, you will find, near the sea, the "Crestarella," one of the first in a numerous series of watch towers built under the viceroys, which characterize – more or less transformed – the landscape of the coast.

Cava de' Tirreni

From Vietri, if you head in along a high valley, you will reach **Cava** (elev. 180 m, pop. 53,160), set in a hollow surrounded by luxuriant hills. Dating back to the Roman period, it was donated in 1058 by Prince Gisulfo II to the abbey, or Abbazia della SS. Trinità. For centuries, it played a predominant role in the trade and commerce of the Kingdom of Naples, enjoying numerous fiscal exemptions (there was also a free port at Vietri) and holding exclusive privileges on the sale of silk tapestries. The layout of the town is quite unusual, in that it is the only town in southern Italy to feature porticoed streets, almost a little "Bologna of the South." Particularly charming is the *Borgo Scacciaventi*, so called for its winding lanes, which block the strong winds, beneath the porticoes of which, protected from the elements, were once set out all the trade goods of the merchants of Cava, and where now you will see the products of local craftsmen. Along *Corso Italia*, the main road (also porticoed, running the length of the town) you may note the *Piazza Roma*, with the town hall, or Municipio, and a public park, or *Giardini Pubblici*. From this last square runs Via Senatore, which leads to the abbey, or Abbazia della SS. Trinità. The route, all uphill, passes by the little church of the *Pietrasanta* (the name, literally "holy stone," recalls the passage of Pope Urban II who, in 1092, on his way to consecrate the church of the Trinità, stopped here to rest on a large rock).

Bright-colored tiles, a typical product of Vietri sul Mare

The abbey, or **Abbazia della SS. Trinità***, was founded in 1011, by a Salernitan noble, who retired there to live a life of contemplation, in compliance with the Benedictine rule of the Cluniac monks. The abbey took on great importance, and its jurisdiction was extended from Rome to Palermo, and it administered its own trade with the East. The present-day church is an 18th-c. reconstruction of the church dating from the 11th c., enlarged on the model of Montecassino. Of the original artworks, there remain on the interior a notable *ambo* (13th c.; rebuilt in 1880) and a *candelabrum* with Paschal candle; of considerable interest, as well, is the 18th-c. *choir*, built to plans by Giovanni del Gaizo, who also designed the façade of the church (1772). In the monastery are a number of rooms of particular note, including the large chapter hall, or *Sala Capitolare* (rebuilt in 1632) with a majolica flooring dating from 1777, wooden stalls from the 16th c., and frescoes dating back to the 17th c. In the "chiostrino," or *little cloisters** (13th c.), with an irregular floor plan, one side features simple recycled columns, surmounted by round-head arches; the other three sides, dating from a later period, still preserve their round arches, but they are set on little twin columns that in turn stand on a balustrade. From the cloisters you will walk down to a remarkable crypt, built in the 12th c. in an ancient Roman chamber, known as the Longobard cemetery, or *Cimitero Longobardo*; here you will find the chapel, or *Cappella di S. Germano* (1280) with frescoes (some of which are attributed to Andrea da Salerno, and others dating from the 15th c.) are preserved in the Gothic chapter hall, or *Sala del Capitolo Vecchio* (13th c.), which you can reach from the little cloisters. The chapel, or *Cappella del Crocifisso*, preserves fragments of a floor dating back to the 15th c. and a bas-relief by Tino di Camaino; adjoining it is another chapel which contains a marble *altar frontal* (11th c.) from the altar that was consecrated by Pope Urban II. The most important area in the entire complex is that of the museum, or *Museo*. Founded in 1953, this three-room museum contains archaeological finds, Roman sarcophagi, marble sculptures, paintings by Andrea da Salerno, G. F. Penni, and of the Neapolitan school of the 17th and 18th c., and other objects, including a nautical chart dating from the 15th c., a small ivory coffer from the 11th c., and illuminated codices (14th/16th c.).

Cetara

After you round the point, or Punta di Fuenti (the panoramic view still embraces the Gulf of Salerno), you will see Cetara (elev. 10 m, pop. 2,446), a picturesque fishing village. This is the easternmost boundary of the dukedom of Amalfi, long established as the maritime port of the abbey of Cava. A typical product of Cetara (whose name is thought by some to derive from the Latin term, "Cetaria," or tuna station) is salted fish sold in little ceramic vases.

Maiori

This town, like the nearby Minori, stands at the mouth of two mountain streams, both called Reginna, and identified as the Reginna Maior and the Reginna Minor, hence the names of the two towns. Maiori (elev. 5 m, pop. 5,904), once enclosed by walls and defended by a major castle (only the ruins survive), is, with Minori, one of the most popular tourist towns of the Amalfi coast, or Costiera, in terms of accommodations and width of the beaches. The town extends along a broad inlet, and presents a modern appearance, in part because it was partially rebuilt following a catastrophic flood in 1954. Occupying a dominant position, along the course of the mountain stream ("torrente"), looms the church of *S. Maria a Mare* (12th c.; rebuilt more than once in the ensuing centuries) with a majolica dome and a campanile from the 18th c. On the interior, with nave and two aisles, with a lacunar ceiling dating from the 16th c., you will find a wooden statue from the

The ancient fishing village of Cetara, on the Amalfi coast

15th c. (*Virgin Mary with Christ Child*) on the main altar, and in the sacristy, a small museum with sacred works of art, including a 15thp-c. English altar frontal made of alabaster. With an outing in a boat, you can reach the grotto, or Grotta Pandone, with numerous stalactites, whose bed takes on an intense blue coloring, especially in the morning.

A detour from Maiori runs through chestnut groves to the high pass, or *Valico della Torre di*

Chiunzi, along a scenic route that, with plentiful curves, climbs up the valley, or Valle di Tramonti. From here you will descend to the plain, or Piana del Sarno (this is the quickest road to Naples). In the luxuriant valley through which runs the mountain stream, or Torrente Reginna Maior, you will find many small towns, villages in the scattered township of Tramonti (elev. 141/1,316 m; pop. 3,922), and in many of them are noteworthy works of art. On the spur that divides the valley in two is the church of *S. Maria di Tramonti*. When you reach the high pass (known as the Valico della Torre di Chiunzi, after a tower that survives from a 15th-c. castle, by Raimondo Orsini) you will continue at a sharp downhill slope, passing through *Corbara* (elev. 167 m, pop. 2,420, renowned for its tomatoes and walnuts), with a vast panoramic view that suddenly opens out upon the Gulf of Castellammare. Nearby stands the town of *Sant'Egidio del Monte Albino* (elev. 60 m, pop. 8,378), of ancient origin, where you will find the abbey, or *Abbazia di S. Maria Maddalena in Armillis*, in which there are artworks by Andrea da Salerno, Giordano, and Solimena.

Minori

This town (elev. 5 m, pop. 3,069), which houses the relics of St. Trophimus, an ancient protectress of Amalfi, appears a bit more intimate and cozy than Maiori and features numerous picturesque corners in the innermost section. Not far from the waterfront, or Lungomare, stands the *basilica of S. Trofimena* (12th/13th c.; rebuilt in the 19th c.) on the interior of which is the interesting crypt, renovated in the 18th c., where there is an urn by G. Ragozzino, with the relics of the patron saint.

In the westernmost sector of the town are the most noteworthy Roman ruins of the coast. This is a *Roman villa**, dating from the 1st c. B.C., which may have belonged to a member of the imperial court. All that survives of the entire complex is the part closest to the beach, corresponding to the ground floor: the *viridarium*, with a pool in the center, surrounded on three sides by a portico, and two clusters of rooms, separated by a large *triclinium*, one of which contains the bath facilities.

Ravello*

The singular beauty of this quiet little town (elev. 350 m, pop. 2,473) has left, over the centuries, its impression on many illustrious authors and artists, from Boccaccio, who wrote about it is a novella of the *Decameron*, to Wagner, who resided here and identified the garden of Villa Rufolo with the garden of Klingsor in *Parsifal*. Arranged on a terrace overlooking the sea, between the valleys of the Dragone and the Reginna, it offers

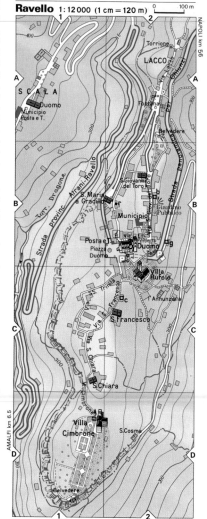

Ravello 1:12 000 (1 cm = 120 m)

a setting of unrivaled beauty. Founded perhaps in the 4th c., it certainly existed in the 9th c., when it formed part of the territory of the dukedom. In 1089 it became the site of the diocese, and was later suppressed and incorporated in the diocese of Amalfi in 1804. It enjoyed its period of greatest splendor in the 13th c., thanks to the important role it played in commercial trade with the East and with Sicily. Rich in history and art, far from the intense life of the coast, Ravello is distinguished by the unusual peace that seems to emanate from the charming little streets and splendid gardens.

At the entrance to the town you will find the church of **S. Maria a Gradillo** (12th c.; renovated; B1-2) in the atrium of which (collapsed 1706), as if it were a seat of local government, or Seggio, the local nobles would assemble to discuss public affairs. The basilican layout ends in three very tall apses, and is surmounted by a dome (rebuilt) set on a high tambour. The church is flanked by a small campanile with twin-light mullioned windows. Adjoining it are the ruins of a 13th-c. *castle*, beyond which is the coral museum, or *Museo del Corallo Camo*, dedicated to the craft of shaping a material found in abundance on the coastline of the gulfs of Naples and Salerno: in particular, note the *Our Lady of the Assumption*, dating from the 16th c., and a *Christ* from the 17th c., both in Italian coral, and a *tobacco box** encrusted with cameos in Louis XVI style.

The Piazza del Vescovado is overlooked by the cathedral, or Duomo (B2), and the square tower that constitutes the entrance to the **Villa Rufolo*** (B, C2), a complex of constructions dating from the 13th and 14th c. (later renovated), in which there is a detectable Muslim influence, arranged on a terrace high above the sea. The villa presents numerous rooms of considerable interest: the *courtyard**, not unlike a cloister, with two orders of loggias with intertwined arches, and the renowned garden, adorned with exotic plants, trees, and brightly colored flower beds, which overlooks a spectacular panorama of the coast. In the summer, concerts are held here, with music by Wagner. In the old chapel there is an *Antiquarium*, with exhibits of architectural fragments, cinerary urns, and Roman and medieval sarcophagi.

The church beneath the villa, visible from the garden, is the church of the **Annunziata** (C2) and dates from the 13th c.; you can reach it from a street that, from the right of Villa Rufolo, descends toward Minori (along the route you will find other small churches and the village, or *Borgo di Torello*, whose church still preserves the porticoed narthex that elsewhere has disappeared). You will then continue uphill along Via S. Francesco, which runs under the cross-vaults of the atrium of the **church of S. Francesco** (C2), of Gothic origin, rebuilt in the 18th c.; on the interior, the transept and the apse preserve their original appearance. Adjoining the church is the monastery, with a small cloisters, in which the Gothic style blurs into a Baroque form. Further along, you will find the **church of S. Chiara** (C1), which was founded in the 13th c. and was rebuilt in the 18th c. The basilican layout (nave and two side-aisles, without transept, with recycled columns) is preceded by a pronaos; there is a handsome majolica flooring dating from the 18th c., and this is the only church of the entire coast that still has its gallery for women (*matronaeum*).

The road continues downhill toward the **Villa Cimbrone*** (D1-2) built in a splendid panoramic location, in the setting of a huge garden, by one of the many English travelers who became honorary citizens of the "Land of Sirens," or "Terra delle Sirene." In the eclectic construction, which reproduces parts of well-known buildings of Ravello, fragments of sculpture of various provenance were recycled as decorative elements. The belvedere is set at the most sharply jutting portion of the spur upon which Ravello stands, and it offers a spectacular *panorama**; in the garden are scattered a series of charming features: the Belvedere di Mercurio (belvedere of Mercury), the Grotta di Eva (grotto of Eve), the Tempio di Bacco (temple of Bacchus),

The incomparable view of the Amalfi coast from the gardens at Ravello

and the rose-garden.

You will then return to the Piazza Vescovado (B2) which constitutes the center of the town, and the limit of automobile traffic. Overlooking it is the cathedral, or **Duomo***, dedicated to St. Pantaleon, founded in 1086 or 1087 by Bishop Orso Papirio, based on the model of Montecassino, and redecorated in the Baroque style in the 18th c. In the facade, which was preceded by a portico demolished in 1786 (of which there survive four columns) the architraves of the three doors are original, as are the recycled marble cornices, dating from classical times. The bronze *door** of the central entrance, by Barisano da Trani, was donated to the church by a leading merchant of Ravello, and is dated 1179 in one of the panels. The interior, with a nave and two side aisles, divided by columns and pillars, was devastated in the 1970s by a "restoration" that suppressed the 18th-c. renovation entirely, demolishing the vaults and the stuccoes, which survive only in the transept. Along the nave are two exquisite *ambos**: the one on the left (donated by Costantino Rogadeo, the second bishop of Ravello) is the oldest, and constitutes the latest surviving example in southern Italy of a typology of Byzantine influence. The ambo, or Ambone del Vangelo, on the right, the work of Niccolò di Bartolomeo da Foggia (1272), presents rich mosaic and marble decorations. To the left of the presbytery is the chapel, or Cappella di S. Pantaleone (1643, rebuilt in 1782), with relics of the patron saint; to the right is a panel painting of *St. Michael*, by G. A. d'Amato (1583); in the crypt is a *museum*, which features sculpture and jewelry dating back to the period between the 12th and 14th c., including the so-called *bust of Silgigaita Rufolo**, a renowned work by Niccolò di Bartolomeo da Foggia. Next to the church stands the *campanile* (13th c.), two stories tall, with large twin-light mullioned windows and intertwined arches (one of the few pieces of architecture that has not yet been ravaged by "restorations"), visible in its entirety from Via Emanuele Filiberto.

You will follow the handsome Via S. Giovanni del Toro, lined with vegetable patches and gardens (there is also a belvedere) and by the *Palazzo Confalone* (now the Hotel Palumbo, while the old courtyard with pointed arches is now the lobby of the hotel) and Palazzo Sasso, until you reach a small square, in which stands the Palazzo d'Afflitto (now the hotel, or Albergo Belvedere), with a portal formed of marble taken from S. Eustachio di Pontone, and the

church of S. Giovanni del Toro* (B2; 12th c., rebuilt in the 18th c.). This church is distinguished by three high semicircular apses and by domes, entirely decorated with the distinctive motifs of intertwined arches, and by a low campanile that recalls, like all the bell towers of the coast, the campanile of the cathedral, or Duomo di Salerno; in the facade, there are traces of the old portico. On the interior are the *pulpit* by Alfano da Termoli (ca. 1200), adorned with light blue Persian basins and 14th-c. frescoes; also dating from the 14th c. are other frescoes in the crypt and a *St. Catherine* in stucco.

The street continues to the Piazza Fontana (A2), beyond which Via Lacco leads to one of the gates of the walled perimeter.

Scala

This small town (elev. 360 m, pop. 1,496) stands across from Ravello and appears dominated by the great mass of its cathedral, or **Duomo***, probably built in the second half of the 12th c.

With a nave and two side-aisles, it preserves its 18th-c. decorations; there are an interesting pair of 16th-c. panel paintings, a pulpit composed in the 18th c., utilizing fragments of a Romanesque ambo and, in the splendid crypt* with vaults supported by two columns, a wooden *Deposition** from early Angevin times, and the later (1332) tomb, or *Sepolcro di Marinella Rufolo** in polychrome stucco.

Of great charm and interest are the many promenades that can be taken along the old roads, often stepped, that link Scala with its villages, or "borghi," and the other towns of the coast, offering lovely views of Ravello, the slopes of the mountains, with cultivated terraces, and the sea.

Atrani

This is one of the most picturesque (elev. 21 m, pop. 1,056) towns, and one that best preserves the characteristics of the architecture of the Amalfi coast, or Costiera. Situated in a small inlet that corresponds to the mouth of the mountain stream, or Torrente Dragone, it is crossed by a road that runs over its riverbed; the settlement stands high atop jagged rock faces, with an intricate network of lanes, covered lanes, stairways, and overpasses, which cross over white houses and colorful vegetable patches and gardens.

In the intimate and charming **Piazza Umberto I***, at the entrance of the town, enclosed on four sides but, with a small opening, still in direct contact with the beach, as in the old days, you will find the **church of**

S. Salvatore de Bireto (A.D. 940, rebuilt in the 19th c.) where the dukes of Amalfi received their investiture, through the coronation with a ducal "biretta," and where they were buried. A few important features of the medieval church still survive: the bronze *door**, similar to the door of Amalfi, cast in Constantinople in 1087, and, on the interior, a *transenna* in marble dating from the 12th c., with a depiction of two peacocks. In a dominant and spectacular location, in the easternmost section of the town, is the monumental complex of the **church of the Maddalena** (1274, repeatedly renovated, and now largely Baroque in style) with a lively majolica dome and an elegant campanile, similar to the Neapolitan bell tower of the Carmine. On the interior, there are several artworks dating from the Renaissance, including a painting by Andrea da Salerno (*Incredulity of St. Thomas*).

Amalfi*

The city (elev. 6 m, pop. 5,683), set practically at the center of the coastline which bears its name, is one of the most famous tourist attractions in Italy, for the beauty of its landscape, the historic and artistic heritage, its remarkable architecture, and its pleasant climate. A legend has it that Amalfi was founded by a number of Roman castaways in the 4th c. A.D.; it is mentioned, however, for the first time as a *castrum* and the site of a diocese at the end of the 6th c. Its remarkable mountainous position ensured its defense against Longobard raids in the 8th c., but was not sufficient in A.D. 838 when Sicardo di Salerno conquered the town; upon his death, the people of Amalfi rebelled; from 839 on it was governed by an authority that took on, with the formal approval of Byzantium, a number of different titles, culminating in that of duke in 958. That point marked the beginning of the ascent of Amalfi, which in the 10th c. and, to an even greater degree, in the 11th c., enjoyed a remarkable commercial expansion, playing the role that was later acquired by Pisa and Genoa. In numerous cities of the Mediterranean there were colonies of Amalfitans (the largest was in Constantinople); the city's prosperity was reflected in its institutions and cultural life, as we can see by the codification of the *Tabula Amalphitana* with an array of maritime protocols and the spread through the west of the nautical compass, discovered through trade with Arabs. The importance of the *Ducatum Amalphitanum* grew with the dynasty founded (958) by Duke Sergio I and culminated with its elevation to the status of the see of an archbishop (987). Once the dukedom had attained its maximum territorial expansion, its political decline began in the

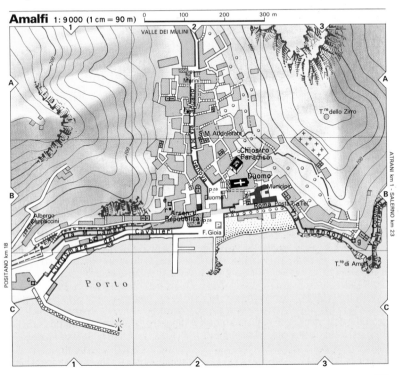

Amalfi 1 : 9 000 (1 cm = 90 m)

11th c. In 1039 it was conquered by the Longobards of Salerno; it regained its independence in 1052, and reinforced its ties with Byzantium, the place of exile of Duke Giovanni, but a few decades later it became impossible for Amalfi to resist the assaults of the Normans, well on their way to unifying southern Italy. After a series of revolts, Amalfi's autonomy was definitively extinguished by the Normans, who called on the Pisans to support them.

In 1137, following a siege and sack, the trading concerns of Amalfi entered definitively into the commercial orbit of their old rival city, Pisa. The end of the dukedom did not immediately translate into cultural decadence, and in fact many of the buildings that constitute the image of Amalfi as a maritime republic, in the city and in nearby towns, can be dated back to the heart of the 13th c.; Amalfi was given as a feudal land holding in 1398 to the clan of the Sanseverino, followed by the Colonna (1405), the Del Balzo Orsini (1438), and the Piccolomini (from 1461 to 1582), and then had practi-

The town is formed by the Piazza Flavio Gioia, overlooking the sea, the terminus of public transportation and tour buses, and by the nearby Piazza Duomo, slightly inland, and dominated by the polychrome mass of the **Duomo*** (B2). You can enter along a monumental staircase, which leads into a porticoed atrium, in which are the entrances to the cathedral, the chapel, or Cappella del Crocifisso, and the old cemetery, known as the Chiostro del Paradiso. The facade and the atrium were completely rebuilt in 1889-91 after the collapse of the older structures; the *campanile**, which existed as early as 1180, was completed in 1276, with the construction of the belfry.

The atrium, with two aisles spanned by cross-vaults set on columns, links two basilicas that originally both had a nave and two side-aisles: the first basilica, the so-called chapel, or *Cappella del Crocifisso* (closed and undergoing restoration following the demolition of the Baroque superstructures), corresponds to the old cathedral erected by Duke Mansone III

The delicate arcading of the Chiostro del Paradiso, Amalfi

cally no more history.

Today there is a contrast between the traffic and bustling crowds of tourists along the waterfront or Lungomare, in the central squares, and on Via Capuano, which covers the mountain stream, or Torrente Chiarito which runs through the city, and the silence and tranquillity of the remaining fabric of the city which, less well known to tourists, constitutes one of the chief sources of charm in any stay on the Amalfi coast, or Costiera.

(959-1004); the second, broader and with a transept, dates back to the period of the archbishop Matteo Capuano (1202-1215) and his brother, the cardinal Pietro, at the time of the deposition in the crypt of the relics of St. Andrew (1208). The cathedral, or Duomo, underwent continuous reconstruction and restoration work, until the most complete restoration (1703-18), which gave it its present-day Baroque appearance, which conceals the medieval structures. Among the works of art that decorate the church, aside from the bronze *door** cast in Constantinople and donated in 1065 by an Amalfitan merchant, we would mention the ceiling, in which there are canvases by Andrea d'Aste, the *marble triptych* in the first chapel on the right (beginning of the 16th c.), the tomb, or *Sepolcro d'Acunto* (turn of the 16th c.) at the far end of the right aisle, the two ambos, recomposed with fragments of the original *ambos*, the silver *altar frontal* (1713) damaged by a theft, the old baptismal basin. Note the *crypt** (with frescoes by Vincenzo de Pino, altar by Domenico Fontana, with *statues of St. Andrew* by M. Naccherino and of *Saints Stephen and Lawrence*, by P. Bernini) decorated in the early years of the 17th c.

When you return to the atrium, you can enter the cloisters, or **Chiostro del Paradiso*** (B2), built (1266-68) at the behest of Bishop Augustariccio as a cemetery for the most illustrious townsfolk, resulting in the demolition of much of the left aisle of the church of the Crocifisso; it is surrounded by a peristyle of pointed arches supported by twinned columns. The charm of the setting is enhanced by the vegetation and the sculptural fragments from various eras, which make it an authentic open-air museum. In a state of terrible neglect are a number of important 14th-c. *frescoes* from the former chapels of the church of the Crocifisso, now visible from the cloisters.

If you leave the Piazza Duomo, with the 18th-c. fountain, or *Fontana del Popolo*, in its center, adorned with a statue of the patron saint, St. Andrew, and you pass through a medieval arch, facing the cathedral, or Duomo, you will head toward the *Piazza dei Dogi* (formerly the Piazza dei Ferrari), where the blacksmiths of the town once had their shops, overlooked by the palazzo that was the home base of the various feudal lords. This zone was called "Arsina" for the presence of the arsenal, or *Arsenale** (B2), of which there survive two aisles, covered by pointed-arch cross-vaults (with entrance from Via Matteo Camera). If you head north, you will cross through a labyrinth of little lanes, often stepped and covered (*Vico dei Pastai, Via Ercolano Marini*, etc.), which lead to the Contrada Campo, from which you can descend along the central thoroughfare formed by Via Capuano, the street that crosses Amalfi along the riverbed of the mountain torrent.

From here, if you head inland, after crossing a modern area of expansion, you will reach the valley, or *Valle dei Mulini*, where there were major paper mills in the Middle Ages, and today there are the traces of various industries from different periods (19th-c. mills and paper mills) and the paper museum, or *Museo della Carta* of the Cartiera Milani.

Not far from the gate, or *Porta dell'Ospedale* is the entrance, studded with recycled marble work, of the loveliest and best known street in the medieval city, Via dei Mercanti (**Ruga Nova Mercatorum***), nearly straight and nearly all covered, which runs the length of the Contrada S. Simone; the street is remarkable for the views and the effects of the light on its white walls. At the end of it, you will follow the Salita dei Curiali which, amidst gardens set between the houses, leads to an intimate little square overlooked by the churches of the *Addolorata* (A-B2) and of *S. Maria Maggiore*, founded in A.D. 986; you will then continue along the Vico S. Maria Maggiore, to the foot of the campanile of the cathedral, or Duomo, beyond which you will walk beneath (arch, or *Arco di S. Anna*) the large staircase. This is an array of streets and views that allow one to observe clearly the remarkable complexity of the urban fabric that is typical of Amalfi and the towns along the coast, especially following the tour of the square and the cathedral, or Duomo. The lane, or *Vico S. Andrea Apostolo* (B2-3) leads into the square where you will see the entrance to the town hall, or Palazzo del Municipio, which houses the city museum, or *Museo Civico*, which features, among other things, the *Tabula Amalphitana*, a codex (probably dating from the 15th c.) which contains the maritime laws and customs of Amalfi, formulated between the end of the 11th and the beginning of the 12th c.

The town hall, or Municipio, overlooks *Corso Roma* (B2-3), an elegant stretch of waterfront that continues in Via Amendola, terminating at the circular tower, or *Torre di Amalfi* convent (C3), one of the many defensive structures built along the coasts of southern Italy in the 16th c.; facing it is the *Albergo Luna* convent (B3), installed in the suppressed monastery, or Convento di S. Francesco (cloisters, with intertwined arches, from the 13th c.), where Ibsen (plaque) wrote *A Doll's House* (1879).

On the far side of the city, in the Rione Vagliendola, you can see, high on the rocky ridge, the equally historic *Albergo dei Cappuccini* (B1), a hotel set in the former monastery, or Ex Convento di S. Pietro della Canonica, founded in the 13th c. and deeded to the Capuchin monks, or Cappuccini, in 1583, famous for its garden, the remains of a 13th-c. cloisters with intertwined arches, and, above all, for one of the most renowned panoramic views of the city and the coast.

From Amalfi, with a detour from the state road, or Statale, you will reach the **highland of Agerola** (elev. 650 m), characterized by a nearly Alpine landscape: dense chestnut forest, green meadows, and houses with pitch roofs. *Agerola* (pop. 7,676) is a scattered township consisting of a series of villages, including *Pianillo* (site of the town hall), *Campora, Bomerano,* and *San Lazzaro*. In the last-named village, near the church of San Lazzaro, is the *Belvedere della Punta** where, on clear days, you can see from Capri to the Monti del Cilento.

Conca dei Marini
This picturesque town (elev. 120 m, pop. 695), comprising a group of houses set high on the ridge of the Capo di Conca, was famous in the past for the flourishing trading activity of its sailors. On the Capo di Conca stands the Torre di Conca, built in the 16th c. to defend against Saracen raids. Not far away, along the state road, or Statale, toward Praiano, is the entrance to the grotto, or **Grotta dello Smeraldo***, so called because of the greenish tint that light acquires as it penetrates the water through the rocks. By elevator, or along a long stairway, one nearly reaches sea level, where, through a natural aperture, one enters the grotto, which was discovered in 1932. Originally, the grotto must have been completely dry, and then, through "bradisismo" (slow seismic phenomena), it was submerged, and the sea halted the development of stalagmites.

Praiano
This small fishing village (elev. 120 m, pop. 1,927) is made up of houses scattered along the ridge of the Monte S. Angelo, which ends in the sea, with the *Capo Sottile*. In the high part of the town stands the parish church of *S. Luca*, in which, aside from a number of paintings attributed to Giovanni Bernardo Lama (16th c.), there is a silver bust of the saint. In an inlet, just outside of the town, is the *Marina di Praja*, a small and charming beach, surrounded by the houses and boats of the fishermen.

Vettica Maggiore
This village in the township of Praiano (elev. 100 m), is endowed with a beach, at the end of a little lane through the olive groves. Here stands the *church of S. Gennaro*, of ancient origin (rebuilt in the 16th c.), with majolica dome and campanile and, on the interior, paintings from the 16th and 17th c., overlooking a remarkable plaza/terrace, partly paved with majolica, that overlooks Positano, offering a lovely view.

Positano*
The overall view, from the sea or from the state road, or Statale, of Positano – its white

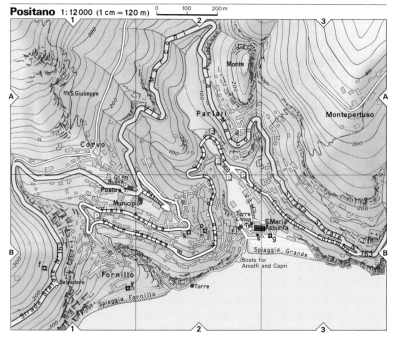

Positano 1:12 000 (1 cm = 120 m) 0 100 200 m

The steeply terraced houses of Positano look out to sea

houses punctuating the lavish vegetation and the gray rock – is quite charming. Arranged in terraces on the green slopes of the Monte Comune and Monte S. Angelo a Tre Pizzi, which converge toward the sea, the houses present a nearly cubic shape, covered by a basket-arch vaulted ceiling and a loggia with arches toward the sea (often with a portico in the front).

According to tradition, Positano (elev. 30 m, pop. 3,784) was founded by the inhabitants of Paestum – who had fled their city, under siege by Saracens – on the site where there already stood a Benedictine abbey dedicated to St. Vitus (Abbazia di S. Vito). Its inhabitants were excellent sailors, and the small village, over the centuries, was the feudal land holding of many important families (Miroballo, Mastrogiudice, Cossa, and others). Not far from the places chosen for the leisure time, or *otia*, or the Roman imperial court, it now constitutes an elegant, exciting, and exclusive tourist resort, popular all year round. In its little lanes, often stepped, there is a succession of little shops, artist's ateliers, restaurants, and bars. In the Piazza Flavio Gioia, which opens toward the sea, is the parish church of *S. Maria Assunta* (B2-3), with a large majolica dome; on the interior (nave and two aisles) you will find a panel depicting the *Virgin Mary with Christ Child*, dating from the 13th c., and a *Circumcision*, by F. Santafede; in the campanile you may note a Romanesque marble slab depicting a pistrix, fish, and a fox.

The town ends at the *Marina Grande* (B2-3), the beach of the fishermen, with a small marina. In the inlets of the coast, there extend other beaches (Fornillo, La Porta, Ciumicello, and Arienzo), and in the rock there are a number of grottoes, some of which housed the earliest signs of human life on the Amalfi coast, or *Costiera*. The most important one is the *Grotta La Porta*, with Paleolithic and Mesolithic remains.

From Positano we recommend an excursion to *Montepertuso* (A3; elev. 355 m), a remarkable little town, and to Nocelle (off map; elev. 443 m), a singular and picturesque little village, which can be reached only by following a long stretch of trails and steps (stunning panoramic view).

Sant'Agata sui Due Golfi

This exquisite little village (elev. 394 m), part of the township of Massa Lubrense, occupies an exceptional location between the Gulf of Salerno and the Gulf of Naples. In the parish church of *S. Maria delle Grazie* (17th c.) there are a notable altar in polychrome marble and precious stones, a Florentine creation dating from the 16th c., and a fine copy of the Raphael's *Madonna della Pace*. One particular attraction of the site is the stroll to the so-called *Deserto**, once the monastery, or Convento dei Padri Bigi, from which you can admired one of the most renowned panoramic views in all Campania, and the excursion to the *Marina di Crapolla*, with the ruins of a medieval abbey and a Roman villa.

10 The Cilento and the Vallo di Diano

The area between the plain, or Piana del Sele, and the gulf, or Golfo di Policastro, is one of the most interesting sub-regions of Campania. This is a mountainous territory, with the exception of the Vallo di Diano; characterized by very jagged coasts, tall peaks and gentle hills, crossed by numerous watercourses, which affected the distribution of settlements

The landscape of the Cilento, between the Piano del Sole and the Gulf of Policastro

and towns. These towns, nearly all dating back to ancient times, stand high on the mountain slopes, or they extend along the river valleys. In ancient times, there was a conflict among various cultures: on the interior were the Lucani and on the coast, the Greek colonists. In Roman times, there sprang up many *municipia* along the road that linked Campania with Calabria. At the beginning of the Middle Ages, many of the lower towns were abandoned by inhabitants, who found shelter on the mountains, especially around the Vallo di Diano, which ran to marshes and swamps. In Norman times the territory, along with the foundation of many castles and fortifications, saw the rise of many new Benedictine foundations, and around them there grew up new towns and settlements. From the 12th c. on, this broad section of the kingdom was given as a feudal land holding to the Sanseverino family, which held it until 1552, making it the theater of the continual rebellions of the powerful family against the royal power.

The Vallo di Diano is a highland which originates from a dry lake bed. It is crossed by a river that originates with the name of Calore, then changes its name to Tanagro, and flows into the River Sele. Over many centuries of history, many efforts have been made to reclaim the Vallo di Diano, from the ancient Romans to the house of Bourbon. A major result was obtained with the work of the Consorzio, or consortium, established in 1936, but the job is not yet done. Both the Cilento and the Vallo di Diano now present a fairly poverty-stricken picture; the inhabitants, deeply tied to the land and to traditions, have often been forced to emigrate. Only slightly populated, the region lives primarily on farming and herding (little fishing is done), and only over the past few years have manufacturing and tourism begun to grow. In the inland areas, there are extensive forests of holm-oaks, ash trees, and chestnuts, while the coast is characterized by Mediterranean maquis.

10.1 From Salerno to Policastro

From Salerno you will head south. Amidst eucalyptus groves and pine forests, you will cross a number of rivers, including, at its mouth, the Sele, near which stands the sanctuary, or Santuario di Hera Argiva. This long stretch of road runs – as far as Paestum – along a broad sandy beach punctuated by small beach resorts, crowded only in the summer. From Paestum, you will return along the state road, or Statale 18, Tirrenica Inferiore, and then you will turn off onto the state road, or Statale 267. Some 13 km later, set on a promontory, you will find Agropoli. From here, you can reach Velia along the network of roads that cuts inland, or else along the state road, or Statale 267, which runs along within sight of the sea, around the Monte Tresino, to reach – in 14.5 km – Santa Maria which, with the neighboring San Marco, constitutes the harbor of Castellabate. You then may continue, among panoramic views, and then you will reach, in 18 km, Acciaroli; in the distance, you will see cape, or Capo Palinuro. You will enter the plain of the River Alento, which reaches the sea not far from Velia. This area, which is luxuriant, is characterized by lush olive groves, vineyards, and prickly pear trees. As you head further into the plain, you will reach the excavations of Velia. Then, when you return to the crossroads, you may continue along the state road, or Statale 447, from which, once you have crossed the Fiumarella, you may turn off to Marina di Ascea, a resort with a handsome sandy beach and numerous accom-

modations, and which has grown greatly over the last few years. The road then runs into the high valley, or Vallone del Fiumicello, with an arid and wild appearance; beyond it, you will once again have a view of the sea, with a fine vista of cape, or Capo Palinuro. You will then pass through Pisciotta, and you will continue along, variously passing long sandy beaches and stretches of rock coastline, until you reach Palinuro (35 km), beyond which you will follow the state road, or Statale 562, which runs through Marina di Camerota to Policastro (37.5 km).

The trip back, on the other hand, may take place through the interior (we recommend an excursion to the Monte Cervati) along the state road, or Statale 18, which, over the course of less than 100 km, runs through villages and towns, as far as Vallo della Lucania, and then returns, on the sea, near the excavations of Paestum.

The mouth of the River Sele, and the Santuario di Hera Argiva

In a spectacular setting, typically marshy, are the scattered monumental remains of one of the most important extra-urban sanc-

tuaries of Poseidonia. Dedicated to Hera and founded at the same time as the city, it marked the boundaries of its territory. The excavations done so for have led to the identification of a early archaic sacellum (ca. 570 B.C.), probably a *thesauros*, of the main temple (ca. 500 B.C.) and of smaller buildings belonging to various eras (including two *stoai*, porticoes serving the faithful). The *thesauros* presents a rectangular plan, with columns on the front; devoid of peristasis, with a roof with four pitches, it was decorated with finely carved architectural elements. The building owes its fame to the carved metopes (now in the Museo di Paestum) representing epic and mythical episodes. Figured metopes also decorated the frieze of the larger temple. The building, with a Doric order, and a cella subdivided into pronaos, *naos*, and *adyton*, originally presented Ionic columns between the antae.

Paestum*

Paestum – its Doric temples, the intact ring of walls – is a major archaeological site, and perhaps even more, a stunning spectacle of majesty and grandeur in the silent variation of light, particularly charming at evening and sunset.

The rediscovery of Paestum and its monuments took place in the middle of the 18th c., when groups of architects began the patient labor of drawing the temples of the city. This was a prelude to the scholarly acquisition of Greek art and the discovery of its values. From that time on, painstaking critical analysis has led to a correct understanding of the architecture of the city, setting aside the myths and focusing on the real documentary role, but Paestum and its excavations have continued to serve test benches for scholarly development. The great campaign undertaken in the 1930s by U. Zanotti Bianco and P. Zancani Montuoro at the mouth of the River Sele led to the discovery of one of the most interesting groups of ancient sculptures in the history of archaeological studies of Magna Graecia. The excavation of the necropolises, which yielded the tomb of the diver, or Tomba del Tuffatore, a rare example of Greek painting from the classical age, has led to a far more thorough exploration of the meaning of the rituals of antiquity and the recomposition of the social fabric that is reflected in tomb furnishings and paintings. The research undertaken in the chief public areas of the city has made it possible to explore the complex question of the institutional transition of a formerly Greek and Lucanian

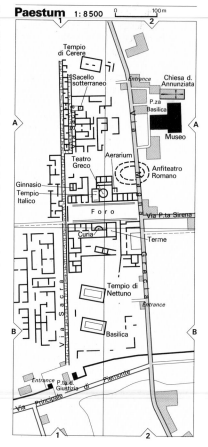

Paestum 1 : 8500

town into the sphere of Roman influence, and to understand better the concept of continuity and transformation in the ancient world.

Poseidonia (the original name of Paestum) was founded by Sybaris, a powerful and opulent city built by Achaean colonists on the Ionic Gulf. It must have been erected at the turn of the 6th c. B.C., the period of the oldest artifacts from the classical period found here. The site upon which the city was built has also yielded up prehistoric finds, and in particular a necropolis dating back to the Eneolithic Age. The earliest layout of the town is virtually unknown. Conjectures, based on the various orientations of the temples with respect to the grid of the roads, call for an early layout that was subsequently canceled and preserved, for reasons of tradition, only in the sacred enclosures. The city was girt with double **curtain walls***, dotted with towers and gates, and originally surrounded by a moat. The present city layout is organized into at least two large east-west plazas, or squares, intersected by orthogonal *stenopoi*, which subdivide the city into modular blocks, that are narrow and elongated. At the end of the 5th c. B.C., the city fell under Lucanian rule, and, during the subsequent century, it prospered greatly.

In 273 B.C. it came under Roman control, and a Latin colony was founded there. It became a diocese in the 5th c. A.D., and the site was definitively abandoned, around the 8th c., due to the difficulties of defense and the unhealthy environment.

In the central sector of the city, the part which has been most intensely explored, you will find the main public and sacred precincts. To the south is the sanctuary, or *Santuario di Hera*. An enclosure wall (*peribulum*) surrounded the sacred area, inside of which stood temples, altars, service structures, and votive dedications. Excavations have revealed an intense array of signs of life in this area, as well as a well-stratified presence of sacred complexes, in some cases indicated only by the evidence of secondary features (architectural terracotta, etc.) and by scattered monumental ruins. To the south stands the structure of the so-called **Basilica*** (B1-2). Of the temple, there survive the external peristasis, the interior colonnade, scanty remains of the epistyle (the array of the stone crowning elements), while the walls of the cella are entirely lost. There is much debate concerning the chronology of the building, which was probably founded as early as the first half of the 6th c. B.C. and renovated after just a few centuries; the structure presents a tendency to soften the style of the Doric order, with links to the Ionic influence, a characteristic that distinguishes the majority of the temples built in Achaean colonies in Magna Graecia. Enneastyle (nine columns on the front), the temple had a cella subdivided into two aisles, preceded by a vestibule, and followed by an *adyton* (probably the site of the treasury of the temple). At the far end of the central room there were two rectangular niches, which led to the hypothesis of the presence of two statues that were worshipped, and, consequently, the dedication of the temple to two different deities (probably, Hera together with Zeus). Of special note are the stone elements, the architectural terracottas (now in the museum, or Museo) which surmounted the

roof, the entasis (central swelling) of the columns, and the expanded silhouette of the Doric capitals, which were decorated, at their top, or "summo scapo," by a collarino of foliate motifs. The original characteristics of this structure become increasingly evident through a comparison with the nearby so-called temple of Neptune, or **Tempio di Nettuno*** (B1-2). Dating from roughly a century later (middle of the 5th c. B.C.), it offers clear evidence of the development of the Doric order in Magna Graecia and the acceptance of influence deriving from the great architectural models of the homeland. Some scholars feel it was dedicated to Hera, while others prefer the theory of Zeus; its fame is due to its excellent state of preservation: hexastyle (six columns on the front), with a cella subdivided into a nave and two side-aisles by two rows of columns in double order, it is possible to observe even now, *in situ*, the succession of load-bearing and crowning elements: the architrave decorated by a *taenia* of *regulae* and guttae, the frieze (metopes and triglyphs), the concluding jutting cornice (*geison*) which should have been crowned by the rim of the sima (now missing).

The rigid forms of the echinus of the Doric capital and the slight entasis of the columns correspond fully to the transformations and canonization of the forms of the Doric order over the course of the 5th c. B.C. The Greek model has been singled out as

The imposing columns of the Basilica, Paestum

the Temple of Zeus at Olympia. On the main front of the temples are placed the altars needed for the celebration of ancient forms of worship.

After the establishment of the Latin colony, profound urban transformations swept the city. The creation of the forum, or **Foro** (A1-2) led to a partial renovation of the sanctuary, or Santuario di Hera. This structure, bounded by a portico in the Doric order, develops to the north of the sacred area; it was surrounded by *tabernae* (shops) and the principal public monuments of the Roman city: on the south side, the *Macellum* (market) and the Basilica (place for commercial transactions and the administration of justice), on the west side, the *Lararium* and another house of worship. The center of the long northern side is occupied by the structure of the *Capitolium*, the chief temple of the city, built, in the classical tradition, on a high podium with moldings and cella, surrounded by columns only on three sides (*peripterus sine postico*, that is, without columns on the rear side). Adjoining the temple, behind it, are the *Comitium*, the place of assembly for citizens during the Roman period, with a circular plan inscribed in a rectangular perimeter and, at a slight distance, the site of the *Curia*.

To the east of these structures, it is possible to tour the amphitheater, or **Anfiteatro** (A2; 1st c. B.C.-1st c. A.D.), which has been only partially excavated and is cut across by the modern road, and, to the right, an area occupied by a pool in which traditionally scholars identify the site of the city gymnasium. Recent discoveries have led to the identification of the **agora** (main square of the Greek city), in the sector immediately to the north of the forum and the amphitheater. The hypothesis has been suggested by the discovery of an ancient assembly site (*ekklesiasterion*) that was eliminated upon the foundation of the Latin colony, with a circular plan, built over the course of the first half of the 5th c. B.C. In the western sector of this area is one of the most interesting and enigmatic monument of the Greek city: the underground sacellum, or *Sacello Ipogeico* (A1). At the center of an enclosure is a partially buried room, with a double pitch roof. On the interior were discov-ered bronze vases containing honey and an Attic vase (end of the 6th c. B.C.) arranged along the perimeter of the room, and a group of five metal spits arranged in the center. Some have hypothesized that this might be the site of a cult dedicated to the nymphs, or, much more interesting, a *heroon*, a celebratory monument, dedicated to the founder of Sybaris, homeland of Poseidonia, built there following the destruction of the Achaean city in 510 B.C.

Even further north, stands the sanctuary of Athena, or Santuario di Atena, which had a monumental presence as early as the turn of the 6th c. B.C.; set on a prominent spot on the *temenos* stands the **temple of Athena*** (A1; so-called temple of Cere) built at the end of the c. Doric, hexastyle (six columns on the elevation), it presents a cella with an *adyton*, preceded by a deep pronaos. The epistyle presents the standard succession of architrave, frieze, and *geison*, punctuated with cornices with moldings. The *geison*, or jutting cornice, features an interesting decoration with caissons'. To the west of the public and sacred areas, are the excavations of the *residential quarters*, with dwellings that can be dated back to the period between the Hellenistic age and the Empire. In the adjoining **Museo Nazionale*** (A2; 1952) you may admire finds from the excavations (bronze *hydriai* vases from the underground sacellum), materials from votive ditches (statues in terracotta including a *Zeus in throne**), sculpted and designed architectural elements (metope* of the Heraion, at the mouth of the Sele), funerary furnishings (decorated Greek and Italic ceramics, including specimens from the local workshop of Assteas and Python) and paintings (slabs from the tomb of the diver, or **Tomba del Tuffatore*** from the first half of the 5th c. B.C.; slabs from the Samnite period, with a recurring depiction of the *Return*

Frescoes from the Tomba del Tuffatore, Museo Nazionale, Paestum

of the Warrior and of the *Return of the Oikos*, the secluded and little-known world of the home, ruled over by women).

Agropoli

Founded almost certainly by the Byzantines in the 6th c., it became an episcopal see, and was occupied between A.D. 882 and 1028 by the Saracens. It was destroyed repeatedly by pirates; the houses, built high on the promontory, seem to blend in with it. Agropoli (elev. 24 m, pop. 18,471) is a lively tourist and beach resort, very popular especially in the summer (beach, or Spiaggia della Baia di Trentova).

Along a ramp and through a battlemented gate, you can enter the old city, silent and charming, with its intricate welter of lanes with narrow stairways, along which, from time to time, you have sudden glimpses of the sea. There you may note the church of *S. Maria di Costantinopoli*, dating from the 17th c., and an old castle (traditionally said to be Saracen, or Castello Saraceno), which was enlarged by the Aragonese, from which you may enjoy a vast panoramic view of the Gulf of Salerno, as far as Capri.

Castellabate

This is a scattered township (elev. 0/356 m, pop. 7,474) with its headquarters in the village of *Santa Maria*. The old Borgo di Santa Maria, which largely preserves its original structure, was one of the first places in the Cilento to become a beach resort; in the sea, an underwater wildlife park has been established.

San Marco, instead, stands on the promontory of Punta Licosa (which closes off the Gulf of Salerno); only recently discovered by tourists, it still has the appearance of a fishing village. Punta Licosa, dominated by the tower, or Torre Licosa, can be reached by sea (at the port, it is possible to rent boats) or on foot along a mule track that leads to *Ogliastro Marina*, set on the opposite slope of the promontory.

Acciaroli

This picturesque little village (elev. 10 m) set at the foot of a promontory, has become popular with mass tourism over the past few decades. Endowed with a little tourist marina and splendid beaches, it was particularly dear to Hemingway who stayed in the hotel "La Scogliera."

Velia*

A promontory in ancient times jutting out into the sea protected two port areas that have since been filled in. A series of hills closed off the horizon behind this town. Here, in 540 B.C., the city of Elea (Velia) was founded by a group of exiles from Phocaea, a city in Asia Minor; these exiles, according to Herodotus, while fleeing the Persians, took refuge first at Alalia, in Corsica, and then landed on the coasts of the Cilento. The city long preserved its Hellenic imprint, and was famous for the philosophical school of Parmenides and Zeno, playing an important roles in the commercial and maritime economy of the region. An early urban layout is documented by the ruins of dwelling found on the two slopes of the acropolis, with houses built with the polygonal technique that derives directly from experiences of the eastern homeland and the first generations of colonists.

Around 480 B.C., Velia underwent a period of profound urban renovation: the acropolis was arranged with new terracings and levels and, probably, destined solely to the construction of sacred buildings and sanctuaries, while public and private construction was concentrated in the lower sections of the site. A series of fortified towns were located on the surrounding hills, proper military bulwarks controlling the routes that, from the hinterland, led to the coastal area.

On the **acropolis** are the remains of the earliest dwellings: built in polygonal style, they were articulated on a number of terraces crossed by a thoroughfare that provided communications with the port area. The terracing done at the turn of the 5th c. B.C. led to the elimination of the residential quarter. On the new levels, a sacred area was built. The *"Ionic" temple* was badly damaged by the medieval fortifications, and little more than the foundations survive: the proportions would seem to encourage the traditionally accepted idea of a temple in the Ionic order. Not far away are the ruins of the *theater* (retaining wall and a number of steps: third c. B.C.) and of a road. The hill was fortified by an enclosure wall with a stone socle and brick elevation. Of it, we have evidence of various phases, and there are smaller linking walls (walls of the northern quarter). A road ran north-south through the fortified area and linked the two ports of the city. Behind the northern walls is a large terrace, with the ruins of an altar ("Ara Pagana"), probably a place of public assembly.

To the south, the furthest stretch of the fortifications, in sandstone, with rusticated decorations, is the result of the renovation of the area in the 4th c. B.C., when, once the old port had silted up, over it was built a res-

A deserted sandy beach near Capo Palinuro

idential quarter, of which you can tour a sector, between the old and the new enclosure walls. If you continue along the ancient turreted fortifications, you will reach the gate, or Porta Marina Sud. Along the sides of the road that runs from here into the city, there are two large public complexes dating from ancient Roman times: the baths (ruins of another bath house dating from Roman times stand to the east) and, further along to the right, a *building* dating from the 1st c. A.D. dedicated to the emperor cult. If you follow the ancient road that led down to the gate, or Porta Marina Sud, you will find the porticoed area (3rd c. B.C.) which – it has been hypothesized – served as the *agora*, or main square of the city, upon which there are little shops, and, to the left, the ruins of the earliest enclosure walls (6th c. B.C.).

If you continue along the road, you will reach two gates: the first dates back to the archaic phase of the fortification (doors in sandstone), the second is the so-called **Porta Rosa*** (middle of the 4th c. B.C.). Retaining walls line the sides of the saddles through which the road ran toward the northern quarter. A monumental round arch closes off the passageway, and on it a smaller arch was set; it thus became possible to walk directly between the two ridges.

Palinuro

This famous tourist attraction (elev. 53 m) with many accommodations, is arranged in a picturesque inlet at the base of the promontory, or Promontorio di Palinuro; before it became popular with mass tourism,

it was considered, along with Marina di Camerota, to be a fairly exclusive spot. The name, of course, is linked to the myth of Palinurus, the helmsman of Aeneas, who died here and fell into the sea; a number of the ruins in the area around the port (situated at a distance of 1.5 km from the town) are commonly believed to be his cenotaph. The jagged coast, bathed by a brightly colored sea, is rich in coves and grottoes, not all of which are accessible from the land, but certainly visible with organized tours from the port.

The first and best known is the Blue Grotto, or *Grotta Azzurra*; after you round the cape you will pass through the Cala Fetente, a cove whose name – Stinking Cove – refers to a sulfur spring, and you will see the *Archetiello*, carved out of limestone. Further along, in the area of the Marina di Molpa are the grotto, or *Grotta delle Ossa*, the walls of which are encrusted with human and animal bones dating from the Quaternary Period, and the grotto, or *Grotta Visco*. On the hill once stood ancient Molpa, which belonged to the Greek colony of Velia, described by Vergil as the *portus velinus*. It was sacked by Goths and Saracens, and was definitively destroyed by the pirate Barbarossa. On the highland that contains the acropolis are now the ruins of a castle.

Marina di Camerota

This town (elev. 20 m) is famous for the splendid sea and for the beauty of its coast, which constitutes the heart of what should one day be the national park, or Parco Nazionale del Cilento, abounds in coastal towers as well as grottoes, like Palinuro. The first grotto, to the south of the town, is the *Grotta della Cala*, where the earliest human remains in the area have been found (the entrance is situated halfway down the hill, on a terrace overlooking the sea, with a fine view of the town as well). Nearby is the grotto, or *Grotta Sepolcrale*, where the dead were buried.

Policastro Bussentino

This town (elev. 14 m), part of the township of Santa Marina (elev. 415 m, pop. 3,314), stands on the site of Pixunte (*Pixus* to the Greeks, *Buxentum* for the ancient Romans), and was destroyed in 1055 by Robert Guiscard; it was a major feudal land holding and a diocese from 1069 (now associated with Teggiano), and it gives its name to the large gulf between Campania and Calabria. Of particular interest is the ancient cathedral, or *Cattedrale** with a crypt with apses on three sides, a handsome campanile adorned by intertwined arches and Renaissance sculptures. The settlement is still protected, enclosed by the medieval walls that follow the outline of the ancient Greek walls.

Reserve, or Area Protetta del Monte Cervati*

You can climb the mountain, elev. 1,898 m, along trails and mule tracks, starting from Sanza, at a distance of 19 km from Torre Orsaia along the state road, or Statale 517 from Policastro, or from *Laurito* (elev. 475 m, pop. 1,013, castle and Gothic church of *S. Filippo d'Argira*) along the provincial road, or Strada Provinciale that runs through the picturesque town of *Rofrano* (elev. 450 m, pop. 2,301) founded around a Basilian cenobium, and the destination of excursions to the Monte Gelbison (see below). The Monte Cervati, upon which you will find the sanctuary, or Santuario della Madonna della

Neve (pilgrimage on 5 August), is a protected natural reserve (Oasi Naturalistica Protetta), mantled with verdant forests with a prevalence of chestnut trees, alders, and ash trees.

Vallo della Lucania

This is the largest farming and trading town (elev. 380 m, pop. 8,330) in the Cilento, almost a capital, a diocese since 1851, and now joined to the older town of Capaccio. Situated on a spur of the Monte Sacro, amidst dense olive groves, it was founded around the middle of the 15th c. in an area that was already densely populated by the farming operations of the lords of Novi (the present-day Novi Velia).

Nearly at the entrance to the town is the seminary, or *Seminario*, and the bishop's palace, or *Palazzo Vescovile*, in which there is a museum, or *Museo*, which contains sacred objects (including the silver Gothic chalice*, or Calice di S. Silvestro, by Ugolino di Vieri) and various paintings, relics of the local artistic culture of the 16th c., from various churches of the diocese.

In the heart of the town stands the cathedral, or *Cattedrale* (S. Pantaleone) with a single nave, majolica dome, and campanile; there are altars made of inlaid marble, a silver statue of the Saint (Pantaleon), and a Neapolitan organ dating from the 18th c. Nearby is the church of *S. Maria delle Grazie*, founded in 1480, in which you may note fine paintings, including a *polyptych* by Andrea da Salerno, dating from 1530 (chapel to the right) with noteworthy period cornices, and, on the left, a *Virgin Mary with Christ Child and St. Francis of Paula*, by G. Santacroce (1515); note the wooden statue of the *Virgin Mary* (1571) on the main altar.

10.2 From Salerno to the Vallo di Diano and Padula

You will leave Pontecagnano, an industrial center just outside of Salerno, in the direction of Battipaglia, a major road and railroad junction for communications between Campania, Calabria, and the Basilicata.

You will then continue on toward Eboli and Polla; this long route runs first of all through the plain, or Piana del Sele, and then continues, for a certain distance, along the course of the River Tanagro, leaving on the right the Monti Alburni.

The state road, or Statale 19, continues to a cross-roads where, if you turn to the left, you cross the Tanagro on a Roman bridge, rebuilt in the 18th c. on its original foundation. Once you leave Sala Consilina you may

choose to tour Teggiano, then you will return to the state road, or Statale, which runs between the highway, or Autostrada, and the River Tanagro as far as Padula.

Pontecagnano-Faiano

This modern farming and manufacturing town (elev. 0/384 m, pop. 22,520), practically joined to Salerno, was built on the site of an Iron Age settlement founded by an Etruscan tribe, known to the Romans as Picentia. Archaeological excavations have unearthed tombs dating back to the Iron Age (9th/8th c. B.C.) and traces of the urban layout (8th/4th c. B.C.).

Among the finds, on exhibit in the *Museo*

dell'*Agro Picentino**, established in 1977, of particular note are the funerary furnishings from the Villanovan culture, the eastern period (princely tombs), and a group of ceramics of the Etruscan Corinthian variety, of local manufacture. Other finds are in the Museo Provinciale di Salerno.

Eboli

This lively (and, thanks to Carlo Levi, famous) farming and manufacturing town (elev. 145 m, pop. 35,139) stands on the slopes of the Monti Picentini, up which extends the picturesque medieval village. Called by the ancient Lucani *Eburnum*, it became a Roman *municipium*, and was an important traffic center on Via Popilia. It preserves, in a modern but pleasant setting, the 18th-c. collegiate church, or *Collegiata di S. Maria della Pietà*, in which there is a notable wooden group of the *Pietà* by G. Colombo, dated 1698. In the old city, up on the hill, are the turreted castle, or *Castello dei Colonna* (15th c.), restored in the 18th c. by L. Vanvitelli, and, in the highest part, the *basilica of S. Pietro alli Marmi* (11th c., considerably renovated) adjoining a monastery of the Capuchins (*Convento Cappuccino*). Of the Norman structure, you can see on the exterior the campanile and two of the three apses; on the interior (nave and two side-aisles, set on recycled columns, with crypt) medieval frescoes (right apse: *St. Anthony* and *St. Francis*).

Pertosa

This farming town (elev. 301 m, pop. 873) situated on the left bank of the River Tanagro, is renowned for the grotto, or **Grotta di Pertosa*** (also known as the *Grotta dell'Angelo* or *Grotta di S. Michele*), which is one of the most extensive (2,560 m) and noteworthy caverns in the south of Italy. Its route follows that of an ancient underground river. It features remains of Neolithic and Eneolithic dwellings; it was inhabited later as well, and it became a place of worship in the 11th c. At the entrance is an embankment, from which a raft runs to the first cavern, with numerous stalactites and a picturesque waterfall; from there, the cave splits into three branches: the *Braccio della Sorgente*, to the right, through which watercourses run, and terminating at the Paradiso; the *Braccio Centrale*, of no particular interest, and the *Braccio Principale*, which you reach at the end and which, in its turn, opens out in various branches. Along the way, you should note the *Braccio delle Meraviglie*, with lavish and fragile concretions, the lovely *Sala della Madonna* and the

Sala delle Spugne or *Sala delle Vergini*, characterized by the purity of its concretions.

Polla

Along the state road, or *Statale*, a few kilometers before Polla (elev. 468 m, pop. 5,638) – which extends along the river banks, serving as the "northern gate" of the Vallo di Diano – are the ruins of the mausoleum of Caius Ultianus Rufus, or *Mausoleo di Caio Ulziano Rufo*, a magistrate of Volcei (Buccino), the largest Roman relic in the Vallo: a square base surmounted by a cylindrical structure covered with a dome.

The territory of Polla was inhabited as early as prehistoric times, as we know from the artifacts unearthed in the grottoes of Polla and Pertosa, but the first real settlement here was in Roman times, where Forum Popili was founded here, to the east of the river, a major trading center and halting place along the consular road, Via Popilia, which linked Capua with Reggio di Calabria. A famous ancient epigraph, the *Elogium* of Polla, set on a modern stele in front of the Taverna del Passo, illustrates the construction of the road in the 2nd c. B.C. In the Middle Ages, the settlement was abandoned in favor of another settlement, atop the hill across the river. A first expansion did not occur until the 16th c., with the construction of various religious complexes; in the two centuries that followed, the town extended to the river banks. The medieval nucleus features a number of interesting elements. Among the twisting lanes (which have been given their original names) are the Renaissance portals of the churches of S. Nicola dei Latini and S. Nicola dei Greci (Sacro Cuore); in the upper part of the town is the square, or Piazzale S. Antonio (broad panoramic view of the entire Vallo) overlooked by the *church of S. Antonio di Padova* (16th/18th c.), preceded by a small atrium with three arches, and with a portal dating from 1541. On the interior, which is asymmetrical, you may note the ceiling, adorned by 40 canvases dating from 1666, by M. Regolia, with *scenes from the Old and the New Testament*, and, in the center, *Our Lady of the Immaculate Conception* ("Immacolata"), the 17th-c. frescoes in the dome, a wooden *Crucifix* by Fra' Umile da Petralia, and a handsome inlaid choir. Adjoining is the Franciscan convent (1593). The town is rich in folk traditions: there are many popular festivals and fairs, during which the women wear the colorful local costume.

Atena Lucana

This is the oldest town (elev. 625 m, pop.

2,364) in the Vallo, and was known in Roman times as *Campur Atina* and in the Middle Ages as Campo Atinate. Indications of the importance of the city in pre-Roman times can be had from the ruins of megalithic walls (4th c. B.C.) and the numerous and important archaeological finds (7th/4th c. B.C.) preserved in the *Antiquarium* situated in a hall of the town hall, or Municipio. A flourishing Roman *municipium* (it even had an amphitheater), it suffered barbarian invasions and moved its inhabited nucleus to the highest part of the hill, where perhaps the acropolis stood. The road grid of the new medieval town was articulated around three concentric ring roads, crossed in a radial pattern by numerous stepped lanes. In the highest point you may note the ruins of a Longobard castle,

Harvesting olives, a typical local product

reinforced in Norman times, in the context of the construction of the new city walls with cylindrical towers.

Sala Consilina

This is perhaps the most important town (elev. 614 m, pop. 12,965) of the Vallo, in terms of its agricultural, commercial, and industrial activities. Arranged on the slopes of the Monti della Maddalena, with the ruins of the oldest part of the town set up high, the modern quarter further down hides the historical center from view.

It was founded in the Middle Ages, possibly by the Longobards on the site of the ancient Marcelliana, destroyed by the Goths; the Normans built a castle here (ruins of the towers) to control the Vallo and the road to Calabria; it was a feudal land holding of the Sanseverino, and over the course of the 18th c. it was embellished with interesting palazzi, built outside of the enclosure walls, and noteworthy for their floor plans, with a typology that is often adapted to suit the landscape, and for the Baroque facades. Among the largest is the *Palazzo Grammatico* (1722), in Via Grammatico, which has carved consoles at the windows and balconies, and a portal with carved ashlars.

Teggiano

This old town (elev. 635 m, pop. 8,543) set high on the summit of the hill that rises on the plain, or Piana del Vallo di Diano. Rich

in monuments, it preserves the Roman road network, and is certainly one of the most important historical towns of Campania, a little museum city, with recycled material scattered everywhere. It preserves intact its appearance as a fortified town, both because the old enclosure walls, with a gate and a number of towers, are almost entirely visible, and because it still stands in isolation on the hill, leaving the plains for grazing, agriculture, and development. Founded in pre-Roman times, it became a Roman *municipium*, changing its original name, Tegia, to Tegianum. Destroyed in A.D. 410, it rose again as Dianum, then Diano, hence the name of the Vallo di Diano. It was given as a feudal land holding to the clan of the Sanseverino, who reinforced it as a stronghold, guarding both Sala Consilina, across the way, the valley, or Valle del Tanagro, and the road to Calabria. It was made an episcopal see in 1850; in 1862 its name was changed to Teggiano. The layout, consisting of narrow winding lanes, is based on two nearly straight thoroughfares, the Discesa S. Andrea-Via Roma, and the Salita Corpo di Cristo-Via S. Giorgio, a vital center of the town, along which stand the most important monuments. You will reach it along Via Matteotti, from which you can see the remains of megalithic walls, incorporated into more recent structures, and the tower, or Torre Varvacane, one of the few surviving towers of the medieval enclosure walls. As if to mark the entrance to the town, at the end of the street, in the Piazza del Municipio, stands the *church of S. Francesco* (14th c.) with a Romanesque portal (1307); on the interior is a wooden choir dating from the 17th c., ambos built with recycled Roman materials, frescoes from the 14th and 15th c., and a wooden ceiling from the 18th c. You will continue along *Via Ro-*

ma where, to the right, you will see the flat apsidal wall of the cathedral, or *Cattedrale* (S. Maria Maggiore) in which are cemented, as in other buildings, Roman funerary aediculae. The church (1274) originally opened out with an atrium on this street, but after the restoration in the wake of the earthquake of 1857, the early structures of the church were altered, and its orientation was inverted. You can still see the *portal** by Melchiorre da Montalbano (1279), the Renaissance portal on the right side, and interesting sculptures on the interior. Among these we would class the *ambo** and the Paschal candle by Melchiorre himself, the monument to Enrico Sanseverino (1336), attributed to pupils of Tino da Camaino, and the Renaissance monument to Orso Malavolta (1479), respectively to the right and left of the entrance wall; a holy-water stoup dating from the 14th c.; two angels (16th c.) at the sides of the altar, a polychrome *Crucifix* dating from the 15th c., and the remains of a late-16th-c. choir.

On Via Roma at the crossroads with the Salita Corpo di Cristo is the old *Sedile*, built by the Teggianese architect Iacobello di Babino (1472), destroyed by the earthquake of 1857 and then rebuilt, which now contains a fountain. You may then continue along the descent, which takes its name from the Angevin *church of S. Andrea*, joined to the bell tower by an overpass; inside are two triptychs from the school of Andrea da Salerno.

At the end of the descent are the churches of the *SS. Annunziata* and of *S. Angelo*. The former, of Angevin origin, is preceded by a pronaos in which you will find a portal dating from 1504. The interior has a Gothic layout and contains artworks from the 15th c. and the 16th c. The latter is thought to have been built on the ruins of an ancient theater (in effect, it reproduces in part the layout); it has an interesting crypt with a nave and two aisles, set on columns, with capitals that are in part recycled.

Along the Salita Corpo di Cristo, in the Piazza IV Novembre, is the *church of S. Pietro*, possibly built on the ruins of the temple of Aesculapius, or Tempio di Esculapio; this church was also founded under Angevin rule. Preceded by a pronaos with three arches, it presents a portal that is similar to the one on the side of the cathedral, or Cattedrale. In the church is the *Museo Civico Dianense*, in which you will find artworks and materials dating from various eras (from Roman times to the 18th c.) taken from buildings that were destroyed in the earthquake, including a tomb by the

school of Tino da Camaino. Behind it is the *church of S. Agostino*, with a frescoed cloisters dating from the 16th c. Facing the Museo, on the other hand, is the *church of S. Martino* and the seminary, or *Seminario* founded in 1564 and repeatedly rebuilt. You then reach the little square, or *Piazzetta della SS. Pietà*, which originally, with the nearby Piazza dei Mori, constituted the Piazza d'Armi, or parade grounds, of the town. The *church of the Pietà* dates back to the late 14th c.; with a pronaos and a fine portal dating from 1475, adorned in the lunette by a bas-relief of the *Pietà*; on the interior, group of the Pietà attributed to Giovanni da Nola. In the monastery, or "convento," now a school and the site of the town council, you may note the Renaissance cloisters, with frescoed vaults. The complex stood behind the northern walls. Lastly, you reach the castle, which is largely in ruins; built in the higher part in 1285 by the Sanseverino family, it was transformed repeatedly in the centuries that followed; the last renovation, done in the 19th c., definitively altered its appearance.

Padula

This town (elev. 699 m, pop. 5,714) occupies an elevated position, dominating the Vallo and the charter house, or Certosa di S. Lorenzo. Perhaps founded in the 9th or 10th c., it was, from the 12th c. on, a feudal land holding of the Sanseverino who, with Tommaso II, rebuilt the castle originally erected by the Normans. It then passed into the hands of the Malaspina-Cybo and, from 1743 on, to the Este. It comprises two urban centers: the first, medieval, is set high on the slopes of the hill and has a triangular shape, a result of the shape of the enclosure wall that ran down from the castle; the second dates back to the expansion of the 17th c., and is less articulated and complex.

In the crypt of the *church of the Annunziata* (15th c., renovated) is the *ossuary* of the 300 patriot of the Expedition of Sapri (1857) led by the patriot, Pisacane; note the interesting monastery, or *Convento di S. Agostino* (now the site of the town council) with a Renaissance cloisters, and the ruins of the *little church of S. Nicola de Donnis*. Not far from the charter house, in the village of Fonti, are the ruins of the *baptistery of S. Giovanni in Fonte* (5th/6th c.), with a central plan and dome, built on a spring that emptied directly into the baptismal font.

At the foot of the hill is the charter house, or **Certosa di S. Lorenzo*** which, with a surface area of 51,500 sq. m, is the largest charter house and, without a doubt, one of the most spectacular monuments in southern Italy. Construction was undertaken at the behest of Tommaso II Sanseverino in 1306 and continued until the 18th c.; almost nothing survives of its original structure; the prevailing architectural style to be seen dates from the Baroque renovation. The monastery was famous because, over the centuries, it represented the most important cultural and economic center of this territory; it was also celebrated for the hospitality of the monks (it is said that Charles V stopped here with his entire entourage, and was treated to a "frittata" made with 1,000 eggs, made by the monks). The monastery was suppressed during the

was housed a private collection (now moved elsewhere because of the risks of collapse) of memorabilia concerning Joe Petrosino (1860-1909), the Italian-American policeman who was born in Padula. Immediately after the entryway, there is a long corridor which links many of the most important pieces of architecture. To the right, stands the *cloisters* which date from 1561, with a fountain in the center, overlooked by the frescoed loggia of the noble guest quarters, or Foresteria Nobile. From there, you can enter the chapel, or *Cappella della Madonna*, also known as the Cappella dei Morti, and the **church***, preceded by a Renaissance portal with a handsome carved wooden *door** (1374). The interior pre-

The main cloister of the Certosa di S. Lorenzo, Padula, one of the largest in the world

decade of French occupation, and stripped of its art treasures, which were largely scattered as they were being transported to Naples. The monastery was then restored to the Carthusians, and then was definitively suppressed in 1866. During the two world wars, it was used as a prison for prisoners of war, both Austro-Hungarian and Allied (with huts erected in the huge park). The damage caused by this use was only exacerbated by abandonment and neglect; since 1982 it has been under restoration, and has nearly entirely been returned to public use. In the charter house, dedicated to St. Lawrence (Certosa di S. Lorenzo), you may note the recurring decorative motif of the grate, symbol of the martyrdom of the saint. Overlooking the **atrium**, dominated by the large Baroque facade (1718-23), are the various service areas (pharmacy, stables, workshops, wine cellars), now partly closed. In one of these rooms

serves its 14th-c. structure, with a single nave and ribbed cross-vaults, recognizable beneath the Baroque stuccoes. Of particular interest are the *altars** in "scagliola" stone, with refined polychrome decorations, with mother-of-pearl inserts (the design of the largest one is thought to be by Giovanni Domenico Vinaccia), the majolica flooring dating back to the 18th c., and the carved and inlaid wooden *choirs** by Giovanni Gallo (choir, or Coro dei Conversi from 1507; choir, or *Coro dei Padri* from 1503). In the chapels, to the right, frescoes and decorations dating back to the 16th/18th c. An inlaid *door* dating from the turn of the 16th c. leads into the sacristy, on the altar of which now stands a bronze *ciborium** by Jacopo del Duca. To the left you may enter the treasury, or *Tesoro*, the chapter hall, or Capitolo, and the old cemetery, or **Cimitero Antico**, transformed into a cloisters in the 18th c., from which you can then enter the chapel containing the 16th-c. tomb of the founder, Tommaso II Sanseverino, the **refectory hall** (with a fresco of the *Wedding at Canae*, by F. d'Elia), and the **kitchens**. These latter, built in an existing refectory hall, of which there survives the frescoed decoration, are one of the most fascinating areas in the charter house, and preserve their large central smoke-hood, as well as a part of the 18th-c. furnishings. From a small adjoining court-

The striking staircase of the Certosa di S. Lorenzo, Padula

yard, one descends into the *wine cellars*, where there is an enormous grape press made of oak and pine, dating from 1785 (the large barrels are pastiche, and were built in the 1960s for a movie that was shot here).

Along the central axis of the complex, to the left, you will find the cloisters, or **Chiostro dei Procuratori**, dating from the 17th c., with a fountain in the center, and shafts of ancient Doric columns in the deambulatory, belonging to the collections of the **Museo Archeologico della Lucania Occidentale**, arranged after the most recent restorations in adjoining halls. The Museo, established in 1957, features finds from the necropolises of Sala Consilina and Padula. Next comes the entrance to the prior's apartment, or *Appartamento del Priore*, with the chapel, or Cappella di S. Michele, decorated with frescoes and stuccoes dating from the 18th c., and a *garden*, to which you may descend from a frescoed loggia.

Following the prior's suite is the entrance to the library, or **Biblioteca**, to which you can climb up along a remarkable stone **staircase**. This library, which was one of the most important ones in the region, is

adorned with a handsome majolica flooring and a ceiling that was painted in the 18th c.; on the original shelves – depressingly empty – is still marked the arrangement of the volumes.

Particularly impressive is the opening, along this walk, of the large cloisters, or **Chiostro Grande*** (12,000 sq. m, one of the largest on earth), begun around the middle of the 17th c. and completed at the end of the 18th c. Toward one of the porticoes is the little cemetery of the monks, enclosed by a marble balustrade. All around are the *quarters of the Carthusian monks*, each consisting of three or four rooms, a small portico giving access to the garden, overlooked by a covered loggia, which leads to a service room; in some cases, you may find an attic used as a workshop. The first rooms on the left can be viewed, and they house periodic exhibitions. At the end of the cloisters is the spectacular elliptical **stairway*** with two ramps (1761-63; attributed to G. Barba) contained in an octagonal tower, from the large windows of which you can enjoy fine views of the park and the surrounding hills. On the walls beneath the first flights of the stairway are painted odd depictions of scenes of the everyday lives of prisoners of war during WWII. The stairway leads to the *gallery*, which originally served as a covered walkway for the monks, and which is now used for temporary exhibitions; in the smaller branch to the right, almost a small permanent Museo dell'Opera, or museum of the construction of the building, you will find paintings, sculptures, furnishings, and ceramics, linked to the charter house, or Certosa, and found during restorations. On the exterior of the stairway is a labyrinth designed with bushes, set in the context of the park, where it is possible to take a walk around the entire monastery.

Outside of the enclosure walls of the charter house, or Certosa, on an axis with the entrance, is the Baroque fountain, or *Fontana di S. Bruno*, which, along the road from the south, marked in a monumental way, the arrival at the large monastery.

Information for Travellers:
Hotels, Restaurants, Places of interest

City by city, town by town, this list includes the hotels, restaurants, campsites, and vacation villages (as well as youth hostels and "agriturismo" locations) recommended with the official classification of the accommodations, expressed in numbers of stars, in accordance with the law, or Legge Quadro per il Turismo of 17 May 1983.

For the restaurants mentioned, we give the following general indications of price level: ¶ less than 45,000 Lire; ¶¶ between 45,000 and 65,000 Lire; ¶¶¶ between 65,000 and 85,000 Lire; ¶¶¶¶ between 85,000 and 105,000 Lire; ¶¶¶¶¶ more than 105,000 Lire.

As of 18th December 1998 each location's telephone code must also be dialled for local calls, indicated in the following list next to the symbol ☎. For those calling from abroad, the local code (including the 0) must be dialled after the international code for Italy, followed by the subscriber's number. The following information has been carefully checked before going to print. We would, however, advise readers to confirm certain data which is susceptible to change, before departure. All observations and suggestions are gratefully accepted.

Naples, or Napoli   ✉ 80100 ☎ 081

Plans on pages 30-31, 72-75

ℹ️ *AA*, Palazzo Reale, tel. 418744; *Ufficio Informazioni*, Piazza del Gesù Nuovo 78, tel. 5512701-5523328 (I C2).

EPT, Piazza dei Martiri 58, tel. 405311, fax 401961 (III, E3); Ufficio Informazioni: Stazione Centrale, tel. 268779 (III C6); Stazione di Mergellina, tel. 7612102 (II D-E1).

Regione Campania, Assessorato al Turismo, Via Santa Lucia 81, tel. 7961111.

Comune di Napoli, Progetto Museo Aperto, tel. 292316 (educational section; for school group tours: tel. 294875).

The historic quarters

This vast area, which corresponds to the historic center of the city, one of the largest in Europe, encloses every aspect of Neapolitan life. The churches (many of them are undergoing restoration, and therefore it is quite likely that you will find them closed to the "general public") are open, if still working as churches, generally between 8 and 12 and between 4 and 6:30 (5-7 in summer). Some of the main churches overlooking the *decumani* of the old center are open (recent development; as of February 1994) by city order, from 10 until 4 on weekdays, and since they are guarded by city employees, they are closed on Sundays. During the same hours, because of temporary prohibitions of traffic and parking, and a more active presence of the traffic police, you will find a more "livable" atmosphere in the old streets and the surrounding areas. The outgoing nature of the Neapolitans, and the courteous generosity of priests, sacristans, nuns, monks, porters, and caretakers of every sort, allows you to obtain, even after a short acquaintance – as in the 18th c. of the Grand Tour – a tour of spaces that are "normally closed," or else to see them after hours, especially considering the small number of tourists. Surprising areas of greenery are found in the cloisters, numerous and unforgettable, to the point that Benedetto Croce stated that a recurrent image in his dreams was that of a Neapolitan cloisters, silent and full of color, an oasis of peace against the walls of which pressed the tumultuous life of the adjoining lanes, or "vicoli." In the center of town, there are countless bar/pastry-shops, trattorias (note the renowned outlets for oil and wine, or "Vini e oli," with a kitchen) and, often sold on counters on the street, pizzerias, "friggitorie," "tripperie," and (in the area around the Porta Capuana) places selling boiled octopus; Naples is a city where you can still get a bite to eat, for next to nothing and at all hours of the day and night.

Due to the working-class and university population, this part of the city has the greatest number of "alternative" theaters, movie houses, clubs, and bars.

The "librerie," or book shops – with interesting stalls selling used books – are especially clustered between Port'Alba, S. Pietro a Maiella, Via S. Sebastiano, and Via Costantinopoli; this last-named street is traditionally lined with antiques shops. Many jewelers (some of whom sell antiques, as well) overlook the Via S. Biagio dei Librai; craftsmen who make crèches and fake flowers are found on the Via S. Gregorio Armeno.

Hotels

*** G.H. Oriente. Via A. Diaz 44, tel. 5512133, fax 5514915. Number of rooms: 132. Air conditioning, elevator; special terms for parking garage (1, D1, **o**).

*** Holiday Inn. Centro Direzionale, Isola E6, tel. 2250111, fax 5628074. Number of rooms: 330. Access to the handicapped. Air conditioning, elevator, garage; indoor pool (III, B6, *off map*).

*** Jolly Ambassador's. Via Medina 70, tel. 416000, fax 5518010. Number of rooms: 250. Air conditioning, elevator; special terms for parking garage (1, D2, **f**).

*** Mercure Angioino. Via Depretis 123, tel. 5529500, fax 5529509. Number of rooms: 85. Rooms only; no dining facilities. Air conditioning, elevator; special terms for parking garage (I, E2, **ae**).

*** Terminus. Piazza Garibaldi 91, tel. 7793111, fax 206689. Number of rooms: 209. Accessible to the handicapped. Air conditioning, elevator; parking garage (3, C6, **k**).

*** Villa Capodimonte. Via Moiatiello 66, tel. 459000, fax 299344. Number of rooms: 60. Access to the handicapped. Air conditioning, elevator; parking, garage, garden, tennis (I, A5, *off map*).

*** Executive. Via del Cerriglio 10, tel. 5520611, fax 5520611. Number of rooms: 19. Rooms only; no dining facilities. Air conditioning, elevator; parking garage, garden (1, D-E2, **q**).

*** Palace. Piazza Garibaldi 9, tel. 267044, fax 264306. Number of rooms: 102. Air conditioning, elevator; special terms for parking garage (1, B5, **h**).

at Agnano Terme, 11 km ⊠ 80125

Hotels, restaurants, campsites and vacation villages

*** San Germano. Via Beccadelli 41, tel. 5705422, fax 5701546. Number of rooms: 105. Air conditioning, elevator, parking, garage, indoor pool, tennis.

*** American Park. Via E. Searfoglio 23, tel. 5706529, fax 5708180. Number of rooms: 96. Air conditioning, elevator, parking, garage, garden.

*** Delle Terme. Via Agnano Astroni, tel. 5701733, fax 7626441. Number of rooms: 62. Accessible to the handicapped. Air conditioning, elevator; parking, garden.

Restaurants

¶ Ciro a Santa Brigida. Via S. Brigida 71/73, tel. 5524072. Closed Sunday, for a period in August. Air conditioning. Neapolitan and classical cuisine (1, E1, **u**).

¶¶¶ San Carlo. Via Cesario Console 18/19, tel. 7649757, fax 2451166. Closed Sunday, for a period in August. Air conditioning, parking. Cuisine of Campania and classical cuisine – seafood (1, F1, **z**).

¶¶ Cavour. Piazza Garibaldi 34, tel. 283122. Air conditioning, parking. Neapolitan cuisine (1, B5, **s**).

¶¶ Mimì alla Ferrovia. Via Alfonso d'Aragona 21, tel. 5538525. Closed Sunday, for a period in August. Air conditioning, parking. Cuisine of Campania (1, A-B5, **rc**).

¶ Cinquantatré. Piazza Dante 53, tel. 5499372. Air conditioning, parking. Cuisine of Campania (1, C1, **t**).

¶ Taverna dell'Arte. Rampe S. Giovanni Maggiore 1/A, tel. 5527558. Closed Sunday, part of August. Neapolitan cuisine (I, D2, **rx**).

Cafes and pastry shops

Gambrinus. Piazza Trieste e Trento 38, tel. 417582-413333. This is one of the oldest and best-known pastry shops in the city, and it preserves delightful rooms decorated with stuccoes and interesting paintings by various major Neapolitan artists of the late 19th c.

Gay Odin. Via Toledo 427/428, tel. 5513491; Via Vetriera 12 (factory), tel. 417843. Founded in 1894 by a Swiss pastry chef, for the past century this shop has made its own chocolate and candies, with seven retail outlets scattered throughout the city, many of them with their original Art-Nouveau furnishing.

Intra Moenia. Piazza Bellini 70, tel. 290720. With the conversion of the Piazza into a pedestrian mall, this has become a favorite meeting place for the young people of Naples.

Pintauro. Via Toledo 275, tel. 417339. This shop is an antique, with handsome Art-Nouveau windows, and is famous for the pastry, or "sfogliatelle," produced fresh continuously.

Scaturchio. Piazza S. Domenico Maggiore 19, tel. 5516944. A must-see on any itinerary through the historic center, due to the high quality of the products. Specialties of the house are the "zeffiro all'arancia" and the "ministeriale," a pastry made with chocolate and rum.

Museums and cultural institutions

Appartamento Storico del Palazzo Reale. Piazza del Plebiscito, tel. 412987. Closed Monday. *Open to the public: weekdays 9-2; holidays 9-1.*

Biblioteca and Galleria d'Arte Moderna. Accademia di Belle Arti. Via Bellini, tel. 5640592. Closed Saturday and Sunday. *Open to the public: 9-2.*

Biblioteca Nazionale Vittorio Emanuele III. Piazza del Plebiscito, tel. 403820. Closed Sunday. *Open to the public: Monday, Friday 9-7; Saturday 9-1.*

Cappella Palatina. Castel Nuovo. Closed Sunday. *Open to the public: 9-7.*

Castelcapuano. Cappella della Sommaria. Palazzo di Giustizia. *Open every Tuesday and Thursday from 9 until 1:30 and from 2:30 until 5.*

Circolo Artistico Politecnico – Museo "Giuseppe Caravita Principe di Sirignano." Piazza Trieste e Trento 48, tel. 417390-418030. Closed Saturday and Sunday. *Open to the public: 9-12.*

Museo Archeologico Nazionale. Piazza Museo, tel. 440166. Closed Tuesday. *Open to the public: 10-10pm; Sunday and holidays 9-8.*

Museo Cappella S. Severo. Via De Sanctis 19, tel. 5518470. Closed Tuesday. *Open to the public: 10-5 (summer 6, Christmas and Easter 7); holidays 10-1:30.*

Museo Civico. Piazza Municipio, Castel Nuovo, tel. 7952003. Closed Sunday. *Open to the public: 9-7.*

Museo Civico Filangieri. Palazzo Como. Via Duomo 288, tel. 203175. Closed Monday. *Open to the public: 9:30-2 and 3:30-7; Sunday 9:30-1:30.*

Museo di Paleontologia. Largo S. Marcellino 10, tel. 204775. *Open to the public: 9-2; Saturday and Sunday 10-1.*

Museo and Gallerie Nazionali di Capodimonte. Parco di Capodimonte, tel. 7441307. Closed Monday. *Open to the public: 10-10 pm; Sunday and holidays 10-8pm.*

Museo Storico-Diplomatico dell'Archivio di Stato. Piazzetta Grande Archivio 5, tel. 204594. Closed Sunday. *Open to the public: 9-6, Saturday 9-1.*

Orto Botanico. Via Foria 223, tel. 449759. *Open to the public, by request, phone from 9 until 2, from Monday to Friday.*

Osservatorio Astronomico. Via Moiariello 16, tel. 293266. *Open to the public, by appointment only.*

Palazzo Reale. Piazza Plebiscito 1, tel. 5808111. Closed Wednesday. *Open to the public: 9:30-10pm.*

Parco del Palazzo Reale. *Open to the public: everyday from 9 until sunset.*

Pinacoteca dei Girolamini. Via dei Tribunali, tel. 292316. Closed Sunday. *Open to the public: 9-1.*

Pio Monte della Misericordia. Via Tribunali 125, tel. 445517. In order to tour, make telephone reservations. Closed Sunday.

Monumental churches

Duomo, or cathedral. Via Duomo, tel. 449097. *Open to the public: 8-12 and 5-7.* The Scavi, or excavations, and the chapel, or Cappella di S. Gennaro, are closed Sunday.

Monteoliveto (S. Anna dei Lombardi). Via Monteoliveto, tel. 5513333. Closed Sunday. *Open to the public: everyday 9-12.*

Pio Monte della Misericordia. Church and art gallery, or Pinacoteca. Via Tribunale 253. *Open to the public: weekdays 9-1:30.*

S. Chiara. Church and cloisters, or Chiostro delle Clarisse. Via Benedetto Croce, tel. 5526209. Cloisters. *Open to the public: 8:30-12:30, 4-sunset (winter), 4-6:30 (summer).* **Museo dell'Opera di Santa Chiara**, tel. 7971256. Closed Wednesday. *Open to the public: 9:30-1, 3:30-5:30; Sunday 9:30-1.*

S. Lorenzo Maggiore and archaeological digs. Piazza San Gaetano, tel. 290580. *Open to the public: Church 8-12:30; Digs 9-11:30.*

S. Maria della Sanità. Catacombe di S. Gaudioso. Piazza Sanità 124, tel. 5441305. *Tour of the catacombs: Sunday, departures at 9:45 and 11:45; telephone to arrange for guided tours at other times.*

S. Maria Donnaregina. Vico Donnaregina. Chiesa Vecchia. *Open to the public: Saturday 9-12:30. Chiesa Nuova, temporarily closed.*

SS. Severino e Sossio. c/o SS. Filippo e Giacomo, tel. 5516666. *Open to the public, only Sunday, 9-12.*

The churches listed here are open *everyday from 9 until 1:30*, except Sunday and holidays, not including the months of March and December.

Cappella Pontano. Via Tribunale, tel. 292316.

Gerolomini. Via Tribunale, tel. 292316.

Purgatorio ad Arco. Via Tribunale, tel. 292316.

S. Giovanni a Carbonara. Via Carbonara, tel. 295873.

S. Maria Maggiore. Via Tribunale, tel. 292316.

S. Paolo Maggiore. Piazza San Gaetano, tel. 454048.

Entertainment, shows, and events

Festa della Madonna del Carmine (July). Fire with fireworks on the campanile of the church of Santa Maria del Carmine. Tel. 5523328.

Festa di San Gennaro (first Saturday in May and 19 September). Church of Santa Restituta and chapel, or Cappella del Tesoro, in the cathedral, or Duomo. Tel. 5523328. This great traditional festival, with processions bearing the silver busts and statues from the cathedral. The populace turns out for the Miracle of St. Januarius, with the liquefaction of the saint's blood.

Festa di Sant'Antonio (17 January). Tel. 5523328. In the lanes and the squares of the city, the populace lights bonfires, both large and small.

Galleria Toledo. Via Concezione a Montecalvario 34, tel. 425824. Festivals: theater, May-October; movies, February-April; music, January-May.

Natale (Christmas) **a San Giorgio Armeno** (for the entire Christmas season). Tel. 5512701. This even is linked to the traditional art of Neapolitan crèches. There are exhibitions of crèches and Christmas fairs in the working-class quarters: Vergini, Sant'Antonio Abate, Pignasecca.

Teatro Bellini. Via Conte di Ruvo 14, tel. 5499688. Founded in 1887, now, entirely renovated, it offers fine theater, dedicating a great deal of space to dance and music.

Teatro Mercadante. Piazza Municipio 74, tel. 5524214-5513396-5513623. This theater is used occasionally.

Teatro San Carlo. Via San Carlo 93/f, tel. 7972111-416305-7972412-7972370. Opera season from December to June.

Shops, crafts, and curiosities

Alla Pignasecca. Flea market near the Piazza Carità, everyday.

Arredi Sacri Catello. Via S. Maria a Costantinopoli 124, tel. 4441696. Holy furnishings.

Box office. Galleria Umberto I 17, tel. 5519188. Sale and reservations for tickets for any show or event in the city.

Bowinkel Ernesto. Piazza dei Martiri 24, tel. 7644344. Since 1879, the display windows of Bowinkel have been recounting the history of Naples, with old and modern prints, bronzes, collections of costumes, photographs, fans, and objets-d'art.

Brinkmann. Piazza Municipio 21, tel. 5520555, Via dei Mille 72, tel. 414475. German rigor and Neapolitan imagination are combined in a century-old crafts tradition of jewelry.

Cartoleria Amodio. Via Port'Alba 24/25/26, tel. 446366.

De Simone. Via Fico S. Brigida 2, tel. 5526424. One of the last fine craftsmen working in straw, wicker, cane, and bamboo.

Enrico Gambardella e F. Via B. Croce 28, tel. 5520874. Paper and cardboard at good prices; paper from Amalfi.

Ferrigno. Via S. Gregorio Armeno 8, tel. 5523148. Giuseppe Ferrigno, in the tradition of his father Salvatore, makes statuettes of shepherds for crèches, and has done for over fifty years.

Francesco Campobasso. Via S. Biagio dei Librai 13, tel. 5521142. Workshop for the production of holy furnishings.

Gaito. Via Toledo 278/279, tel. 421104. Designers and manufacturers of original jewelry, once suppliers of the royal house.

Galleria d'Arte Framart Studio. Via Nuova S. Rocco 62, tel. 7414672-7414427. Exclusive shows, especially for this gallery; it gives space to great masters and young artists involved in creative experimentation.

Gastronomia L.U.I.S.E. Via Toledo 266/269, tel. 407852. Fine food shop, with French and Neapolitan food: *zeppole*, *timballi*, *tartine*, pâté, pizzas, and *arancini*.

Gioielleria Caso. Piazza S. Domenico Maggiore 16, tel. 5516733-5520108; Via Bisignano 9, tel. 403940-405639. Antique and period jewelry and watches, and more; exquisite and remarkable jewels in coral, including the rare coral of Sciacca.

Gioielleria Pagano. Piazza Orefici 2, tel. 5544030.

La Casa della Penna. Corso Umberto I 88, tel. 204763. This shop sells and repairs all sorts of pens.

Libreria Antiquaria Colonnese. Via S. Pietro a Maiella 33, tel. 459858. Rare and out-of-print books, collectors' postcards, prints, photographs, newspapers, and magazines.

Libreria Antiquaria Lombardi. Via S. Maria di Costantinopoli 4/bis, tel. 441332. Aside from old books, there is also a notable collection of scientific books.

Libreria Antiquaria Regina. Via S. Maria di Costantinopoli 103, tel. 290925. Supplier of prestigious Italian libraries, including the library of the Quirinal.

Libreria Clean. Via D. Loy 19, tel. 5524419. This bookshop specializes in publications concerning architecture, urban planning, and design.

Libreria Feltrinelli. Via S.T. D'Aquino 70/76, tel. 5521436-5524468. One of the best supplied and functional bookstores in Naples; it is open throughout the day and in August.

Libreria Guida. Via Port'Alba 20/23, tel. 446377; Via Merliani 70, tel. 459822. This historic bookshop is one of the cultural treasures of the city. It exports to Africa and Asia and has customers all over Italy.

Libreria Lucio Pironti. Via Maddaloni 3, tel. 5510691. Text books and rare books.

Libreria Treves. Via Toledo 249/250, tel. 415211. A remarkable assortment of Italian and non-Italian fiction.

Mercatino del Ponte di Casanova. Market just beyond the Porta Capuana. Everyday from 8 until 2.

Mercato di Porta Nolana. Via Carmignano. This market is renowned for seafood. Everyday from 8 until 2.

Mercato di S. Antonio Abate. Via S. Antonio Abate. Every day from 8 until 2.

Nilo Carta e Cartoni. Via S. Biagio dei Librai 1, tel. 5521333. Articles in paper, remarkable and rare.

Orologeria Telesco. Via P.E. Imbriani 31, tel. 5519330. Restorations, repair, and cleaning of all sorts of clocks and watches, with a craftsmen's love of a challenge.

Ospedale delle Bambole. Via S. Biagio dei Librai 81, tel. 203067. This doll hospital is near the Duomo, and is one of the most charming shops in Naples.

Professione Musica. Via S. Sebastiano 65/66, tel. 291585-459215.

Riciclò. Via Giordano Bruno 54, tel. 5529158. Articles made only from recycled paper.

Stendardo. Rua Catalana 101, tel. 5513124. Saturday closed. Manufactures articles in copper, brass, and bronze.

Strumenti Musicali Loveri. Via S. Sebastiano 8, tel. 459569-450279.

Strumenti Musicali Miletti. Via S. Sebastiano 46; tel. 459895.

Trucchi. Piazza Trieste e Trento 49, tel. 417874. A perfect place for collectors and enthusiasts of watches and clocks.

Ugo Esposito. Via S. Gregorio Armeno 46, tel. 5516205. Statues of shepherds.

Vomero, Mergellina, S. Lucia

The Vomero is a modern quarter with environmental and social characteristics that set it apart from the historic center. Clearly middle class, it is no different from the quarters built in other Italian cities in the years of the late 19th c. and the turn of the 20th c. It is a city within a city, and it has its elegant center in the Piazza Vanvitelli, the "shopping streets" – in particular, the Via Scarlatti – museums, theaters, movie houses, and its own night life. There are also – though they are rarer – *mercatini*, *friggitorie*, and cheap pizzerias.

Pizzofalcone seems to epitomize all of the stereotypes about Naples and the Neapolitans because it encloses, in a fairly small space, illustrious monuments, a large theater, a prestigious cultural institution (the Istituto Italiano di Studi Filosofici), a popular site of exhibitions and conferences, nearly every day another, restaurants, trattorias, markets ("mercatini"), smuggling, and laundry on the lines in the Pallonetto. At the foot of the hill winds a waterfront road, or Lungomare, with the most elegant hotels, yacht clubs, and the occasional club along the roads around S. Lucia, the Chiatamone, and the Piazza Vittoria and the Piazza dei Martiri. Between these two squares and Mergellina, with a northern boundary along the Via dei Mille and the Via Crispi, you will find most of the movie houses and many of the most elegant and popular bars and clubs. There are full fledged "bivouacs" of more-or-less motorized young people in the Piazza dei Martiri and Piazza Amedeo and in the Via Carducci and the Via Martucci.

Another center of night life, especially in the summer – very popular as well with those who come from the hinterland and from the provinces – is the area of Mergellina. A number of very popular bars and ice creams shops enliven the streets that climb up the hill of Posillipo, which is almost entirely residential, with the exception of the sailing clubs (in the first stretch), a movie house, and the little theater, or Teatrino di Villa Patrizi in the higher section.

Hotels

★☆★ **Britannique**. Corso Vittorio Emanuele 133, tel. 7614145, fax 660457. Number of rooms: 88. Air conditioning, elevator; parking, parking garage, garden (3, E2, **a**).

★☆★ **Continental**. Via Partenope 44, tel. 7644636, fax 7644661. Number of rooms: 166. Accessible to the handicapped. Air conditioning, elevator; parking, parking garage, swimming pool (3, F4, **c**).

★☆★ **Excelsior**. Via Partenope 48, tel. 7640111, fax 7649743. Number of rooms: 102. Air conditioning, elevator; special terms for parking garage (3, F4, **d**).

★☆★ **Grand Hotel Parker's**. Corso Vittorio Emanuele 135, tel. 7612474, fax 663527. Number of rooms: 83. Accessible to the handicapped. Air conditioning, elevator; parking, parking garage (3, E2, **e**).

★☆★ **Grand Hotel Vesuvio**. Via Partenope 45, tel. 7640044, fax 5890380. Number of rooms: 167. Accessible to the handicapped. Air conditioning, elevator; parking garage (3, F4, **n**).

★☆★ **Miramare**. Via N. Sauro 24, tel. 7647589, fax 7640775. Number of rooms: 31, no dining facilities. Air conditioning, elevator; special terms for parking garage (3, E4, **g**).

★☆★ **Paradiso**. Via Catullo 11, tel. 7614161, fax 7613449. Number of rooms: 74. Air conditioning, elevator; special terms for parking garage (3, F1, **i**).

★★ **Royal**. Via Partenope 38, tel. 7644800, fax 7645707. Number of rooms: 275. Accessible to the handicapped. Air conditioning, elevator; parking garage, swimming pool (3, F3, **l**).

★★ **Santa Lucia**. Via Partenope 46, tel. 7640666, fax 7648580. Number of rooms: 102. Air conditioning, elevator; special terms for parking garage (3, F4, **m**).

★★★ **Canada**. Via Mergellina 43, tel. 682018, fax 680952. Number of rooms: 12. Rooms only; no dining facilities. Elevator; special terms for parking garage (3, F1, **p**).

★★★ **Rex**. Via Palepoli 12, tel. 7649389, fax 7649227. Number of rooms: 40, 37 with bathroom and shower. Rooms only; no dining facilities. Air conditioning; special terms for parking garage (3, F4, **j**).

★★★ **Splendid**. Via A. Manzoni 96, tel. 7145630, fax 7146431. Number of rooms: 44. Air conditioning, elevator; parking, garden (3, F1, off map).

Restaurants

🍴🍴🍴 **Cantinella**. Via Cuma 42, tel. 7648684, fax 7648769. Closed Sunday, for a period in August. Air conditioning, parking. Cuisine of Campania and classical cuisine (3, E4, **r**).

🍴🍴🍴 **Sacrestia**. Via Orazio 116, tel. 664186, fax 7611051. Closed Monday, for a period in August. Air conditioning, parking, garden. Cuisine of Campania and classical cuisine (3, F1, **y**).

🍴🍴🍴 **Girulà**. Via Vetriera a Chiaia 7/A, tel. 425511, fax 425511. Closed Sunday, August. Air conditioning. Neapolitan cuisine (III, E3, **rm**).

🍴🍴🍴 **Rosolino**. Via N. Sauro 5/7, tel. 7649873, fax 7640547. Closed Sunday evening. Air conditioning. Cuisine of Campania and classical cuisine – seafood (3, F4, **x**).

🍴🍴 **Bersagliera**. Borgo Marinaro 10/11, tel. 7646016. Closed Tuesday, for variable vacation periods. Air conditioning. Neapolitan cuisine – seafood (3, F4, **rd**).

🍴🍴 **Don Salvatore**. Via Mergellina 5, tel. 681817, fax 661241. Closed Wednesday. Air conditioning, parking. Cuisine of Campania – seafood (3, F1, **v**).

🍴🍴 **Posto Accanto**. Via N. Sauro 2, tel. 7648600. Closed Sunday evening. Air conditioning, parking, garden. Cuisine of Campania and classical cuisine (3, F4, **w**).

🍴🍴 **Sbrescia**. Rampe S. Antonio a Posillipo 109, tel. 669140. Closed Monday. Air conditioning, parking. Neapolitan and classical cuisine – seafood (3, F1, **ra**).

🍴🍴 **Vadinchenia**. Via Pontano 21, tel. 660265. Closed Sunday, August. Air conditioning. Cuisine of Campania and Lucania (III, E2, **rg**).

🍴 **Umberto**. Via Alabardieri 30, tel. 418555. Closed Sunday, August. Air conditioning. Cuisine of Campania – seafood (3, E3, **rb**).

Youth hostels

🏠 **Mergellina**. Salita della Grotta a Piedigrotta 23. Beds, 200. For information: Ugo Persico, tel. 7612346.

Cafes and pastry shops

Bellavia. Via L. Giordano 158, tel. 5789684; home production, tel. 5563151.

Caffetteria Bernini. Viale Michelangelo 9/A.

Daniele. Via Scarlatti 104/106, e Via E. Alvino 43/47/51, tel. 5780555-5780941-5785167-5785267; Saturday and Sunday open until 10 pm.

Gay Odin. Via L. Giordano 21/A, tel. 5783380; Via F. Cilea 189, tel. 7146847. Founded in 1894 by a Swiss pastry chef, for the past century this shop has made its own chocolate and candies, with seven retail outlets scattered throughout the city, many of them with their original Art-Nouveau furnishing.

La Caffettiera. Piazza Vanvitelli 10/B, tel. 5782592. Open from 7 until midnight.

Mandara. Via F. Cilea 135, tel. 5604651. Dairy products and ice cream.

Museums and cultural institutions

Acquario, or aquarium. Villa Comunale, tel. 5833263. Closed Monday. *Open to the public: (summer) weekdays and Saturday 9-6; Sunday and holidays 9-6; (winter) 9-2.*

Castel S. Elmo. Largo S. Martino, tel. 5784030. Closed Monday. *Open to the public: from Tuesday to Sunday, 9-2.*

Catacombe di S. Gennaro. Via Capodimonte; entrance near the church of the Madre del Buon Consiglio, tel. 7411071. *Guided tours only Friday, Saturday and Sunday; departure of the tours, 9:30, 10:15, 11, 11:45.*

Catacombe di S. Severo. Piazzetta S. Severo, tel. 454684. *Make telephone reservations for tours of these catacombs.*

Church of the Nunziatella; c/o Scuola Militare Nunziatella, tel. 7641451-7641520. *Open to public only Saturday and Sunday, for the Holy Mass at 10 am.*

Istituto d'Arte e Museo Artistico Industriale. Piazzetta Salazar 6, tel. 7646133. *You can tour this institute of the manufacturing arts only by calling ahead.*

Museo Nazionale della Ceramica "Duca di Martina." Villa Floridiana, entrance from Via Aniello Falcone or from Via Cimarosa 77, tel. 5788418. Closed Monday. *Open to the public: 9-2; Saturday 9-7.*

Museo Nazionale di S. Martino. Museum and gardens. Largo S. Martino 5, tel. 5781769. Closed Monday. *Open to the public: 9-2; Saturday 9-7.*

Osservatorio Astronomico di Capodimonte. Salita Maiarello 16, tel. 440101. *This observatory is open to the public, by appointment only.*

Stazione Zoologica. Villa Comunale, tel. 5833263. This zoo is closed Monday. *Open to the public: (summer) 9-6; (winter) 9-5.*

S. Teresa a Chiaia. Via dei Mille, corner of Via V. Colonna, tel. 414263. *Open to the public: every day, 7:30-11.*

Villa Floridiana. On the Vomero; villa and park. Tel. 7441307. *Open to the public: from 9 to one hour prior to sunset.*

Villa Pignatelli. Via Principessa Pignatelli. Closed Monday. *Open to the public: 8-2.*

Shops, crafts, and curiosities

Effetto Gioco. Via Solimene 37, tel. 5564606.

Fiera Antiquaria. Villa Comunale. Antiques fair, from 8 until 4 pm, on the second Sunday of every month.

Gioielleria Gallotta. Via L. Giordano 30, tel. 5787790-5788541.

La Bottega della Carta. Via L. Giordano 17/a, tel. 5780076.

Mercatino della Torretta. Market, between Viale Gramsci and the Via Mergellina, mornings only.

Mercatino di Antigano. Every morning, near the Piazza degli Artisti on the Vomero.

Mercatino di Poggioreale. Sunday morning.

Soave. Via Scarlatti 130, tel. 5567411. Fine cheeses and dairy products.

Top Music. Via G. Merliani 53, tel. 5562789.

Marechiaro, Posillipo

Restaurants

🍴 **A' Fenestella**. Calata Ponticello a Marechiaro 25, tel. 7690020, fax 5750686. Closed Wednesday, lunch and Sunday evening; every Sunday in July and for a period in August. Air conditioning, parking. Neapolitan cuisine – seafood (3, F1, *off map*).

🍴 **Giuseppone a Mare**. Via F. Russo 13, tel. 5756002, fax 7640195. Closed Monday, for a period in August e Christmas-New Year's Day. Air conditioning, parking. Cuisine of Campania and classical cuisine – seafood (3, F1, *off map*).

🍴 **Poeta**. Piazza S. Di Giacomo 133, tel. 5756936, fax 5756936. Closed Monday, for a period in August. Air conditioning, parking, garden. Cuisine of Campania – seafood (3, F1, *off map*).

🍴 **'O Calamaro**. Viale Campi Flegrei 30/A, tel. 5704387. Closed Sunday. Air conditioning. Neapolitan cuisine (3, F1, *off map*).

Spas and hot springs

at Agnano Terme, 11 km

Terme di Agnano. Via Agnano Astroni 24, tel. 5702122-5704260-5704521. Spa, offering therapies based on mud baths, hot baths, and inhalations; massage therapy.

Cafes and pastry shops

Bar dell'Ovo. Via Partenope 6, tel. 7644280.

Caffè Megaride. Via Eldorado 1, Borgo Marinai, tel. 7645300. Closed Tuesday. Open from 8:30 to 2 am.

Carraturo. Via Arangio Ruiz 75/79, tel. 681795.

Chalet Ciro. Via F. Caracciolo, facing the Via Orazio, tel. 669928. Closed Wednesday. Open from 6 to 1 am; in summer and on weekends, open also until 3 am.

Gay Odin. Via V. Colonna 15/B, tel. 418282; Via Chiaia 237, tel. 422824. Founded in 1894 by a Swiss pastry chef, for the past century this shop has made its own chocolate and candies, with seven retail outlets scattered throughout the city, many of them with their original Art-Nouveau furnishings.

Gelateria Bilancione. Via Posillipo 238/B, tel. 7691923. Closed Wednesday.

Gelateria Il Gelatiere. Via S. Pasquale 15, tel. 406750.

Gelateria Remy Gelo. Via Galiani 30, tel. 668480. Closed Monday. Open from 9 until 11 pm.

Gran Bar Riviera. Riviera di Chiaia 123, tel. 665026; Via dei Mille 60, tel. 440400.

La Caffettiera. Piazza dei Martiri 25/26, tel. 7644243. Open from 7 until midnight.

Le Bar. Via Eldorado 7, Borgo Marinari, tel. 7645722. Closed Wednesday. Open from 9:30 pm until 3 am.

Moccia. Via S. Pasquale a Chiaia 21/22/77, tel. 411348-425067. Pastry shop and bakery.

'O Café e 'Onna Rosa. Via Eldorado 2, Borgo Marinai, tel. 7640860. Open only in the evening.

Museums and cultural institutions

Museo delle Carrozze. Riviera di Chiaia 200. Closed for restoration.

Museo Principe Diego Aragona Pignatelli Cortes. Riviera di Chiaia 200, tel. 669675. Closed Monday. *Open to the public: 9-2.*

Parco di Posillipo. Free entrance to this park, everyday from 9 until one hour before sunset.

Parco Virgiliano. Free entrance to this park, everyday from 9 until one hour before sunset.

Entertainment, shows, and events

Festival delle Ville Vesuviane (July). Array of performances and events in the villas of the Vesuvian area of the city and at Herculaneum (Ercolano). Tel. 5512701.

Athletic activities

Acquaflash. At Licola (beltway exit), tel. 8047122. Aquatic park open only in summer.

Bowling Oltremare. Viale J. F. Kennedy, tel. 624444. Open everyday from 10 until 1 am.

Capitaneria di Porto. Molo Pisacane, tel. 206133-207056.

Molosiglio, Santalucia (Largo Marinai), Mergel-lina, and Posillipo. Tourist marinas, suited for all sorts of vessels.

Parco dei Divertimenti Edenlandia (fun park). Viale J. F. Kennedy, tel. 2394090. Open Saturday, Sunday and all holidays from 10 until midnight; from April to September, open weekdays from 3 pm until midnight. For the other months of the year, the schedule varies; we recommend calling ahead.

Piscina Scandone. Pool, Via Giochi del Mediterraneo, Fuorigrotta, tel. 5709159.

Port: Principal Stazione Marittima on the Molo Angioino. Piazza Municipio. Boats for the islands of the Gulf of Naples (ferryboats and hydrofoils) departing from the Molo Beverello and from Mergellina.

Stadio S. Paolo. Fuorigrotta, tel. 2395623.

Tennis Club Napoli. Villa Comunale, Via Le Dohrn, tel. 7614656.

at Agnano Terme, 11 km

Centro Ippico Agnano. Via R. Ruggero 12, tel. 5702695. Riding school.

Ippodromo di Villa Glori. Horse racing track, Via Ippodromo, tel. 5704201-5702610.

Shops, crafts, and curiosities

Aldo Tramontano. Via Chiaia 149, tel. 414758; Via Bisignano 6, tel. 412888; Via Monte di Dio 1/E, tel. 7646123. Fine high-fashion leather goods.

Arethusa Manifesti. Posters, Riviera di Chiaia 202/B, tel. 411551.

Bowinkel Umberto. Via Santa Lucia 25, tel. 7640739. Since 1879, the display windows of Bowinkel have been recounting the history of Naples, with old and modern prints, bronzes, collections of costumes, photographs, fans, and objets-d'art.

Canestrelli. Via Chiaia 131, tel. 401954. Dowries and embroideries.

Cartoleria P&C. Largo Vasto a Chiaia 86, tel. 418724. Pens and stationery, fine and original.

Concerteria. Via M. Schipa 23, tel. 7611221. Sells tickets for concerts and shows.

Drogheria Codrington. Via Chiaia 94, tel. 418257.

Drogheria Del Vecchio. Via Cavallerizza a Chiaia 33, tel. 414568.

Fidanzini. Via Chiaia 149/A, tel. 416447. Creations and compositions of flowers and fruit.

Galleria d'Arte Dina Carola. Via Orazio 29, tel. 669715.

Galleria d'Arte Lia Rumma. Via Gaetani 12, tel. 7644213.

Galleria d'Arte Lucio Amelio. Piazza dei Martiri 58, tel. 422023.

Galleria d'Arte Studio Morra. Via Calabritto 20, tel. 7643737.

Galleria d'Arte Trisorio. Riviera di Chiaia 215, tel. 414306.

Gioielleria Brinkmann. Via dei Mille 72, tel. 414475.

Gioielleria Gallotta. Via Chiaia 139, tel. 421164.

Gioielleria Ileana della Corte. Via Santa Lucia 65, tel. 7648765.

Gioielleria Knight. Piazza dei Martiri 52, tel. 7643837.

La Barberia. Via F. Crispi 15, tel. 660553. Closed Monday.

La Bottega della Carta. Via Cavallerizza a Chiaia 22/23, tel. 421903.

La Libreria dei Ragazzi. Largo Ferrantina 1, tel. 404826.

Legatoria Villa di Chiaia. Riviera di Chiaia 202/A, tel. 400475.

Libreria Antiquaria Casella. Via C. Poerio 92/E, tel. 7642627.

Libreria Antiquaria Grimaldi. Via Bausan 58, tel. 406021.

Libreria Antiquaria Regina. Via Michelangelo Schipa 92, tel. 7611616.

Libreria Guida. Piazza dei Martiri 70, tel. 418155.

Libreria Marotta. Via dei Mille 78/80, tel. 418881.

Libri & Libri. Via Carducci 32, tel. 417152.

L. Nappa. Via G. Filangieri 65, tel. 413143. Design their own fine jewelry.

London House. Via G. Filangieri 26, tel. 415793; Viale Maria Cristina di Savoia 2, tel. 669710. Apparel, linen, and products of all sorts, including foods, all imported from Great Britain.

L.U.I.S.E. Via S. Caterina a Chiaia 68, tel. 417735. Fine foods.

Mandara. Via S. Caterina a Chiaia 4, tel. 417348. Fine cheeses and dairy products.

Marinella. Riviera di Chiaia 287, tel. 2451182, Piazza Vittoria 287, tel. 7644214. Ties made to measure, once for Lord Byron, now for the President of Italy.

Menichiello. Piazza C. Rodinò 15, tel. 417270. Fine fruit and vegetables.

Mercato del Casale di Posillipo. Market, every Thursday from 8 until 2 pm.

Pistola. Via Santa Caterina a Chiaia 12, tel. 422058. Craftsman, making gloves for over a century.

Acciaroli   ✉ 84041 ☎ 0974

Page 187

Hotels, restaurants, campsites, and vacation villages

at Pioppi, 8 km   ✉ 84060

★★★ **La Vela**. Via Caracciolo 96, tel. 905025, fax 905140. Seasonal. Number of rooms: 42. Elevator; parking, parking garage, garden.

❚❙ **Grigliaro**. Via Caracciolo 96, tel. 905025. Seasonal. Air conditioning, parking, garden. Cuisine of the Cilento – seafood.

Agriturismo (real Italian country living)

at Ascea, 15 km

Casa Leone. At Terradura. This 12-hectare farm

---

has olive groves, chestnut groves, and citrus groves, not far from the sea. For information: Armando and Gino Troccoli, tel. 977003.

Agropoli   ✉ 84043 ☎ 0974

Page 187

ℹ️ *Pro Loco*, Piazza Umberto I, tel. 827341.

Hotels, restaurants, campsites, and vacation villages

★★★ **Carola**. Via Pisacane 1, tel. 826422, fax 826425. Number of rooms: 34. Elevator; parking, parking garage, garden, private beach.

★★★ **Serenella**. Via S. Marco 140, tel. 823333, fax 825562. Number of rooms: 32. Accessible to the handicapped. Air conditioning, elevator; parking, garden, private beach.

❚❙ **U' Saracino**. Via Trentova, tel. 824063. Closed Tuesday in the low season, for a period in November. Air conditioning, parking, garden. Cuisine of Campania – seafood.

⛺ **Arco delle Rose**. Contr. Isca, Litoranea Paestum-Agropoli, tel. 838227, fax 838227. Seasonal.

Youth hostels

🏠 **La Lanterna**. Via Lanterna 8, At San Marco. 56 beds. Open, 15 March/30 October. For information: Tiziana Caprio Mamone, tel. 838003.

Museums and cultural institutions

Castello di Rocca Cilento. *To arrange for a tour, telephone the Municipio di Lustra, tel. 830074.*

Museo di Storia Naturale del Cilento. At Matonti di Laureana. *To arrange for a tour, telephone the Municipio, tel. 832022.*

Amalfi   ✉ 84011 ☎ 089

Plan, page 177

ℹ️ *AA*, Corso Roma 19/21, tel. 871107 (B2).

Hotels, restaurants, campsites, and vacation villages

★★★★ **Il Saraceno**. Via Augustariccio 25, tel. 831148, fax 831595. Seasonal. Number of rooms: 56. Air conditioning, elevator; parking, garden, swimming pool, private beach (C1, *off map*).

★★★★ **Luna Convento**. Via P. Comite 33, tel. 871002, fax 871333. Number of rooms: 45. Elevator; parking, parking garage, garden, swimming pool, private beach (B3, **g**).

★★★★ **Miramalfi**. Via Quasimodo 3, tel. 871588, fax 871287. Number of rooms: 48. Elevator; parking, swimming pool, private beach (C1, *off map*).

★★★ **Dei Cavalieri**. Via M. Comite 26, tel. 831333, fax 831354. Number of rooms: 60. Air conditioning, elevator; parking, special terms for parking garage, garden, private beach (C1, *off map*).

★★★ **La Bussola**. Lungomare dei Cavalieri 16, tel. 871533, fax 871369. Number of rooms: 63. Elevator; parking, parking garage, private beach (B1, **b**).

¶¶¶ **Eolo**. Via P. Comite 3, tel. 871241, fax 871024. Closed Tuesday (except in summer), end of November – Christmas. Cuisine of Amalfi with a touch of originality (B3, **m**).

¶¶ **Gemma**. Via Frà Gerardo Sasso 10, tel. 871345. Closed Wednesday(except in summer, mid-January/mid-February). Air conditioning. Classic cuisine – fish (B2, **p**).

¶¶ **La Caravella**. Via M. Camera 12, tel. 871029. Closed Tuesday, November. Air conditioning. Cuisine of Amalfi – seafood (B2, **r**).

Cafes and pastry shops

Andrea Pansa. Piazza Duomo 40, tel. 871065. Since 1830, local specialties, from "delizia al limone" to "tegole al cioccolato" or "tegole alla nocciola," from white profiteroles to citrus peels covered with chocolate.

Museums and cultural institutions

Centro di Cultura e Storia Amalfitana. Via Annunziatella, tel. 873143. *Open to the public: Tuesday, Thursday and Saturday 9-1; Monday, Wednesday and Friday 4-8 pm.*

Museo Civico. Piazza Municipio, tel. 871066. Closed Saturday and Sunday. *Open to the public: 8-2; Tuesday and Thursday also 4-7.*

Museo della Carta. Valle dei Mulini, tel. 8736211. *Visits on request.*

Entertainment, shows, and events

Regata Storica delle Antiche Repubbliche Marinare (regatta, 1 June, every 4 years). Tel. 871107.

Shops, crafts, and curiosities

Cartiera Amatruda. Via Fiume, tel. 871315. This is probably the oldest crafts paper shop in Italy; since the year 1200, the Amatruda have been handing down their craft from one generation to the next.

D'Antuono. Piazza Duomo 11, tel. 872368. In this little shop, along with art books and old prints, you can buy stationery, albums, and notebooks, made with the fine paper of the mills of Amalfi.

Mostacciulo. Piazza Duomo 22, tel. 871552. Coral craftsmen.

Atena Lucana ✉ 84030 ☎ 0975

Page 190

Hotels, restaurants, campsites, and vacation villages

★☆★ **Kristall Palace**. At the highway exit, tel. 71152, fax 71153. Number of rooms: 22. Accessible to the handicapped. Air conditioning, elevator; parking.

Atrani ✉ 84010 ☎ 089

Page 176

Hotels, restaurants, campsites, and vacation villages

¶ **Le Arcate**. Via G. Di Benedetto 4, tel. 871367. Closed Monday in the low season, mid-January/mid-February. Cuisine of Amalfi – seafood.

Bacoli ✉ 80070 ☎ 081

Page 103

ℹ️ *Ufficio Beni Culturali e Turismo*, c/o Municipio, Via Risorgimento 36, tel. 8553285.

Hotels, restaurants, campsites, and vacation villages

¶¶¶ **La Misenetta**. Via Lungolago 2, tel. 5234169, fax 5231510. Closed Monday (except in summer), Christmas-New Year's Day and for a period in August. Parking. Cuisine of Campania and classical cuisine – seafood.

Museums and cultural institutions

Cento Camerelle and Piscina Mirabile. Inquire with the caretaker, Signora Basile, Via A. Greco 10, or else at the Ufficio Beni Culturali del Comune, tel. 8553285. *Open to the public: 9-one hour before sunset.*

at Marina di Bacoli

Tomb, or Sepolcro di Agrippina. Via Agrippina. Contact caretaker, Sig. Giovanni Castiglia, or else inquire at the Ufficio Beni Culturali del Comune, tel. 8553285. *Open to the public: 9-one hour before sunset.*

Athletic activities

Polly Magoo. Viale Olimpico 75, tel. 5234763. Sports facilities.

Shops, crafts, and curiosities

I.M.A.T. Via Scalandrone 89, tel. 8687974. Fine ceramics.

Lobster. Via Faro 34, tel. 5234487. Lobsters and shellfish, alive and frozen.

Baia ✉ 80070 ☎ 081

Page 101

at Bacoli, km 3

ℹ️ *Ufficio Beni Culturali e Turismo*, c/o Municipio, tel. 8553285.

Hotels, restaurants, campsites, and vacation villages

¶¶¶ **Dal Tedesco**. Via Temporini 12, tel. 8687175, fax 8687336. Closed Tuesday, Christmas-Epiphany (6 January). Parking, garden. Cuisine of Campania – seafood.

Museums and cultural institutions

Museo Archeologico Campi Flegrei. Castello di Baia, tel. 5233797. *Open to the public: 8-5; Sunday 8-2.*

Parco Archeologico. Temples of Diana and Venus. Via Fusaro 35, tel. 8553285. *Open to the public: everyday, from 9 until one hour before sunset.*

Athletic activities

Circolo Nautico e Subacqueo Poseidon. Diving and sailing. Molo di Baia, tel. 8687198.

Local guides and excursions

Servizio Guide del Comune, guides free of charge, tel. 8553285.

Boat rental, or Noleggio Barche, near the port of Baia. Excursions with local fishermen.

Battipaglia   ☒ 84091 ☎ 0828

Hotels, restaurants, campsites, and vacation villages

¦ **Commercio**. Via Variante-S.S. 18, tel. 671321, fax 673689. Number of rooms: 81. Accessible to the handicapped. Air conditioning, elevator; parking, parking garage.

⚠ **Maldive First Class**. Via Litoranea 31, tel. 624103. Seasonal.

at Lido Spineta, 9 km   ☒ 84090

*** **Etap Club Paestum**. Via Spineta Nuova, tel. 624121, fax 624242. Seasonal. Number of rooms: 295. Accessible to the handicapped. Elevator; parking, garden, swimming pool, tennis.

Boscotrecase   ☒ 80042 ☎ 081

ℹ c/o *Municipio*, Assessorato al Turismo, tel. 5373838-5373371.

Capri (Isola di, or Isle of Capri)
☒ 80073 ☎ 081

Map on page 145, plan on page 148

at Capri

ℹ *AA*, Piazzetta I. Cerio, tel. 8375308 (B2); Via Padre Cimmino, tel. 8370424 (B2). Information: Via Marina Grande, tel. 8370634 (A1); Piazza Umberto I, tel. 8370686 (B2).

at Anacapri

Ufficio Informazioni, Via G. Orlandi 19/A, tel. 8371524.

Hotels, restaurants, campsites, and vacation villages

at Capri   ☒ 80073

¦¦¦ **Grand Hotel Quisisana**. Via Camerelle 2, tel. 8370788, fax 8376080. Seasonal. Number of rooms: 150. Air conditioning, elevator; garden, indoor and outdoor swimming pools, tennis (B2, **a**).

¦ **La Pazziella**. Via P. Reginaldo Giuliani 4, tel. 8370044, fax 8370085. Number of rooms: 20. Rooms only; no dining facilities. Air conditioning; garden, swimming pool (B3, **q**).

¦ **Luna**. Viale Matteotti 3, tel. 8370433, fax 8377459. Seasonal. Number of rooms: 56. Air conditioning, elevator; special terms for parking garage, garden, swimming pool (C2, **h**).

¦ **Punta Tragara**. Via Tragara 57, tel. 8370844, fax 8377790. Seasonal. Number of rooms: 47. Air conditioning, elevator; garden, swimming pool (C3, **g**).

¦ **Scalinatella**. Via Tragara 8, tel. 8370633, fax 8378291. Seasonal. Number of rooms: 30. Rooms only; no dining facilities. Accessible to the handicapped. Air conditioning, elevator; swimming pool (C3, **j**).

¦ **Villa Brunella**. Via Tragara 24, tel. 8370122, fax 8370430. Seasonal. Number of rooms: 20. Air conditioning; garden, swimming pool (C3, **k**).

*** **Gatto Bianco**. Via Vittorio Emanuele 32, tel. 8370446, fax 8378060. Seasonal. Number of rooms: 37. Rooms only; no dining facilities. Air conditioning, elevator; garden (B2, **c**).

*** **Villa Sarah**. Via Tiberio 3/A, tel. 8377817, fax 8377215. Seasonal. Number of rooms: 20. No dining facilities. Garden (B3, **p**).

¦¦¦ **Quisi**. Via Camerelle 2, tel. 8370788, fax 8376080. Seasonal. Air conditioning, garden. Classic cuisine (B2, **a**).

¦¦¦ **Canzone del Mare**. A Marina Piccola, Via Marina Piccola 93, tel. 8370104, fax 8370541. Seasonal. Cuisine of Campania (C1, **ra**).

¦¦¦ **Capannina**. Via delle Botteghe 12 bis, tel. 8370732, fax 8376990. Seasonal. Air conditioning. Cuisine of Campania – seafood (B2, **rd**).

¦¦ **Casanova**. Via Le Botteghe 46, tel. 8377642. Closed Epiphany (6 January)/mid-March. Air conditioning. Cuisine of Campania, refined – seafood (B2, **rb**).

at Anacapri   ☒ 80071

¦ **Europa Palace**. Via Capodimonte 2/B, tel. 8373800, fax 8373191. Seasonal. Number of rooms: 90. Air conditioning, elevator; parking, parking garage, garden, indoor and outdoor swimming pools.

*** **San Michele**. Via G. Orlandi 1, tel. 8371427, fax 8371420Seasonal. Number of rooms: 59. Elevator. Parking, garden, swimming pool.

** **Bellavista**. Via Orlandi 10, tel. 8371463, fax 8370957. Seasonal. Number of rooms: 15. Garden, tennis.

¶ **Cucciolo**. A Damecuta, Via La Fabbrica 52, tel. 8371917. Seasonal, closed Tuesday in the low season. Parking, garden. Cuisine of Campania.

¶ **Gelsomina alla Migliara**. Via Migliara 6, tel. 8371499. Closed Tuesday, mid-January/mid-February. Garden. Cuisine of Campania.

Cafes and pastry shops

at Capri

Alberto. Via Roma 9-11, tel. 8370622. Pastry shop that produces the best "torta caprese."

Bar Caso, tel. 8370600. **Bar Tiberio**, tel. 8370268. **Gran Caffè**, tel. 8370388. **Piccolo Bar**, tel. 8370325. The cafes of the Piazzetta Umberto I.

Limoncello di Capri. Via Roma 79, tel. 8375561. Aside from this lemon liqueur, invented at the end of the 19th c., you can also sample other fine products of the island.

at Anacapri

Bar Grotta Azzurra. Via Orlandi 240, tel. 8372081. Excellent ice cream.

Museums and cultural institutions

at Capri

Biblioteca Comunale. Library, Certosa di S. Giacomo, tel. 8370450.

Certosa di San Giacomo. Museo Diefenbach and small cloisters (Chiostro Piccolo), Piazzetta Certosa di S. Giacomo, tel. 8376218. Closed Monday. *Open to the public: (weekdays) 9-2; (holidays) 9-1.*

Museo del Centro Caprese. Piazzetta Cerio 8/a, tel. 8370858. Closed Saturday and Sunday. *Open to the public: everyday 10-12.*

Palazzo Tiberio, or Palace of Tiberius. Villa Imperiale. Tel. 8375308. *Open to the public: (weekdays and holidays) from 9 until one hour before sunset.*

at Anacapri

Villa Imperiale di Damecuta. Tel. 8371524. *Open to the public: 9-2, free of charge.*

Villa S. Michele. Via Capodimonte 34, tel. 83 '1401. *Open to the public: November-February 10:30-3:30; March 9:30-4:30; April and October 9:30-5; May-September 9-6.*

Entertainment, shows, and events

at Capri

S. Costanzo (14 May). Festa Patronale, or Feast of the Patron Saint. Tel. 8370686.

at Anacapri

S. Antonio da Padova (13 June). Festa Patronale, or Feast of the Patron Saint. Tel. 8371524.

Athletic activities

at Capri

Circolo Sportivo Caprese. Via Roma, tel. 8377147.
Circolo Tennis Yacht Club Capri. Via Camerelle 41, tel. 8370261.

at Anacapri

Sport Club Capri. Anacapri, Via G. Orlandi 10, tel. 8372612.

Shops, crafts, and curiosities

at Capri

Canfora. Via Camerelle 3, tel. 8370487. Amedeo Canfora makes all his shoes strictly by hand (if desired, to order), and they are elegant and inexpensive.

Carthusia. Via Camerelle 10, tel. 8370529. Essences of Capri. The perfumes of Capri are not exported, and can only be purchased on the island or ordered by mail.

Chantecler. Via V. Emanuele 51, tel. 8370544. One of the finest jeweler's of Capri. Here you can find brooches made with stones of every sort, jewelry made with pearls and diamonds, birds made of amethyst, all in excellent artistic style.

Gigino Esposito. Via I. Cerio 6, tel. 8376296. In this tailor shop, for the past 30 years, trousers made to order have been prepared in just a few days.

La Campanina. Via V. Emanuele 18, tel. 8370643. In the display windows of this shop glitter large rings with stones of every color, diamonds, pearls, and enormous coral necklaces.

La Conchiglia. Viale Botteghe 12, tel. 8376577. This bookshop, and, since 1989, also a publishing house issuing old and unpublished writings on Capri, features its own production, as well as rare texts about the island's history, prints and lithographs.

Siniscalco-Gori. Via Camerelle 89, tel. 8376798. Antique objects, furniture, and paintings.

at Anacapri

Giuseppe Faiella. Via V. Emanuele 49. Following the decree of the township, or Comune di Capri (no. 23 of 19-7-1960), prohibiting the use of wooden globs anywhere within the town limits, Giuseppe Faiella took care of the problem by making comfortable and silent cloth shoes, typical of Capri, with a woven-rope sole and canvas uppers.

Local guides and excursions

at Capri

Tour around the island. Tel. 8370634. Every morning (except winter) with departure at 9 am; the ride lasts about 2 hours.

Blue Grotto, or Grotta Azzurra. Tel. 8370634. Motorboat from Marina Grande. *You may enter the grotto in a rowboat, for a fee, from 9 until one hour before sunset.*

Capua   ✉ 81043 ☎ 0823

Plan, page 166

ℹ️ c/o *Municipio*, Piazza Giudici, tel. 961322.

Hotels, restaurants, campsites, and vacation villages

★★★ **Mediterraneo**. S.S. Appia at 202.150 km, tel. 961575, fax 622611. Number of rooms:

50, of which 34 with bath or shower. Accessible to the handicapped. Elevator; parking, parking garage, garden, swimming pool (C2-3, *off map*).

Museums and cultural institutions

Museo Provinciale Comunale. Via Roma 68, tel. 961402. Closed Monday. *Open to the public: 9-1:30; Sunday 9-1.*

Cafes and pastry shops

Gran Caffè. Piazza dei Giudici 1, tel. 961623.

Caserta ⬜ 81100 ☎ 0823

Plan, page 155

ℹ️ *EPT*, Palazzo Reale, tel. 326300; *Uffici Informazioni*, Corso Trieste corner of Piazza Dante, tel. 321137 (D2).

Hotels, restaurants, campsites, and vacation villages

*★**★** **Jolly**. Viale Vittorio Veneto 9, tel. 325222, fax 354522. Number of rooms: 107. Accessible to the handicapped. Air conditioning, elevator; parking, special terms for parking garage (D2, **a**).

★★★ **Centrale**. Via Roma 122, tel. 321855, fax 326557. Number of rooms: 40. Air conditioning, elevator; parking, special terms for parking garage (D3, **d**).

🍴 **Ciacco**. Via Majelli 37, tel. 327505. Closed Sunday, except in summer. Air conditioning. Cuisine of Campania and classical cuisine – seafood (D2, **r**).

Museums and cultural institutions

Palazzo Reale. Closed Monday. *Open to the public: everyday, 9-1:30; Sunday 9-9:30pm.*

Parco di Palazzo Reale. *Open to the public: everyday, 9–one hour before sunset.*

at Casertavecchia, 10 km ⬜ 81020

🍴 **La Castellana**. Via Torre 4, tel. 371230. Closed Thursday. Garden. Cuisine of Campania, fresh pasta - mushrooms.

🍴 **Mastrangelo**. Piazza Duomo 5, tel. 371377. Closed Tuesday in winter. Garden. Cuisine of Campania.

at San Leucio, 4 km ⬜ 81020

🍴 **Antica Locanda**. Piazza della Seta 8/10, tel. 305444. Closed Sunday evening and Monday, for a period in August. Air conditioning. Cuisine of Campania.

🍴 **Leucio**. Via Panoramica, tel. 301241. Closed Sunday evening and Monday, part of August, Christmas and Easter. Air conditioning, parking. Classical cuisine.

Castellammare di Stabia
⬜ 80053 ☎ 081

Page 138

ℹ️ *AA*, Piazza Matteotti 58, tel. 8711334.

Hotels, restaurants, campsites, and vacation villages

*★**★** **La Medusa**. Via Passeggiata Archeologica 5, tel. 8723383, fax 8717009. Number of rooms: 52. Air conditioning, elevator; parking, parking garage, garden.

*★**★** **Stabia**. Corso Vittorio Emanuele 101, tel. 8722577, fax 8722577. Number of rooms: 96. Air conditioning, elevator; parking, parking garage, garden.

★★★ **Dei Congressi**. Viale Puglie 45, tel. 8722277, fax 8722277. Number of rooms: 80. Accessible to the handicapped. Air conditioning, elevator; parking.

Museums and cultural institutions

Antiquarium. Via Marco Mario, c/o Liceo Plinio Senior, tel. 8707228. *Open to the public: everyday (except Monday) from 9 until 6 pm.*

Villa Arianna and **Villa S. Marco**. Passeggiata Archeologica (Varano), tel. 8714541. *Open to the public: from 9 until one hour before sunset, free of charge.*

Spas and hot springs

Antiche Terme Stabiane. Piazza Amendola, tel. 8714422, various treatments; Nuove Terme Stabiane, Viale delle Terme 3-5, tel. 8714422. Therapies based on: hot springs, mud packs, inhalations; and massage therapy.

Cava de' Tirreni ⬜ 84013 ☎ 089

Page 172

ℹ️ *AA*, Corso Umberto I 208, tel. 463723.

Hotels, restaurants, campsites, and vacation villages

🍴 **Vincenzo**. Via Garibaldi 7, tel. 464654. Closed Monday July-August. Air conditioning, garden. Cuisine of Salerno – pasta, seafood.

at Corpo di Cava, 3 km ⬜ 84010

*★**★** **Scapolatiello**. Piazza Risorgimento 1, tel. 443611, fax 443611. Number of rooms: 49. Air conditioning, elevator; parking, garden, swimming pool.

Cafes and pastry shops

Gran Caffè Respighi. Via Mazzini 5, tel. 343039. Local meeting spot for artists and poets.

Museums and cultural institutions

Abbazia di S. Benedetto. Abbey, *open to the*

public: weekdays, 9-12:30; holidays, except major religious holidays, 9-10:30.

Entertainment, shows, and events

Sagra di Monte Castello (Ottava del Corpus Dominus) and Disfida dei Trombonieri (first Sunday in July). Banner-spinners, including the famous Sbandieratori di Cava.

Eboli ⊠ 84025 ☎ 0828

Page 190

Hotels, restaurants, campsites, and vacation villages

★★★ **Grazia**. Via Nazionale 20, tel. 366038, fax 366038. Number of rooms: 56. Elevator; parking, parking garage, garden.

★★★ **Paestum**. At Foce Sele, tel. 691003, fax 691003. Seasonal.

Ercolano, or Herculaneum
⊠ 80056 ☎ 081

Plan, page 124

ℹ️ *Ufficio Informazioni Turistiche*, Via IV Novembre 82, tel. 7881243.

Hotels, restaurants, campsites, and vacation villages

★★★ **Punta Quattroventi**. Via Marittima 59, tel. 7773041, fax 7773757. Number of rooms: 37. Air conditioning, elevator; parking, garden, indoor and outdoor swimming pools, private beach.

Museums and cultural institutions

Antiquarium. Archaeological digs. Piazza Museo 1, tel. 7390963. *Open to the public: everyday from 9 until one hour before sunset.*

Ischia (Isola d', or Island of Ischia)
⊠ 80077 ☎ 081

Map on page 110, plan on page 112

at Ischia

ℹ️ *AA*, Via Colonna 102, tel. 991464 (A3). *Ufficio Informazioni*, Via Jasolino, tel. 991146 (A1).

Hotels, restaurants, campsites, and vacation villages

at Ischia ⊠ 80077

★★★ **Grand Hotel Punta Molino Terme**. Lungomare C. Colombo 23, tel. 991544, fax 991562. Seasonal. Number of rooms: 82. Air conditioning, elevator; parking, garden, indoor and outdoor swimming pools, private beach (C2, **d**).

★★★ **Continental Terme**. Via M. Mazzella 74, tel. 991588, fax 982929. Seasonal. Number of rooms: 244. Air conditioning, elevator; parking, garden, indoor and outdoor swimming pools, tennis, private beach (C1, *off map*).

★★★ **Grand Hotel Excelsior**. Via E. Gianturco 19, tel. 991522, fax 984100. Seasonal. Number of rooms: 74. Air conditioning, elevator; parking, garden, indoor and outdoor swimming pools, private beach (B2, **b**).

★★★ **Jolly delle Terme**. Via De Luca 42, tel. 991744, fax 993156. Seasonal. Number of rooms: 208. Accessible to the handicapped. Air conditioning, elevator; parking, garden, indoor and outdoor swimming pools, tennis (B1, **g**).

★★★ **Regina Palace**. Via E. Cortese 18, tel. 991344, fax 983597. Seasonal. Number of rooms: 63. Air conditioning, elevator; parking, garden, indoor and outdoor swimming pools, tennis, private beach (B2, **e**).

★★★ **Bristol Hotel Terme**. Via V. Marone 10, tel. 992181, fax 993201. Seasonal. Number of rooms: 61. Elevator; special terms for parking garage, garden, swimming pool (B2, **a**).

♦♦♦ **Damiano**. Nuova Circonvallazione, tel. 983032. Seasonal. Cuisine of Ischia and classical cuisine (B1, *off map*).

♦♦♦ **Gennaro**. Via Porto 66, tel. 992917, fax 983636. Seasonal, closed Tuesday in the low season. Air conditioning. Cuisine of Ischia and classical cuisine (A2, **r**).

★★ **Internazionale Ischia**. Via Foschini, tel. 991449, fax 991472. Seasonal.

at Casamicciola Terme ⊠ 80074

★★★ **Elma**. Corso Vittorio Emanuele 57, tel. 994122, fax 994253. Number of rooms: 73. Accessible to the handicapped. Air conditioning, elevator; parking, garden, indoor and outdoor swimming pools, tennis, private beach.

★★★ **Manzi**. Piazza Bagni 1, tel. 994722, fax 980241. Seasonal. Number of rooms: 62. Air conditioning, elevator; garden, swimming pool, tennis, private beach.

★★★ **Gran Paradiso**. Via Principessa Margherita 20, tel. 994003, fax 994311. Seasonal. Number of rooms: 46, 45 of which with bath or shower. Elevator; parking, swimming pool, private beach.

★★ **Monti**. Calata S. Antonio 7, tel. 994074, fax 900630. Seasonal. Number of rooms: 26. Parking, garden, indoor and outdoor swimming pools.

at Forio ⊠ 80075

★★★ **Mezzatorre**. At Sammontano, Via Mezzatorre 23, tel. 986111, fax 986015. Seasonal. Number of rooms: 55. Air conditioning, elevator; parking, garden, swimming pool, tennis, private beach.

★★★ **Parco Maria**. At Cuotto, Via Provinciale Panza 212, tel. 909040, fax 909100. Number of rooms: 98. Parking, garden, indoor and outdoor swimming pools, private beach.

★★★ **La Bagattella**. At San Francesco, Via T. Cigliano 8, tel. 986072, fax 989637. Seasonal. Number of rooms: 53. Air conditioning, elevator; parking, garden, indoor and outdoor swimming pools.

¶¶¶ **Romantica**. Via Marina 46, tel. 997345. Closed Wednesday in the low season, for a period in January. Cuisine of Campania.

¶¶ **Il Melograno**. Via G. Mazzella 110, tel. 998450. Closed Epiphany-March. Parking, garden. Cuisine of Campania – fish.

¶ **Da Peppina di Renato**. Via Bocca 23, tel. 998312. Seasonal, closed Wednesday (except from June to September). Parking. Cuisine of Campania.

at Lacco Ameno ✉ 80076

‡‡‡ **Regina Isabella e Royal Sporting**. Piazza S. Restituta, tel. 994322, fax 900190. Number of rooms: 134. Accessible to the handicapped. Air conditioning, elevator; parking, parking garage, garden, indoor and outdoor swimming pools, tennis.

★‡★ **San Montano**. Via Montevico, tel. 994033, fax 980242. Seasonal. Number of rooms: 67. Air conditioning, elevator; parking, special terms for parking garage, garden, indoor and outdoor swimming pools, tennis, private beach.

★★★ **Don Pepe**. Via Campo 25, tel. 994397, fax 996696. Seasonal. Number of rooms: 70. Air conditioning; parking, garden, indoor and outdoor swimming pools.

★★★ **Grazia Terme**. Via Borbonica 2, tel. 994333, fax 994153. Seasonal. Number of rooms: 58. Air conditioning, elevator; parking, garden, swimming pool, tennis.

★★★ **Villa Angelica**. Via IV Novembre 28, tel. 994524, fax 980184. Number of rooms: 20. special terms for parking garage; garden, indoor and outdoor swimming pools.

at Sant'Angelo ✉ 80070

★‡★ **Park Hotel Miramare**. Via C. Maddalena 29, tel. 999219, fax 999325. Seasonal. Number of rooms: 54. Garden; indoor and outdoor swimming pools, tennis, private beach.

★★★ **San Michele Terme**. Via S. Angelo 60, tel. 999276, fax 999149. Seasonal. Number of rooms: 52. Garden; swimming pool.

★★ **Casa Celestino**. Via Chiaia delle Rose, tel. 999213, fax 999805. Seasonal. Number of rooms: 20.

Spas and hot springs

at Ischia

Ischia Termal Center. Via delle Terme, tel. 984376. Therapies: hot springs; mud packs; massage therapy.

Parco Termale Giardini Eden. Via Nuova Cartaromana, tel. 993909-985015. Long-term daily stays, with a number of thermal pools, restaurants, and other services.

at Casamicciola

Parco Termale Castiglione. Via Castiglione 36, tel. 982551. Long-term daily stays, with a number of thermal pools, restaurants, and other services.

at Forio

Parco Termale Giardini Poseidon. Spiaggia Citara, tel. 907122. Long-term daily stays, with a number of thermal pools, restaurants, and other services.

Cafes and pastry shops

at Ischia

Bar Calise. Via A. Sogliuzzo, tel. 991270. This is a sweets shop where you can enjoy many specialties: the Napoleone (fruit pie), the San Domingo (coffee cake), and *parfé* (*parfait*), a form of chocolate, strawberry, and coffee ice cream.

La Dolce Sosta. Ischia Porto, Corso V. Colonna 101, tel. 991678.

at Casamicciola

Calise. Piazza Marina 26, tel. 994080.

at Sant'Angelo

Dal Pescatore. Tel. 999206. Excellent pastries.

at Forio

Da Elio. Via G. Castellaccio 5 bis, tel. 997668. Famous ice cream shop of the island, popular with young people.

Museums and cultural institutions

at Ischia

Castello Aragonese. Ischia Ponte, tel. 992834. *Open to the public: (from March to November) everyday, from 9 until sunset.*

at Lacco Ameno

Santa Restituta. Sanctuary and museum. Piazzetta S. Restituta, tel. 986313. *Open to the public: 9:30-12, 4-7:30.*

Villa Arbusto. Corso Rizzoli, tel. 900315. Parco. Closed Sunday afternoon. Open to the public: all year, from 8 until 6 pm. Museo Archeologico being installed.

Athletic activities

at Ischia

Capitaneria di Porto. Via Jasolino, tel. 991417.

Shops, crafts, and curiosities

at Ischia

Appuntamento Vino. Via Porto 23, tel. 982981. Tasting of wines produced by the Casa Perrazzo.

Dominique. Corso V. Colonna 184 (women), tel. 991221; Corso V. Colonna 159 (men), tel. 991754. The Boutique di Luciano Marino offers the classic names of French and Italian fashion, with an emphasis on casual and athletic lines. Note the interiors with majolica and wood, of clear derivation from Ischia.

Enoteca D'Ambra. Ischia Porto, Via Porto 24, tel. 991046 and in the Località Panza, State road 206 16, tel. 907210, where there is also a museum of peasant culture, or Museo della Civiltà Contadina. Since 1888, the D'Ambra family has been selected new grapes from the vineyards of Ischia and developing wines such as the champagne Kalimera.

Gallerie delle Stampe Antiche. Ischia Ponte, Via. L. Mazzella 83, tel. 992408. Prints, oil paintings, and water colors, dating from the 17th, 18th, and 19th c.

Ischia Sapori. Ischia Porto, Via Gianturco 2, tel. 984482. Here you will find a collections of all the perfumes of the island: extra virgin olive oil with aromas of lemon, citrus marmalades and jellies, acacia and chestnut honeys; aromatic spices, almond and chocolate cakes, and such fine wines as the Cru Vigna Spadara, the Cru Tufaceo, or the Andrezzata.

at Casamicciola

Ceramiche Mennella. Via S. Girardi 47, tel. 994442. Production of traditional ceramics of the island.

at Forio

Taki. Via G. Mazzella, tel. 989149. 20. The master craftsman Taki creates stunning majolica decorations for interior decoration, with the distinctive colors of the island: ochre, dark blue, and burnt Sienna. Note the bricks painted with religious themes.

Local guides and excursions

at Ischia

Noleggio Imbarcazioni, or boat rentals. Tel. 992383-905114-995261.

Maiori   ⊠ 84010 ☎ 089

Page 173

ℹ️ *AA*, Corso Reginna (Palazzo Zitara), tel. 877452-853672.

Hotels, restaurants, campsites, and vacation villages

★☆★ **Panorama**. Via S. Tecla 8, tel. 877202, fax 877998. Seasonal. Number of rooms: 79. Accessible to the handicapped. Air conditioning, elevator; parking garage, swimming pool, private beach.

★☆★ **San Pietro**. Via Nuova Chiunzi 139, tel. 877220, fax 877025. Seasonal. Number of

rooms: 40. Elevator; parking, garden, swimming pool, tennis, private beach.

★★★ **Miramare**. Via Nuova Chiunzi 5, tel. 877225, fax 877490. Seasonal. Number of rooms: 46. Rooms only; no dining facilities. Air conditioning, elevator; parking, special terms for parking garage, private beach.

★★★ **San Francesco**. Via S. Tecla 54, tel. 877070, fax 877070. Seasonal. Number of rooms: 44. Elevator; parking, parking garage, garden, private beach.

🍴 **Mammato**. Via Amendola, tel. 877036. Closed Tuesday in the low season, holiday closure varies. Cuisine of Amalfi – seafood.

Museums and cultural institutions

Collegiata S. Maria a Mare. Church and museum. Tel. 877090. *Open to the public: 8:30-12, 4-7:30.*

Athletic activities

Delegazione di Spiaggia. c/o Municipio. Tel. 877110. For information on landing small boats.

Shops, crafts, and curiosities

Ceramica Bottone. Via Casale dei Cicerali. Traditional products of Ischia.

Marina di Camerota   ⊠ 84059 ☎ 0974

Page 188

ℹ️ *Pro Loco* (seasonal), Via Porto, tel. 932900.

Hotels, restaurants, campsites, and vacation villages

★★★ **Delfino**. Via Bolivar 45, tel. 932239, fax 932239. Number of rooms: 23. Accessible to the handicapped. Parking, parking garage, garden.

★★ **Bolivar**. Via Bolivar 34, tel. 932059, fax 932036. Seasonal. Number of rooms: 14. Elevator; parking.

🍴 **Valentone**. Piazza S. Domenico 5, tel. 932004. Closed Sunday in the low season, October-December. Cuisine of the Cilento.

🏕️★★★ **Black Marlin Club**. At Torre Mingardo, S.S. 562 at 2,9 km, tel. 931108, fax 938147. Seasonal.

🏕️★★★ **Happy Camping Village**. Contr. Arconte, S.S. 562 at 8.2 km, tel. 932326, fax 932769. Seasonal.

🏕️ **Villaggio Vacanze T.C.I.** At Torre d'Arconte, tel. 932116, fax 932012. Seasonal.

Shops, crafts, and curiosities

at Camerota, 6 km

Ciociano. Via Pubblici Uffici 6, tel. 935065. Crafts production of terracotta and clay.

Massa Lubrense   ✉ 80061 ☎ 081

Page 144

[i]   *Ufficio Turistico Comunale*, Viale Filangieri 13, tel. 8089571.

Hotels, restaurants, campsites, and vacation villages

‡   **Delfino**. A Marciano, Via Nastro d'Oro 2, tel. 8789261, fax 8089074. Seasonal. Number of rooms: 67. Air conditioning, elevator; parking, garden, swimming pool, private beach.

***   **Bellavista**. Via Partenope 26, tel. 8789181, fax 8089341. Number of rooms: 36. Accessible to the handicapped. Air conditioning, elevator; parking, parking garage, swimming pool, private beach.

¶¶   **Antico Francischiello-da Peppino**. Via Partenope 27, tel. 5339780. Closed Wednesday. Air conditioning, parking. Neapolitan cuisine.

at Marina del Cantone, 10 km   ✉ 80068

¶¶¶   **Taverna del Capitano**. Piazza delle Sirene 10/11, tel. 8081028, fax 8081892. Closed Monday (except in summer), for a period between January e February. Air conditioning, parking. Cuisine of Campania, refined.

Δ**   **Nettuno**. Via Vespucci 39, tel. 8081051, fax 8081706. Seasonal.

Minori   ✉ 84010 ☎ 089

Page 174

Hotels, restaurants, campsites, and vacation villages

‡   **Villa Romana**. Corso Vittorio Emanuele 90, tel. 877237, fax 877302. Number of rooms: 53. Air conditioning, elevator; parking, parking garage, garden, swimming pool, private beach.

¶¶   **Giardiniello**. Corso Vittorio Emanuele 17, tel. 877050. Closed Wednesday in the low season, November. Garden. Cuisine of Campania – seafood.

Cafes and pastry shops

Gambardella. Corso Vittorio Emanuele 37/39, tel. 877299. Specialties: "cioccolatini al limone" and "cioccolatini all'arancia."

Museums and cultural institutions

Villa Romana. Via Santa Lucia, tel. 852893. *Open to the public: from 9 until one hour before sunset.*

Entertainment, shows, and events

Concerti di Mezza Estate, Music, Ballet, Opera (July-August). Tel. 877135.

Athletic activities

Gruppo Sportivo Minori. Via Dietro la Chiesa 12, tel. 851122.

Shops, crafts, and curiosities

Ruocco. Corso V. Emanuele 23, tel. 851900. Crafts production of ceramics.

Miseno   ✉ 80070 ☎ 081

Page 104

Hotels, restaurants, campsites, and vacation villages

***   **Cala Moresca Hotel Club**. Via Faro 44, tel. 5235595, fax 5235557. Number of rooms: 28. Accessible to the handicapped. Air conditioning, elevator; parking, swimming pool.

Ottaviano   ✉ 80044 ☎ 081

Hotels, restaurants, campsites, and vacation villages

‡   **Augustus**. Viale Giovanni XXIII 61, tel. 5288455, fax 5288454. Number of rooms: 41. Rooms only; no dining facilities. Air conditioning, elevator; parking, parking garage, swimming pool.

Paestum   ✉ 84063 ☎ 0828

Plan, page 184

[i]   *AA*, Via Magna Grecia 152, tel. 811016, fax 722322.

Hotels, restaurants, campsites, and vacation villages

‡   **Mec Paestum Hotel**. At Licinella, Via Tiziano 23, tel. 722444, fax 722305. Number of rooms: 54. Accessible to the handicapped. Air conditioning, elevator; parking, parking garage, garden, swimming pool, private beach.

‡   **Ariston**. At Laura, tel. 851333, fax 851596. Number of rooms: 110. Air conditioning, elevator; parking, parking garage, garden, indoor and outdoor swimming pools, tennis, private beach.

***   **Cristallo**. At Laura, Via P. della Madonna 39, tel. 851077, fax 851468. Number of rooms: 36. Parking, garden.

¶¶   **La Pergola**. At Capaccio Scalo, Via Nazionale 1, tel. 723377. Closed Monday except in summer, and for variable vacation periods. Parking, garden. Cuisine of the region – fish, mushrooms.

¶¶   **Nettuno**. Via Principe di Piemonte 2, tel. 811028. Closed Monday, Christmas. Parking, garden. Cuisine of Campania and classical cuisine – seafood.

Δ   **Torino**. At Linora, Via Licinella, tel. 811851, fax 811851. Seasonal.

Agriturismo (real Italian country living)

at Capaccio, 14 km

Azienda Agricola Seliano. Località Seliano. Accommodations in two renovated mid-19th-c. country houses. Fruit farm and livestock. Riding stables, swimming pool, cooking courses. For information: Cecilia Baratta, tel. 723634-724544.

Museums and cultural institutions

Museo Archeologico Nazionale e Scavi. Tel. 811023. Closed 1st and 3rd Monday of the month. *Open to the public: 9-6:30.*

Palinuro   ✉ 84064 ☎ 0974

Page 188

ℹ️   *Pro Loco* (seasonal), Via Parrocchia 1, tel. 938144, fax 931147.

Hotels, restaurants, campsites, and vacation villages

*★★   **Grand Hotel San Pietro**. Corso C. Pisacane, tel. 931466, fax 931919. Seasonal. Number of rooms: 49. Air conditioning, elevator; parking, swimming pool, private beach.

*★★   **Il Gabbiano**. Corso C. Pisacane, tel. 931155, fax 931121. Seasonal. Number of rooms: 45. Air conditioning, elevator; parking, garden, swimming pool.

*★★   **Arco Naturale**. At Mingardo-Molpa, tel. 931157, fax 931975. Seasonal.

★★★   **Marbella Club**. At Piana Mingardo, tel. 931003, fax 938364. Seasonal.

Agriturismo (real Italian country living)

Azienda Agricola S. Agata. At S. Agata Nord. A renovated 18th-c. farmhouse, in the hills, surrounded by ancient olive trees. Trekking, boating, and cooking courses. For information: tel. 931716-933015.

Pertosa   ✉ 84030 ☎ 0975

Page 190

ℹ️   *Pro Loco*, Via Grotte, tel. 397037.

Local guides and excursions

Grotte, or caves. Via Muraglione. *Guided tours every hour from 1 April until 30 September, 8-7; from 1 October until 31 March, 9-12 and 2-4.*

Pompei, or Pompeii   ✉ 80045 ☎ 081

Plan on pages 128-129

ℹ️   *AA*, Via Sacra 1, tel. 8508451 (C6, *off map*); *Ufficio Informazioni*, Piazza Porta Marina Inferiore 11 (B2-3); Via Colle S. Bartolomeo 10 (C6, *off map*) tel. 167013350.

Hotels, restaurants, campsites, and vacation villages

★★★   **Bristol**. Piazza Vittorio Veneto 1/3, tel.

8503005, fax 8631625. Number of rooms: 50. Elevator; parking garage (C6, *off map*).

★★★   **Diomede**. Viale Mazzini 46, tel. 8507586, fax 8631520. Number of rooms: 24. Rooms only; no dining facilities. Elevator; parking, parking garage (D6, *off map*).

★★★   **Forum**. Via Roma 99, tel. 8501170, fax 8506132. Number of rooms: 19. Rooms only; no dining facilities. Air conditioning, elevator; special terms for parking garage, garden (C6, *off map*).

🍴   **Il Principe**. Piazza B. Longo 8, tel. 8505566, fax 8633342. Closed Sunday evening and Monday (except April/June and September/October) Christmas. Air conditioning. Cuisine of Campania and classical cuisine – refined (C6, *off map*).

🍴   **Zi' Caterina**. Via Roma 20, tel. 8507447. Closed Tuesday. Air conditioning, parking. Neapolitan cuisine (C6, *off map*).

Cafes and pastry shops

Peluso. Via Lepanto 6, tel. 8631238. Excellent pastries and ice cream.

Museums and cultural institutions

Museo Vesuviano. Via Colle S. Bartolomeo 10, Villino B. Longo, tel. 8503232. Closed Sunday. *Open to the public: 8-2.*

Museo del Santuario della Madonna del Rosario. Piazza del Santuario, tel. 8507000. *Open to the public: from 9 until 1 and from 3 until 6:30.*

at Pompei Scavi

Zona Archeologica. Pompei Scavi, or excavations of Pompeii, tel. 8610744. Closed: Christmas, New Year's Day, Easter and Easter Monday, Feast of the Assumption (15 August). *Open to the public: generally from 9 until one hour before sunset. The chart with the exact schedules (which vary every 15 days) can be seen at the entrance to the excavations, or else by inquiry at the Azienda di Soggiorno.*

Entertainment, shows, and events

Festa della Supplica della Madonna del Rosario (8 May and first Sunday in October). Piazza del Santuario, tel. 8507000.

Teatro Antico. Theater, with classical performances (June-September). Tel. 8507255.

Shops, crafts, and curiosities

Calabrese. Via Plinio 59, tel. 8631568. Fine ceramics.

Casa del Corallo. Via Plinio 111, tel. 8614634; Piazza Porta Marina 13/14, tel. 8612763. Crafts production of coral.

Vetrina Incantata. Via Carlo Alberto 23, tel. 8505470. Typical craftsmanship of Pompeii.

Pontecagnano-Faiano   ✉ 84098 ☎ 089

Page 189

Hotels, restaurants, campsites, and vacation villages

★★★ **Europa**. Via Europa 2, tel. 848072, fax 848528. Number of rooms: 40. Elevator; parking.

Museums and cultural institutions

Museo Nazionale dell'Agro Picentino. Piazza Risorgimento, tel. 383505. *Open to the public: 9-2.*

Positano   ✉ 84017 ☎ 089

Plan, page 180

ℹ️   *AA*, Via del Saracino 4, tel. 875067, fax 875760 (B2).

Hotels, restaurants, campsites, and vacation villages

★★★ↄ **San Pietro**. Via Laurito 2, tel. 875455, fax 811449. Seasonal. Number of rooms: 60. Air conditioning, elevator; parking, garden, swimming pool, tennis (B3, *off map*).

★★★ **Le Agavi**. Via G. Marconi 127, tel. 875733, fax 875965. Seasonal. Number of rooms: 70. Air conditioning, elevator; parking, garden, swimming pool, private beach (B1, **f**).

★★★ **Buca di Bacco**. Via Rampa Teglia 4, tel. 875699, fax 875731. Seasonal. Number of rooms: 53. Air conditioning, elevator (B3, **g**).

★★★ **Villa Franca**. Via Pasitea 318, tel. 875655, fax 875735. Seasonal. Number of rooms: 28. Elevator; special terms for parking garage, swimming pool (B2, **k**).

★★★ **Casa Albertina**. Via della Tavolozza 3, tel. 875143, fax 811540. Number of rooms: 21. Elevator; special terms for parking garage (B2, **o**).

★★★ **Pupetto**. Via Fornillo 37, tel. 875087, fax 811517. Seasonal. Number of rooms: 30. Elevator; parking, garden (B1, **y**).

🍴 **Cambusa**. Piazza A. Vespucci 4, tel. 875432. Air conditioning. Cuisine of Campania – seafood (B2-3, **s**).

Cafes and pastry shops

La Zagara. Via Mulini 8, tel. 875964. You may sample the Positanese (a fine chocolate cake) and more than 40 different types of pastry, magnificent pies, 15 different fresh-fruit "granite," and 5 citrus cocktails. All of this in a lovely garden under lemon trees, with the wonderful smell of orange-blossoms.

Museums and cultural institutions

Church of S. Maria Assunta. Via Marina, tel. 875480. *Open to the public: everyday, 8:30-12:30, 15:30-7:30.*

Entertainment, shows, and events

Premio Positano "Leonide Massine" per l'Arte e la Danza (September), arts prizes. Tel. 875067.

Athletic activities

Ufficio Locale Marittimo. Via del Brigantino, tel. 875486. For information on docking small boats.

Shops, crafts, and curiosities

Ceramiche Assunta. Via Colombo 97, tel. 875008. Traditional ceramics of Vietri, in splendid colors and patterns: dishes, glasses, cups, vases, and trays, to order as well.

Costanzo Avitabile. Piazza A. Vespucci 1-5, tel. 875366. In just a few minutes, you can have a pair of the famous sandals of Positano, made to order.

Emporio la Sirenuse. Via C. Colombo 103, tel. 811468. Refined linen, cotton, cashmere, and silk knitwear, made by hand.

Giuseppe Di Lieto. Via Corvo 37, tel. 875265. This painter describes himself as a "landscape artist of the Amalfi coast and of mermaids."

La Bottega di Brunella. Via Pasitea 76, tel. 875228. Men's, women's, and children's wear; for those who want to be original, choose unusual patterns and fabrics here.

Maria Lampo. Via Pasitea 12-4, tel. 875021. For the past 45 years, Maria has been making swim suits, beach dresses, bermuda shorts, and trousers, for men, women, and children, in the traditional fabrics of Positano.

Nadir. Via Pasitea 44, tel. 811690. Here, folk and country styles are the rule. Aside from big names, there is crafts production, making use of original American fabrics to create quilts and patchwork clothes.

Pozzuoli   ✉ 80078 ☎ 081

Plan, page 98

ℹ️   *AA*, Via Campi Flegrei, tel. 5261481-5265068 (A1).

Hotels, restaurants, campsites, and vacation villages

★★★ **Santa Marta**. At Arco Felice, Via Licola Patria 28, tel. 8042404, fax 8042406. Number of rooms: 34. Accessible to the handicapped. Elevator; parking (A1, *off map*).

★★ **Mini Hotel**. S.S. Domiziana at 61.7 km, tel. 5263223, fax 5263223. Number of rooms: 23. Rooms only; no dining facilities. Air conditioning; parking, garden (B3, off map).

🍴 **Ninfea**. Via Italia 1, tel. 8661326, fax 8665308. Closed Tuesday in low season. Air conditioning, parking, garden. Cuisine of Campania (A1, *off map*).

Vulcano Solfatara. A La Solfatara, Via Domiziana at 60 km, tel. 5267413, fax 5263482. Seasonal.

Spas and hot springs

Terme Puteolane. Corso Umberto I 195, tel. 5261303. Therapies based on: hot baths, mud packs, inhalations.

Museums and cultural institutions

Amphitheater, Mausoleums, Baths of Neptune. Tel. 5265068-5266639. *Open to the public: 9-2:30 (winter), 9-4:30 (summer)*.

at Cuma, see plan on page 106

Parco Archeologico Cuma, Acropoli. Via Cuma, tel. 8543060. *Open to the public: everyday from 9 to sundown*; the exact hours, which vary from month to month, are posted at the entrance to the archaeological park.

Solfatara. Via Solfatara 161, tel. 5262341. Guided tours.

Athletic activities

Campo Sportivo Solfatara. Via Coste d'Agnano 4, tel. 5268800.

Complesso Sportivo Damiani. Via Domiziana, tel. 8042666. Tennis, swimming pool, and go-kart track.

Gondola d'Averno. Lago d'Averno, tel. 8665344. Water-skiing.

Shops, crafts, and curiosities

Fochi. Via Pisciarelli, tel. 5265244. Local craftsmanship.

Mani Abili. Via Pergolesi 150, tel. 5269419. Local craftsmanship.

Praiano ✉ 84010 ☎ 089

Page 170

ℹ c/o *Municipio*, Via Umberto I, tel. 874944.

Hotels, restaurants, campsites, and vacation villages

★★★ **Tritone**. A Vettica Maggiore, Via Nazionale, tel. 874333, fax 874374. Seasonal. Number of rooms: 58. Air conditioning, elevator; parking, garden, swimming pool, private beach.

★★★ **Margherita**. Via Umberto I 70, tel. 874227, fax 874628. Number of rooms: 28. Elevator; parking, parking garage.

★★★ **Tramonto d'Oro**. At Vettica Maggiore, Via G. Capriglione 119, tel. 874008, fax 874670. Number of rooms: 40. Accessible to the handicapped. Air conditioning, elevator; parking, swimming pool.

Ψ **Open Gate**. Via Roma 38, tel. 874148. Closed Tuesday in the low season. Parking. Cuisine of Campania and classical cuisine – seafood.

▲ **Tranquillità**. S.S. 163 at 21.5 km, tel. 874084, fax 874779. Seasonal.

Procida ✉ 80079 ☎ 081

Page 108

ℹ *AA*, Via Roma, Stazione Marittima, tel. 8101968.

Cafes and pastry shops

Dal Cavaliere. Via Roma 42, tel. 8101074. "Granita al limone."

Bar Grattino. Via Roma 121, tel. 8967787. They offer an excellent "granita."

Local guides and excursions

Noleggio Barche, or boat rentals. Spiagge Corricella e Chiaiolella, tel. 992383-905114, 8969400.

Ravello ✉ 84010 ☎ 089

Plan, page 174

ℹ *AA*, Piazza Duomo 1, tel. 857096 (B2).

Hotels, restaurants, campsites, and vacation villages

★★★ **Palumbo**. Via Toro 16, tel. 857244, fax 858133. Number of rooms: 21. Air conditioning; parking, parking garage, garden (B2, **b**).

★★★ **Rufolo**. Via S. Francesco 1, tel. 857133, fax 857935. Number of rooms: 30. Air conditioning, elevator; parking, parking garage, garden, swimming pool (C2, **c**).

★★★ **Graal**. Via della Repubblica 8, tel. 857222, fax 857551. Number of rooms: 33. Accessible to the handicapped. Air conditioning, elevator; parking garage, garden, swimming pool (B2, **g**).

Ψ¶ **Confalone**. Via Toro 16, tel. 857244, fax 858133. Closed, mid-January/February. Air conditioning, parking, garden. Cuisine of Campania and classical cuisine (B2, **b**).

Ψ **Cumpa' Cosimo**. Via Roma 44/46, tel. 857156. Closed Monday in the low season. Cuisine of Campania (B2, **r**).

Museums and cultural institutions

Museo del Corallo "Camo." Piazza del Duomo. Closed Sunday. *Open to the public: 10-12, 3-5 (summer); 10-12, 3-5 (winter)*.

Museo del Duomo. Piazza del Duomo. *Open to the public: 9-1, 3-7*.

Villa Cimbrone. Via S. Chiara. *Open to the public: 9-8 pm (summer); 9-sunset (winter)*.

Villa Rufolo. Piazza del Duomo. *Open to the public: from 9 to sunset*.

Entertainment, shows, and events

Festival Musicale Wagneriano (July). Wagner, Gardens of Villa Rufolo. Tel. 857096.

Shops, crafts, and curiosities

Ceramù. Via Roma 58, tel. 858181. Ceramic for flooring, with design decorations.

Giardini di Ravello. Via Civita 14, tel. 872264. Home-made lemon, tangerine, and fennel liqueurs.

Sala Consilina   ✉ 84036 ☎ 0975

Page 191

[i]   *Pro Loco*, Corso Vittorio Emanuele 25, tel. 21165.

Hotels, restaurants, campsites, and vacation villages

★★★   **La Pergola**. At Trinità, Via Trinità 239, tel. 45054, fax 45329. Number of rooms: 28. Elevator; parking, parking garage.

Museums and cultural institutions

Antiquarium. Ex Convento dei Cappuccini, tel. 21052. Closed Sunday. *Open to the public: 9-2.*

at Padula, 10.5 km

Certosa. Tel. 77745. *Open to the public: 9-6. Departure, guided tours: 10-11-12-3.*

Salerno   ✉ 84100 ☎ 089

Plan, pages 166-167

[i]   *AA*, Via Roma 258, tel. 224744, fax 252576. (B1); Via Torrione, tel. 790469.

    EPT, Via Velia 15, tel. 224322, fax 251844. (B3); Piazza Ferrovia, tel. 231432 (C4).

Hotels, restaurants, campsites, and vacation villages

★★★   **Jolly delle Palme**. Lungomare Trieste 1, tel. 225222, fax 237571. Number of rooms: 104. Air conditioning, elevator; parking, special terms for parking garage (B1, **b**).

★★★   **Fiorenza**. Via Trento 145, tel. 338800, fax 338800. Number of rooms: 30. Rooms only; no dining facilities. Air conditioning; parking, parking garage (C5, *off map*).

★★★   **Plaza**. Piazza Vittorio Veneto 42, tel. 224477, fax 237311. Number of rooms: 42. Rooms only; no dining facilities. Air conditioning, elevator; special terms for parking garage (C4, **a**).

❙❙   **Brace**. Lungomare Trieste 11/13, tel. 225159. Closed Sunday, Christmas. Air conditioning, parking. Cuisine of Campania – seafood (B1, **r**).

❙❙   **Del Golfo**. Via Porto 57, tel. 231581. Closed Monday in the low season. Parking. Cuisine of Campania – seafood (B1, **s**).

Youth hostels

🏠   **Irno**. Via Luigi Guercio 112. Beds, 100. For information: Lucio Giovannone, tel. 790251.

Cafes and pastry shops

Pasticceria Pantaleone. Via Mercanti 73/75, tel. 227825. Intact interiors dating from 1868.

Caffè e Dolcezze (Gay Odin). Via Roma 228.

Museums and cultural institutions

Castello di Arechi. Colle Bonadies, tel. 227237. *Open to the public: 9-1.*

Collezione di Ceramiche Alfonso Tafuri. Larghetto Casavecchia 11, tel. 227782. Closed Sunday. *Open to the public: Monday-Saturday 9-1; Thursday 4-7.*

Museo Archeologico Provinciale. Via S. Benedetto 28, tel. 231135. *Open to the public: 9-7:30; Sunday 9-2.*

Museo Diocesano. Piazza Plebiscito, tel. 239126. *Open to the public: 9-one hour before sunset.*

S. Matteo, Cathedral and Museum. Via Duomo, tel. 231387. *Open to the public: everyday, 9-12, 4-7:30; Sunday 9-1.*

Sezione Didattica della Scuola Medica Salernitana, museum of the Medical School of Salerno; c/o Church of S. Gregorio. *Open to the public: Monday-Saturday 9-1; 4-7:30; Sunday 9-1.*

Entertainment, shows, and events

Festival Internazionale del Cinema, film festival (October). Tel. 254404.

Salerno-Festival. Major concerts (July-September). Tel. 224744.

Viva l'estate. Summer arts season (July-September). Tel. 224744.

Athletic activities

Capitaneria di Porto. Via Molo Manfredi, tel. 255000.

Club Velico Salernitano. Piazza Concordia, tel. 236235.

Lega Navale Italiana. Piazza Concordia, tel. 226924.

Tennis Club degli Arechi. Via Risorgimento, tel. 229995.

Tennis Club Lido Kursaal. Lungomare Gen. Clark, tel. 335029.

Shops, crafts, and curiosities

Borsari dell'Antica Salerno. Via Sedile di Portanova 14.

Sant'Agata sui Due Golfi

    ✉ 80064 ☎ 081

Page 181

Hotels, restaurants, campsites, and vacation villages

★★★   **Sant'Agata**. Via dei Campi 8/A, tel. 8080363, fax 8080800. Seasonal. Number of rooms: 28. Accessible to the handicapped. Elevator; parking, special terms for parking garage.

¶¶ **Don Alfonso 1890**. Corso S. Agata 11, tel. 8780026, fax 5330226. Closed Monday and Tuesday (only Monday in high season, for a period between January and February. Air conditioning, parking, garden. Refined cuisine.

Santa Maria Capua Vetere

☒ 81055 ☎ 0823

Plan, page 157

ℹ c/o *Polizia Municipale*, Via Mazzocchi, tel. 846455 (C2).

Hotels, restaurants, campsites, and vacation villages

★★★ **Milano**. Viale De Gasperi 102, tel. 843950, fax 843323. Number of rooms: 29. Rooms only; no dining facilities. Air conditioning; parking (A2, **a**).

Museums and cultural institutions

Amphitheater and antiquarium. *Open to the public: 9-one hour before sunset.*

Museo Archeologico dell'Antica Capua. Via D'Angiò 48, tel. 844206. Closed Monday. *Open to the public: 9-7.*

Santa Marìa di Castellabate

☒ 84072 ☎ 0974

ℹ *Pro Loco*, c/o Municipio, Via Roma, tel. 961098.

Hotels, restaurants, campsites, and vacation villages

★★★ **Grand Hotel Santa Maria**. Via Velia, tel. 961001, fax 961200. Seasonal. Number of rooms: 61. Elevator; parking, private beach.

Agriturismo (real Italian country living)

at San Marco, 3 km ☒ 84071

Podere Licosa. Lungomare Perrotti. Villas in a pine grove, surrounded by a farm with olive groves, at just 50 m from the sea. For information: Tommaso Perrotti, tel. 961137.

Museums and cultural institutions

Antiquarium. Via Naso. Open to the public, by inquiry at the tourist office (Ufficio Turistico), tel. 961098.

Sapri

☒ 84073 ☎ 0973

Hotels, restaurants, campsites, and vacation villages

A
★★★ **Bungalow Residence** and **Parco Pisacane**. At Oliveto, S.S. 18 at 14 km, tel. 391541, fax 391004. Seasonal.

Scario

☒ 84070 ☎ 0974

Hotels, restaurants, campsites, and vacation villages

★★★ **Approdo**. Via Nazionale 10, tel. 986070, fax 986303. Number of rooms: 25. Parking, garden.

★☆★ **La Francesca Sud**. At Punta Garagliano, tel. 986068, fax 986068. Seasonal.

at Bosco, 6 km ☒ 84040

¶ **Romeo**. Via Provinciale 35, tel. 980004. Closed Wednesday, October. Parking. Cuisine of the Cilento.

Sorrento

☒ 80067 ☎ 081

Plan on pages 142-143

ℹ *AA*, Via De Maio 35, tel. 8074033 (B3).

Hotels, restaurants, campsites, and vacation villages

★☆★ **Bellevue Syrene**. Piazza della Vittoria 5, tel. 8781024, fax 8783963. Number of rooms: 73. Accessible to the handicapped. Air conditioning, elevator; parking, garden, private beach (B2, **h**).

★☆★ **G.A. Excelsior Vittoria**. Piazza T. Tasso 34, tel. 8071044, fax 8771206. Number of rooms: 106. Elevator; parking, garden, swimming pool (B3, **c**).

★☆★ **Grand Hotel Ambasciatori**. Via Califano 18, tel. 8782025, fax 8071021. Number of rooms: 103. Accessible to the handicapped. Air conditioning, elevator; parking, garden, swimming pool, private beach (B4, **m**).

★☆★ **Grand Hotel Capodimonte**. Via del Capo 14, tel. 8784555, fax 8071193. Seasonal. Number of rooms: 131. Accessible to the handicapped. Air conditioning, elevator; parking, garden, swimming pool (C2, **j**).

★☆★ **Grand Hotel Royal**. Via Correale 42, tel. 8073434, fax 8772905. Seasonal. Number of rooms: 96. Accessible to the handicapped. Air conditioning, elevator; parking, garden, swimming pool, private beach (B4, **e**).

★☆★ **Imperial Tramontano**. Via Vittorio Veneto 1, tel. 8782588, fax 8072344. Number of rooms: 115. Access to the handicapped. Air conditioning, elevator; parking, garden, swimming pool, private beach (B3, **d**).

★☆★ **La Solara**. Via del Capo 118, tel. 5338000, fax 8071501. Number of rooms: 38. Air conditioning, elevator; parking, garden, swimming pool, private beach (B1, *off map*).

★★ **La Minervetta**. Via del Capo 25, tel. 8073069, fax 8773033. Number of rooms: 12. Parking, private beach (B1, **a**).

¶¶ **Caruso**. Via Sant'Antonino 12, tel. 8073156, fax 8072899. Closed Monday. Air conditioning. Cuisine of Campania and classical cuisine – seafood (C3, **t**).

🍴 **Favorita-o' Parrucchiano**. Corso Italia 71/73, tel. 8781321, fax 8772905. Closed Wednesday from mid-November to mid-March. Parking, garden. Cuisine of Campania, refined (C3, **s**).

☆☆☆ **Nube d'Argento**. Via Capo 21, tel. 8781344, fax 8073450. Seasonal.

at Sant'Agnello, 2 km ✉ 80065

☆☆☆ **Grand Hotel Cocumella**. Via Cocumella 7, tel. 8782933, fax 8783712. Seasonal. Number of rooms: 61. Accessible to the handicapped. Air conditioning, elevator; parking, garden, swimming pool, tennis, private beach (A5-6, **n**).

Agriturismo (real Italian country living)

at Meta, 4 km

La Pergola. At Traviri, Via T. Astarita 80. Small farm with citrus and olive groves, and livestock. Local cuisine. For information: Nicola D'Esposito, tel. 8083240.

Cafes and pastry shops

Davide Il Gelato. Via R. Giuliani 41, tel. 8781337.

Fauno. Piazza Tasso 1, tel. 8781021. Bar popular with the local young people.

Piemme. Corso Italia 161, tel. 8072927. With old recipes, candies, and home-made liqueurs, "limoncello" and mint and basil liqueurs. We recommend the "follovielli," stuffed "involtini" with raisin and lemon leaves.

Museums and cultural institutions

Museo Correale di Terranova. Via Correale 48, tel. 8781846. Closed Tuesday. *Open to the public: 9-2.*

Shops, crafts, and curiosities

Anna Maria. Via Tasso 47, tel. 8781748. Lace and embroideries.

Apreda. Via Tasso 6, tel. 8782351. Renowned cheese-makers of the Amalfi coast.

Di Maio. Via degli Archi 16, tel. 8784656. One of the most renowned makers of wooden intarsias in the Sorrento area. He produces a series of inlaid wooden boxes in accordances with the designs of ancient Sorrento mosaics; he also makes small inlaid tables, popular throughout the world.

Laboratorio Rosbenia. Piazza Lauro 34, tel. 8772341. Hand-embroidered linen, dowries with embroideries and lace, in accordance with the oldest local tradition.

La Bottega del Gioiello. Corso Italia 179, tel. 8785419. This is one of the best-known goldsmith shops of the city; in particular, the master goldsmiths are rightly proud of the coral and finely carved cameos.

Luigi Coppola. Vicolo 3° Rota 13, tel. 8784217. This may be the best known master craftsman working in copper in Sorrento. For more than 60 years he has been working this red metal, seated on an exceedingly old stool, handed down from generation to generation of craftsmen in his family over the centuries, along with his tools.

Luigia Gargiulo. Corso Italia 44. Embroideries, dowries, and linen in the traditional style.

Olga. Via Cesareo 18. Situated on the Decumano Maggiore, among shops of every sort. This store is devoted to children, and its windows display hand-made items by local embroiderers.

Pastificio Riccio. Viale degli Aranci 101, tel. 8782772.

Ruoppo. Piazza Tasso 18. In the courtyard of Palazzo Correale, Claudio Ruoppo creates floral compositions with grapes, sheaves of wheat, lemons, and pomegranates.

Stinga. Via Luigi di Maio 16. Mosaics of wood, inlaid frames, coral.

Solascion. Via S. Nicola 13, tel. 8781425. Fine ceramics.

Torre Annunziata ✉ 80058 ☎ 081

Page 120

ℹ️ *Pro Loco*, Via Sepolcri 16, tel. 8623163.

Museums and cultural institutions

Pastificio Setaro. Via Mazzini. Pastries; *open to the public: by request. tel. 8611464.*

Scavi di Oplonti. Tel. 8621755. *Excavations open to the public: 9-one hour before sunset.*

Spas and hot springs

Terme Vesuviane Nunziante. Via Marconi 36, tel. 8611285. Therapy based on: hot baths, mud packs, inhalations; massage therapy.

Local guides and excursions

Collegio Regionale Guide Alpine Campania. Via Panoramica 302, tel. 7775720.

Torre del Greco ✉ 80059 ☎ 081

Page 120

ℹ️ *Pro Loco*, Corso V. Emanuele 208, tel. 8814676.

Hotels, restaurants, campsites, and vacation villages

☆☆☆ **Sakura**. Via E. De Nicola 26, tel. 8493144, fax 8491122. Number of rooms: 65. Accessible to the handicapped. Air conditioning, elevator; parking, parking garage, garden, swimming pool.

☆☆☆ **Marad**. Via S. Sebastiano 24, tel. 8492168, fax 8828716. Number of rooms: 79. Air conditioning, elevator; parking, special terms for parking garage, garden, swimming pool.

Museums and cultural institutions

Museo del Corallo. Piazza Luigi Palomba, tel. 8811360. Visits by request.

Vallo della Lucania ✉ 84078 ☎ 0974

Page 189

ℹ️ c/o *Municipio*, Piazza Vittorio Emanuele, tel. 714112.

Hotels, restaurants, campsites, and vacation villages

★★★ **Mimì**. Via O. De Marsilio 1, tel. 4302, fax 72879. Number of rooms: 27. Accessible to the handicapped. Elevator; parking, garden, swimming pool.

Museums and cultural institutions

Museo Diocesano. *Open to the public: Thursday 9:30-12:30; by request, tel. 4142. Tel. 4501 At Monte Gelbison, 14.5 km.*

Santuario della Madonna di Novi Velia. *Open to the public: May-September.*

Velia (Scavi di) ✉ 84070 ☎ 0974

Page 187

ℹ️ c/o *Municipio*, Via Pellacara, Palazzo Ricci, tel. 977008.

Museums and cultural institutions

Zona Archeologica. Excavations, tel. 971409, 972134. *Open to the public: 9-one hour before sunset.*

Vico Equense ✉ 80069 ☎ 081

Page 140

ℹ️ *AA*, Via San Ciro 16, tel. 8015752, fax 8799351.

Hotels, restaurants, campsites, and vacation villages

★★★ **Capo la Gala**. At Scraio, S.S. Sorrentina at 14 km, tel. 8015758, fax 8798747. Seasonal. Number of rooms: 18. Elevator; parking, garden, swimming pool, private beach.

★★★ **Le Axidie**. At Marina di Equa, tel. 8028562, fax 8028565. Seasonal. Number of rooms: 30. Air conditioning; parking, garden, swimming pool, tennis.

★★★ **Aequa**. Via Filangieri 46, tel. 8015331, fax 8015071. Number of rooms: 62. Air conditioning, elevator; parking, garden, swimming pool.

Spas and hot springs

Lo Scrajo. S.S. 145, tel. 8015731. Therapy based on: hot baths, mud packs, aerosol.

Cafes and pastry shops

Exotic Ice Cream. Via Filangieri 107, tel. 8016400. Home-made pastries and ice cream.

Museums and cultural institutions

Antiquarium. Via Vescovado. *Open to the public: from Monday to Friday, 9:30-1.*

Museo Mineralogico. Via San Ciro 2, tel. 8015668. Closed Monday. *Open to the public: 9-1; 5-8 pm (summer); 4-7pm (winter).*

Shops, crafts, and curiosities

Caseificio Savarese. Via R. Bosco 197, tel. 8027575.

Pastificio Starace. Via Filangieri 53, tel. 8027497.

Vietri sul Mare ✉ 84019 ☎ 089

Page 172

ℹ️ *Pro Loco*, Piazza Matteotti, tel. 211285.

Hotels, restaurants, campsites, and vacation villages

★★★ **Lloyd's Baia**. Via De' Marinis 2, tel. 210145, fax 210186. Number of rooms: 120. Accessible to the handicapped. Air conditioning, elevator; parking, parking garage, swimming pool, private beach.

★★★ **Bristol**. Via C. Colombo 2, tel. 210800, fax 761170. Number of rooms: 22. Elevator; parking, garden, swimming pool, private beach.

Museums and cultural institutions

Museo della Ceramica Vietrese. Torretta di Villa Guariglia (Raito), tel. 211835. Closed Monday. *Open to the public: 9-1, 3-6.*

Shops, crafts, and curiosities

Ceramiche Solimene. Via Case Sparse, At Fontana Vecchia, tel. 210188. Vases, dishes, statues, and ceramics of all sorts, including wall and floor tiles.

ICA Maioliche Vietresi di G. Giordano. Via Travertino 17, tel. 211894. Crafts production of ceramics.

Index of Places

Index of places, sights, and monuments, with most place names in Italian (refer to first mention in text of guidebook)

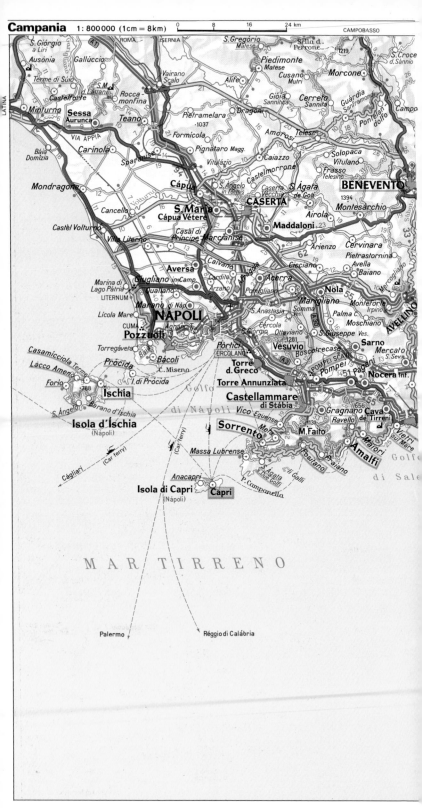

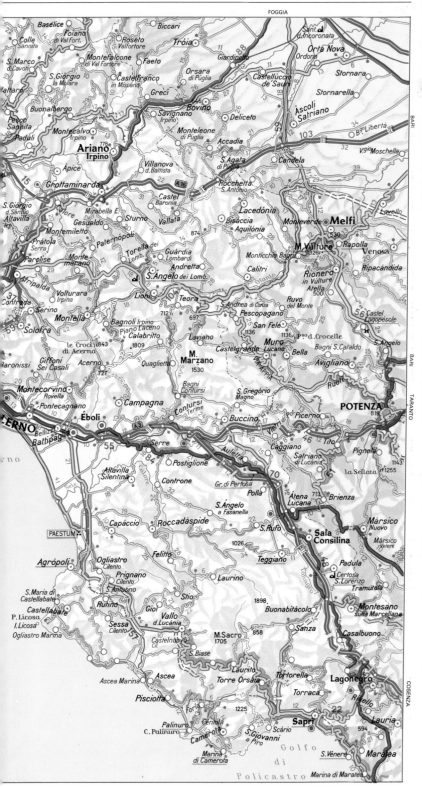

Italy: Useful Addresses

Citizens of Australia, Canada, New Zealand, and the United States can enter Italy with a valid passport, and stay for a period of not more than 90 days; citizens of Great Britain and Ireland, as members of the European Union, can travel either with valid passport or with valid identification card.

Foreign Embassies in Italy

Australia:
Corso Trieste 25, Rome, tel. (06) 852721

Canada:
Via G.B. de Rossi 27, Rome, tel. (06) 445981

New Zealand:
Via Zara 28, Rome, tel. (06) 4402928

United States of America:
Via Vittorio Veneto 119/A, Palazzo Margherita, Rome, tel. (06) 46741

Great Britain:
Via XX Settembre 80/A, Rome, tel. (06) 4825441

Ireland:
Piazza Campitelli 3, Rome, tel. (06) 6979121

Foreign Consulates in Italy

Australia:
Via Borgogna 2, Milan, tel. (02) 777041

Canada:
Via Vittor Pisani 19, Milan, tel. (02) 67581

New Zealand:
Via G. D'Arezzo 6, Milan, tel. (02) 48012544

United States of America:
– Lungarno A.Vespucci 38, Florence, tel. (055) 2398276
– Via Principe Amedeo 2/10, Milan, tel. (02) 290351
– Piazza Repubblica 2, Naples, tel. (081) 5838111
– Via Re Federico 18/bis, Palermo (consular agency), tel. (091) 6110020

Great Britain:
– Via S. Paolo 7, Milan, tel. (02) 723001
– Via Crispi 132, Naples, tel. (081) 663511

Ireland:
Piazza San Pietro in Gessate 2, Milan, tel. (02) 55187569

Italian Embassies and Consulates Around the World

Australia:
12 Grey Street - Deakin, Canberra, tel. (06) 273-3333
Consulates at: Adelaide, Brisbane, Melbourne, Perth, Sydney.

Canada:
275 Slater Street, 21st floor, Ottawa (Ontario), tel. (613) 2322401/2/3
Consulates at: Montreal, Toronto, Vancouver.

New Zealand:
34 Grant Road, Wellington, tel. (4) 4735339 - 4729302

United States of America:
1601 Fuller Street, N.W., Washington D.C., tel. (202) 328-5500/1/2/3/4/5/6/7/8
Consulates at: Boston, Chicago, Philadelphia, Houston, Los Angeles, Miami, New York, New Orleans, San Francisco.

Great Britain:
14, Three Kings Yard, London W.1, tel. (0171) 3122200
Consulates at: London, Manchester, Edinburgh.

Ireland:
63/65, Northumberland Road, Dublin 4, tel. (01) 6601744

ENIT

In order to have general information and documentation concerning the best known places in Italy, you can contact the offices of the Ente Nazionale Italiano per il Turismo (ENIT), run by the Italian government; they are open Mon-Fri, from 9 to 5.

Canada:
Office National Italien du Tourisme/Italian Government, Travel Office, Montreal, Quebec H3B 3M9, 1 Place Ville Marie, Suite 1914, tel. (514) 866-7667/866-7669, fax 392-1429

United States of America:
– Italian Government Travel Office, New York, N.Y. 10111, 630 Fifth Avenue, Suite 1565, tel. (212) 2454822-2455095, fax 5869249
– Italian Government Travel Office, Chicago 1, Illinois 60611-401, North Michigan Avenue, Suite 3030, tel. (312) 644-0996, fax 644-3019
– Italian Government Travel Office, Los Angeles, CA 90025, 12400, Wilshire Blvd., Suite 550, tel. (310) 820-0098/820-1898, fax 820-6357

Great Britain:
Italian State Tourist Board, London W1R 6AY, 1 Princes Street, tel. (0171) 408-1254, fax 493-6695

GRAND HOTEL
COCUMELLA
★ ★ ★ ★ ★

The Grand Hotel Cocumella, on the eastern side of Sorrento was one of the stops on the Grand Tour and would have faded into oblivion had not an ambitious architect in 1978sunk lire and talent aplenty into recapturing its brilliance. The efforts have paid off and the property now has what many sophisticated travellers feel is a advantage: its tranquil setting 15 minutes' walk from Sorrento's central square. The main building was originally a Jesuit monastery of the 16th century and became hotel since 1822 much of the tranquil and historical aura still remains. The ambience is more Old World than what most vacationers expect when heading a beach resort. Its name origins from the nymph "Colomeide" (Honey botton) so called by the Jesuit fathers for its favourable position and for the fertility of its orange and lemon orchards. There is also who states that the name has another antique origin deriving from the "coccume", vases of hearthwater with spout and handle used to contain water that were produced here. The discovery of the caves confirm this second hypothesis.

The roman cistern, used to accumulate a remarkable quantity of spring water, supplying even the villa of emperor Tiberio in Capri, has now benn transformed into large conference room.

The antique cloisfer with a volcanic grey tuff well in the centre is today a wonderful dining room that still conserves its antique conventual atmosphere.

The annexed chapel, a real jewel, is usually used for concerts which are numerous during the summer season.

The Cocumella has a very relaxing feel, it is surrounded by a century old park and the vast gardens are extensive and beautiful which streches down to a terrace overlooking the famous gulf of Naples and Vesuvius. Immersed in

the park are also a swimming pool very large and well kept and tennis court. The private solarium is easily reached by the hotel's lift.

The 60 rooms are all different from each other, decorated with original furnishing and some still have an authentic fireplace and they are well executed in traditional style with lamps and armoires. The hotel dispose of two restaurant: "Scintilla", also called "Pasta, Paste e Antipasti" as its name already describes, is specialised in the local Mediterranean cuisine, in a romantic settin overlooking the garden.

During the summer period the "Agrumeto" restaurant by the pool is open for a light buffet lunch. The last novelty is the "Vera", the 30 mt sail boat built in 1880, available for charters and for excursions to Capri and the Amalfi coast. The solicitous staff has a polite smile as if to reiterate the Cocumella's slogan: "Learn to Like Yourself". This genial traditional resort is just the place to do that.

Via Cocumella, 7 - 80065 Sant'Agnello - Sorrento
Telefax +39 081 8783712 - Tel. +39 081 8782933
E-Mail: hcocum@tin.it